Photoshop® CS2

Sherry London

WILEY

Wiley Publishing, Inc.

Gone Wild

Photoshop® CS2 Gone Wild

Published by
Wiley Publishing, Inc.
111 River Street
Hoboken, N.J. 07030-5774
www.wiley.com

Copyright © 2006 by Wiley Publishing, Inc., Indianapolis, Indiana

Published simultaneously in Canada

Library of Congress Control Number: 2005926044

ISBN-13: 978-0-7645-9813-5

ISBN-10: 0-7645-9813-9

Manufactured in the United States of America

10 9 8 7 6 5 4 3 2 1

1K/RZ/RQ/QV/IN

About the Author

Sherry London is a graphic designer, fiber artist, teacher, and author of a number of books on Photoshop, Illustrator, and Painter including Photoshop 7 Magic (with Rhoda Grossman), Photoshop Textures Magic, and Photoshop Special FX How To. Her Photoshop-designed fiber art has been featured in Fiber Arts magazine and exhibited at juried Embroiderer's Guild of America Fiber Forum group shows nationwide.

Sherry is the owner of London Computing: PhotoFX, a digital art studio. She has taught for the prestigious Thunder Lizard Photoshop Conference and the Professional Photographer's of America seminars. She currently teaches a number of Photoshop courses via the Internet through colleges and universities worldwide. To find a college or university near you, go to Education To Go's website at www.ed2go.com.

Sherry writes for a number of magazines. Her articles and reviews have appeared in *MacWeek, MacUser, MacWorld, Computer Artist, Electronic Publishing, Desktop Publishing,* and *Pre-* magazines. She currently writes the QuickTips column for *Photoshop Users* magazine as well as feature articles and reviews for both *Photoshop User* and *Mac Design* (now *Layers* magazine). Sherry's web site is www.sherrylondon.com.

Credits

Acquisitions Editor
Tom Heine

Project Editor
Timothy J. Borek

Technical Editor
Darren Winder

Copy Editor
Kim Heusel

Editorial Manager
Robyn Siesky

Vice President & Group Executive Publisher
Richard Swadley

Vice President & Publisher
Barry Pruett

Project Coordinator
Maridee Ennis

Graphics and Production Specialists
Jennifer Heleine
Lynsey Osborn

Quality Control Technician
Charles Spencer

Proofreading
Arielle Menelle

Indexing
Sherry Massey

For my son, Dan — this book is for you —
and for many Thanksgiving dinners yet to come.

Preface

Photoshop CS2 Gone Wild is a different type of Photoshop book. It doesn't try to teach you Photoshop; it shows you how to work with Photoshop on real projects that you can follow step by step. The projects are funky and weird, but exciting; definitely not the usual stuff. They push the edge of what Photoshop can do.

There are two ways to teach a subject: *deductive* and *inductive*. The deductive approach to Photoshop would have you master each of the commands and functions and then put them together in a project. I much prefer the inductive approach — work the projects, and in the process of completing them, you learn Photoshop. You also retain much more of what you learn, because you'll have seen how to apply it. "Use it or lose it" is really applicable to Photoshop. If you work with the program and keep at it, the learning curve simply fades away. This book is not a detailed reference guide to Photoshop, but if you work though it, I promise that you'll have a super understanding of Photoshop and a lot of practical experience when you're done.

I make the assumption that you aren't brand-new to Photoshop. You should at leave have a clue as to how to use layers and layer masks. My instructions are detailed enough to get you through the rest. Even though the projects might be wild, the Photoshop techniques used in this book are rock solid and totally practical. I also wanted to create a book exclusively devoted to *nondestructive editing;* this is the first book that focuses on creating images that preserve every bit of data in your originals.

How to Use This Book

Photoshop CS2 Gone Wild is not only nondestructive, it's nonlinear. I've arranged the tasks (projects) into chapters related by the subject matter. I mixed up the tasks so you don't get bored working all the Displacement techniques in one chapter or all the techniques that simulate 3D in another. However, just because I used a plant picture on a technique doesn't mean that you have to keep using plant pictures. The techniques work happily with varied subject matter. You can find a cross reference of Photoshop techniques used in the various projects on the book web site at www.photoshopgonewild.com. Please work through the book in any order, following any picture that catches your eye.

The Book CD-ROM and Web Site

All the images needed to work the various tasks are included on the CD-ROM that comes with this book. You get every photo, starting image, and supplementary file needed. Just open the image from the CD-ROM and work on it in Photoshop. The supplementary files (patterns, styles, gradients, brushes, and shapes) can just as easily be moved into Photoshop.

If you use a Mac, double-click on any PAT, ABR, CSH, or ASL document. The file automatically attaches itself to the correct location in Photoshop. On Windows, make sure that Photoshop is open. Then, drag the file from the CD and drop it into the open Photoshop application window. It is immediately available from the expected location.

The images are divided into chapter folders. Most folders contain both an OtherAssets folder and a ZIP file that is labeled starting with *ComstockImages*. Please read the README_FIRST file on the CD-ROM to see how to unzip these files on both Mac and Windows. The ZIP files require a password, which is located at the bottom of the ComstockLicense.html file on the CD-ROM. This password works for every ZIP archive.

All of the OtherAssets folders files are uncompressed. If you use a Mac, double-click on any PAT, ABR, CSH, or ASL document. The file automatically attaches itself to the correct location in Photoshop. You can also drag it onto the open Photoshop icon in the Dock. On Windows, make sure that Photoshop is open. Then, just drag the file from the CD-ROM and drop it into the open Photoshop application window. It is immediately available from the expected location.

If creating the effects in the book doesn't keep you busy, try your hand at the bonus tasks on the *Photoshop CS2 Gone Wild* CD-ROM. We've provided six bonus tasks as separate PDF files in a folder named Bonus Tasks, which also contains all the source images and supporting files required to complete the bonus tasks.

Be sure to visit the book web site, www.photoshopgonewild.com to get extra material that didn't fit on the CD-ROM or to just hang out a bit. I update the site with relevant links and materials as I find them.

However, another major advantage in using Smart Objects is that it gives you a non-destructive image transformation. So long as you transform the Smart Object in its layer in the main image (not in the Smart Object file itself), and use of Edit ➪ Transform (including the new Warp command) can be reversed, altered, or removed at any time. If you need to change the angle of a rotation, for example, you can simply enter the new rotation amount and you see no loss of image quality. The command goes back to the untouched original image to calculate the changes.

Warp

The Warp command jumps from the Type options to the Edit ➪ Transform command in CS2 and takes on a new dimension. In addition the standard text warping presets, you can create your own warp. The Warp icon, when chosen on the Options Bar of the Edit ➪ Transform command, shows a nine-grid mesh — almost like a Tic-Tac-Toe grid. The corners of the mesh have handles that work like Bezier curves. You can either reshape the warp by dragging the handles or by pushing on the pixels inside the mesh grid. You can also move the grid lines themselves. If you warp a layer that holds a Smart Object, the warp can be changed or removed without data loss.

If you don't have CS2, the closest command to use to replace the warp is probably the Liquify command. You can also try the Distort command, but that only gives you four points to warp. To work the projects that require warping, you need to duplicate the layer to be warped or create a merged layer to use.

Vanishing Point

The Vanishing Point filter enables you to paste, paint, or clone in perspective. You can create perspective grids on an image, and these grids remain with the image when the image is saved. You can go into and out Vanishing Point as often as you want. You should use a new layer every time you go into Vanishing Point, and anything you want to paste must already be on the clipboard.

If you don't have CS2, just use the Clone Stamp tool as best you can.

Groups and Clipping Masks

Adobe plays the 'name change' game in CS2. Layers Sets are now called Groups and take over the Command/Ctrl+G shortcut that belonged to clipping masks (Group with Previous) in earlier versions of the program. The new shortcut for clipping masks is Command/Ctrl+Option/Alt+G. The command to create a Layer Set (or Group) is no longer on the context menu from the Layers palette. However, the shortcut is the easiest way to create it.

If you don't have CS2, this one is really no change. You just need to know that "group" means "layer set."

Linking Layers

The Link icon in previous versions is missing from the columns on the Layers palette in CS2. However, you can still use it at the bottom of the Layers palette. You won't want to, though, as soon as you realize the new power that exists. To apply a command to multiple layers, you can just Shift-click to target a contiguous range of layers or Command/Ctrl-click to target layers that aren't above or below each other. The language in the book, however, says, "Select layers x, y, z ." I've used a shortcut to keep the instructions down a bit. When you are told to "select" multiple layers, that does not mean to load them as selections; instead, it means to click, Shift-click, or Command/Ctrl-click to highlight the various layers.

If you aren't using CS2, you can either link the layers where is possible to perform the needed instructions on multiple layers or else work with one layer at a time.

About Non-Destructive Editing

For years, I have told students, "Show me a designer who never had a client request a change and I will show you a designer who never had a client." Change is inevitable — even if it is only you who has that better idea in the middle of the night.

I've watched as each version of Photoshop brings us closer to the ideal of being able to easily change anything in an image at any time. To build an image nondestructively requires some forethought and ingenuity, and a solid understanding of some of Photoshop's more esoteric features. The main idea is to not remove so much as a single pixel from the image just in case you might need it later. This is a packrat's idea of heaven. The main principles to follow are:

* Embed your starting image in the file and never remove or edit it.
* Always create and work in layers.
* Use layer masks rather than the Eraser tool.
* Use Layer Styles that can always be adjusted.
* Use vector layers such as Solid Color Fill, Gradient Fill, and Pattern Fill layers.
* Use Shapes when possible.
* Always color correct using Adjustment layers.
* Apply filters to a duplicate of the layer, then mask or reduce opacity of the filter layer.
* Clone stamp and heal an image in a blank layer.
* Use layer blend modes to mix layers together.
* Use knockout options to recover areas of the untouched originals.
* Make your files self-documenting by naming the layers and by organizing layers into logical groups.
* Save your files in PSD format with all layers intact (hard drives are cheap these days).

A fringe benefit to nondestructive editing is that, by making an image modular, you can easily reuse portions of that image in another project.

Photoshop CS2 New Features

Photoshop Gone Wild is written to take best advantage of the new features in Photoshop CS2, especially the new Smart Object technology.

Smart Objects

Smart Objects are the most significant change to structuring a Photoshop file since Adobe introduced layers in version 3.0 in 1995. Smart Objects hold an entire raster or vector (Illustrator) file and protect it from change. However, you can edit the Smart Object file itself and any changes that you make are updated into the main file. If you use multiple copies of the Smart Object file and change one copy, all of the linked copies are also updated.

A Smart Object is stored in a PSB file inside of the main PSD file. It can hold multiple layers inside of it. Since these layers can be turned on and off, Smart Objects give you a marvelous way to try out different looks and effects. When you are done editing the Smart Object file, I ask that you click the Close box on the file window and then click Yes to the prompt to save your changes. When you next make the main file active, the changes to the Smart Object show up on your main file.

I use Smart Objects in many instances where I would previously have put the layers into a Layer Set and changed the blend mode of the layer set to Normal so that the layers interacted with the image as if they were a single object. I also found that Smart Objects replaced most of my need to create a merged layer above a group of layers. If you don't have Photoshop CS2, you can use either of those two strategies (a layer set or a merged layer) to mostly replace the Smart Object technology that I use.

Acknowledgments

John Nack at Adobe Systems: thanks for providing such a swift beta enrollment and for your excellent help in interpreting the features of Photoshop CS2 upgrade.

The Photoshop engineering team at Adobe: thanks for creating such fabulous new features in CS2 and for giving the world this incredible gift called "Photoshop."

Traci Torres at Comstock: I am so grateful for your help in securing exciting photos to use in this book.

Rhoda Grossman: my love and big hugs for helping me out with five great techniques.

Kiska Moore: I helped set your feet on the Photoshop path, but the rest of your journey has been your own. Thanks so much for bringing your expertise to bear on retouching Lisa.

Lisa Boch: I am really grateful to you for modeling your recent weight gain for me. I hope this gives you the motivation you wanted — though I would not have noticed the extra weight had you not made a point of it.

Darren Winder: What I can say? Your help through the years has been indispensable. For this book, and for your help online, I am deeply grateful.

Kathryn Bernstein: Kathryn, I value our friendship as much as I treasure your design expertise. You manage to provide much needed perspective when I am about ready to give up. Thank you so much!

Thom La Perle: Watching you learn Photoshop has been like introducing you to something you already knew instinctively how to do. It was incredible to see your work over three courses. Thank you so much for sharing your Winged Lady with us.

Liz Goldman: Thanks for sharing your creativity with your classmates and your instructor.

David Xenakis: Thanks for letting me use your wonderful photos of Greece. Thanks also for your friendship and collaboration over the years.

Dan Bacon: Thank you so much for the superb wolf photos that you sent to me and for sharing your skill so freely.

Karl Switak: I appreciate your licensing the banded sand snake photo to go with Thom's Winged Lady image.

Andrew Buckle: Thanks for allowing me to include some of your wonderful brushes and shapes in the book. I really appreciate it.

Bryan Peterson, Kerry Drager, Tony Sweet, Brenda Tharp, Jim Zuckerman, and Susan and Neil Silverman at BetterPhoto.com: I can't thank you enough for your excellent courses at betterphoto.com. It's because of you that I am able to contribute my own photos, without embarrassment, to this book. I am a much better photographer now than I was before taking your courses.

Judy Donovan: This has been another excellent adventure. I hope we share many more together. Hopefully Reiko has recovered from the photo shoot. Just don't show him his picture in the blue dress.

Margot Hutchinson, my agent at Waterside Productions: Words fail me. Thank you for bringing me this book and finding me great things to write and places to teach. This book is also for you — and Sammy.

David Karlins: Thanks for your encouragement and help as we each went down the path in parallel.

Tim Borek and Tom Heine: You both poked and prodded and challenged me to move out of my comfort zone. An old business legend talks about the manager who gave his underling a report to write. A day after the report was finished, the manager handed it back and asked, "Is this the best you can do?" The employee took it back and worked on it some more. Again he was asked, "Is this the best you can do?" This scenario was repeated several more times until in anger and frustration, the employee finally screamed, "Yes, this is the best that I can do." The manager calmly said, "Good, now I'll read it." Guys, this is the best that I can do! (And despite my screaming, it is better than it would otherwise have been). Thank you both.

My students: You have enriched my life as much as I hope I have influenced yours. It has been an awesome experience teaching you from all over the English-speaking world in the comfort of my own home. As I see you get turned on to Photoshop and watch your skills grow, I feel that I am finally accomplishing something that really makes a difference in someone's life. I love your enthusiasm and love to see the creativity that emerges. Your problems help me to see how Photoshop needs to be taught.

Dan London: You are, of course, the very best thing I have done with my life. Thank you for your help with the images and for catching my faux pas with the acoustic guitar before I made a public fool of myself.

Norm London: If Dan is our best production, then you are the very best co-producer I could possibly have. Thank you for putting up with me all these years. I love you.

Contents

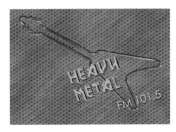

three people **88**

four places **122**

Contents

five faces **156**

six groups **216**

Contents

nine paranormal **318**

ten playing with your food **348**

index . . . .

metallics

Metallics is all about creating metal effects in Photoshop. From metal patterns and chrome text ("Chromicity") to "Flaming Metal" with its mixture of flames and photo collage, these tasks show you how to fashion and use metallic effects. Kathryn Bernstein's "Metal with Style" is a stunning introduction to creating your own metallic styles. An adaptation of a metallic etching technique developed by Liz Goldman lets you create a keepsake coin of your favorite good luck person. "Heavy Metal" constructs a brushed metal surface suitable for many different types of background designs.

Chromicity

The chrome diner is a fixture in American life. In this tribute to the breed, you create flashy chrome text and build a patterned background based on the hammered metal of diner fronts and street vendor hot dog carts. I show how you can control (or lose control) over the shine of the chrome and vary the font used in the task (you'll try both a thick and a thin font). Your font choice really matters here. Chrome works on any font, but larger and fatter fonts need different settings, and skinny fonts can get much too reflective very quickly. Sunglasses anyone?

THE PLAN

- Build the background image pattern
- Construct the background image
- Build Adjustment layers for the text
- Add the text
- Emboss and (if needed) blur

TIP

Always name your layers so they tell you what you did. Repeating the process is easier when you have a clue what you did to it the first time!

1 Start by making a pattern for the background. Create a new image 300 pixels square with a white background. Set your colors to the default of black and white. Choose Select ➪ All and the Edit ➪ Stroke, 10 pixels, Inside. This adds a 10-pixel border to the image. Then choose Filter ➪ Blur ➪ Gaussian Blur, 30. Click OK. Choose Edit ➪ Define Pattern and name it **Outline Blur**. Double-click on the layer and rename it **Blur 30 on Stroke 10**. This is the first of two tiles to create in this file.

2 Duplicate the Blur 30 on Stroke 10 layer. Choose Filter ➪ Stylize ➪ Emboss. Set the Angle to **35** degrees, Height to **47**, and Amount to **66%**. Click OK. Rename the layer **Emboss, 35, 47, 66**. This creates the second tile. Choose Edit ➪ Define Pattern and name it **Embossed Blur**. Save the file as **TileBase.psd** and close it.

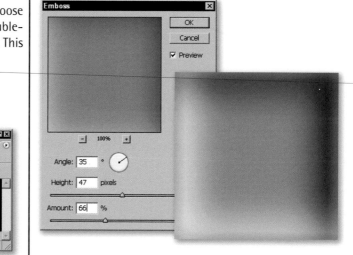

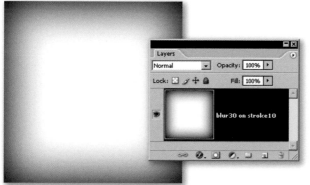

3 Create a new file 1,200 pixels square. This file is four times the size of the pattern base file so it can hold four repeats in each direction. Create a new layer named **Outline Blur** and fill it with the Outline Blur pattern. Next, add a new layer named **Embossed Blur** and fill it with the Embossed Blur pattern. Choose Image ➪ Rotate Canvas ➪ Arbitrary, 45 degrees CW. Click OK. Your canvas gets larger and forms diamonds. Try to keep your zoom level to **25%** or **50%** depending on your screen size. Turn off the eye on the Background layer and Embossed Blur layer and then make Outline Blur the active layer.

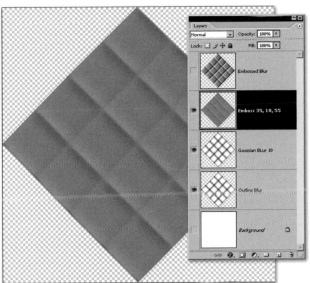

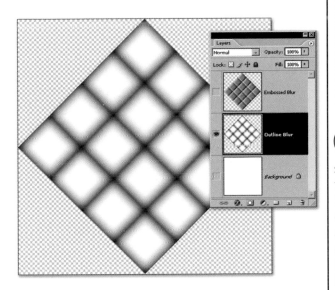

4 Duplicate the Outline Blur layer as **Gaussian Blur 10**. Command/Ctrl click the layer thumbnail in the Layers palette to load the selection. Then choose Filter ➪ Blur ➪ Gaussian Blur, 10. Click OK. Duplicate that layer and choose Filter ➪ Stylize ➪ Emboss. Set the Angle to **35** degrees, the Height to **18**, and the Amount to **55**. Click OK. Deselect. Rename the layer **Emboss 35, 18, 55**. Click on the three visible layers in the Layers palette to select them and press Command/Ctrl+G to group them. Name the group **Outline Blur**.

5 Make the Embossed Blur layer active and visible. Add an Invert Adjustment layer. Choose the 100-pixel soft brush and click the Airbrush icon. Reduce the Opacity to **31** and the Flow to **22**. Add a new layer above the Invert layer and call it **Airbrush 100 @ 31, 22**. You need to darken the areas between tiles. The easiest way is to make a tic-tack-toe grid. On the new layer, click the outer edge of the pattern area to set a brushstroke. Release the mouse button. Move the brush to the opposite side of that "ditch" in the patterns, press Shift, and click. You leave a totally straight diagonal line. Repeat this to make a grid. Reduce the layer opacity to 50%. (The darker lines on the figure outside the diamond just show extensions of the lines and won't show up on your image).

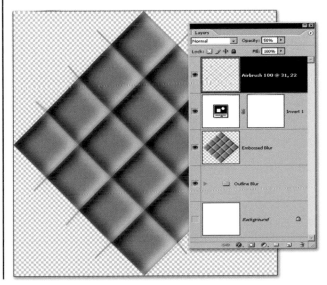

6 Copy the file MetalCurve.acv from the companion CD to the Photoshop Curves Presets folder on your hard drive or any other convenient location. Add a Curves Adjustment layer. Click Load and choose the MetalCurve.acv that you just copied. A bit bright, don't you think? Tone it down by setting the layer opacity to about **22**. Then add a Levels Adjustment layer. Drag the White Point slider to about **203** to add more white to the tile. Click all of the layers above the Outline Blur group and press Command/Ctrl+G to make a Layer Set group from them. Name it **Embossed Blur**.

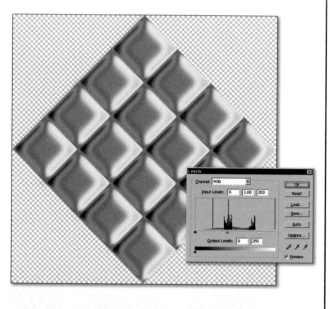

TIP

The Adobe Settings folder contains the Presets folder that contains a folder for Curves. On both the Mac and Windows, the Settings file is inside of the Photoshop application folder.

7 Press Shift+Command/Ctrl+Option/Alt+E to create a merged layer. Name it (what else?) **Merged Layer**. Open the Outline Blur group and duplicate the Emboss 35, 18, 55 layer. Drag it to the top of the layer stack. Collapse the Outline Blur group and make the top layer active. Command/Ctrl-click the layer thumbnail to load a selection. Choose Filter ➪ Blur ➪ Gaussian Blur ➪ 15 and then click OK. Deselect. Add **BLUR 15** to the layer name. Reduce the layer opacity to **47%**.

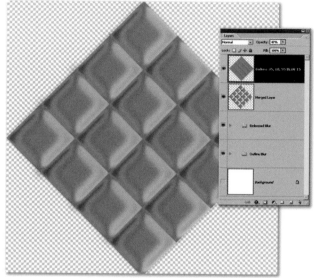

8 You have a choice now. You need to define the pattern tile, and you can do it in a painful, precise manner with guides at the centers of the four inner diamonds, or you can choose a Fixed Size style on the Rectangular Marquee tool and set the fixed size to 424 x 424. I suggest the latter method. Then place the marquee in the center of the image — but you can be sloppy about it. Any 424-pixel section of the diamond will work. Choose Edit ➪ Define Pattern and name the pattern **Chrome Tile**. Deselect. Save the file as **TileBuild.psd** and close it.

TIP

Your original tile was 300 pixels square. You made a diamond out of it. Therefore, if you draw a line diagonally across the square, that line is horizontal when you rotate the square. It's the equivalent of the hypotenuse of a right triangle. The hypotenuse of a right triangle is equal to the square root of the sum of the opposite sides. Bottom line: that number happens to be 424 — the needed pattern tile size. Every now and then, geometry proves useful!

9 Open the image DinerScene.psd. Now you can finally create the real image. Create a new file 1,200 pixels wide x 800 pixels high. Add a Pattern Fill layer and choose the Chrome Tile pattern that you just created. and drag the DinerScene image into the upper-left corner of the working image. Name the layer **DinerScene**. Close DinerScene.psd to get it off your desktop.

Photo: www.comstock.com

10 Make the DinerScene layer active. Press Command/Ctrl+T and hold the Shift key as you drag the lower-right corner of the bounding box to the bottom of the image. Press Return/Enter to commit the transformation. Add a layer mask. With white as your foreground color and black as the background color, choose the Gradient tool and the Foreground to Background gradient (Linear Gradient, Normal mode, 100% opacity). While pressing and holding Shift, drag the Gradient cursor from a bit less than the left side of the image to just a bit before the diner scene image ends. Release the mouse button. The diner scene fades seamlessly into the chrome tile pattern.

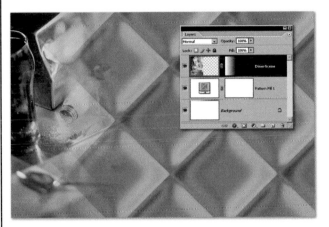

TIP

Normally, I would advise you never to enlarge an image because it loses quality. However, you're not enlarging it all that much and the image is fading into the chrome. Whenever possible, try to start with an image that is at least as large as you need (or larger). Using Bicubic Softer helps if you absolutely must enlarge something, but I don't think you get decent results above about a 200 percent size increase.

(11) Finally, you can create the type that's the main feature of this technique. Choose a relatively thin decorative typeface. I used the font, Orlando, designed by Tim Rolands Digital Design (www.myfonts.com/fonts/timrolands/orlando/). If you want to use just this text (and not this font or your own font); you can download the words "American Diner and Grille" already set and rasterized from the book Web site. I include several typeface examples in the thin-face.psd file. Type **American Diner & Grille** at 130 points or drag one of my rasterized type layers into the image. If you set your own type, rotate the type -11 degrees to give it a nice slant.

(12) Create a new layer about the type and name it **Embossed Type**. Fill it with 50 percent gray. Command/Ctrl-click on the text layer to load it as a selection, and then add a layer mask to the Embossed Type layer. Next, Command/Ctrl-click on the Embossed Type layer mask thumbnail (or the text layer again) to load the text as a selection. Make the Embossed Type *image* portion of the layer active and choose Select ⇨ Feather, 3, and click OK. Fill the selection with black and then deselect. Turn off the eye on the text layer.

(13) This is a setup step so that you can better judge the needed Emboss filter settings. Press and hold Option/Alt as you add a Curves Adjustment layer from the Add New Fill or Adjustment layer icon on the bottom of the Layers palette. In the New Layer dialog box, choose the Use Previous Layer to Create Clipping Mask check box. Click OK. In the Curves dialog box, click Load and choose the MetalCurve.acv file that you used previously. Click OK. Then press and hold Option/Alt and add an Invert Adjustment layer. Again, in the New Layer dialog box, click the Use Previous Layer to Create Clipping Mask check box. Click OK.

(14) Now you're ready to create chrome. Click between the layer and the layer mask on the Embossed Type layer to remove the link. Make the layer active. Choose Filter ➪ Stylize ➪ Emboss. Start by setting the Angle to **35** degrees and moving the Amount slider to **100**% with the Height Slider at 1. Next, move the Height slider slowly to the right as you watch the preview. By the time the Height slider gets to **16**, you have crazy striped lines on the text, and if you move the Height to **60**, the type starts to look like a demented zebra. Drag the Height back to about **6** pixels and then experiment with the Amount slider. As you move the Amount to the right, you begin to get vertical zebra stripes. That's okay if you like the effect, but it's a bit bright for me. As you drag the Amount slider below **100** percent, you begin to get a brushed metal effect instead of chrome. I like the effect best at about **136** percent, so that's the one I used. Click OK.

(15) Press and hold Option/Alt as you add a Levels Adjustment. In the New Layer dialog box, click the Use Previous Layer to Create Clipping Mask check box, and then click OK. Drag the White point to the left until you have some solid white. This setting differs every time you use this task. The value you want depends on the white levels already in the embossed text. I set this to 240, but you need to determine your best setting. Click OK. Then add up to a 3-pixel Gaussian Blur to the embossed text to see if you like the slightly softer shine. Finally, add a Drop Shadow effect using the settings shown here. This version of the image is done.

(16) Save the first diner file. Choose Image ➪ Duplicate ➪ OK. Delete the Embossed Type layer mask and fill the layer with 50 percent gray to remove the type from the image and leave you with a clean slate. You can leave the Drop Shadow layer style attached. Click the eye on the Embossed type layer to hide the entire clipping mask set. Turn eye back on for the layer and then double-click the text layer to reopen it for editing. I used BigBand by Linotype (www.myfonts.com/fonts/linotype/bigband/) as the fat typeface, again at 130 points. It's one of the many possibilities in the FatFaces.psd file.

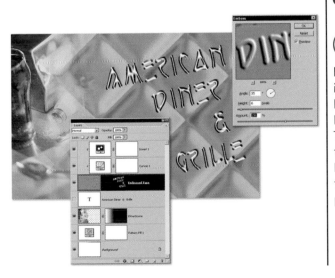

If you want a color other than silver for your metallic and chrome effects, you can add a Hue/Saturation adjustment layer over it and clip it to the type.

(18) Save the image as **DinerFatFont.psd**.

A short recap

Metallic text is fascinating in the way it glints and glitters. The special metallic curve is part of the secret to getting good metal. To make the text, you need to fill a layer with gray and place your text to emboss in black, after you feather the original type. Masking the feathered type with the original gives you the cut-off look that keeps a hard edge on the type. Above the embossed type, you have a triple-decker clipping mask sandwich of the metal Curves layer, an Invert layer, and a Levels layer. You can fine-tune the type effect by altering the white point in the Levels layer or by slightly blurring the embossed text. You could also reduce the intensity of the metal curves. You used a few tricks on the background of this image, too. The metal curve at a low opacity helped to make chrome tiles. You also got to review high school geometry.

(17) Load the text as a selection, and add a layer mask to the Embossed Type layer. Show the Embossed Type layer and hide the text layer. Load the mask as a selection and make the Embossed Type layer active. Choose Select ⇨ Feather, 5 and click OK. Next, fill the selection with black and deselect. Turn off the link between the layer and the layer mask, and then choose Filter ⇨ Stylize ⇨ Emboss. You'll notice you can push the settings higher now. I used a Height of 9 and an Amount of 150. Adjust the white point on the Levels layer if you wish. Unless you want to try out all of the other fat faces, you're done.

Heavy Metal

You'll find lots of tutorials on the Internet for creating brushed metal. Immodestly, I think this one is the best! You get full control over lighting changes on the metal, and it's infinitely editable. You can also decide at any moment if you want rivets to sink or protrude. If you don't like the spacing of the rivets, that's easy to change, too. Then add a guitar and metallic text. Who could ask for anything more?

THE PLAN

- Create the basic brushed metal
- Combine two pieces with a Clouds filtered layer mask
- Create the rivets pattern and add it
- Create the metallic text

1 Open a new file, 800 pixels x 600 pixels in RGB mode at 72 ppi with a white background. Add a new layer and make a selection with the Rectangular Marquee tool that is about 30 pixels wide and the full height of the image. Fill it with light gray (RGB: 176, 176, 176). Deselect. Choose Filter ⇨ Noise ⇨ Add Noise, Monochromatic, Gaussian, 20%. Click OK. Name the layer **Stretched Noise, 20**.

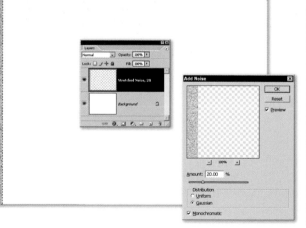

2 Press Command/Ctrl+T to choose the Edit ⇨ Transform command. Drag the center handle on the right side of the bounding box until it reaches the right side of the image. Commit the transformation. This stretches the noise and creates lines that add texture to the brushed metal.

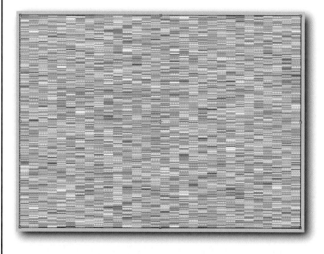

TIP

The amount of noise influences the color of the brushed metal that emerges. The darker the noise, the darker the result. Your starting color also changes the effect. Try 400% noise against white to see the difference.

3 Duplicate the Stretched Noise layer as **Noise, 60.** Choose Filter ⇨ Noise ⇨ Add Noise and change the amount to **60%**. Click OK. Next, duplicate that layer as **Motion Blur**. Choose Filter ⇨ Blur ⇨ Motion Blur, change the Angle to **41** degrees, and set the Distance to **99** pixels. Click OK. Rename the layer to **Motion Blur 41, 99** so that you record the settings.

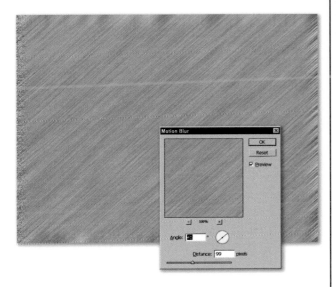

4 The basic brushed metal is done, but the edges are really funky. Choose the Crop tool and select the center area so that you cut off the odd-looking borders. Click Hide in the Options bar and commit the Crop.

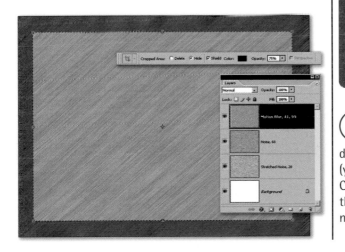

5 Click on the top three layers to select them, and then Ctrl/right-click and choose Group into New Smart Object. This tucks the original layers away for safekeeping. Rename the Smart Object as **Basic Brushed Metal.** Drag the Basic Brushed Metal smart object to the New Layer icon at the bottom of the Layers palette to duplicate it. You don't need to give it a new name. Press and hold Option/Alt and add a Hue/Saturation adjustment layer. In the New Layer dialog box, choose Use Previous Layer as Clipping Mask. Just change the Lightness to **-35** and click OK.

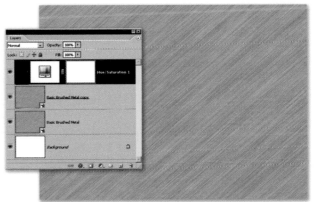

TIP

Why Hue/Sat and not Levels? Again, if you prefer Levels (or even Curves), use it. I found that mucking around with Levels created a more interesting result—but that wasn't the look I was going for. All I really want to happen is to slightly darken the layer. You could even leave out the Hue/Sat layer and change the Blend mode of metal copy to Multiply if you prefer that effect.

6 Make the Basic Brushed Metal Copy layer active. Add a Layer Mask. Press D to change the colors to the default of black and white. Choose Filter ⇨ Render ⇨ Clouds (yes, in the mask). Then choose Filter ⇨ Render ⇨ Difference Clouds. Repeat that filter a few times until you like the way the images blend. Don't worry if the blend isn't smooth. The next step fixes that.

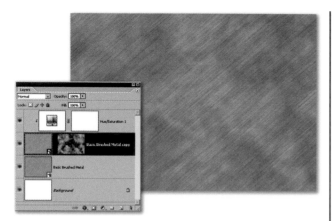

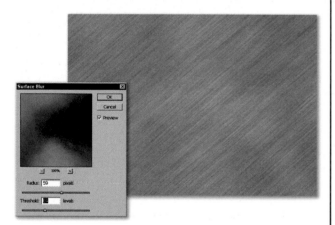

(7) With the cloud-filled layer mask still active, choose Filter ⇨ Blur ⇨ Surface Blur. The settings you use are a personal choice. You can watch the preview and move the sliders. I found that a Radius of 59 and a Threshold of 89 gave me a lovely, soft result.

(8) Next, you need to create the rivets on the metal. Minimize the brushed metal for now. Create a new file 13 pixels wide and 16 pixels high. Fill it with black and make the foreground color white. Choose the 9-pixel hard brush. Stamp once in the small image. Duplicate the layer. Press Command/Ctrl+Option/Alt+C to access the Canvas Size dialog box. Check the Relative box. Set the Width to **100** percent; don't change the height. Click the center-left Anchor square, then click OK. Choose Filter ⇨ Other ⇨ Offset. Set the horizontal offset to 13 pixels (or half of the document width). Set the vertical offset to 8 pixels (half the document height). Click OK. Then choose Edit ⇨ Define Pattern. Name the pattern **Rivets**. Click OK.

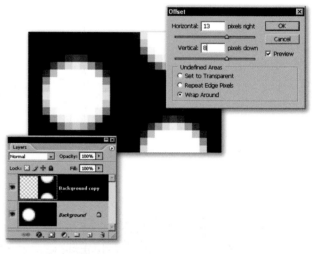

TIP

The Surface Blur filter is new to Photoshop CS2 and is quite different than the Gaussian Blur. Gaussian Blur is a blur-it-all-and-mix-it-up filter while Surface Blur is more discriminating and blurs areas without making uniform mud. I thought you'd like to know that an Adobe engineer, when asked about the purpose of the new blur filters (in addition, there are Shape Blur and Box Blur) replied that he was sure people would find something to do with them!

TIP

Photoshop can only create rectangular patterns and tile a pattern just by repeating the pattern unit over and over again in straight lines. That really limits what a pattern can do. Think of wallpaper patterns — so many of them repeat in rows with every other row offset halfway down. That is technically known (in pattern design lingo) as a *half-drop* repeat. The principle of a half-drop repeat is that the pattern unit moves down half the height of the repeat on subsequent rows. I just gave you the easiest way to create one. Start with a blank canvas and add the pattern design. Duplicate the layer and then double the width of the file. Offset the top layer by half the current image height and width and define the pattern. So long as the pattern element does not touch any of the four borders of the image, you'll get a perfect seamless repeat every time.

9 Add a new layer to the image and name it **Rivets**. Choose Edit ⇨ Fill, with Pattern and choose the Rivets pattern. Click OK. Add a layer mask. Fill the layer mask with the same pattern (now you see white dots). Change the Fill opacity for the layer to **0** (yes, that does make the pattern go away). Add a Bevel and Emboss layer style to the Rivets layer. It's a super-simple layer style. Change the Depth to **1** percent and the Direction to Down. Both Size and Soften are set to **0**. The other settings are standard, as you can see in the figure. Click OK to exit.

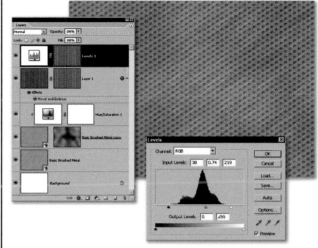

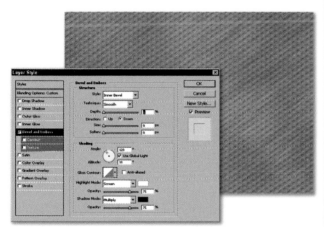

TIP

Could you have used a Pattern Fill layer here? Yes. However, with a pattern fill layer, you could not have seen any result from the Bevel and Emboss layer style unless you added a mask anyway. The mask would only get in your way if you decide to change the pattern scale or move the pattern. As those are the two main reasons for using a pattern fill, I didn't bother.

10 I find the image a bit lacking in contrast. Load the layer mask of the Rivets layer as a selection and then add a Levels adjustment layer. This masks the Levels layer so the adjustment only alters the rivet area. I have no way to predict what values work best for you as this depends on the layer mask on the Basic Brushed Metal copy layer. For me, sliding the black and white points to just outside of the actual image data and then adjusting the Gamma slider to 0.74 worked best.

TIP

If you feel the metal is still too bumpy, double-click one of the Smart Object layers to open it. Duplicate the Motion Blur layer in the smart object file. Use a Gaussian Blur to taste or try a Shape Blur of about 5 using the Checkmark shape. Then click the Close box on the smart object and click OK when prompted to save the file. When you make the brushed metal image active again, both smart object layers update to show the blur. If you don't like it, just undo it. If you pass the undo point, then reopen the smart object and just toss that top blur layer.

11 Before you start a new task, always clean up. Select all of the layers except for the Background layer and press Command/Ctrl+G to group them into a layer set. You're going to place a rock guitar shape and apply a metal layer style to it to set off the background image. Drag the file FlyingV.csh into the open Photoshop application. The shape appears in the Shapes palette. Choose the Custom Shape tool and select the FlyingV guitar. In the Geometry Options palette, click the Defined Proportions option button. Click the center icon on the Options bar to select Paths. Choose Image ⇨ Rotate Canvas and rotate the image **90** degrees clockwise. Then drag the guitar from near the top of the image almost to the bottom of the image. By the way, I lightened the background image on the figure so you can see the guitar shape better.

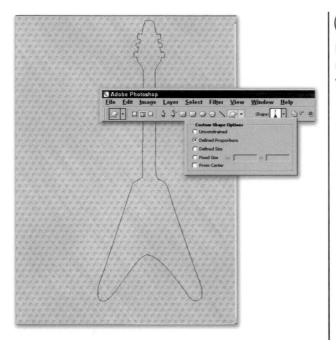

(13) Drag the HeavyMetal.asl file into Photoshop. It installs itself in the Styles palette. With the Guitar layer active, click the Heavy Metal style. If you want to make a style similar to this one by yourself, Task 3 shows you how.

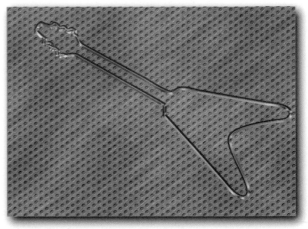

(12) Rotate the canvas **90** degrees counterclockwise to put it back. Add a new layer above the group folder and name it **Guitar**. With the Shape tool still active, press Command/Ctrl+T. Type **29 degrees** into the Angle field and then move the shape closer to the center of the image. Commit. Choose the Pencil tool and the 9-pixel hard brush. Click the Stroke Path icon in the Paths palette.

(14) You're ready to create some metal type using a really old trick (Photoshop 3 old; so old it's new again!). Choose a wide or fat typeface (or open my already rasterized version of the freeware Metal Lord font). Type the words Heavy Metal at about 70 points. Then, before you commit it, press and hold Command/Ctrl and rotate it **–19** degrees. The typeface I used needs serious kerning (actually tracking because the free font has no kerning information in it). If your letters are wide apart, use the tracking control to tighten the spaces and then select the individual letter pairs to tighten the spacing as needed. Commit the type.

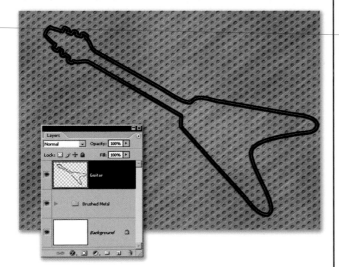

TIP

You can download the Metal Lord font at http://sanctuary.maidenrules.com/. You just need to scan the page fairly carefully to find it. If you want to go directly to the download screen, the link is http://sanctuary.maidenrules.com/Metal Lord.TTF (yes, there's a space in it).

TIP

Unlike the way I prefer to work, creating this metallic text can't preserve the text as vector. I wish it could, but the layer styles just don't seem to do as good a job for this as the old-fashioned CHOPs (channel operations). I've updated the task though to make it as adjustable as possible. You place and feather the text onto the gray layer and then emboss it. Instead of adding a metallic curve after, I have you add it before so that you better judge the settings you want. I have you add the Invert layer for the same reason — so you can see your result before you do the pieces that aren't adjustable (emboss and blur). Now, about that Invert layer . . . Common sense says, "Why not just invert the Curve?" but that doesn't do it. The curve is magic, but the result almost always needs to be inverted to make it shiny.

(15) Add a new layer above the type layer and name it **Raster Type**. Fill the layer with 50 percent gray. Copy the file MetalCurve.acv to the Photoshop Curves Presets folder on your hard drive or any other convenient location. Command/Ctrl-click the Heavy Metal type thumbnail in the Layers palette to load the type as a selection. With the type selected, but with the Raster Type layer active, add a new layer mask. Then press and hold Option/Alt as you add a new Curves adjustment layer from the menu at the bottom of the Layers palette. Click the Use Previous Layer for Clipping Mask check box and click OK. In the Curves dialog box, load the MetalCurve.acv curve and then click OK. Next, press and hold Option/Alt as you add an Invert Adjustment layer above the Curves adjustment layer, then choose Use Previous Layer to Create Clipping Mask. This is all prep work for the next step.

(16) Load the text layer mask (or the text layer) as a selection by Command/Ctrl-clicking on its Layers palette thumbnail. Make the gray section of the Raster Type layer active. Choose Select ⇨ Feather ⇨ 3 and click OK. Fill this selection with black. Wow! Now you can see a real difference. (Peek at the posterized histogram, too.) The next step is to emboss the text. Click the link between the layer mask and the layer to only emboss the text (if you leave the layer linked, you also emboss the mask). Then deselect. Choose Filter ⇨ Stylize ⇨ Emboss. Set the Angle to **35** degrees. Try a Height of **3** pixels and an Amount of **65** percent. These settings give you a brushed metal, which is appropriate for the background image. Reduce the Opacity on the Curves layer to **69** percent to enhance the soft metal look of the text. Rename the Raster Text layer **Emboss, 35, 3, 65** or whatever settings you used.

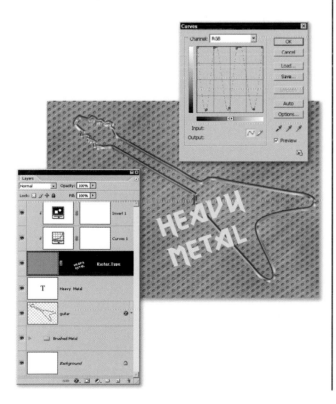

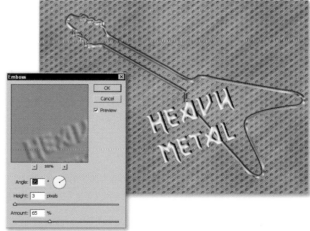

(17) Let's finish the Heavy Metal text with a drop shadow and a stroke. Add a Stroke layer style. Set the Size to **1**, the Position to Outside, the Blend Mode to Normal, and the Fill Type to Color. Choose white as the color. Click the Drop Shadow style choice and add a drop shadow of **125** degrees, Distance: **5** px, Spread: **0%**, Size: **5** px. The rest is just standard — normal contour and **0** noise with the default opacity and blend mode settings you can see on the figure. Click OK.

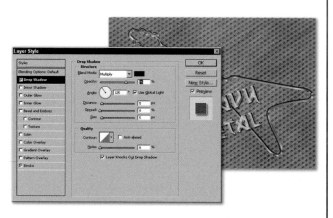

(18) The only item left is to add the call letters **FM 101.5**. I used Century Gothic, Regular, 48 points, Smooth in white. Any condensed, narrow font should do. Add the same drop shadow setting as you used on the Heavy Metal text. Angle the type to about **-19** degrees and move it into position. You're on the air!

A short recap

Playing with metal is fun. Forcing Photoshop to do the work of a 3D-rendering program can be even more fun. The real beauty of the brushed-metal background is the play of color. You get that variation in tone simply by using the Clouds and the Difference Clouds filter in the layer mask of darkened copy of the image. You have a lot of flexibility to adjust your image even after you've saved and closed it. You can change the color or mix of the background and you can alter the direction of the rivets. By altering the pattern in the pattern layer and in the mask of the Levels layer above it, you can even change the actual rivets that you use. If you don't care for the spacing, you can change it without having to tear apart your image. You don't have quite as much freedom on the text (a brushed-metal variation of the first task in Chapter 1), but you can still alter the shine on it should you wish.

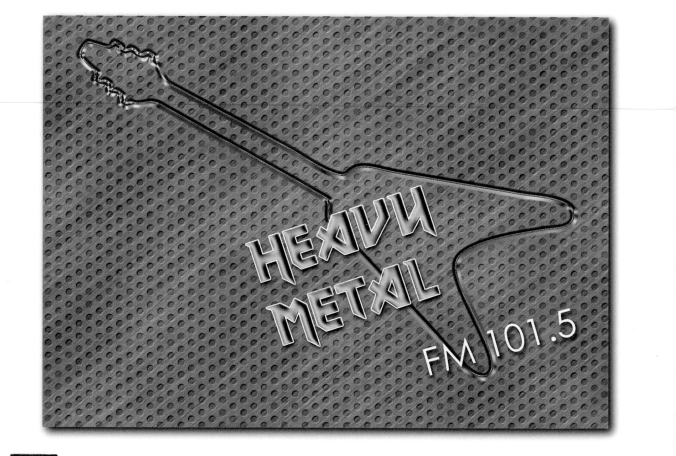

Metal with Style

Mis en place is the name cooks give to the process of cutting up veggies and other foods in advance so that they are on hand when needed (recipes usually contain many ingredients or components that need to be cooked first). Let's chop up some metal style sauce that can be served with an infinite number of main courses. For a real challenge, try to match the pictures without reading the settings. Kathryn Bernstein designed the image used in this task and created the layer style.

THE PLAN

- Create a metallic layer style with custom contours
- Create a Smart Object
- Use the Smart Object as both cast shadow and reflection
- Alter the Smart Object

TIP

The View ➪ New Guide command is very precise. I like it because you don't need to show the rulers first. I prefer to keep my units set to pixels. If you don't work in pixels, then you need to explicitly type the px into the New Guide dialog box.

1 Create a new image 400 pixels x 400 pixels. Set your foreground color to RGB: **0, 50, 83,** and add a Solid Color Fill layer. Choose View ➪ New Guide and add a horizontal guide at position 280 px. Add a vertical guide the same way at position 230 px. Choose the Custom Shape tool and select the Fleur-de-Lis shape. In the Custom Shape options box, set the Fixed Size to 306 px x 308 px. Click the From Center check box.

2 Make sure that the Shape tool is set to create shapes (the icon on the left of the Options bar). Place your cursor on the intersection of the guides and click to leave the shape layer. Press Command/Ctrl+T. Drag the object straight down until the crossbar on the Fleur-de-Lis is over the intersection of the guides. Drag the center point of the bounding box onto the intersection of the guides. Set the Angle on the Options bar to **-41** degrees and then commit. Choose View ➪ Extras to hide the guides, and then click under the Shape 1 Vector Mask entry in the Paths palette to hide the shape vector preview.

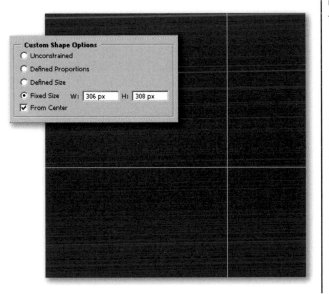

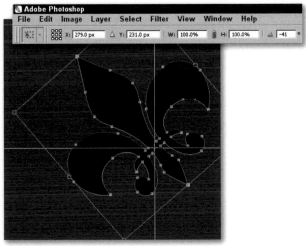

TIP

Altering the location of the center point of the bounding box causes the transformation to occur from the new location. You set the center point at the intersection of the guides so that it rotates from that point.

(3) Metal is shiny, so this gradient sets the tone for the entire style. It's the first of the many layer effects that create a metallic layer style. Open KB-Blues.grd from the CD-ROM and drag it into Photoshop to add this Gradient preset. Choose Gradient Overlay from the Add a Layer Style menu at the bottom of the Layers palette. Set the Blend Mode to Hard Light, Opacity to 100 percent, and choose the KB-Blues gradient preset that you just loaded. Use a Linear style gradient at an angle of 124 degrees, and set the scale to 130 percent. It's important that after you enter the settings, you drag the gradient on the image until the bands of color fall in the same place as shown. Don't exit the dialog box yet.

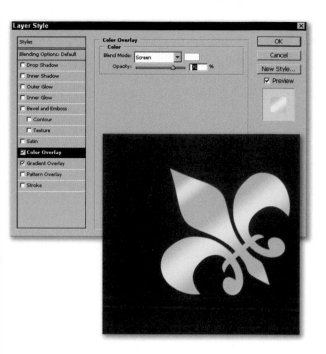

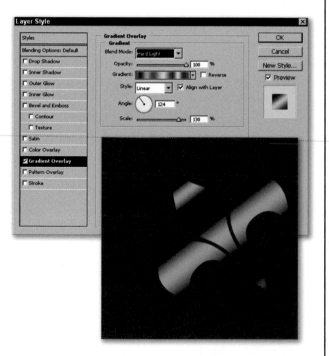

(4) Click to add a Color Overlay effect and then set the focus of the dialog box there. Choose white as the overlay color. Use Screen mode and 75 percent opacity. Leave the dialog box open.

(5) Next, click on the Inner Shadow to add that to the style in progress. You want the shadow to cover just the tips of the Fleur-de-Lis. The settings that do that are: Blend Mode: Color Burn, Opacity 100 percent, and Angle to –81 degrees. Use Global Light: Not checked, Distance: 6 px, Choke: 0, Size 62 px. Click the arrow to the right of the Contour field and choose the Rounded Steps contour. Click somewhere in the Layer Style dialog box to close the Contour menu. Don't check Anti-Alias and leave Noise set to 0. Again, don't exit yet.

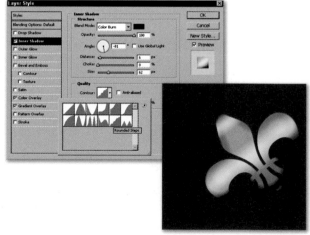

NOTE

You might wonder how one goes about designing a new style. There aren't any rules here. The one thing that Kathryn knew as she designed the inner shadow is that she wanted the tips of the shape covered. The rest was experimenting to see what combination of settings worked. Start by getting the inner shadow where you want it. You can do that just by dragging the shadow around on the image. You need to adjust the Size; Photoshop moves the Angle and the Distance as you drag. The mode change darkens the image for dramatic shadows. The Contour has a major effect on the final result. Sometimes, you'll need to go back and alter one setting after you've added another effect.

6 Next, add a Satin Effect. Satin causes lights and shadow play. The aim of this effect is try to get a line that mimics the upward V of the Fleur-de-Lis. You also want the Fleur-de-Lis to have blue feet! Change the color of the Satin effect to white. Choose Screen for the Blend Mode at **100** percent Opacity. The Angle is **–49** degrees. Set a Distance of **46** px and a Size of **18** px. Again, use the Rounded Steps Contour. This time, however, anti-alias it for smoothness. Uncheck the Invert box.

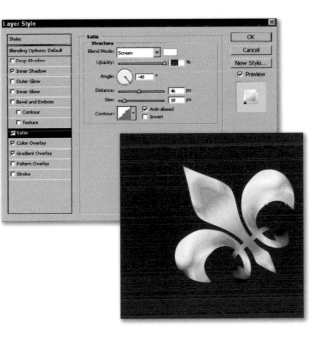

TIP

If the curves on the feet of the Fleur-de-Lis aren't a shade of blue, then go back and adjust the Gradient Overlay effect.

7 The Bevel and Emboss effect is next, and it's by far the most complex of any of them. Use an Inner Bevel Style and a Smooth Technique. Depth is **560%** in an Up direction. The Size is **7** px and the Soften is **0**. Soften was the easiest thing to set because I knew the metal style needed a hard edge. Okay, that's the end of the easy stuff in this dialog box. Lighting makes or breaks the whole look of the Style. Don't use Global Light. Set the angle to **121** degrees and the Altitude to **27** degrees. The Highlight and Shadow modes are standard as are the opacities (Screen at **100** percent and Multiply at **75** percent). Saving the worst for last, choose the Sawtooth 1 Glass Contour from the drop-down menu. Click the Anti-aliased check box.

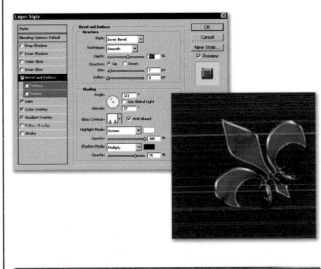

TIP

Kathryn wants me to warn you *never* to use the Create Layers command unless you have saved your style and you also have a back-up copy. She painstakingly created the style only to lose it all to layers before she saved the file or the style. This left me, just as painstakingly, to re-create the entire effect based on the layers that Create Layers created. Not a fun evening.

8 You need to modify the Gloss Contour to get a better play of light on the rim of the Fleur-de-Lis. Click the Gloss Style preview (not the menu arrow) to open a dialog box that's similar to a Curves dialog box. Drag the point of the rightmost saw tooth up one full grid square so that both Input and Output are **75**. Then move the left sawtooth point so that the Input is **35** and the Output **53**. This lightens the fill on the Fleur-de-Lis. Click OK to close the Gloss Contour dialog box. Are we done? One more dialog box to go, so keep the Layer Styles open.

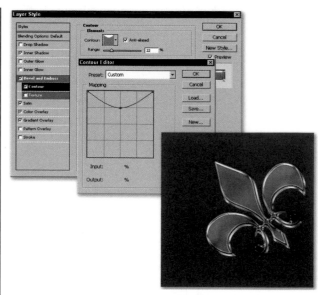

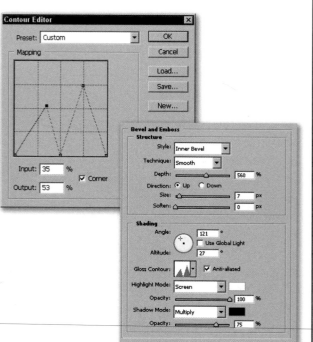

9 In the list of Layer Styles on the Left, click to open the Contour effect under the Bevel and Emboss. Choose the Cone Inverted preset and click on the preview to edit it. Drag the center point up so that the Input of 50% becomes an Output of 75%. Click OK to exit the Contour editor. Set the Range to **22**. Turn on Anti-aliased. Click the New Style button on the right and save the finished styles as **KB-Blues**. Click OK to exit.

10 I keep talking about the blues — KB-Blues. Where's the blue? The name actually comes from Kathryn singing the blues when she lost the style, but you do need to add a blue-toned Hue/Saturation layer. Choose the Hue/Saturation layer from the Add New Fill or Adjustment Layer menu at the bottom of the Layers palette. Click Colorize. Set the Hue to **218** and the Saturation to **31**. Whoops! Now the background is bluer. There is a fix, and it's a tricky one. Select both the Hue/Sat and the Shape layer and group them (Command/Ctrl+G). Change the Blend mode of the new group to Normal (from Pass Through). Name the Group **Fleur-de-Lis**.

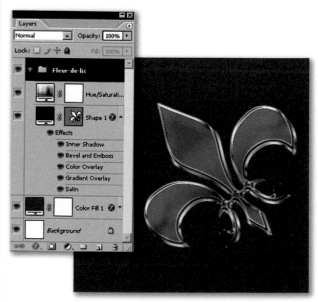

NOTE

The setting of Saturation 31 depends upon your monitor and your RGB workspace. I had my workspace set to sRGB when I wrote this task (and Kathryn's original file was also in sRGB). If your profile is set to Adobe RGB, adjust the saturation to suit after you've grouped the layers.

TIP

Why wouldn't making a clipping mask work? The object is almost all layer style, and clipping groups don't really affect layers styles. All you see is a very tiny change. If you have time to play, make a duplicate of the image so far. In the duplicate, change the Hue/Sat layer to a Solid Color Fill of RGB **255, 0, 255**, which is an intense magenta. Make a Clipping Mask with the Shape layer. Try out every one of the Blend modes. Then put the layer back to Normal mode, turning off the Satin effect, the Gradient overlay, and the Inner Shadow. Then turn off the Color Overlay. You'll see how each partially blocks the Solid Color Fill layer. So why does grouping work? If you change the Blend mode for the Group to Normal, the Hue/Sat layer only colors the Shape layer, because that's the only other layer in the group. Normal mode encapsulates the result so that the group pretends that it's a single layer.

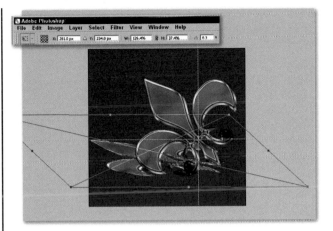

11 *Mis en place* is done. It's time to cook! Control/right-click on the Fleur-de-Lis Group layer and choose Group into New Smart Object. The entire group is replaced by a single entry and can be used in multiple locations. Drag the Fleur-de-Lis Smart Object to the New Layer icon at the bottom of the Layers palette and name it **Cast Shadow**. Drag it below the original Smart Object. Press Command/Ctrl+H to show your Guides again. Choose Edit ⇨ Free Transform. Drag the Center point control to the intersection of the guides. Type the numbers X: **281.0 px**, Y: **234.0**, W: **126.4%**, H: **37.4%** and Angle **0.3** degrees into the Options bar fields. Press and hold the Command/Ctrl key and move the center-top control point until the tip of the Fleur-de-Lis at the left edge of the image at the guide-line. Press and hold the Command/Ctrl key and drag the center-bottom control point until the left leaf of the Fleur-de-Lis on the cast shadow is just touching the left leaf of the original Fleur-de-Lis. Commit.

12 Doesn't look much like a cast shadow yet. Let's fix it. Hide Extras. Reduce the layer opacity to 25%. Press and hold the Option/Alt and add a Solid Color Fill layer from the Add New Fill or Adjustment Layer menu. In the Layer Properties dialog box, choose Use Previous Layer to Create Clipping Mask. Click OK. Choose black as the fill color. Click OK. Make the Cast Shadow layer active and add a layer mask. Choose the Gradient tool with the Copper gradient. Select the Radial style and click Reverse in the Options bar. Set the mode for the Gradient tool to Normal at **100%** opacity. Place the start of the gradient cursor line on the center bar of the cast shadow Fleur-de-Lis. Drag the Gradient cursor to the left side of the image until it is on a line with the top edge of the original Fleur-de-Lis. Release the mouse. You've now created a complex cast shadow.

(13) Next, you need to create a reflection. Drag the Fleur-de-Lis Smart Object to the New Layer icon at the bottom of the Layers palette and then name it Reflection. Choose Edit ➪ Transform ➪ Flip Vertical. Drag the object straight down until it is just below the original. The two objects should have a 2-pixel gap between them. Choose the Gradient tool and reset it. Press DX to set your colors to the default and make white the foreground color. Uncheck the Reverse check box. Choose the Foreground to Background gradient preset and create a layer mask for the Reflection layer. Drag the Gradient cursor from the start of the reflection to the bottom of the image. This image is done, but it can be totally changed in the blink of an eye.

below the bottom of the Fleur-de-Lis. If the scissors is styled, choose a Style of None on the Styles palette. Then click the KB-Blues style in the Styles palette. Turn off the visibility of the layer that contains the Fleur-de-Lis shape. Click the Close box on the Smart Object and click Save. Voila! You have a totally new dish with reflection and cast shadow in place. The figures show the Fleur-de-Lis Smart Object layers and then the final image Layers palette. You may certainly rename the Smart Object to **Scissors** if you wish.

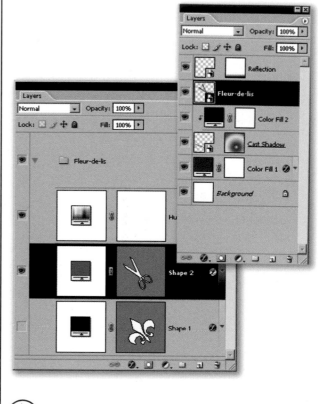

(15) Save your work.

(14) Select the Custom Shape tool and load the Objects set of shapes. Append to the current set. Leave the geometry options set as they were for the Fleur-de-Lis. Double-click on the Fleur-de-Lis Smart Object to open it. Choose the Scissors1 shape in the Shapes palette (it's in the set you just loaded). Make the Shape 1 layer active. Click on the center bar of the Fleur-de-Lis to set the scissors shape. Choose Edit ➪ Free Transform and rotate the object **180** degrees. Drag it so that the handle of the scissors is just

TIP

Rotate a shape to the angle you want it before you apply the style. When you rotate a styled object, the style does not seem to rotate along with it properly. If it does, you have placed both objects in the upright position and then are able to add a transformation to the Smart Object that rotates any content in the Smart Object.

A short recap

Adding a layer style can be a complex thing, but once it's done, you can constantly reuse it — so the pain is fleeting. Try working with custom contours. Try out all of the different contours when you get the time so you can get an idea of what each one does. This task was actually very straightforward. You used Smart Objects to build the image, the cast shadow, and reflection. Just make sure that you not only save the style to the Styles palette, but also use the Edit ➪ Preset manager to save a style set to your hard drive. Save it twice — once to the Adobe Presets folder and then to a safe location on your hard drive that won't be affected by Adobe updates. Make sure that you, unlike Kathryn, don't end up singing the blues!

Flaming Metal

Flames can be a metaphor for a hot night on the town enjoying some sizzling live jazz. Where better to look than Bourbon Street in New Orleans, where the sound never sets? Maybe you also have some images that don't do well on their own and can use the excitement of a metallic flame effect. This one would look right at home on the local jazz scene. Consider this my tribute to the Big Easy.

THE PLAN

- Create a displacement map
- Draw the starting lines
- Use Displacement, Wind and Blurs to build complexity
- Create the metal embossing
- Adjust the background colors
- Add a complementary image and blend it in

TIP

The Displacement filter uses the black and white values in a displacement map to determine how to alter the pixels in the filtered image. The file used as a Displacement map must be a flat file and saved in PSD format. It can't be bitmapped. A grayscale file works fine. You can also use an RGB, CMYK, or Multichannel file. In the RGB and CMYK images, only the first two channels are used. The first channel controls the left/right movement and the second channel controls the up and down movement. These channels can contain the same or different images. You get interesting variations if you either rotate the image in the second channel or invert the image. If you have the time or wish to play, try creating several displacement maps from the clouds image. In one, rotate the Green channel. In the other, invert it.

(1) Your first step is to make a displacement map that you'll use on the main image. Create a new image 775 pixels square at 72 ppi. Press D to set your colors to the default of black and white. Choose Filter ➪ Render ➪ Clouds. Save the image as **Cloudsmap.psd** and close it.

(2) Create a new file 775 pixels square, or the same size as the displacement map you plan to use. (Hmmm... I'm tired of writing that one out. From now on, I'll refer to displacement maps as *dmaps!*). Add a black Solid Color Fill layer over the blank Background layer. Add a new layer and name it **Lines**. Then, using white, paint a number of semi-wiggly vertical lines on the new layer in varying widths, degrees of hardness, lengths, and textures. You can try some of the fancy shapes or effects brushes as well. The figure shows my starting set of lines.

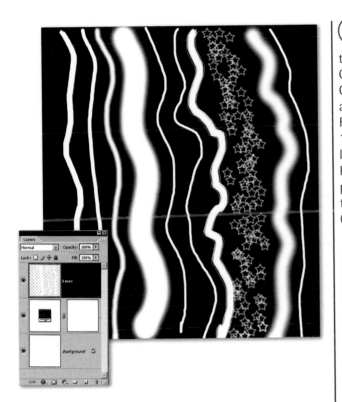

4 Hide the eyes on the bottom two layers so that only the Wind and the Gradient Fill layers are visible. Make the Gradient Fill layer active. Press Shift+Command/Ctrl+Option/Alt+E to make a merged layer above the Gradient Fill layer. Name it **Windy Colors**. Hide the Wind and the Gradient Fill layers and turn on the black Solid Color Fill layer. Duplicate the Windy Colors layer as **Displace, 50, 100** and turn off the Windy Colors layer. Make the Displace layer active. Choose Filter ➪ Distort ➪ Displace. Choose a Horizontal scale of **50** percent and a Vertical scale of **100** percent. Also select Wrap Around and Stretch to Fit, and then click OK. In the next dialog box, choose the Cloudsmap.psd file you created in Step 1. Click OK.

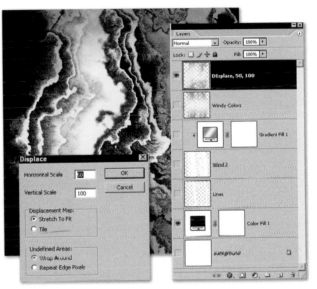

3 You need to thicken the lines without blurring them. Duplicate the Lines layer as **Wind, Right, 2**. Turn off the Lines layer and make the Wind, Right, 2 layer active. Choose Filter ➪ Stylize ➪ Wind and then click Wind and From Right. Click OK. The lines are better, but not thick enough. Press Command/Ctrl+F to filter it again. It's time to add a gradient over the lines so that we can move some colors around in the next steps. Press and hold Option/Alt and add a Gradient Fill layer from the bottom of the Layers palette. Select Use Previous Layer as Clipping Mask and click OK. Then add a Linear Yellow, Orange, Yellow gradient (from the standard presets) at an angle of **90** degrees.

TIP

The Vertical scale seems to work best in this technique at 100. However, the Horizontal scale has much more play in it. If you don't like the displacement you get, or want to fiddle some more, try different values for the Horizontal scale.

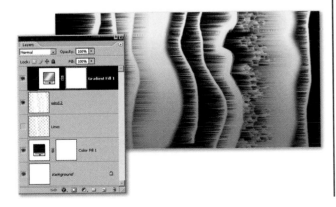

5 Duplicate the Displace, 50, 100 layer as **Wind, 10.** Turn off the eye on the Displace, 50, 100 layer. You want to add wind that moves down next, but the Wind filter only goes right or left. No problem! Choose Image ⇨ Rotate Canvas ⇨ 90 CCW. Then choose Filter ⇨ Stylize ⇨ Wind, and select Wind, from Left. Click OK. Well, that's a bit meager. Press Command/Ctrl+F to taste. I did it nine more times. Always clean up after yourself; choose Image ⇨ Rotate Canvas ⇨ 90 CW to put the file back where it started. You should begin to see flame-like possibilities in the image.

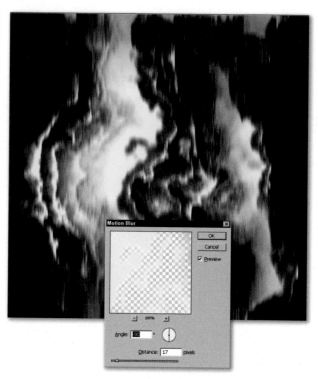

7 You need to make the flames a bit more wispy, so you motion blur again, but at an odd angle. Duplicate the Motion Blur layer and name it **Motion Blur2, 52, 25.** Turn off the first Motion Blur layer and make the top layer active. Choose Filter ⇨ Blur ⇨ Motion Blur and set the Angle at **52** degrees and the Distance at **25** pixels or to taste. Click OK.

TIP

Do you want to keep looking at all of those turned-off layers? If you find that a turn-off, select all of them and create a Group (also known as a layer set). Then, as you turn off each layer after this, just drag it into the Group folder for safekeeping.

6 Duplicate the Wind, 10 layer as **Motion Blur, 90, 17.** (If you don't use those settings, then update your layer name). Turn off the Wind layer and make the top layer active again. Can you guess what's next? Big surprise. Choose Filter ⇨ Blur ⇨ Motion Blur and set the Angle to **-90** degrees and the Distance to **17** (or where you like it). Click OK to exit. Now, you should definitely start seeing flames.

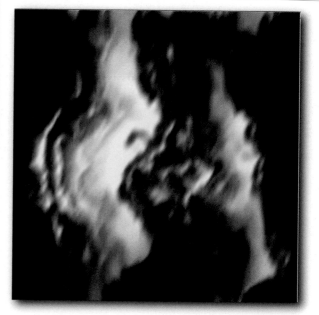

8 Just when you thought you had the pattern, it's time to change it. (It was getting old anyway.) Duplicate the Displace layer and drag it to the top of the layer stack. This layer is the basis for the final flames, but it takes several steps to get there. Name this layer **Displace White**. Press D to set your colors to the default and then press Shift+Command/Ctrl+Delete/Backspace. This fills the layer with white, but preserves the transparency of the layer at the same time.

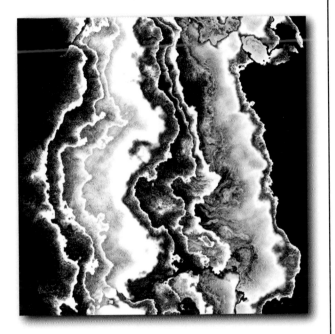

TIP

You can either lock the layer before you fill or use the Edit ⇨ Fill command and turn on Preserve Transparency. I much prefer the keyboard shortcut — the Shift key — along with the Fill command shortcuts (Command/Ctrl+Delete/Backspace to fill with the background color, and Option/Alt+Delete/Backspace to fill with the foreground color). The shortcuts are great for short attention spans. I tend to forget that I locked the layer. I always forget to turn Preserve Transparency *off* again if I use it in the Fill command.

---

9 Make sure the Displace White and the Solid Color Fill 1 layer are the only visible layers. Press Shift+Command/Ctrl+Option/Alt+E to make a merged layer above the Displace White layer. Name it **Blurred Displace**. Turn off the Displace White layer and make the Blurred

Displace layer active. What follows is an old Kai Krause tip for making fuzzy objects smooth. It starts with a blur, so add a Gaussian Blur filter of **4.0**.

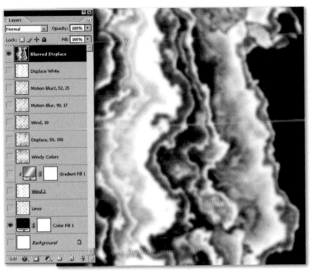

10 Add a Levels Adjustment layer above the Displace Blur layer. You need to get fairly crisp edges on the white shapes and thin them down a bit. The thinned shapes will be the final metal flame, so their shape is important and has no standard setting. Drag the Black Input slider to the right until the shapes start to get compact. Then drag the Gamma slider toward the black point slider. The closer the gamma is to the black point, the whiter the shapes become. You need to leave at least some gray in them.

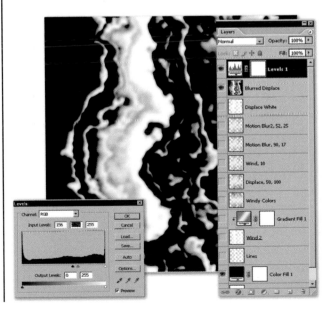

11 Create a merged layer above the Levels 1 layer (Press Shift+Command/Ctrl+Option/Alt+E. Name it **Flames**. (Yes, the end is almost in sight.) You need to add some wind to this. Choose Image ⇨ Rotate Canvas ⇨ 90 Degrees CCW. Then choose Filter ⇨ Stylize ⇨ Wind, from Left. Click OK. Rotate the canvas **90** degrees CW. Turn off the Levels 1 and the Displace White layers. Turn back on the Motion Blur 2 layer, though you won't see it yet. Make the Flames layer active. Command/Ctrl-click / on the RGB channel thumbnail in the Layers palette to load the values in the Flames layer as a selection. Then add a layer mask. Now you can see the yellow-orange flames of the Motion Blur 2 layer.

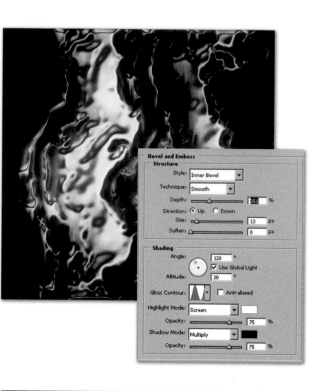

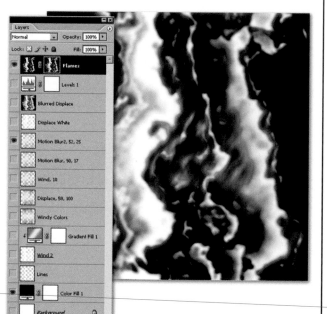

12 Time to make the metal. Add a Bevel and Emboss layer effect. Choose the following settings: Style: Inner Bevel; Technique: Smooth; Depth: **351**%; Direction: Up; Size: **13** px; Soften: **0** px. For the Shading, choose Angle: **120**, Global Light On; Altitude: **30** degrees; Gloss Contour: Ring, Anti-aliased off; Highlight Mode: Screen at **75**% opacity; Shadow Mode: Multiply at **75**% opacity. Click OK. If you don't like the settings, feel free to edit them. Drag the Fill opacity for the layer toward 0 as you prefer.

TIP

With Fill opacity set to **0**, you can see through to the flames. If you want more white to show, back off and increase the Fill opacity a bit more.

13 You could be done at this point, but my image looks a bit empty of smoke, and where there's fire, there has to be smoke (or something like that...). Duplicate the Motion Blur2 layer and name it **Motion Blur3**. Turn off the Motion Blur2 layer and make the Motion Blur3 layer active. You're on your own as to settings, but I used an Angle of **81** and a Distance of **166**.

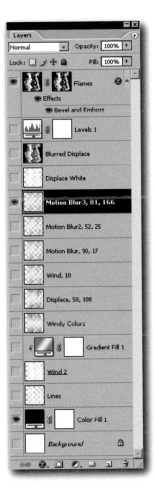

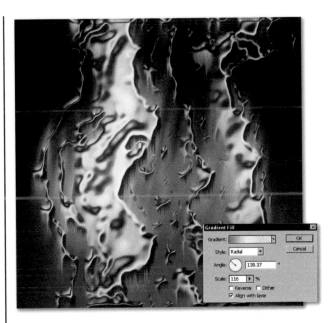

(15) Drag the file HotJazz.asl into the open Photoshop application to add two new layer styles to the Styles palette. I used the font Kurt Bold (it's from FontFont) at 200 points, Sharp. If you want to use the same type, open HotJazz.psd and use that instead of live type. Then add the HotJazz1 style to the text layer. Duplicate the layer and assign the HotJazz2 style. (I thought the first type layer needed some dimensionality as well as a bit less glitz).

(14) The one tweak left for the flames is to add more flaming color to the image. Make the black Solid Color Fill layer active and then add a Gradient fill layer above it. In the Gradient Editor, choose the same Orange, Yellow, Orange gradient that you use for the flames. Click the Opacity stop on the top right and choose white for the color (click on the white patch in the Toolbox). That makes the gradient transparent at the end of its range. Click OK to close the Editor, and then change the Gradient style to Radial. Drag the gradient until the center of it is near the bottom of the image. Adjust the Scale. I set it to **116** percent. I also created a Group out of all the unused layers at this point. You might want to slightly reduce the opacity of the layer.

Two layers of type with different layer styles assigned are often better than one. Because you can't add two different bevels to the same piece of type, duplicating the layer and changing the style frequently gets the job done.

You're seeing the end result of a very long decision-making process. How did I know that I wanted the layers in that order, that I wanted the FinalFlames layer to use Pin Light and the BourbonStreet layer to use Hard Light? I wish I could tell you that I am a genius and I just knew — but that would be lying. (Well, maybe I am a genius, but I certainly didn't know in advance what blend modes I wanted.) I arrange and rearrange the layers and methodically try every blend mode that exists to see what I prefer. When I find a combination I like, I save it as a snapshot in the History palette. When I finish with all of the blend modes and permutations, I look at the snapshots and save a new copy of the image for each snapshot I really like. Then I pick the one I like best.

16 Make the top layer active and create a merged layer above it (press Shift+Command/Control+Option/Alt+E). Name the merged layer **FinalFlames**. Change its blend mode to Pin Light and drag it below the two type layers. Make the Flames layer active and then open the image BourbonStreet.psd and drag it into the flames image. Press and hold Shift as you drag to make the two images register. Change the blend mode of the BourbonStreet image to Hard Light.

17 Finally, what would jazz in New Orleans be without the wail of a sax? Open the image sax.psd and drag the saxophone into the image above the FinalFlames layer. Name the layer **Sax**. Rotate the layer approximately **20** degrees and drag it into the lower-left corner near or on top of the lamppost. Add a layer mask and use a large soft brush with black to softly blend the sax into the image. Save your work.

A short recap

Flames and metallic effects are endlessly fascinating. The combination of the two is almost irresistible. Explore the many ways you can combine and recombine the layers. You start from a blank canvas, and you never get the same results twice. There's a lot of layer duplication going on in this task. Redundant perhaps, but once you toss something, it's gone for good. By saving all of the named layers, you

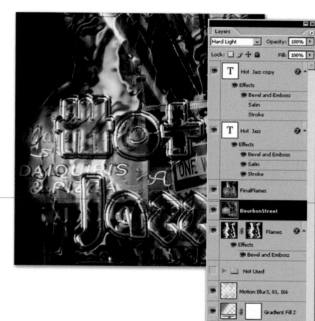

can trace your way back through the task at any point — even months later. The most critical determining factor in the final image is the original dmap. The method used to save the dmap (the look of the second channel) is also a determining piece. Play around with this. Try altering the original gradient color or the Solid Color Fill layer. Black is best when you create the image, but it doesn't need to remain black. Finally, try mixing up blend modes as you add foreground elements to this background image. *Laissez les bon temp rouler!*

Burnished

Did you ever have metal embossing kits as a child? This exercise shows you how to create a similar but more sophisticated look resulting in a keepsake coin. Any favorite child, family member, or co-worker would be happy to volunteer for the position on the coin. In the process, you take a few detours to explore both the Layer Styles and the various changes that you can make to an image. This task is not a recipe. Every image you use with it requires a slightly different treatment. The better you understand how this works, the more likely you are to use it in the future.

THE PLAN

- Select a photo to use
- Choose or create a metallic layer style
- Apply the effect and modify the layer style
- Finish by creating a coin

(1) Open the file LittleGuy.psd. While you are at the Web site for the book, also drag the file LizGold.asl and drop it into the open Photoshop program to add to your Styles palette (on the Mac, double-click the file to install it). Press Command/Control+Option/Alt+I to open the Image Size dialog box. With Resample Image and Constrain Aspect Ratio on, set the height of the image to 900 pixels. Change the Interpolation Method to Bicubic Smoother and click OK.

Photo: www.comstock.com

TIP

Styles are readily available in many locations. Adobe has an entire collection of free styles on its Web site. You're more likely to modify a style than to create one from scratch. However, if you want the practice of creating your own style from the start, then take a look at Chapter 1, Task 3.

(2) Double-click the Background layer thumbnail in the Layers palette and accept Layer 0 as the layer name. Click OK. Press Command/Ctrl+Option/Alt+C and make the canvas 1168 x 1038 (Relative unchecked) and anchor in the center. Click OK. Add a Gradient Fill layer and choose the Spectrum Gradient. Set the Style to Reflected and the Angle to **-160** degrees. Click OK.

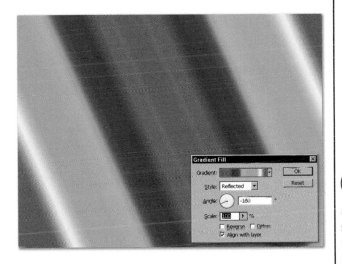

TIP

The choice of a gradient is one of the most important decisions in this task. You can change your mind after the fact, but it's messy. The thing to ask yourself here is if you want a shaded or a solid background. The tonal variation in the gradient is more important than the colors. The reflected Spectrum gradient gives you a metallic reflection on the finished coin. A gradient using the darkest and lightest background color in the original Little Guy image gives you an almost solid background.

(3) Duplicate Layer 0 as **Masked Boy** and send the duplicate layer to the top of the layer stack. Using the Pen tool, create a path around the boy and then save and load the path as a selection. (If the Pen tool is not your thing, just make any selection that you can around the child). With the selection active, add a Layer Mask. Then choose Image ⇨ Adjustments ⇨ Shadow/Highlights. Accept the default amount. It adds a needed separation between the hat and the boy's hair.

(4) Command/Ctrl-click the RGB Channel thumbnail in the Channels palette to load the value of the image as a selection. Press Shift+Command/Ctrl+C to copy this selection. Then press Command/Ctrl+V to paste the selection into a new layer. (The figure shows only the Light Tones layer.) Name the layer **Light Tones**.

TIP

Loading the values of a solid layer converts the image into grayscale (in the processing logic) and then puts marching ants around the lightest values in the image. Any pixel that is lighter than 128 shows in the marching ants. However, the only value that is totally unselected is solid black — and this image has no areas of solid black. Therefore, when you paste the selected area into its own layer, you see much more than just the area that was marqueed. (Of course, if you don't turn off the eyes on the other layers, you don't see any change at all!)

5 To get an idea of what styles can do to an image, open the Styles palette and apply any style. After you play a bit (and hopefully store up design ideas for later), make the Masked Boy layer active. Add a white Solid Color Fill layer between that and the Light Tones layer. Then make the Light Tones layer active. Again, click randomly to try out different styles. You'll see a huge difference. Click the LizGold style that you previously dragged into Photoshop. Click the eye on the Color Fill layer on and off to see the difference. Then drag the white Color Fill 1 layer under the Masked Boy layer. Again, you see a large difference.

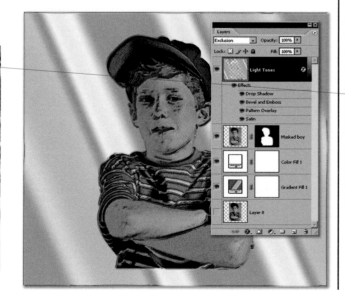

6 Let's fiddle with the style a bit. Double-click the Light Tones thumbnail to open the Layer Styles dialog box. Click the Bevel and Emboss settings. Change the Size of the bevel to **4**. Change the Gloss Contour from Cone to Ring-Double. Click OK.

7 The mottled texture in the skin is not attractive. It's coming from the Contour section of the Bevel and Emboss. Open the Bevel and Emboss dialog box again and click the text on the left that says Contour. Than change the Contour from the custom contour that Liz creates to the standard Rolling Slope Descending contour. Turn off the Satin effect; it makes no difference to the image if it's on or off. Click the Pattern Overlay effect to turn it off. This makes a big difference in the result. You might want to see what happens with other patterns, but you need to keep the Wood pattern as that pattern is what produces the gold. Click OK to save your changes and exit. The boy looks a bit like the Phantom of the Opera, but at least the rest of him no longer looks diseased. You'll fix that problem soon.

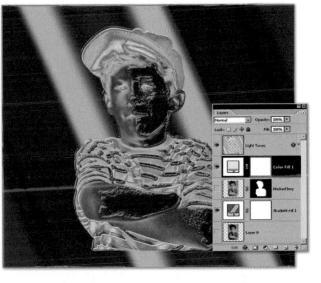

TIP

When you download pre-made styles and apply them, or you use the Adobe-provided styles, you'll often discover that you only like *part* of what the style is doing. You then need to deconstruct the style to figure out which part is causing the undesirable changes. You do this by turning the various parts of the Layer Style on and off and seeing what changes. You can learn a tremendous amount about building layer styles just by taking a complex style and analyzing what makes it work and what happens when you alter a piece of it.

TIP

When the coin is done, these color explorations don't matter. However, the burnished metal is such a neat task for images that you *don't* want to change into coins, I want you to see various ways you can alter your results.

8 We have a white Solid Color Fill under the partially transparent Light Tones layer. Changing the color of the fill can make a huge difference, and is one of the best methods, on your own, to vary the way this task looks. Turn off the eye on the Masked Boy image. Double-click the Solid Color Fill layer to reopen and see what happens as you randomly select colors. That gives you an idea of the types of changes you can make. Then choose RGB: **243**, **236**, **210**. Click OK. It's cream-colored neutral.

9 Command/Alt-click the thumbnail of the Light Tones layer to load the transparency of the layer (that gives you the same result as turning off all the layers and loading the values of the original in the Channels palette, and it's a lot faster too). With the selection active, add a white Solid Color Fill layer above the Light Tones layer. The selection automatically becomes the new mask. Copy the layer styles from the Light Tones layer and paste them onto the new Solid Color Fill layer. Change the Blend mode to Normal from Exclusion mode on the top layer. While you're at it, rename the top layer **LayerMasked**.

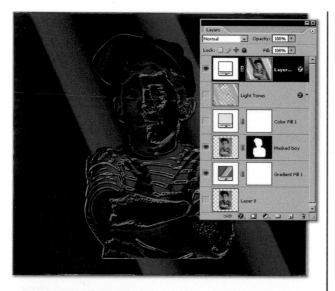

TIP

You might wonder if changing the color of the Solid Color Fill layer matters; it doesn't. The LayerMasked layer reacts the same way to color change whether you use a Solid Color Fill layer or not. The Pattern Overlay in the layer style blocks the original color of the layer. If you want to recolor the image or experiment with other fill colors, turn off the Color Overlay. Of course, you lose the gold tones.

(10) If you take the Little Guy image and put it in a layer and apply our modified LizGold style, all you get is a dark solid with a metallic edge. However, if you apply the style to just the dark areas of the image, you get a totally different look. Load the transparency of the Light Tones layer by Command/Ctrl-Clicking its thumbnail in the Layers palette. Then press Shift+Command/Ctrl+I to invert the selection. Make the LayerMasked layer active and then add a new white Solid Color Fill layer. Name the new layer **Dark Tones**. Paste the layer style onto the Dark Tones layer. You've now reconstructed the original image, but you do see a totally metal effect rather than a dark solid.

(11) Make the Dark Tones layer active and click the LizGold style in the Styles palette to replace the current style. Make the LayerMasked layer active and replace its style with the LizGold style as well. Turn on the eye on the Light Tones layer. Make the Color Fill 1 layer active, change the Blend Mode to Linear Light and delete the layer mask on the layer. Load the mask of the MaskedBoy layer by Command/Ctrl-clicking the thumbnail in the Layers palette. Add a new layer mask to the Color Fill 1 layer. Now the color in the layer only affects the child — and not the background area.

(12) Double-click the thumbnail of the Gradient Fill 1 layer and then open the Gradient Editor. Drag the magenta, blue, and yellow sliders off the gradient. Drag the final red slider off as well. Drag the green slider to the right edge of the Gradient bar and place the cyan slider at **58** percent. Click OK and then click OK again to set the new gradient. Save your work.

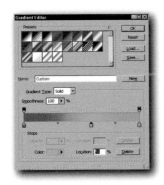

(13) Select all of the layers. Then Control/Right-click the layer entry on one of the selected layers and choose Group into New Smart Object. Name it **Boy**. Then press Command/Ctrl+Option/Alt+C and change the canvas size (Relative off) to 1200 pixels x 1000 pixels. Anchor in the center and click OK (some clipping will occur, click OK). Choose View ⇨ New Guide and set a guide at Vertical pixel 36. Then choose View ⇨ New Guide and set a Horizontal guide at pixel 65. Choose the Elliptical Marquee tool and change the Style on the Options bar to Fixed Size. Set the Width to 1109 pixels and the Height to 857 pixels. Uncheck Anti-alias. Click at the intersection of the guides on the image to place the marquee and then click the Add Layer Mask icon at the bottom of the Layers palette. Hide the Guides. Add a new layer and then choose Layer ⇨ New Background from Layer.

(14) To add a lip to the coin, load the layer mask as a selection by Command/Ctrl-clicking the layer mask thumbnail in the Layers palette. Choose Select ⇨ Modify ⇨ Border, 12 pixels and click OK. Add a new layer and fill the selection with your foreground color (the color doesn't matter). With the selection still active, click the Add Layer Mask icon on the Layers palette. Apply the LizGold style but turn off the Drop Shadow in the list of Effects. Name the layer **Lip**.

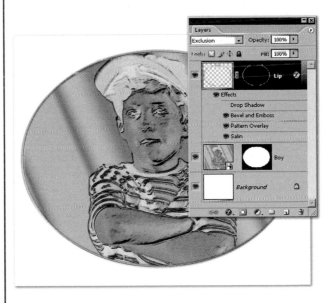

TIP

We're cheating a bit here. The final coin is in a skewed, distorted perspective so you can see the edge of the coin, but I don't like the result of distorting the actual image. So, I create a perspective where the child remains at actual size and aspect ratio but the coin shape is in perspective.

15 To create the coin's edge, clear the guides from the image. Next, choose View ➪ New Guide and set it at Vertical pixel 38 and another new guide at Horizontal pixel 92. Turn Anti-alias back on. Click at the intersection of the guides to leave the marquee. Click the Save Selection as Channel icon on the Channels palette and name the alpha channel **Coin Edge 1**. Deselect. Make the Coin Edge 1 channel active by clicking it in the Channels palette. Then show the RGB channel by turning on the eye on the RGB channel — don't click the channel (only the Coin Edge 1 channel should be highlighted in the Channels palette). Choose the Rectangular Marquee tool and reset it. The Style is Normal. Drag the marquee from the center of the canvas on the left edge of the coin to the right edge of the coin and down to cover almost to the bottom of the image. Press Shift+Command/Ctrl+I to inverse the selection and fill the selection in the channel with black. Deselect. Turn off the eye on the Coin Edge 1 alpha channel and make the RGB channel active.

16 Make the Background layer active and add a new layer named **Black Edge**. Load the Coin Edge 1 alpha channel by Command/Ctrl-clicking its thumbnail in the Channels palette. Fill the selection on the layer with black. Reduce the layer opacity to **61**%. Create a new image 9 pixels wide and 1 pixel high. Double-click the Hand tool to zoom into this image 1600%. Add a new layer and turn off the Background layer in the tiny file. You need to make a pattern for the edge of the coin. Choose the Pencil tool and the 1-pixel brush. Set your foreground color to RGB: 8, 6, 4 and an opacity of 72%. Click in the image at pixel 2, 5, and 8 (from the left). Then change the foreground color to RGB: **7, 7, 7** at **14**% opacity. Click to fill pixels 3, 4, 6, and 7. Choose Edit ➪ Define Pattern and name the pattern **Coin Edge**. You can close the pattern file now. Working back in the coin image, add a new layer above the Black Edge layer. Name it **Gold Edge**. Load the Coin Edge 1 alpha channel again and choose Edit ➪ Fill, with Pattern and select the Coin Edge pattern. Click OK. Add a Pattern Overlay style and choose the Wood pattern that you use throughout this task to make the gold color. Change the Blend mode of the layer to Overlay.

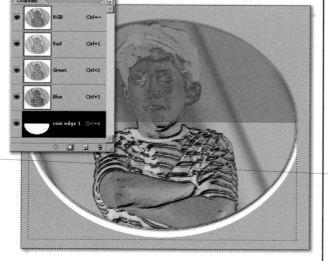

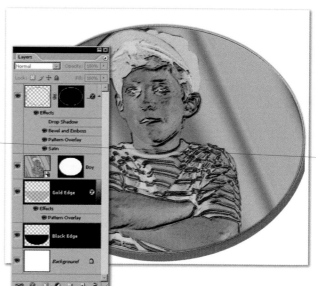

17 To make a drop shadow, Command/Ctrl-click the layer mask of the Boy Smart Object layer to load it as a selection. Press and hold Shift and Command/Ctrl-click the Black Edge layer to add it to the current selection. Make the Lip layer active and add a new layer above it. Name the layer **Shadow**. Fill the selection with the black on the Shadow layer. Set the Fill opacity to **0**. Add a Drop Shadow style. Set the Angle to **144** degrees with Global Light checked. Set the Distance to **43** pixels and the Size to **51** pixels. Use the default values for everything else. Click OK.

18 To add the type, Choose the Elliptical Shape tool. In the Ellipse Options palette on the Options bar, click the check box to draw from the center. Set the Shape tool to Create Paths. Click in the approximate center of the image and drag (before you release the mouse button) until you have the shape centered on the coin. Any serif font works for the type, but I used Adobe Garamond at 60 points, Sharp. Click the Center Text icon on the Options bar. Then click the left-center of the path to start the text. I typed **In Jimmy We Trust**. Commit. Add another Elliptical Shape path exactly on top of the first one (same size, same options). Click the center of the right side of the path. Then type more text for the right side of the coin. Add the LizGold style to both type layers. Save your work.

TIP

If you don't like the centering of the text, you can press the space bar until the text moves where you want it to go. Yes, that's cheating, but it sometimes works. The correct way to move type along a path is to choose the Direct Selection or the Path Selection tool. Click at the start of the text and you see an I-beam with an arrow. Drag the type around the path (being careful not to flip the type).

A short recap

When Liz first showed me her idea for burnished metal, I flipped over it. However, using her methods, I could not manage to get the effect to look good on any image that I tried (and I tried a lot of them). If you try this task on an image and don't like the way it looks, use a Solid Color Fill layer and put the light or dark values into the layer mask. Then use the Levels command on the layer mask. When you use the Levels command in the layer mask of a Color Fill layer, you are affecting the opacity of the pixels in the image, which dramatically alters the way the metal style appears. The image you used for the coin didn't need a Levels adjustment, but if you try this with landscapes (which really work quite well), you'll probably want to adjust the levels.

chapter

2

patterns 'n' pieces

Designing components makes it possible for you mix and match as you work. By having a lot of patterns, backgrounds, and text effects ready-made, you can pull an image together faster and you're ready for anything. Here is a bunch of ready-to-wear tasks that should be fun to do. The chapter includes two type treatments: outlined text that can go from bright to elegant as the situation warrants, and glass type that looks elegant in almost any typeface. You can create a wild background based on square pixels (and mix in a custom foreground) and you can use a filter to create a huge variety of pattern elements. Finally, for those of you who are addicted to interlocking patterns, I show you how to create an interlock from a scribble and how to create an Escher-style interlocking pattern from a photo.

Outline/Inline

How many hours did you spend doodling on your notepad during another boring class? Perhaps scribbling the name of a loved one over and over? It isn't quite the same in Photoshop (for one thing, now it's time out from work or — gasp — from your own precious free time). But, you can use brighter colors than in high school math. It would have been really hard to explain to the algebra teacher why you had 12 Magic Markers on your desk! This is a very simple technique but a powerful one. You'll find a lot of uses for it both on text and around objects or selections.

THE PLAN

- Create the basic text
- Repeat the text object until you have enough outlines
- Add other areas (objects) of interest
- Add a paper-lined background pattern

TIP

If you don't have a suitably wide font, you can start with type that is already rasterized. I posted two starting versions using Bees Knees. One loves Norman and the other one loves Susan. Pick the most appropriate. I wouldn't want your co-workers to peek over your shoulder and walk away with strange looks in their eyes!

(1) Create a new file 900 pixels x 900 pixels. Pick a very heavyweight font (I use Bees Knees) and type the name of your current love interest at approximately 125 points. Add a Gradient Overlay effect. Click the Gradient Preset arrow and select the Spectrum Gradient. Click OK. Set the Style to Radial and leave the Angle at **90** degrees. Set the Scale to **150**%. Click OK. Press Command/Ctrl+T and type **-27** degrees into the Angle field. Commit.

(2) Set your colors to the default of black and white. Add a Stroke effect. First, select the Gradient Fill Type. Choose the Transparent Stripes preset. Change the Style to Radial. Leave the Angle at **90** degrees. Choose an Inside position. I know I'm not giving you these fields in the same order as they appear, but this is the way I decide what settings to use. Now that you have that much set up, you can drag the Size and Scale sliders to find the best mix. I quickly determine that I need to check the Reverse check box, too. Reversing the gradient puts the black line at the very outside of the type. I use a Size of **9** pixels and a Scale of **139**%. Adjust to taste. A different font and a different typeface mean that all bets are off as to the suitability of my settings. Before you close the dialog box, check the Bevel and Emboss check box on the left to enable it. This gives the most basic bevel, and it's just fine; no need to even peek at the settings! Save the style if you think you'll use it again. Then click OK to exit.

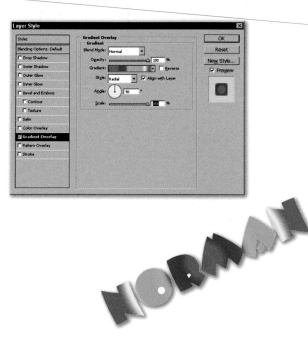

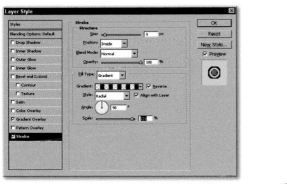

4 Drag the Gradient Type layer to the New Layer icon to duplicate it. I usually have you rename layers, but in this case, the default increment name is probably just as helpful. If you want to rename it, just add (red) to the back of the Gradient Type copy name. Choose the Type tool, and without selecting the text, type **130** into the Font Size field. Remove the current layer style by clicking the None style on the Styles palette or by dragging the styles to the Layers palette trashcan. Then add a Stroke effect using the default red color and a 9-pixel outside stroke.

3 Drag the type layer to the New Layer icon at the bottom of the Layers palette to duplicate it. Name the new layer **Gradient Type**. Make the lower type layer active and rename it **Blue Button**. Choose the Type tool, and without selecting the text, type **130** into the Font Size field. Then open the Styles palette and click the Blue Button style that ships with Photoshop. This gives the type a bit more dimensionality.

TIP

You have a number of possible ways to build this effect. My original method simply creates a merged layer for the text and then adds a stroke to that. However, you might want to change the actual text at some point, and the construction method in the instructions makes it easy to alter the text, the font, the size, or the colors. It is a totally nondestructive way to build the effect. Should you need to change the text, you need to change it one layer at a time. (I would copy the second layer's text and then paste it into each successive layer—the type on the first layer is smaller.) If you need to alter the font size, select all of the layers, choose the Type tool, and alter the font size field.

5 The rest of the text outlines are built up the same way – you just keep duplicating the previous layer and moving it lower in the layer stack. To create the rest of the layers: Duplicate the Gradient Type Copy layer and open the Stroke effect. Give it a 14-pixel magenta stroke on the outside (click on the color swatch to see the Color Picker and then click on magenta in the image). This gives you a stroke of 9 pixels under the original red stroke plus 5 pixels to view the magenta color. Duplicate that layer and drag it down in the stack. Open the Stroke dialog box and choose a very light blue-white from the top of the text. This stroke has a total amount of 23 pixels. The next duplicate layer adds a 3-pixel black stroke to the current stroke amount (for a total of 26 pixels). Then add an additional 3 pixels (total of 29 pixels) to the stroke in bright blue (chosen again from the image) to another duplicate layer.

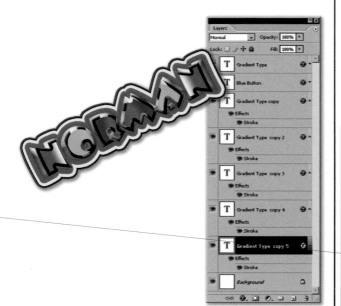

6 The last gradient stroke is a bit different. Duplicate the Gradient Type copy 5 layer. Choose Gradient for the Fill Type. The stroke amount is 64 pixels. Leave the Angle at **90** degrees and the Scale at **100%**. Choose the Shape Burst Gradient. Shape Burst applies the gradient run around the text so that each color in the gradient encircles the entire shape and the color in the gradient moves from the inside of the shape to the outside. Click the Gradient Editor and choose the Spectrum gradient. Space the gradient so that it doesn't start changing colors until you see it come out from under the layer on top. Then move the magenta, blue, cyan, and green color stops closer to the red color stop on the left (just drag them). Click the green color stop to make it active and press and hold Option/Alt as you

drag a copy of that stop to the right. Move the yellow color stop closer to the red on the right and Option/Alt-drag a copy of the yellow stop toward the left. You can enlarge or contract any band of color in this manner. Click OK when you like the result. Click OK to exit the Stroke dialog box.

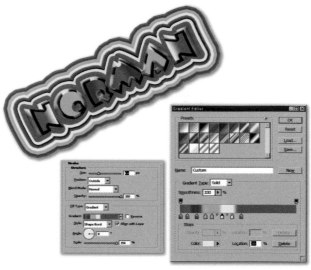

TIP

If you position the dialog box so you can see both it and the text, you can see the effect of the changes in the gradient as you make them. There's no need to duplicate my gradient alterations. Have fun and see how wild you can make the stroke. You can add colors to a gradient anywhere just by clicking and then double-clicking the new stop to open the Color Picker. If you use the Live Text method to build the image, the Shape Burst with a Spectrum gradient is trickier. Alter the gradient to get it out to the edge of the previous layer's stroke before you start changing colors. To do that, move all of the color stops closer to the color on the left of the gradient.

7 Let's change the magenta stroke to stripe it. Make the Gradient Type Copy 2 layer active. Drag it to the New Layer icon to duplicate it, but leave it on top of the original layer. Add **blue** to the end of the layer name. Double-click the Stroke effect on the new layer to reopen the Stroke dialog box. Change the Fill Type to Gradient and the Gradient Style to Reflected. Click the Gradient Editor field and select the Transparent Stripes preset. Double-click the Color Stop on the left and pick a blue from the image. Click OK on the Color Picker and then double-click the color stop on the right. Choose the same blue for it as well. Click OK to exit the Color Picker and the Gradient Editor. Leave the Scale of the gradient at **100**% and the Angle at **90** degrees. Click OK. The new blue color appears over the original magenta layer that is duplicated. Select all of the layers except the Background layer and press Command/Ctrl+G to Group them. Name the group **Text**.

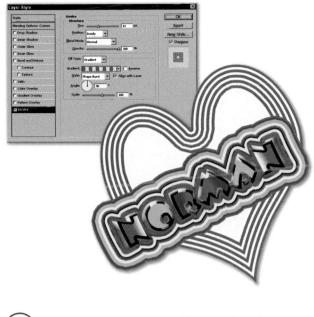

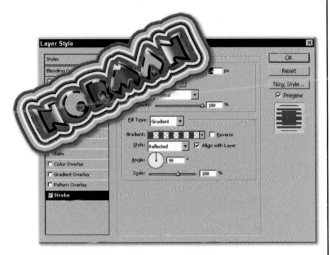

8 Move the Text group closer to the center of the image. Make the Background layer active. Choose the Custom Shape tool and the heart shape. In the Custom Shape Options dialog box, click Fixed Size and set the Width to 637 px and the Height to 664 px. Set the Style to None. The color does not matter. Click to set a heart shape in the image. After you release the mouse button, press Command/Ctrl+T and type **–27** degrees into the Angle field. Commit. Position the heart closer to the right side of the text as shown. Set the Fill opacity to **0**. Make red your foreground color. Add an Inside Stroke effect. Choose a Gradient type with the Shape Burst gradient. Pick the Transparent Stripes preset. Notice, this time the stripes go around the entire object (or will as soon as you pick the size). Click OK. The red foreground color means that you get red stripes without doing anything special. Set the Size to about **81**. Click OK.

9 Type the word **I** in any wide serif font. I use 350-point Warnock Pro. Rotate it to **–27** degrees and move it into place.

10 Let's create some lined notebook paper. For some reason, the paper always has light-blue lines. Create a new file 1 pixel wide and 20 pixels high. Yep — you can just about see it. Double-click the Hand tool to enlarge it to 1600% and give yourself a fighting chance to paint in it. RGB:**110, 173, 210** looked like a good line color to me, but feel free to choose purple lines if that makes you happy. With the Pencil tool and the 1-pixel brush, leave a 1-pixel dot in the image. I put mine at the top, but it can go anywhere. Choose Edit ➪ Define Pattern and name it **School Book**. Click OK. Make the Background layer active and add a new Pattern Fill layer. Choose the School Book pattern and click OK.

11 Finally, you might like to give the text more of a dimension. You can reuse the Blue Button layer for that. Bring the Blue Button layer to the top of the layer stack. Open the attached styles and turn off the eye on the Color Overlay and the Gradient Overlay. Set the Fill opacity to **0**. Now you can decide which one you prefer.

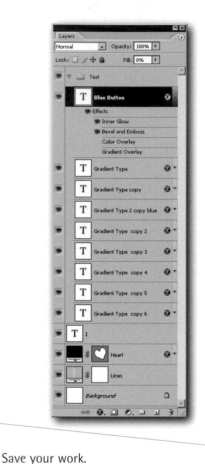

12 Save your work.

A short recap

You can't add multiple strokes to an object in Photoshop (at least, not nondestructively). However, you can fake it out. One way is to add a stroke, make a copy of the layer—stroke and all—and stroke that. In this way, your base image gets larger with every copy. That can make it hard to change, but if you alter the layer order so that the smallest layer is on top, you can change any stroke. However, you can also build as I did, by making the stroke itself get larger with every new layer added. You need to remember to keep bringing the newest layer under the previous layer so they don't cover up the smaller strokes. This way, you can build as complex an object as you want, and one that can be altered at the slightest hint of indecision.

The Highway

Ever wonder why there are so many highway metaphors? Photoshop, too, is also a highway with many exits, twists, and turns. Follow this colorful exploration for a trip down several of them. By repeatedly copying layers before you filter or alter them, you leave yourself a road to follow back, so you can revisit old haunts and explore other paths. The main component is the square, which can be built in different ways. Finally, because an undecorated highway is just empty, you see how to blend a photo into it in a way that gives you the best of both images. You can always use a new background technique and can never have too many ways to create. The Highway leads you down another path for background construction of a modular component.

THE PLAN

- Create a difference gradient and make it into squares
- Blur
- Find Edges, Invert and set to Different mode
- Explore other winding trails
- Pick a road and embed a photo

1 Create a new image 450 pixels wide x 750 pixels high with a white background. Choose the Gradient tool. Load the Color Harmonies 2 Set of Gradients and click Append. Choose the MGY.grd gradient from the newly loaded presets. You may use the Spectrum Gradient if you prefer, but it uses much stronger colors.

Gradient Editor dialog box — Presets, Name: Magenta, Green, Yellow; Gradient Type: Solid; Smoothness: 100 %

(2) Change the Blend mode on the Gradient tool Options bar to Difference. Use a Linear Gradient and leave the Opacity at **100%** and the Mode at Normal. Drag the Gradient cursor from the top of the image to the bottom, pressing and holding Shift to constrain the direction. Then drag the Gradient cursor from the left to the right, also with the Shift key pressed. This is the base image.

TIP

If you start recording an Action for the next two steps, things will go faster because you use this step several times in this task. Name the Action **Highway**.

(3) Duplicate the background layer as **Blocks**. Choose Filter ⇨ Pixelate ⇨ Mosaic, Cell size: **16**. Click OK.

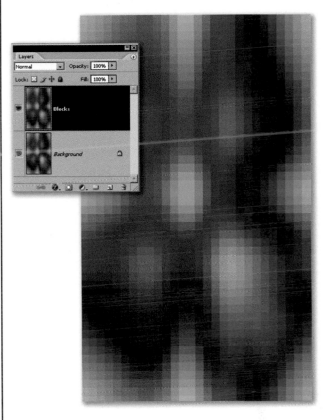

(4) Duplicate the Blocks layer as **Blur**. Choose Filter ⇨ Blur ⇨ Gaussian Blur, 1.0. Click OK. Duplicate the Blur layer as **Find Edges**. Choose Filter ⇨ Stylize ⇨ Find Edges. Change the blend mode for this layer to Difference and choose Image ⇨ Adjustments ⇨ Invert. That's all there is to the basic task. Though you can stop here, there's so much more that you can do.

TIP

If you're recording an Action, stop recording now.

Task 7 ● The Highway

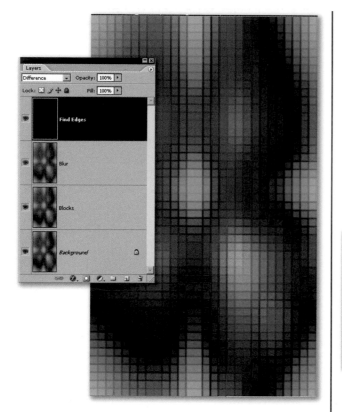

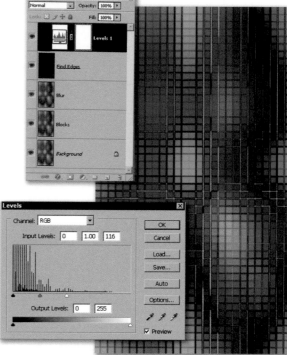

⑤ Sometimes the inverted Find Edges gives bright, glowing colors. This isn't one of those times! (It depends on the base gradient). If you want a brighter grid, it's easy to get. Press and hold Option/Alt as you choose a Levels layer from the New Fill or Adjustment icon at the bottom of the Layers palette. Check the Use Previous Layer to Create Clipping Mask check box. Click OK. Drag the Input White Point slider to the left until you like the results. I use a White Point value of 116. Click OK.

⑥ So, what else can you do? Want a more high-tech highway? Create a merged layer at the top of the layer stack (Shift+Command/Ctrl+Option/Alt+E). Choose Filter ⇨ Distort ⇨ Glass and use the settings shown. Click OK. Name the top layer **Glass**.

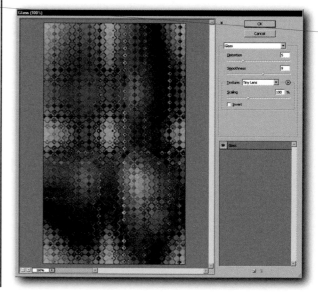

TIP

Why those settings? The real reason is that I like them. You can pick whatever you want. I think the Tiny Lens at a Distortion of 5 and a Smoothness of 9 is a sweet spot. You can still retain that design if you increase the Scaling. Distortion of 5 doesn't look like glass yet. It looks like wiggly tadpoles with a single eye. At 4, there isn't any eye; at 6, a second eye starts to form.

TIP

Whenever possible set up Blend modes and turn on all needed layers before filtering to get the benefit of as accurate a preview as possible.

7 Want more complexity in the Step 5 ending image? Hide the Glass, Blocks, and Blur layers. Make the Background layer active and duplicate it as **Motion Blur 1**. Change the Blend mode to Difference. Choose Filter ⇨ Blur ⇨ Motion Blur. Set the Angle to **90** degrees. Drag the Distance slider until you see a change in the image that you like. I set it to 575 pixels.

8 If you prefer the original colors but like the additional complexity, you needn't sacrifice one for the other. Just duplicate the Motion Blur 1 layer as **Motion blur 2**. There is nothing else to do. The Blend mode does it all.

9 You can also widen the byways a bit. In addition to the layers already hidden, turn off the two new Motion Blur layers and make the Background layer active. Duplicate the Background layer as **Find Edges 2**. Choose Stylize ⇨ Find Edges. Invert the layer and then change the Mode to Difference. You don't see much change yet. Press and hold Option/Alt as you choose a Levels layer from the New Fill or Adjustment icon at the bottom of the Layers palette. Check the Use Previous Layer to Create Clipping Mask check box. Click OK. Drag the Input White Point slider to about **34** and the Gamma slider to about **1.83**. Now that pops!

10 Okay, we've dragged that out enough. Let's reuse the Background layer one more time, but choose Layer ⇨ Duplicate Layer, Destination: New to put the layer into its own file and flatten it. Using the gradient as in Step 1 and still in Difference mode, drag from top to bottom, then from left to right, and then from top to bottom again. This forms an almost geometric pattern.

11 Play your saved action or repeat Steps 2 to 4. Then duplicate the Find Edges layer as **Find Edges 2**. You guessed it! Apply the Find Edges filter again. Change the mode to Difference and invert the layer.

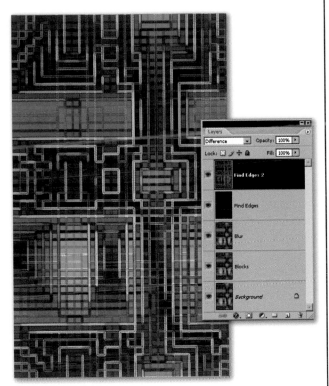

12 You'll get more punch from the double outline if you see less of it. Add a layer mask on the Find Edges 2 layer and fill the mask with black. Square brushes are hard to find in the default set, but this works: Select the Eraser tool in Block mode. Press D for defaults and then X, if needed, to exchange the colors so the background color is white (Photoshop isn't always consistent when a mask is active). Now use the Eraser tool in the mask to reveal the highway and the route you want to travel. If you get off at the wrong exit, not to worry. Just reverse your colors and retrace your steps.

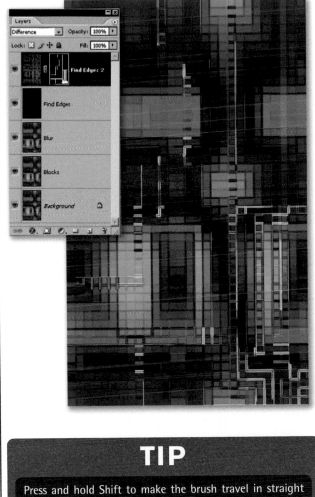

TIP

Press and hold Shift to make the brush travel in straight lines.

(13) Choose Image ⇨ Rotate Canvas ⇨ 90 degrees CW, then open the image teen.psd and, pressing and holding Shift to center the image, drag it in to the highway image as the top layer. Name the layer **Teen**. Dig that hair! Do *you* feel like masking it? It can be done, and the white mask background makes it easier, but let's not. Instead, start by pressing Command/Ctrl+T and scaling the girl's photo 170 percent (type **170** in the Width field and click the link between width and height to scale in proportion). Commit the transform.

Photo: www.comstock.com

(14) Instead of masking the layer, we just drop out a lot of the white, leaving a glow behind her hair. First, duplicate the Teen layer two more times, then hide these two new copies. Make the Teen layer active. Double-click on the Teen layer to open the Layer Style dialog box. Drag the Blend-If This Layer white slider toward the left until most of the white drops out. It will be around a value of **153**. Of course, most of the image has also dropped out. The white point slider has two pieces. Press and hold Option/Alt and slide the right half of the slider to the right again. As you drag it back toward the right, the transition gets smoother. Drag the right half back to value **254**. (Yes, I know she's missing part of her skin, which isn't a very attractive look.)

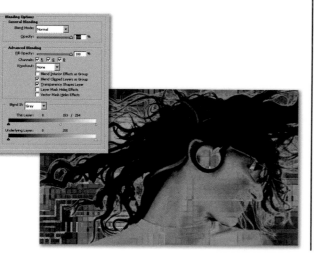

(15) Turn on the eye on the next layer up, rename the layer **Skin**. Press and hold Option/Alt and add a layer mask from the bottom of the Layers palette. This masks the layer completely. With white and a soft brush, paint the teenager's face, shirt, and earphones back in.

(16) At this point, the young lady is stretched out over the canvas but isn't really interacting with it. She doesn't seem to be involved with the highway at all. Let's start to change that. Turn off all of the teen layers. Choose Image ⇨ Duplicate ⇨ Merged Layers only ⇨ OK. Just let the merged copy stay there on the desktop and go back to the layered highway image. Turn on all three of the teen layers. Rename the top layer **Blouse**. Choose the Pen tool and make a path around the blouse (remember to select Paths on the Options bar). Then click the Load Path as Selection button in the Paths palette.

TIP

If you don't know how to use the Pen tool, you ought to learn, because it is a really precise way to make a selection. However, you can use the Magic Wand tool with a Tolerance of about 40 and hack away at the blouse to select it all if you prefer. You can also use the Color Range command and save an alpha channel that you need to modify until it selects just the area you want. You can also paint the selection in QuickMask mode. Believe me; once you master it, the Pen tool is so much easier!

TIP

If you want to get all the colors in the highway image into the blouse, you need to have only the blouse selected when you apply the adjustment. If the blouse is masked or simply not selected at all, the result is dramatically different.

(17) You should now have a selection, however, you got it. Choose Image ➪ Adjustments ➪ Match Color. In the Match Color dialog box, choose the new merged document as the Source image (the name of your image is almost undoubtedly going to be different than mine shown in the figure). The colors of the highway image mix to form a new color for the rather bland blouse. Click the Add Layer Mask icon on the Layers palette to change the selection into a mask. You may close the merged duplicate image without saving it.

(18) We're getting there. I think the teen needs a bit more glow around her hair. The white around it is already glowing a bit and we need to accentuate that look without obliterating the image underneath. Make the Find Edges 2 layer active. Add a Solid Color Fill layer of RGB: **229, 179, 91**. Click OK. Press D to set the Foreground/Background colors to their default of black and white. Press and hold Option/Alt as you choose Filter ➪ Render ➪ Clouds. You get a high-contrast Clouds fill on the mask of the Solid Color Fill layer that makes the highway image blend softly in and out and makes the hair glow.

Filtering a layer mask can make very interesting blends on an image. Clouds is an excellent filter to slide things together. Because there are no hard edges in the mask, all of the transitions are soft and gentle. You can use the Levels command on this mask, but I don't care for the blobs of color it creates. I like the softness. I might have preferred an inner or outer glow layer style, but even though you have a Blend-If set for the Teen layer, Photoshop sees that layer as being solidly opaque. If you want each hair to glow, make a precise selection and then a layer mask. I find that the Clouds filter on a Solid Color Fill layer does just about as a good job in this instance — with much less work.

19 Next, add a layer style that you can see on the full Blend-if layer. A bevel and emboss only alters the perimeter of an opaque layer, but the changes are still visible. You can use that effect to get a shadowed glow along the outer edge of the image. Make the Teen layer active and add a Bevel and Emboss. For Style, choose the Inner Bevel; set Technique to Smooth. Set Depth to **251**% and click the Up option button for Direction. Size is **120** px and Soften is **0** px. Leave the Angle at the default **120** degrees and set Altitude at **30** degrees with a standard Gloss Contour. Set the Highlight mode to Color Dodge and assign it the same RGB: **229, 179, 91** that you used for the glow layer. Change the Opacity to **100**%. Choose RGB: **129, 35, 135** for the shadow color. Change the Shadow mode to Color Burn, and set its opacity to **100**%. Click OK to exit the Layer Style dialog box.

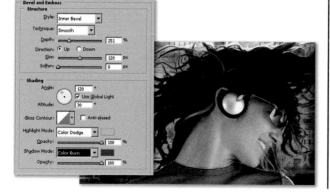

20 Now, mix back some of the final Highway image with the young girl. The Tip tells why this somewhat mysterious process works. Select the three teen layers and the Solid Color Fill layer. Press Command/Ctrl+G to make it into a Group/Layer Set. Name the group **Teen**. Select the remaining ungrouped layers, Control/right-click and choose Group into New Smart Object. Make the Teen group active and Expand the group. Make the Blouse layer active and then add a black Solid Color Fill layer (named **Knockout**). Fill the Layer Mask on this layer with black to hide the effects of the layer. On this new layer, double-click to open the Layer Style dialog box. Drag the Fill opacity slider to **0** and change the Knockout to Shallow. The image looks no different yet, so it isn't shown in the figures here.

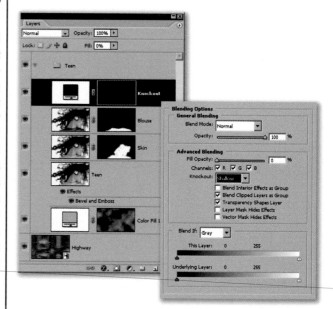

What did you do in this step? What's the point? The goal is to bring back some of the Highway image in its final form and mix it into the earphones, the blouse, and the sunglasses of the teen. Photoshop has a number of ways to do that. You can mask all the way back down to the Find Edges 2 layer, but I think that's really messy. You can duplicate the layers into a merged layer, bring the duplicate above all of the layers, and mask it. That works reasonably well but adds an extra layer. My choice is to use the Knockout control in the Layer Styles dialog box. Knockout allows you to cut through all of the layers in a reverse masking process. You can bring back detail from the Background layer by choosing Deep Knockout. However, in this case, the Background layer doesn't contain the full image that we want to reveal. That full image is layered. You can, of course, merge those layers into the Background layer, but that rather defeats the care we took to leave the layers in the first place! So, because we can't use Deep Knockout, what other option do we have? Photoshop also has a Shallow Knockout mode. You can activate Shallow Knockout in two ways: the base layer of a Clipping Mask group can be used for Shallow Knockout or the layer directly under a Group/Layer Set can be used for Shallow Knockout. The Teen group layers don't seem to be a natural fit for becoming a Clipping Mask group, so the Group method seems the best alternative. Again, we have the problem of needing a single layer to use as the layer under the Group. However, if we make a Smart Object of the original Highway layers, the problem is solved without any extra layers. You can't do a Deep Knockout to a Smart Object, because it isn't the official Background layer, but it's quite suitable for use in Shallow Knockout. And the 0 percent Fill opacity business? Oh yes, Knockout only shows up when the Fill opacity of the layer used for Knockout is 0. You can add layer effects to that layer (we won't), but the Fill must be at 0. Knockout is very useful in certain circumstances (like this one), but I won't deny the complexity of the issue. Except for the intricacies of CMYK or color management, this is almost as deep and technical as you can get. An empty layer that's set to Knockout doesn't do very much, (nor does a Solid Color Fill layer that is masked in black), but if you put something white or gray in that layer mask, it acts as a mask through which to reveal the detail in the designated layer. You could simply use the paintbrush in a regular layer set to Knockout to reveal detail from the Smart Object. However, if you paint in a regular layer and decide you don't like some of the results, you need to use the Eraser tool to get rid of areas you don't want. I prefer convenience over increased file size, so I had you use a Solid Color Fill layer with an automatic layer mask. Anywhere you add white or gray to the mask, you reveal the Smart Object. If you don't like the effect somewhere in the image, press X and paint with black to fix it easily.

21 You're finally ready to paint on the Knockout layer. Make the Knockout layer active and fill with the foreground color (it doesn't matter what it is; you don't see it anyway). The entire Teen group seems to disappear, and all you see is the Highway. Press and hold Option/Alt and click the Add Layer Mask icon. That hides the layer. Now, you can paint in the layer mask with white. Use the 65-pixel soft brush and click over the earphones to pull the Highway image into them. Leave some reflective silver on the edges. Click over the lens of the teen's sunglasses. Use the 9- or 10-pixel brush at 50% opacity to brush in some color on the wire of the earphones. With the 17-pixel brush and 50% opacity, bring the Highway into the ribbing on the neckline of the teen's blouse. Change the opacity to 30% and paint over the lighter colored areas of the blouse. Finally, with a 100-pixel soft brush at 10% opacity, slowly bring some transparency (and highway) into the edges of the teen's hair. Save the image.

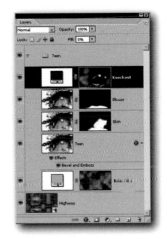

22 Save your work.

A short recap

There's so much that you can do with the Highway task. Try duplicating the base gradient layer and making 8-pixel Mosaic blocks and Find Edges. Then group the layers and mask them so that only some of the smaller areas of block are visible. Try creating diagonal gradients or dragging the gradient cursor in random directions and lengths. The basic task is easy—gradient, make blocks, blur, find edges, and invert in difference mode. The variations are a totally different journey each time. If you then use the Highway image as a background, you have even more ways to make the foreground react with the background image to create a unified composition. Try out the Knockout controls on your own images as well.

Through the Styled Glass

What happens when you want to apply three different sets of styles to one set of text? Typically, you're out of luck. An object can have one drop shadow — pick one, any one, but just one. I am congenitally indecisive and I always want more. I much prefer "and" to "or." The solution? Duplicate the object and add a different style to it, and then mix and match. That's how glass text is born, and we use it here in the context of a wedding template. The base template is designed by Kathryn Bernstein, and you see how to modify it for different photos and type styles.

THE PLAN

- Select a photo
- Choose colors
- Expand the template
- Set type
- Add layer styles

1 Open the image KBtemplate.psd. It consists of five Solid Color Fill layers with the colors blocked out by vector masks. It's remarkably easy to change and recombine colors. The middle three layers use different opacities to mix with each other, and the top layer is styled so that all you see is a shadowed frame and an outer edge.

2 Open the image FirstDance.psd. Choose Image ⇨ Image Size. Change the Height to 400 pixels. Choose the Bicubic Smoother Interpolation Method. Constrain Proportions and Resample Image should be selected. Click OK. Make the KBtemplate active. Command/Ctrl-click the Alpha 1 channel to load it as a section. Using the Rectangular Marquee tool, drag the marching ants into the FirstDance image. Drag the Insert Picture alpha channel and drop it into the FirstDance image. Click the eye on the alpha to show the red coating and make the alpha channel active. Drag the alpha selection with the Move Marquee tool until you like the cropping. Load the alpha channel and copy (Edit ⇨ Copy) the selection to the clipboard. Make the KBtemplate image active and click the Shape 1 layer. Choose Edit ⇨ Paste (or drag and drop). Now your image is in the correct position. Name the layer *Image*. You can close the FirstDance image.

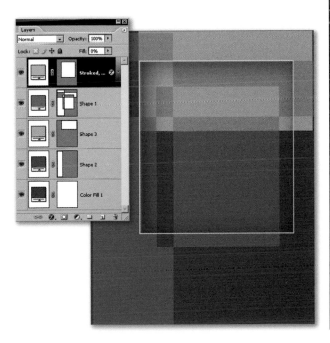

Photo: www.comstock.com

3 The next step is to add a bit of light to the template. Make the Shape 1 layer active. Press and hold Option/Alt and click the New Layer icon at the bottom of the Layers palette. In the New Layer dialog box, change the Mode to Soft Light and click the Fill with Soft-Light neutral color (50 percent gray). Click OK. Name the layer **Light**. Choose Filter ➪ Render ➪ Lighting Effects. Choose the Default style and click OK.

4 Add a layer mask to the Light layer. Using black in the mask with the 100-pixel soft brush, brush out the effect on the top-right corner. Remove the light from the entire peach stripe.

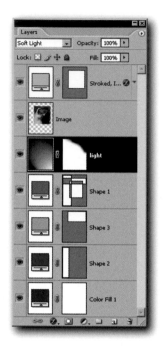

5 Select all of the layers in the image and right-click. Choose Group into New Smart Object. Name the Smart Object **Main Focus**. We need to enlarge the canvas, so choose Image ➪ Canvas Size. Deselect Relative, and set the width to 629 pixels and the height to 807 pixels. Leave the anchor in the center square and click OK. Add a black Solid Color Fill layer, named **Bottom**, and drag it under the Smart Object layer.

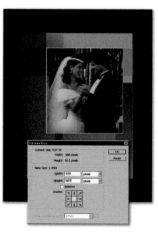

6 Press Command/Ctrl+T and click the upper-left button in the Reference point location on the left of the Options bar. This moves the center point of the bounding box to the top-left corner of the Smart Object. Then type **115** into the X: field and **167** into the Y: field to move the Main Focus Smart Object to my preferred location. If you don't prefer that location, use the Move tool and drag it anywhere you wish. Commit.

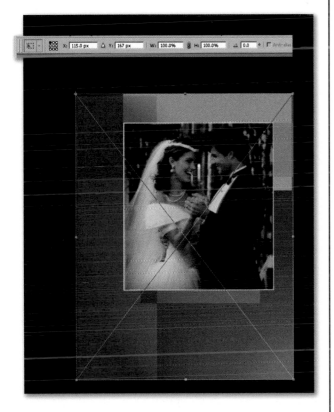

Why Use a Smart Object?

The template image in this example is filled with Solid Color Fill Layers. If you increase the size of the canvas, the Solid Color Fill layers also expand to their new size and lose the focus of the image. Making them into a Smart Object first keeps them from expanding. Your other options are to individually mask each layer or make a Layer Set Group out of them and mask the Group folder layer. I prefer the Smart Object route because of its elegance (a programmer's term). I can manipulate the entire set of layers as if they were a single layer, edit anything I want to alter, but protect the layers from any type of unintentional change.

7 Make the Bottom layer active. Click the RGB channel. Choose the Shape tool and the Rectangular shape. Press and hold Option/Alt and click on a spot of dark rust on the curtains behind the groom to set your foreground color. Drag and set the Rectangle shape to cover from the top left of the image to the bottom and as far right as the right edge of the top purple stripe. Name the layer **Left Side**. Then press and hold Option/Alt and click on the peach stripe. Add a new Rectangular Shape layer so that it is about the same distance above the top purple square as the height of the square and stretches to the right and bottom edges of the image. Name this layer **Right Side**. Select the three new layers and group them (Command/Ctrl+G) as **Extended Layers**. Now you're ready to create the glass text.

Clicking the RGB channel allows you to pick a color even when a Color Fill layer is active. One of the best ways to customize a template that you create is to choose colors for the Solid Fill colors from the image itself. That way, the template always looks as if it belongs to the image. By using Solid Color Fill layers, you can preview any color change before you make and try out many different colors.

Many different fonts will work with this. Not all of them will get a glassy look. If you want to try Hopeless Heart, it's available at www.myfonts.com. However, I also placed a rasterized version of it on the book Web site and it works as well as the real type; it just can't be edited or changed. To see which font I wanted to purchase for this task, I looked at Script fonts on myfonts.com. I then asked for a display of the words On Our Wedding Day at 48 points. I took a screen shot of a group of fonts and deleted the extra material on the page until I had only the black-and-white type left (black type on a white page). I then loaded the page as a selection and inverted it. I added three Solid Color Fill layers in the text color I wanted and added the glass text styles to each layer. I offset each mask slightly. That way, I could preview a lot of fonts at the same time and decide which I liked best. I put one of these samples on the Web site.

8 Choose a lighter version of the peach stripe and create your text. Type **On Our Wedding Day** and divide the line after the first two words. I used Hopeless Heart at 60 points, but you may use whatever font is available. (Monotype Corsiva or any relatively thick script font works well.) Duplicate the text layer twice so that you have three identical text layers. Put the three type layers into a Group (press Command/Ctrl+G). Open the group folder. Hide the eyes on the top two layers.

9 Add a Drop Shadow effect to the visible layer. Use an Angle of **132** degrees, a Distance of **18** pixels, a Spread of **5** percent, and a size of **8** pixels. Assign a Cone contour, Anti-aliased, with **0** Noise to the drop shadow. Add a smooth Inner Bevel of **100** percent depth and an **11-pixel** Size with Soften set to **0**. Assign a Ring Gloss Contour and an Altitude of **32** degrees. In the Contour subheading, choose the Gaussian contour with an anti-aliased 50 percent Range. In the Blending Options Advanced Blending section, change the Fill Opacity to **50%**. Close the Layer Style dialog box.

10 Turn on the eye on the middle text layer and make it active. Add a Drop Shadow effect using a Distance of **36** pixels, a Spread of **5** percent, and a Size of **8** pixels. Change the color of the drop shadow to neutral gray (RGB: **128, 128, 128**) by clicking the color patch in the Drop Shadow dialog box. Add a Cove-Shallow contour. Click OK to close the dialog box. Turn on the eye on the top text layer. Shift-click the top text layer so that both it and the middle layer are selected. Tap the down-arrow key twice and the right-arrow key twice to slightly offset the text.

TIP

You can alter the distance between the copies of the type. A larger font could be moved farther away. Make sure that you can see the glow from the edge of the bottom text layer when you move the type.

11 Deselect the center layer and leave the top layer active. Add a Smooth Inner Bevel with a Depth of **151** percent and a Size of **7** pixels. Soften is set to **0**. Leave the Angle at **132** degrees and the Altitude at **32** degrees. Assign a Ring Gloss Contour. You don't need to assign a shape Contour setting in addition to the Gloss. Add the default Outer Glow to the text, but select a lighter version of the foreground color as your glow color. Click OK to close the dialog box. Move this layer of text two taps of the down- and right-arrow keys. Move the group folder for the type where you think it looks best (all the layers then move together).

12 To see how easy this now is to change, open the image Couple.psd and select a portion of it as you did in Step 2. Double-click the Main Focus Smart Object to reopen it and then paste the couple image above the original image. Move it to the same location. Click the Close box and then click OK to save the Smart Object. Shift-click to select all three type layers and then choose the Type tool. You can now pick any font in your list as a replacement for all three sets of type at the same time. I choose Brush Script Std this time. Then pick a different color for the Left Side and the Bottom layers. I chose a deep green of the trees for the Bottom layer and the yellow-gold of the groom's flower for the Left Side. Finally click the Main Focus Smart Object and add a drop shadow with a Distance of **11** and a Size of **16**.

Photo: www.comstock.com

13 Save your work.

TIP

The top layer mostly controls the shine on the type. If you prefer a more satiny look, reduce the Fill opacity to about **48** percent. Also, try a different spacing to see what that does to the type.

A short recap

Templates are all the rage now in wedding photography, sports photography, and scrapbooking. A good template lends itself to easy changes based on the images that you include. In this example, you see how easy it is to make changes to both the colors of the template and the type. You can also expand the template while protecting the integrity of the original. The glass type is created from three layers of identical type. By applying different layer styles to each copy and offsetting the copies, you can build up much more complexity than is possible in a single type layer. Again, my thanks to Kathryn Bernstein for the use of her original template. Any changes that I make to it are not the designer's fault!

Tessellations

M. C. Escher was the greatest pattern artist who ever lived. His interlocking lizard pattern is totally awesome. You, too, can try your hand at creating a pattern built on the same principles as Escher's lizard. This lizard image exhibits four-point rotational symmetry (what an intimidating mouthful that name is!). That symmetry's much easier to create than it sounds, though Escher's genius was in seeing how to make a lizard from just two lines. See what creatures you can unlock!

THE PLAN

- Draw the pattern lines and rotate them
- Build the base shape
- Create the repeat
- Define, test, and refine the pattern
- Add cartooning or artwork

TIP

Are you still wondering what a tessellation is? A tessellation is a shape that tiles when you place repeated copies next to one another by either rotation or repetition. Creating patterns (symmetries) is fun, but there's a huge amount of technical theory behind them. For example, there are actually 17 different combinations of rotation, reflection, and gliding in which patterns can tile seamlessly. I'll try to keep the jargon to a minimum.

(1) Open the image Pattempl.psd and duplicate it. Close the original. Turn on the eyes to the left of both alpha channels in the Channels palette. I created a cheat sheet for you to use as you build the base lines that form the tessellation. You see a square outlined in green. That square is your pattern template. You need to connect its corners in the next steps.

(2) Add a new layer (named **Bottom Line**) to the top of the layer stack. Choose the Brush tool with the 1-pixel brush. Zoom in until the light-red area of the template fills most of your screen. Starting in the bottom-right corner of the green-outlined square, draw a wiggly line to the bottom-left corner. Try to start and end the line precisely at the corner pixels. The diagonal lines in the template show the safe areas. You can draw the line over a diagonal, but realize that you might need to modify it later. (In this task, *modify* means *do over.*)

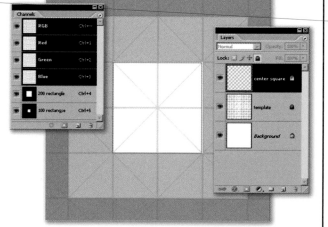

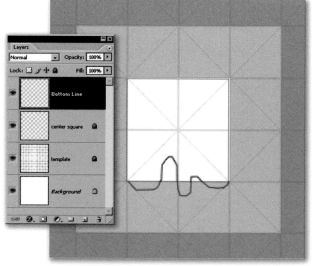

3 Duplicate the Bottom Line layer as **Left Side**. Choose Edit ➪ Free Transform (Command/Ctrl+T). Drag the rotation point from the center of the bounding box to the bottom-left pixel on the green-outlined square. Zoom in by pressing Command/Ctrl+Spacebar until you can see well enough to move it. You need the rotation point to land on that specific pixel. Either type **90** degrees in the Angle field of the Options bar, or press and hold Shift as you rotate the bounding box **90** degrees. Click the check mark to commit. Notice that the areas that are out of the square on your first line are inside the square on the new line.

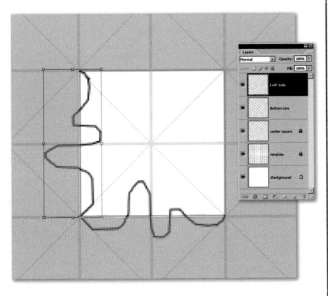

TIP

In case you're curious, you have just created a two-fold rotation. Actually, if you decide that you enjoy this stuff, the book, Introduction to Tessellations, by Dale Seymour and Jill Britton, is an excellent source of more information.

4 Add a new, blank layer and name it **Top Line**. Using the Brush tool with the 1-pixel brush, start at one of the corner pixels on the top of the green-outlines square and wiggle your way to the opposite end. On my image, you can see I'm in the danger zone. However, nothing else is close to that area. My rotation (where the outside goes in) will make a narrow shape, but nothing overlaps.

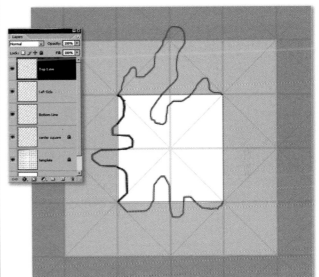

5 Duplicate the Top Line layer as **Right Side**. Choose Edit ➪ Free Transform and move the rotation point to precisely the top-right corner outlined in green. Rotate the line **-90** degrees. Commit. You now have a complete shape (or you will when you fill it).

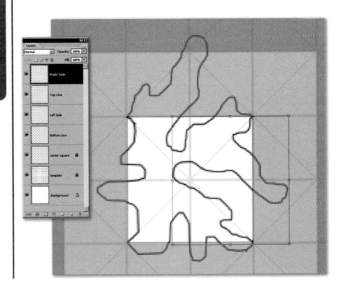

(6) Turn off the bottom three layers from the original template image and create a merged layer of the Bottom and Top Line and the Right and Left Side layers (press Shift+Command/Ctrl+Option/Alt+E). Name the layer **Shape**. Select the four line layers (Right Size, Top Line, Left Side, and Bottom Line) and group them into a Layer Set (press Command\Ctrl+G). Name the group **Lines**. Hide the Group from view by clicking the eye to the left of it on the Layers palette. Turn off the eyes on the two alpha channels as well. Set the Magic Wand tool to a Tolerance of **0**, Contiguous On, and Anti-alias Off. Make the Shape layer active. Click outside the shape to select the outer area of transparency. Choose Select ➪ Inverse and then choose Select ➪ Modify ➪ Contract, 1 pixel. Fill the selection on the Shape layer with red or whatever you want as the color of the first shape (you can pick two or four colors for this). Then choose Select ➪ Inverse and press Delete or Backspace. Blur the shape very slightly (Filter ➪ Blur ➪ Gaussian Blur, **0.3** pixels. Click OK.

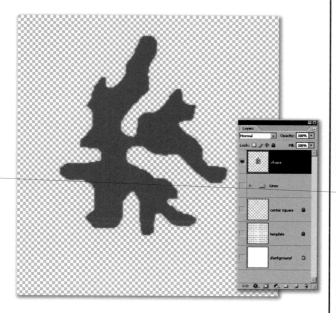

(7) Duplicate the Shape layer three more times. Make Shape Copy active and Command/Ctrl-click the thumbnail in the Layers palette to load the layer transparency as a selection. Fill this selection with yellow (or any different color) and then choose Edit ➪ Free Transform to rotate the layer **90** degrees. Change the layer name to show

the color and the rotation amount. Do the same thing for the other two layers above it. Fill the shape in the next one up with blue and rotate it **180** degrees. Make the shape in the top layer green and rotate it **-90** degrees.

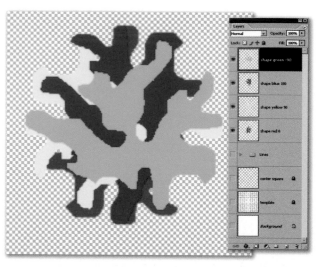

TIP

You can press Shift+Option/Alt+Delete/Backspace to fill the opaque pixels on a layer with the foreground color. The main advantage of this is that you don't need to bother making a selection. The Shift key tells Photoshop to preserve the layer transparency.

(8) The next step is to define each of the layers as a pattern. Highlight all four shape layers and turn on the 200 rectangle alpha channel. If the shapes don't fit inside the clear area, use the Move tool to move the four layers until they are totally inside of the clear rectangle. Make the Shape-Red 0 layer the only visible layer. Turn off the alpha channel. Load the 200 rectangle channel as a selection. Choose Edit ➪ Define Pattern. Name it **Shape-Red 0**. Hide the red layer and turn on the yellow layer. The 200 rectangle alpha channel is still loaded. Choose Edit ➪ Define Pattern and name it **Shape-Yellow 90**. Define the other two layers as patterns, making sure that only one layer is visible at a time (**Shape-Blue 180** and **Shape-Green -90**). Click to select each of the shape layers and press Command/Ctrl+G to group them. Name the Group **Shapes**.

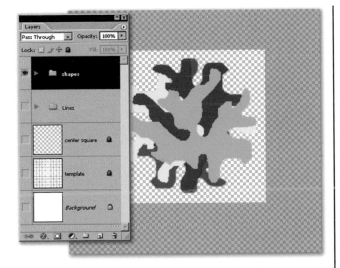

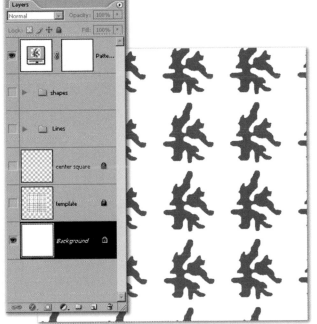

TIP

Why a selection that is 200 pixels? Why not? But there happens to be a valid reason for this one. Your original pattern square is 100 pixels. This particular symmetry features a four-fold rotation and takes all four pattern tiles for a single repeat. Therefore, it needs two tiles across and two tiles down. That's 200 pixels in each direction. One of the little-known rules about patterns is that if you create multiple patterns using the same repeat size, you can make the two patterns blend with each other seamlessly. They might not interlock, but they tile and repeat along the same grid. In our case, the patterns also interlock, but each of these separate shapes needs to be defined as an individual pattern using the same 200-pixel repeat size first.

(9) Deselect. Hide the eye on Shapes Group in the Layers palette. Nothing but the transparency indicator should be visible. Choose Image ⇨ Canvas Size and with Relative checked, add 300 pixels to each dimension (to get up to an 800 pixel square image). Then add a Pattern Fill layer and choose the Shape-Red 0 pattern. Click OK. You don't need to move the pattern on the image even if the first pattern tile seems cut off.

(10) Add another Pattern Fill layer above the red pattern layer and choose the Shape-Yellow 90 pattern. Click OK. Move this pattern directly under the red pattern until it locks in place. You can move a pattern anywhere in the Pattern Fill layer just by using the Move tool.

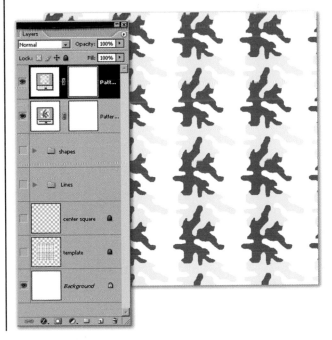

11 Add the green and the blue patterns the same way, using Pattern Fill layers. If you decide that you need to change the colors (as I do at this point), you can either rasterize the pattern fill layers and add a Color Overlay style to them or go back into the Shapes group and recolor the shapes and repeat the process of defining the pattern and then placing the pattern fill layers. You have a totally interlocking pattern, but you aren't quite done yet.

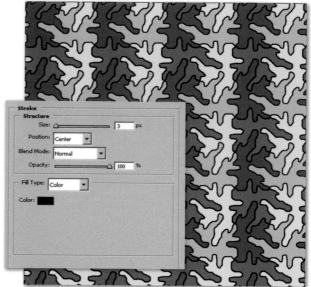

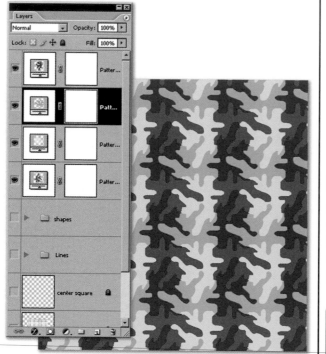

12 You may notice as you move the pattern tiles, that the pieces don't interlock perfectly. You can spend an hour or two hacking at the image with the Pencil tool and the Eraser tool, but I have a feeling you have better ways to spend your time. Not my idea of fun either! The Gaussian blur edge causes part of the problem, but not all of it, and it makes it much easier to solve the problem. Cover the edges with a Stroke effect and no one will know about the dust or clothes under your bed. Rasterize the top layer in the stack. Add a Stroke effect in black of 3 pixels on the Center and click OK. Rasterize whichever layer makes the shape lean diagonally to the right and down from the top layer. Add the same Stroke style to it and move it up in the Layers palette to the top or to the layer just under the top layer.

13 This step is both long and optional. If any of the shapes remind you of something, you can add cartooning to them. First, Group the four pattern layers to neaten the Layers palette (name the group **Shape Patterns**). Then, add a new layer for each of the shape colors. Using the Brush or the Pencil tool with a 3-pixel brush, paint in the detail for one shape of each color.

TIP

You can't get a 200-pixel marquee around all of the image detail at one time unless you paint pieces of different shapes inside of the marquee. I find that hard to do. Even though it seems (okay, is) finicky, it's still faster and less prone to errors to draw all of the detail for one of each in its own layer and make it into it's own pattern.

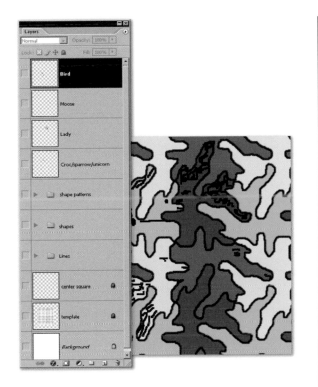

14 Then turn off all of the layers but one detail layer. Load the 200-rectangle layer and define the detail as a new pattern. When you have all four detail layers designed and defined (basically the same process that you used to add each shape to the image), create a pattern layer for each one. Turn on the shape pattern group and move each detail pattern where it belongs.

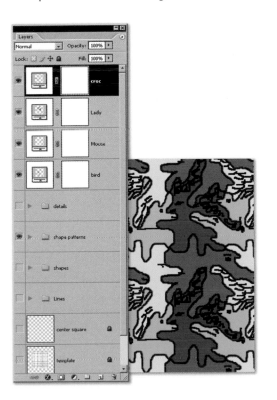

TIP

If the detail doesn't fit inside of the 200-pixel marquee when you load the alpha channel, move the marquee until it is around the detail image. The position of the marquee on the image isn't important — it can be anywhere. It just has to be a 200-pixel marquee.

15 At this point, you have a whole Layers palette littered with bits and pieces of this image. The good thing is that it's relatively easy to go back and change whatever might need changing. The downside is that it's a mess to try to use this pattern. The solution? You need to define one tile that has a bit of everything in it and will tile seamlessly. Impossible? Not at all. All you need to do is to place the 200-pixel marquee anywhere in the image and define the pattern. Everything was built on a 200-pixel grid. Therefore, any 200-pixel segment carries all of the information needed to re-create the entire pattern. Group the four Detail pattern layers together and make sure the group is visible (name it Detail Patterns). You also need to have the Shape Patterns group visible (which it should be anyway). Load the 200-rectangle alpha channel as a selection. You don't need to move it. Click the RGB channel in the Channels palette. Choose Edit ➪ Define Pattern and name it **Escher Test**. Save the file as **EscherBuild.psd** and close the file.

16 Choose File ⇨ New and create a file 1,000 pixels square. Add a pattern fill layer and choose the Escher Text pattern. Voila! It's all there. Do I hear any cheers???

> ## TIP
>
> After all this hard work, save the pattern and all of its preliminary patterns as a new pattern set. In the Edit ⇨ Preset Manager ⇨ Patterns palette, click to select all of the related patterns. Choose Save Set. You can put it in the Adobe Pattern presets folder, but save it somewhere else as well. That way, if you need to upgrade or reinstall Photoshop, you won't lose your custom presets. This tip applies to all of your custom sets and to your third-party plug-ins as well.

A short recap

You can layer one pattern on top of another and arrange them in any way you want so long as the size of the pattern as defined is the same. Escher's work depended on the way in which shapes and lines were created, and you are able to re-create his methods in Photoshop. Although this one might have gone a bit slowly, the process is actually quite fast when you get the hang of it. Set up a square that is one-half the pixel count of the final pattern size you want. Draw the first line and rotate it. Draw the second line and rotate it. Build the shape and then make four copies. Color, rotate, and define the patterns. Build the pattern file and then create the interlocking image. Then create the outline. Add details if you wish and then define the final tile.

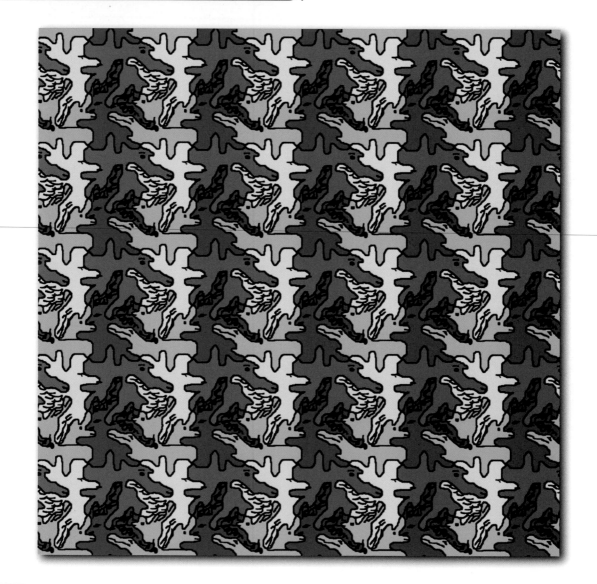

Repeat That Again, Sam

In this exercise, you get to try your hand at making a photo interlock and repeat. Few feelings in life are quite as satisfying as solving a difficult puzzle or working out the solution to a complex problem. That could be why I love creating tessellations (shapes that interlock in an infinite repeat). Making geometric lines and squiggles tessellate is challenge enough. The trick is to find a geometric shape that tessellates and also works with your starting photo — or, as in this case, to find a photo the works with a specific shape.

THE PLAN

- Create the basic shape
- Build the first interlocking pair
- Duplicate and rotate the interlocking pair to form the inner and outer rosettes
- Duplicate and interlock the full pattern unit
- Define the pattern and use it

(1) Open the image Chameleon.psd. Set your background color to black and choose the Measure tool (it lives in the Eyedropper slot). Drag the Measure cursor along the left edge of the branch. Then choose Image ⇨ Rotate Canvas ⇨ Arbitrary. Click OK. The angle is already set by the Measure tool (it should be about 32 degrees on the Rotate Canvas dialog box regardless of the angle shown the Measure tool). Then press Command/Ctrl+Option/Alt+C and check the Relative box. Add 300 pixels to the image height and anchor in the center. Click OK.

TIP

Using the Measure tool to straighten an image is a huge timesaver. Just drag the tool along a straight line in the image that you want to be vertical (or horizontal) and choose Image ⇨ Rotate Canvas ⇨ Arbitrary. Photoshop automatically enters a clockwise angle.

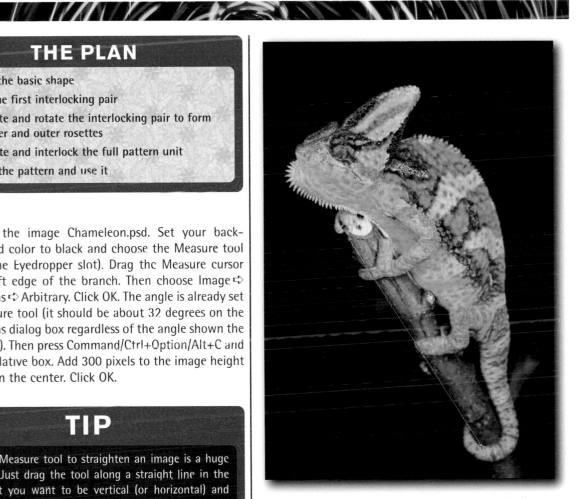

www.comstock.com

2) On the Mac, double-click the file *triangle.csh* to load the 30-30-120 triangle it contains into the Shapes palette. On Windows, drag the file *triangle.csh* into the open Photoshop application and it will attach itself to the Shapes menu as a 30-30-120 triangle. Choose the Custom Shape tool and select the 30-30-120 triangle shape. In the Geometry Options, click the Fixed Size option button and set the Width to 190 px and the Height to 653 px. Set your foreground color to red. Choose Image ⇨ Rotate Canvas ⇨ Flip Horizontal so that the chameleon faces the same way as the triangle (you'll flip them both back in a minute). Click to set the triangle shape on the image and, without releasing the mouse button, drag the shape over the chameleon so that the triangle's right side is up against the branch (with the chameleon's little legs outside the shape) and the bottom left side touches the chameleon's tail. The figure shows the positioning before releasing the mouse. When you release the mouse, you see a red shape.

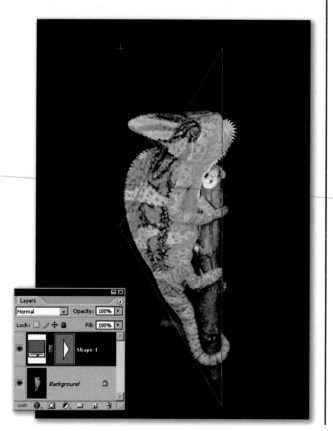

TIP

The only reason to set a fixed size on the triangle shape is so your results match mine. If you do this on your own, use the Defined Proportions option. You need the 120-degree angle on this triangle in order for the tessellation to work correctly. You can also tessellate an equilateral triangle.

3) Add a new layer to the image and name it **OuterRotation1**. Draw a loose Lasso selection around the chameleon's ear and back so that it covers the ear and back and some of the red shape and some of the background black. Choose the Magic Wand tool and set the Tolerance to 35, Anti-alias off, Contiguous on, and Sample All Layers On. Press and hold Option/Alt and click the black area inside the marching ants. Then press and hold Option/Alt and click the red area inside the marching ants. The marquee shrinks to select only the chameleon's ear and back area that protrudes from under the triangle shape.

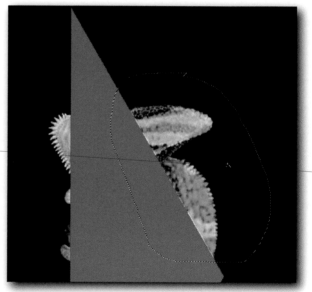

④ Choose Select ⇨ Modify ⇨ Expand, 1 pixel and Select ⇨ Modify ⇨ Smooth, 2 pixels. Choose the Lasso tool and press and hold Option/Alt and remove the extra area about the ear and back from the selection. Do the same thing to the additional selection at the bottom of the ear and back area. If it's easier for you, you can do this in QuickMask mode. After you remove the extra selection on either side of the chameleon, press and hold Command/Ctrl+Option/Alt and click on the Shape 1 layer mask to remove the triangle shape from the selection. Fill the selection on the new layer with red and deselect. If you need to touch up any areas, use the Pencil tool and do it now. Once you rotate this shape, you won't be able to alter it.

TIP

At the end of Step 3, you have a really close selection of the jaggies on the chameleon's ear and back. You're eventually going to rotate this area and knock it out of the red shape on the other short side of the triangle. It would be great to preserve this jagged area, but believe me; it's not worth the effort. By the time the tile gets rotated in all directions, the jaggies are history anyway. I'm showing you the pixel version of creating the shape. If you're a pro with the Pen tool, use that to trace the ear and back instead. The trick is that you're got to combine the top shape with the triangle and remove the rotated copy from the triangle shape. It can be done in Photoshop and I've done it, but it's an ugly process. If you have Illustrator, it's much easier to chop up shapes there. You might want to make your outer shapes in Photoshop and then export the triangle and outer shapes as paths to Illustrator and build your final tile shape there. Then bring the tile shape back in as a shape or path.

⑤ Duplicate the layer and press D to choose the default colors. Name the layer **InnerRotation1**. Press Shift+Option/Alt+Delete/Backspace to fill the small shape with black while preserving the transparency. Press Command/Ctrl+R to turn on the rulers and zoom in on the 120-degree angle section of the triangle. Drag a horizontal and vertical guide so that they meet at the exact point of the triangle. Press Command/Ctrl+T and then zoom out (Option/Alt+Spacebar) until you can see both the center of the selection's bounding box and the intersection of the two guides. Drag the center point of the bounding box to the intersection of the guides (zoom in to make sure of the placement). Then type **-120** in the Angle field on the Options bar. Click Commit.

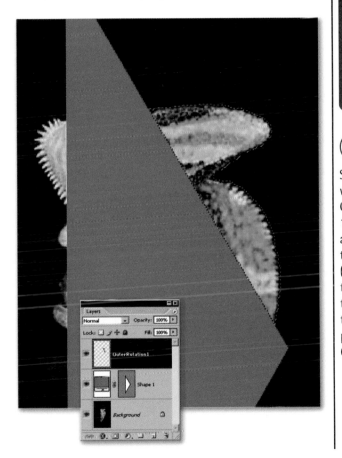

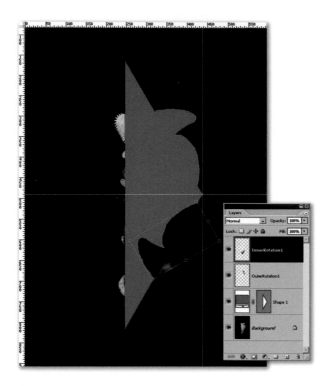

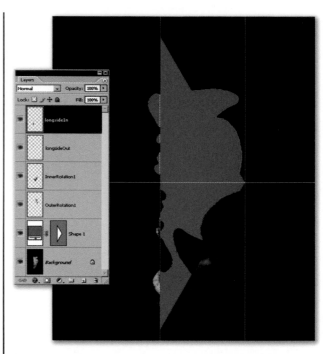

(6) In order to tessellate, all three sides must contain some rotation, and you want to catch the little paws on the branch. However, the triangle has run out of sides to rotate, because it only has three and you've used up two. So, we break the remaining side in half and create a shape to come out over the top half and knock out on the bottom half of the remaining side. Repeat Steps 3 to 5 using a new layer named **LongsideOut**. However, this time, you want to lasso the snout and paw area on the top half of the long side of the triangle. Fill the selection with red on the new layer, and duplicate the layer as **LongsideIn**. Fill the duplicate with black (remember to press and hold Shift to lock transparency). Drag a new vertical guide so that it sits along the straight long edge of the triangle. Press Command/Ctrl+T and drag the center point of the bounding box to the intersection of the left-most vertical guide and the horizontal guide. Set the Angle to **180** degrees and commit.

TIP

When you try to drag the center point on this bounding box, Photoshop is likely to become very stubborn and refuse to let you move it. Instead, it will insist on moving the entire layer contents. However, you can be meaner than Photoshop! Click the bottom-center dot in the Reference Point Location gadget on the Options bar. Once the center point moves to the bottom of the bounding box, Photoshop recovers from its hissy fit and permits you to move the reference point to the intersection of the guides.

7 Set the Tolerance on the Magic Wand to 200 with Contiguous and Sample All layers turned on and Anti-alias turned off. Click the red area to select all of the new shape. Add a new layer, named **Final Shape**, and fill the selection marquee with red. Deselect. Choose Filter ➪ Blur ➪ Gaussian Blur, **0.5** pixels. Click OK. Drag a duplicate of the Background layer to the top of the layer stack and Control/right-click to choose Create Clipping Mask. Turn off all the layer eyes except for the top two layers. Press Shift+Command/Ctrl+Option/Alt+E to create a merged layer at the top of the layer stack. Name the merged layer **Chameleon Shape**. This is the shape that needs to tessellate.

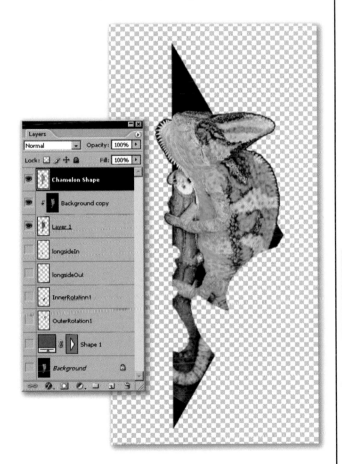

8 Control/right-click on the Chameleon Shape layer and choose Duplicate Layer into a new image and click OK. Save the original file as **ChameleonBuild1.psd** and close it. Choose View ➪ New Guide and place a Vertical guide at pixel 287. Choose View ➪ New Guide and place a Horizontal guide at pixel 478. Move the chameleon shape so that the right point of the original triangle is directly over the horizontal guide and the vertical guide sits on the anti-aliased pixels to the left of the top point of the triangle. You need to zoom all the way in to see this properly. Press Command/Ctrl+T. If the center reference point does not fall exactly on the guideline, press and hold Command/Ctrl and move the guide. Don't move the image. Press Esc after you fix the guide.

TIP

Yes, I know this is a finicky pain. However, if you don't get the shape precisely correct, you won't get a good tessellation. Stick with me; it gets less fussy real soon now!

9 Duplicate the Chameleon shape layer; no valid need to rename it. Press Command/Ctrl+T. Check to see that the Center reference point is exactly on the guide. If it is, drag it to the intersection of the guides. Type **180** degrees in the Angle field and commit. There's no need to second-guess this transformation so long as your guides are properly placed. Photoshop anti-aliases the result, making it hard to count or proof. You need to take it on faith at this point. The close-up shows how the area where the two shapes meet has less opacity. It's fine for now. Hide the Guides.

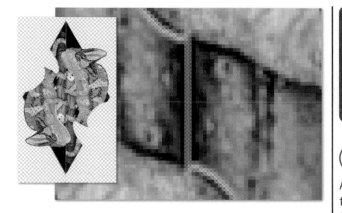

I add the Bevel and Emboss to give the image a little bit of depth and help differentiate between the pattern elements. However, it's hard to judge the rotation with the emboss showing so we turn it back on later.

10 Make the Chameleon Shape copy layer active and add a Bevel and Emboss. Choose a Smooth Inner Bevel of **510**% and a Size of **8**. Click OK. Control/right-click the layer and choose Copy Layer Style. Paste the layer style onto the Chameleon Shape layer. Then open the Layer Styles dialog box again and choose a Cove Deep Gloss Contour. Click OK. Disable the Effects on both layers. Select both layers in the image and choose Group Intro New Smart Object name Chameleon Shape. Press Command/Ctrl+Option/Alt+C and add 300 pixels to the width of the image. Click OK. The figure shows the bevel and emboss (before I turn it off).

11 Press Command/Ctrl+T and type **277** px into the Height field on the Options bar. Click the Constrain Aspect Ratio link icon between the Width and Height fields to shrink both sides proportionally. Click Commit. Turn the Guides back on. Press and hold Shift and slide the Smart Object straight up until its lower point rests on the horizontal guide. Duplicate the Chameleon Smart Object layer as **Chameleon Shape 2**. Press Command/Ctrl+T and click the center bottom dot in the Reference Point Locator gadget in the Options bar. This should make the center of rotation indicator appear exactly at the intersection of the guides. Type **180** degrees into the Angle field on the Options bar and click OK.

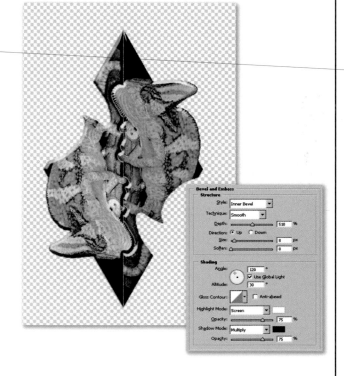

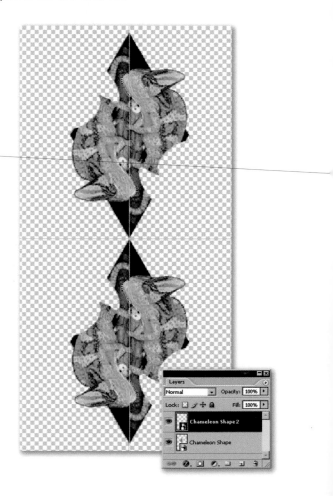

12 Select both Smart Objects and drag them to the New Layer icon at the bottom of the Layers palette to duplicate them. Leave the two new layers selected. Press Command/Ctrl+T and type **60** degrees in the Angle field. The center point is exactly in the right spot, so just click Commit. The layers are still selected. Drag them to the New Layer icon again and leave them selected. Press Command/Ctrl+T and type **60** degrees in the Angle field. Click Commit. You've made the inner rosette of the rotation. Rename all of the layers for their position as if they were hours on a clock face.

13 Duplicate the 6 o'clock shape layer and drag it to the bottom of the Layers palette. Press Command/Ctrl+T and then drag the center reference point on the bounding box to the lowest tip of the triangle. Zoom in all the way to place the rotation point precisely. Type **–120** degrees in the Angle field on the Options bar and click Commit. The shape locks in place around the outside of the rosette. Rename the layer **Chameleon Shape SE** (for Southeast).

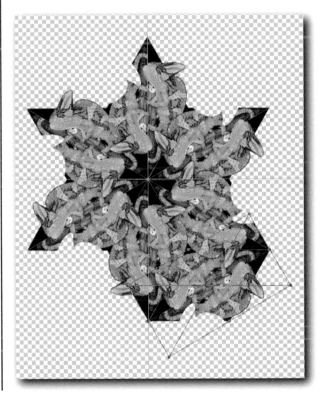

14 Duplicate the SE layer. You need to make it travel across the circle, but the Smart Object remembers its original rotation amount so the numbers you need are a bit odd. Choose View ➪ Smart Guides. Make the duplicate the only active layer and press Command/Ctrl+T. Drag the center reference point into the center of the image where the guides intersect. Type **60** degrees in the Angle field. This time, before you click to Commit, take a look at where the image lands. You might need to slightly adjust its position (not the angle; the location). Drag it until the smart guides flash hot pink and the shape lines up. Then click OK. Name the new layer **Chameleon Shape NW**.

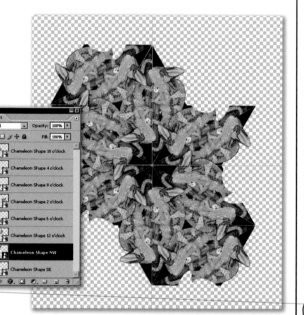

TIP

Because the angle is correct, you can even nudge a bit after the transformation if necessary. I was able to make the guides flash on the left side during the transform, but I could not get the top aligned until afterward.

15 Select both the SE and the NW layers and drag them to the New Layer icon at the bottom of the Layers palette to duplicate them. Leave them selected. Press Command/Ctrl+T and type **60** into the Angle field on the Options bar. The center of rotation is right in the center where it belongs. Click Commit. Drag the two selected layers

to the New Layer icon and leave them selected. Press Command/Ctrl+T again and again type **60** degrees in the Angle field. Click Commit. The rosette is complete. You now have one full repeat element (but not a definable pattern quite yet). Rename the layer to show their correct orientation. If you need more room, add 300 pixels to the width of the canvas (Command/Ctrl+Option/Alt+C anchored in the center). Save this image as **ChameleonBuild2.psd**. Then choose Image ➪ Duplicate ➪ OK (don't merge the layers) and close the original.

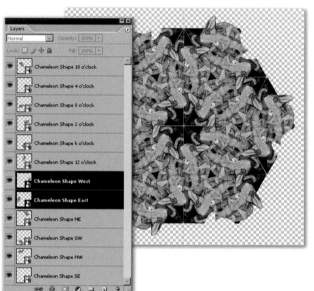

16 Select all of the layers in the new image, Control/right-click and choose Group into New Smart Object. Rename the Smart Object as Chameleon Repeat. The next step is to measure the rosette to calculate your pattern repeat. Drag guides to the top, bottom, and sides of the rosette as if it were a solid hexagon (don't count the pieces of the chameleon that are popping out. Turn Snap on the View menu. Then drag the Rectangular Marquee so that it snaps to the guides. Read the measurement off of the Info palette. Mine says 642 pixels wide and 556 pixels high. Your measurements are likely to be different by even as much as 10 pixels in either direction. Your final pattern size is 1.5 times the width and the actual height measurement. Therefore, my pattern repeat unit is 964 pixels high by 556 pixels high. To obtain enough room to make the final tile, press Command/Ctrl+Option/Alt+C, and set the canvas size to 1000 pixels wide by 700 pixels high, Anchor in the center.

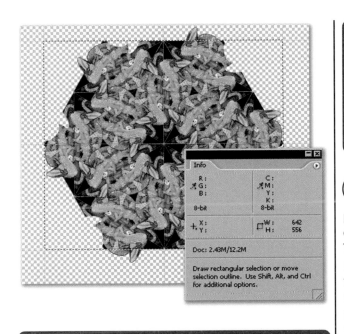

TIP

Why am I telling you where to put the cursor? I really don't mean to insult you...I just want you to not drag the rosettes out of the image by accident. If you place your cursor at the spot where the current layer will meet and interlock with the original, you won't have a problem.

(18) Select all three Smart Object layers and drag them to the New Layer icon at the bottom of the Layers palette to duplicate them. Let them stay selected. Place your cursor on the left edge of the rosette and drag to the right. This time, don't press Shift because you need to offset the rosettes by about half. You need to do this by sight until they snap in place. Select the original three Chameleon Repeat layers again and this time, place your cursor on the right and drag left until they snap into place about half a rosette height down. Add a black Solid Color fill layer and drag it to the bottom of the layer stack. You may hide the guides now. Choose the Rectangular Marquee tool and select Fixed Size from the Style drop-down on the Options bar. Set the fixed size to the width and height that you calculated in Step 16. Place the marquee in the image choose Edit ⇨ Define Pattern. Name the pattern **Plain Chameleon**.

TIP

If you're agonizing about the semitransparent areas and whether to place your guides in anti-aliased areas of the hexagon, relax. We add a black background to get rid of the transparency and a margin of error of a pixel or two won't matter here.

(17) Duplicate the Chameleon Repeat Smart Object layer. Place your cursor near the top of the rosette, press and hold Shift, and drag the tile down until it snaps into place at the bottom of the original tile. Yes, you should see a smidgen of transparency as the tiles meet. Duplicate the original Chameleon Repeat Smart Object layer again. This time, place the cursor at the bottom of the tile and drag up until the tile snaps into place at the top.

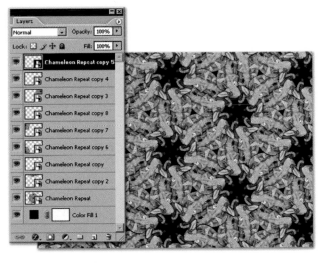

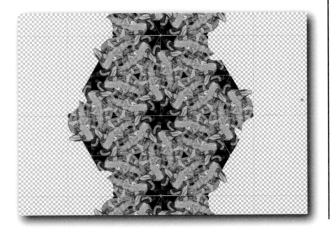

TIP

If Edit ⇨ Define Pattern is grayed out, make the top layer in the layer stack active, or click on the RGB channel in the Channels palette. You'll be able to define the pattern.

(19) Remember the Bevel and Emboss you added so long ago? Let's activate it now and dress up the pattern a bit. Now? How? Double-click one of the Smart Object layer thumbnails. The image that has all of the rosette smart objects opens. Double-click one of the Smart Object layer thumbnails in this new file and you see the original two repeats and the inactive Bevel and Emboss styles. Click the eyes on the layer styles to turn them back on. Make the top layer in the file active. Press and hold Option/Alt and choose the Photo Filter from the New Fill or Adjustment layer icon menu at the bottom of the Layers palette. In the dialog box, click Use Previous Layer to Create Clipping Mask. Click Color and then click the color swatch to open the Color Picker. Set the new color to RGB: **0, 5, 213**. Click OK to close the Color Picker. Set the Density of the effect to **100%**. Click OK to close the Photo Filter dialog box.

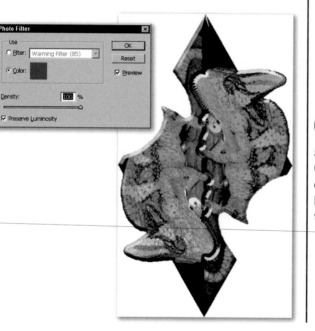

(20) Click the close box on the double-chameleon file and click Save. The rosette file acquires the bevel and color change. Click on rosette file close box and again choose Yes. The pattern tile file suddenly updates as well. You already have the correct marquee active in the image. Choose Edit ⇨ Define pattern and name it **Decorated Chameleon**. Save the file as **FinalTile.psd** and close it.

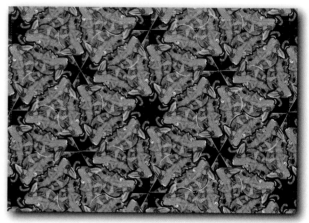

(21) Create a new file 2000 x 2000 pixels. Add a pattern layer and choose the plain chameleon pattern. Then add another new pattern layer and choose the Decorated Chameleon tile. Now you can decide which you prefer. Of course, if you don't like either of them, go back to the FileTile.psd image and add a different color or effect and try that.

A short recap

You've now completed one of the most complex tessellation patterns around. It's just one of many different geometric shapes that will tessellate. Any triangle will tessellate on a plane without rotation or reflection. However, only a right triangle or 30-30-120 Isosceles triangle will form this type of rosette repeat. Although we still left some background around the repeat shape, we produce a shape that interlocks and we did it from an undistorted photo. If you enjoy playing with photo patterns, you have so many more images like this that you can create. Patterns are one of my favorite things in life and I really hope that you enjoyed this exploration.

chapter 3

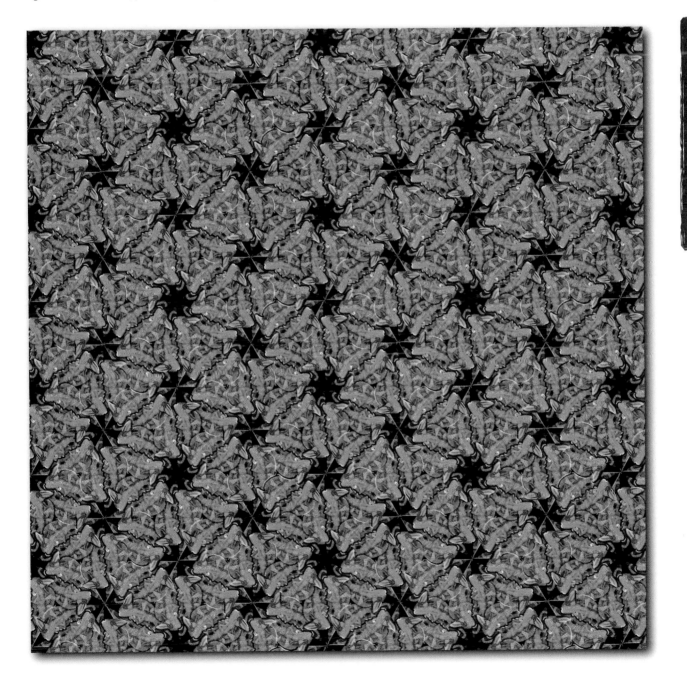

People who need people. (Okay, let's not go there). Most people enjoy manipulating photos of other people. In this chapter, you find a number of strange things to legally do to other people. Rhoda Grossman shows you how to create a warped image to make someone's head seem a lot bigger and, well, warped. She also shows you a number of different ways to recolor an image in her tribute to Andy Warhol. Kiska Moore shows off her retouching skills as you see how you can make someone lose weight without going to the gym or using a personal trainer. If only someone would enable the computer to deliver the results right to our hips! I show you an advertising technique to make an image stand out, and I finish with a totem pole that tells the story of a very special little boy.

Strange Perspective

What a large head you have! A traditional way to get this forced perspective effect involves standing on a ladder. That's a bit dangerous for many of us, so we rely on Photoshop to distort an image that was shot by a photographer with both feet firmly on the ground. This technique was designed and written by Rhoda Grossman.

THE PLAN

- Separate the head from the body
- Distort the head using Transform and Liquify effects
- Create foreshortening on the body

① Open cutekid.psd. Choose Image⇨Image Size and change the Width and Height to **150%** with Bicubic Smoother Interpolation. Click OK. Then choose Image⇨ Canvas Size and, with the Relative check box checked, add 150 pixels to the image height. Anchor in the center and set the Canvas Extension to white. Click OK. The image comes with a clipping path, which you use to make a quick selection of the whole body, separating it from the background. Command/Ctrl-click the path to load the selection. Set your colors to the default of black and white. Then press Command/Ctrl+Option/Alt+J to cut the young lady and place her into her own layer. Fill the Background layer with white to remove the stray pixels.

Photo: www.comstock.com

2 Make Layer 1 active. Choose the Lasso tool and drag it carefully along the lower edge of her chin, some-what less carefully around the neck, collar, and the areas where hair touches her dress. Complete the selection by dragging loosely around her head, or press and holdOption/ Alt to make a polygon that completes the selection. Switch to Quick Mask mode to touch up important areas: the chin, of course, and where her hair meets the dress.

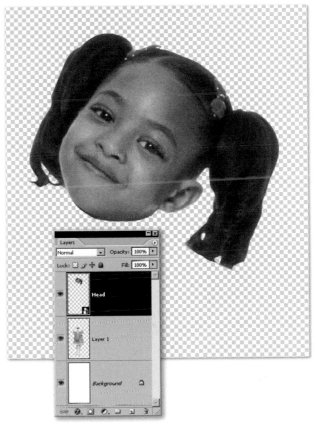

TIP

You may prefer to use the Pen tool for creating or altering paths precisely, before converting them to selections. But if you have a reasonably steady hand and a graphics tablet, as I do, you may be comfortable without relying on the vector tools.

3 Use Command/Ctrl+Option/Alt+J to create a new layer for the head. Name the layer **Head**. Make this layer a Smart Object with the Group into New Smart Object command, so you can transform it nondestructively. You may want to rotate the head somewhat toward vertical with the Free Transform command to avoid getting a stiff neck while you work on this project.

4 To use Liquify on a Smart Object, open the Smart Object for editing by double-clicking the layer icon. Duplicate the original layer in the Smart Object file by dragging it to the New Layer icon at the bottom of the Layers palette. Name the layer **Liquify**. Choose Filter⇨ Liquify. With a brush size set to about 45 pixels, I used the Warp brush to shape the chin into a dainty elfin point. Because I was in the neighborhood, I reshaped her ponytail with a combination of Pucker and Bloat strokes. I also bloated the eyes just a tiny bit. Turn off the eye on the original layer, leaving only the liquefy layer visible. Click the close box on the Smart Object file and click Yes to the prompt to save the file.

(5) Type Command/Ctrl+T to transform the Head Smart Object layer. Type **150** in the Width field on the Options bar and click the Constrain Proportions icon to automatically set the Height to the same percentage. Then click the Warp icon on the Options bar. You see a grid that can be maneuvered to distort the shape of the head. This dandy feature gives you much more control than the Distort command, which only allows the manipulation of corner points. Push or pull the segments of the grid, and manipulate the anchor points and handles until you achieve an effect that approaches a bird's-eye view of the little girl. Commit.

(6) Time to work on the body. First, clean up any stray pixels left over from the selection of the head. Repair the upper edge of the collar by using the perfect collar on the other side. Make a loose lasso selection of the pristine collar. Use Command/Ctrl+J to make the selection a new layer. Name the layer **Collar**. Move it into position and rotate it with the Free Transform command. Use the Clone Stamp tool on this layer with Sample all Layers checked to merge the new collar seamlessly into the old one.

7 Select the Collar and the body layers and Control/right-click one of the layer entries and choose Group into a Smart Object. Name the Smart Object layer **Body**. With the Body Smart Object layer active, press Command/Ctrl+T and then click the Warp icon. Warp the body into a trapezoid shape, making the height smaller in the process.

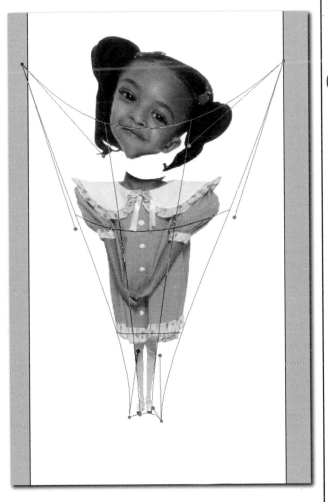

8 Open the Body Smart Object for editing. Make the Collar layer active in the Smart Object file and press Shift+Command/Ctrl+Option/Alt+E to make a merged layer. Name the layer **Liquify**. Turn off the other layers in the file but leave the Liquify layer visible and active. Choose Filter⇨Liquify to enter the Liquify environment once again, and use the Warp brush to make her neck thinner. Switch to the oddly named Push Left tool and use it to lower the top edge of her collar. This tool is highly directional. Drag from right to left to push pixels down. Give her collar a bit of a winged look. Click OK when you're happy with the results. Close the Smart Object file and save the changes. Move her head on her new neck shape. If you need to adjust the results, press Command/Ctrl+T in the Body layer in the main image. Make any last changes that you want.

9 Crop the image if you wish. Save your work.

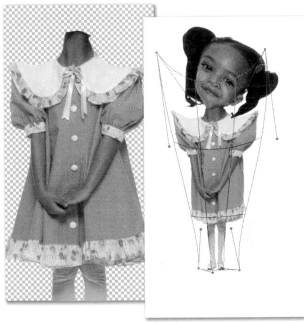

TIP

You can edit the warped Body Smart Object as often as needed without image degradation. If you want to start over, change the Warp in the Options bar from Custom to None and Commit. Then warp the body again.

A short recap

We started with a perfectly normal little girl and made a Munchkin. Using a combination of Warp and Liquify effects you distorted a photo to mimic forced perspective. You took advantage of Photoshop's new Smart Object feature, and you were smart not to climb up on that ladder.

Model Material

Lisa is a fitness instructor, but in the past year, she has become a fitness consultant and she no longer works out of a gym. Consequently, she has had a lot of trouble getting to a gym to work out. Unhappy with a 15-pound weight gain, she wanted a "virtual" makeover to inspire her to get thin again. Photoshop is the super spa. The idea with this task is to start with the larger problems and work down to the smaller ones. All the slimming is done with the Liquify filter and the makeup primarily with the healing brush. The photography is my effort, but the task is the work of Kiska Moore, who has had many years as a traditional photo retoucher prior to learning Photoshop.

THE PLAN

- Slenderize tummy and thighs
- Remove tan lines; soften knees
- Modify frown
- Soften lines, freckles, and veins
- Remove blemishes

1 Open the image Lisa.psd and duplicate the Background layer.

Photo: Sherry London

2 Choose Filters⇨Liquify Filter. Freeze all but the tummy and waist area. Use the Pucker tool with a brush size of about 190. Tap the center of the tummy lightly. Don't hold the mouse button down. The Liquify tools are extremely powerful. If you overdo, you can reset. Mask the waist area and clear (erase) thighs. Mask the hands. Use Forward Warp tool to gently push outside of the thighs inward.

4 Create a new layer. With the Eyedropper tool, sample the chest color, and choose a soft brush with a low opacity (15%). Build up the paint over the tan lines to make Lisa's skin tones blend with the surrounding areas. Go up to the collarbone and pick up a darker color; paint on the shoulder, right under the hair. Add a very light Noise filter set to **2** with the Distribution section set to Uniform and the Monochromatic option checked.

3 The next step removes Lisa's tan line. On the background copy lasso, along the bathing suit, the tan line area. Copy to a new layer. Use the Healing Brush, set to darken, on the strap lines first. Work from middle of the chest outward toward the suit. You will pick up extra freckles that will be softened later. When you get close to the blue suit, the Healing Brush starts to smudge. Stop using the Healing Brush at this point.

5 Now to work on her knees, which are a bit knobby. On a new layer, use the Healing Brush at normal to soften the dark areas around the knees. Lower the layer opacity to about 50%.

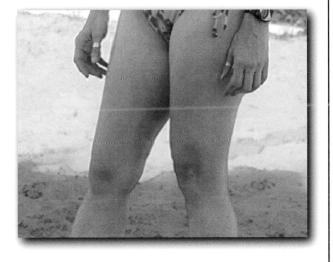

6 Next, you fix her smile. Activate the background copy. Loosely select the face and copy the selection to its own layer. Choose Filter➪Liquify. Mask above and below the mouth. Use the Forward Warp tool to bring each side of the mouth outward just a bit. Don't close the Liquify filter yet.

7 Mask around the cheeks as shown. Use the Forward Warp tool to lift the cheeks and lines along nose slightly upward and out. Smile and feel what your face muscles do. Mask all but eyes, and lift the top and bottom lids of each eye slightly. Click OK to exit the Liquify filter.

8 Retouch the face. Create a new layer, and with the Healing Brush go over the frown lines and lines from nose to mouth. Lower the layer opacity if need be. Create another new layer. Use the Clone Stamp tool on the circles under her eyes. Adjust layer opacity.

9 Now you fine-tune. Create a new layer. Move in close — about 400 to 500 percent magnification. Using the Healing Brush, start on the chest to soften some freckles, but leave most of them. Move over to the arms and work on the veins. Move to the stomach area; smooth around the navel. Move toward her left arm; there are some very faint clothing marks. Move to the legs, and smooth somewhat. Check for blotchy areas.

10 Create a new layer and merge visible. Select the eyes. Use a Brightness/Contrast adjustment layer. Increase both brightness and contrast. Clean up any color spill with a black brush on the mask. Duplicate this layer for a little more pop to the colors.

11 Save your work.

A short recap

Don't we all want to lose a few pounds and make those lines magically disappear? Photoshop does it easily, but also makes it much too easy to end up with a plastic person.

A real person has flaws. You want to leave some of them. After a digital makeover, your victim (uh...subject) should look better — but recognizable. Kiska retouches with a very gentle hand. You should do the same.

Warhol Coloring

The silkscreen portraits that came from Andy Warhol's art factory in the 1960s have a distinctive look. The original source photo is reduced to a minimum and a few bold, flat colors are added. Several variations, which differ only in color, are typically combined in a grid. Whether the subject is Marilyn Monroe or Bill Gates, this style is worthy of revival with digital techniques. This technique was designed and written by Rhoda Grossman.

THE PLAN

- Make a high-contrast monochrome version of the source photo
- Create simple shapes for color fills
- Choose your method for making a grid of color variations

(1) Open the source photo, prettybrunette.tif. Remove color nondestructively by using a Hue/Saturation Adjustment Layer. Move the Saturation slider to the extreme left.

Photo: www.comstock.com

(2) You reduce detail and create high contrast in this step. Choose a Levels adjustment layer. Move both the black and white sliders under the histogram toward the center and adjust the Gamma slider as needed. These adjustments compress the value range and minimize midtones. Be careful to keep a few subtle cues to the modeling of the face, like the shadow under her nose and a hint of the nasolabial folds. Preserve a few highlights in her hair as well.

TIP

The next few steps are devoted to simplifying the image further by dividing it into three or four areas for flat color fills. There are several ways to approach this, as is the case with many Photoshop tasks. The Posterize Adjustment Layer and the Cutout Filter are quick ways to achieve reduction in tonal variation, but I wanted more control and decided to use a combination of Selection tools and commands.

③ Select the darkest pixels with the Magic Wand. Set the tolerance higher, to about **50**, and deselect the Contiguous option. This should pick up most of the hair and vest, leaving some highlights in the hair unselected, which is good. You have not picked up enough of the dark pixels needed to define the facial features. You add to the current selection by pressing and holding Shift as you use the Magic Wand with new settings: reduce the tolerance to **24** or lower if needed, and select the Contiguous option. Now you can add eyebrows, nostrils, the shadow under the nose, and some of the mouth. If you want to make the lips a separate color, as in Warhol's Marilyn, there's no need to include those pixels now. Save your selection and test it by filling a new layer with a dark color. Turn off visibility of the photo so you can easily see if changes are necessary.

TIP

For a quick way to fill a selection with the foreground color, press Option/Alt+Delete/Backspace.

④ Use Quick Mask mode to clean up the selection. Paint with white where you want to add pixels to the selection, such as the hair on the left side of the image. Paint with black if you want to remove pixels from the selection. Avoid any temptation to work precisely or in a painterly way, as the Warhol look is casual and bold.

5 Select the white background and the shirt collar and sleeves with the Magic Wand in Contiguous mode, and Tolerance set to about **50** once again. Shift-click as you add sections. Save the selection and test it with a fill of a contrasting color. There are sure to be some areas that need to be added to the selection. Use Quick Mask mode for this. Save the cleaned-up selection, replacing your earlier version by using the Replace Selection operation. Yes, I have experimented with both green and purple hair. By the time this project is finished I'm sure to use both!

6 To create the selection for the face and neck, load both of the selections you have already saved, making sure to use the Add to Selection operation. Then inverse the selection. The result requires some cleanup in Quick Mask mode, as before. Save it. Your saved selections can be seen in the Channels palette. Choose a third color for this fill that strongly contrasts with the other two colors.

TIP

An alternative to repairing saved selections in Quick Mask mode is to paint directly on the channel with black or white. Recall that white pixels are selected, while black ones are unselected.

7 Now that all three areas are filled with color it's easy to see any remaining flaws. Ragged edges and bits of white showing between colors are unsightly. These can be repaired with the techniques you have been using, although the selection that includes just the background and shirt lends itself to a more efficient method. Load that selection and choose Select⇨Modify⇨Expand. Two pixels should do the trick. Save the modified selection as an alpha channel.

9 Ready to make some color variations? Duplicate the image and flatten the copy. Duplicate the copy twice more. You use a different method for each of the copies. First, add a Curves adjustment layer to one of the copies and use the Pencil tool to scribble in the graph. You are certain to get some unusual color effects, and when you like one, click OK and save the results.

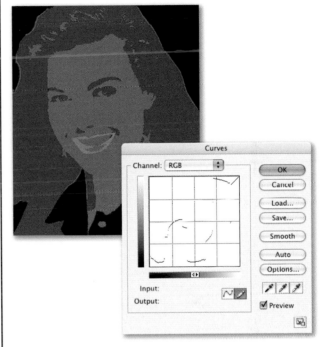

8 You can make this image more exciting by adding a fourth color for her mouth. Target the background and use the Magic Wand with tolerance set to around **50** and the Contiguous option selected. Click a dark pixel on her lower lip and shift-click the corners of her mouth to add them to the selection. Reduce tolerance to the default **32** and add more of the midtones. Tweak in Quick Mask mode if you must. Save the selection and fill it with another bright, saturated color.

10 Choose a fresh copy and create a Gradient map adjustment layer this time. Try several of the gradients in the default presets, or switch to another library if you want. I settled on the Orange, Purple, Red gradient, but reversed it to maintain the original tonal relationships.

(11) Finally you use colors from a completely different image and apply them to your last copy. I chose this young girl in denim overalls and a daisy on her hat. Open the image Daisy.psd on the CD-ROM for the book. Choose Image⇨Mode⇨Indexed Color and choose the Local (Perceptual) option for the palette. Choose Image⇨Mode⇨ Color Table. Save the color table and name it **DaisyGirl.act**.

Photo: www.comstock.com

(12) Make the copy of your working Warhol image active, and choose Image⇨Mode⇨Indexed Color, and load the Daisy.act color table you just saved. Unless you are a purist who won't meddle with the wisdom of chance, adjust the results. In this case, I want to increase the contrast between the blue and green areas. One way to do that is to load the selection for the shirt-plus-background, then increase brightness and contrast.

(13) It's time to combine your four variations into a grid. Choose the one you want to be in, say, the upper-left corner, and use Canvas Size to increase the pixel dimensions to the right and down. Drag and drop each of the other copies into position. Make any color changes you like to improve the composite using Adjustment Layers. I increased contrast and reduced brightness to enrich the colors in the copy that used a Gradient map (step 10).

A short recap

Imitating the pop-art look of a Warhol silkscreen portrait began with simplifying a source photo. Then, a small number of areas were selected for flat color fills, using some of Photoshop's advanced selection techniques. Choosing the colors for several variations, you explored options relying on chance to some degree. Finally, you combined the variations into a grid.

Standout

The cartoon look has been popular in many different ads and TV spots. You, too, can silhouette a person and create a styled image that is recognizable but also looks like a framed cardboard cutout. The Styles palette is the star of this production and lets you add the gradient strokes that make this look work. You can take the technique as far as your imagination permits and encase your friends, family, and coworkers in the colors of their choice. Become your own gradient designer!

THE PLAN

- Prepare the base images
- Create an altered background image
- Add the cutouts, gradient strokes, and overall color

① Open the image Tree.psd from the book Web site. Choose Image➪Image Size and resample the image to **120** percent. Choose Bicubic Smoother and click OK. As you can see in the layers, the tree is not the only occupant of the original image. I saved you the bother of removing the interloper.

② Press Shift+Command/Ctrl+Option/Alt+E to add a merged layer to the top of the stack. Name this layer **Difference Clouds**. Make the Clone Stamp layer active and add a white Solid Color Fill layer to the image. This layer functions as a false background layer and just provides a white base for the background image. Then set your colors to the default of black and white, and choose Filter➪Render➪Difference Clouds. You might want to repeat this another time or two to see if you prefer the result. If you don't, just step backward in the History palette. Set the layer opacity of the Difference Clouds layer to **37%**.

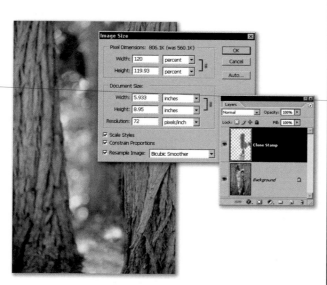

Photo: www.comstock.com

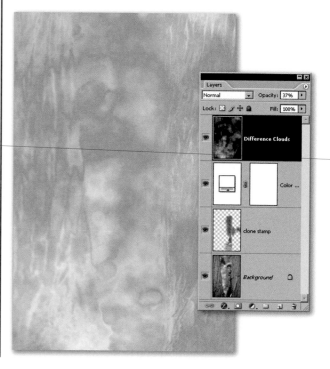

3 Duplicate the Difference Clouds layer and name it **Mosaic**. Change the Blend mode to Linear Light. Choose Filter➪Pixelate➪Mosaic, 15. Click OK.

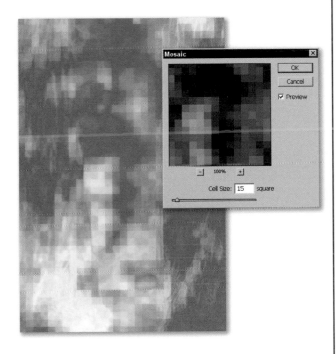

4 Turn off the eyes on all but the bottom two layers and make the Clone Stamp layer active. Press Shift+Command/Ctrl+Option/Alt+E to add a merged layer. Turn on all of the layers. Drag the new layer to the top of the layer stack. Name it **Color Burn** and change the Blend Mode to Color Burn. Set the Opacity to **85%**. The background isn't done yet, but you have a better chance to judge what you want to do with the background once the foreground is in place.

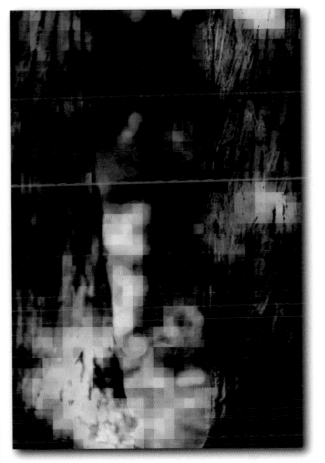

5 Open the image Teen.psd from the book Web site. Notice that this image contains two paths in the Paths palette. Duplicate the Background layer as **Close Path** and make Path 1 active in the Paths palette. Press and hold Command/Ctrl and click the Add Layer Mask icon to add Path 1 as a vector mask. Then duplicate the Background layer again as **Loose Path**. Make Path 2 active in the Paths palette and press and hold Command/Ctrl and click the Add Layer Mask icon to add Path 2 as a vector mask.

TIP

You need to get the paths and the teen into the tree image all lined up together. I've made this more difficult than necessary because I cropped the original teen image. The only way the paths are going to make it to the tree image in sync with the teen is if they travel as vector masks. The paths, by the way, are part of the original stock photo. When you purchase stock art from a company such as Comstock, art is usually shot against white backgrounds that include clipping paths, which is a major benefit.

Photo: www.comstock.com

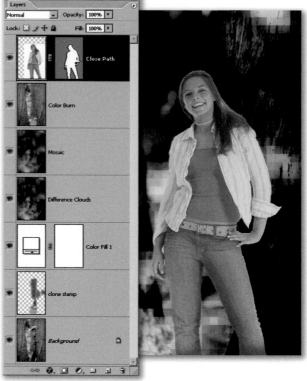

6 Select both the Loose and Close Path layers and drag them both at the same time into the Tree image. They should appear at the top of the Layer stack. Make the Loose Path layer active and drag the Vector Mask entry in the Paths palette to the New Path icon at the bottom of the Paths palette. It's automatically named Path 1. Rename it **Loose Path**. You may now discard the Loose Path layer. If you need or want to use the looser path, you have access to it.

7 The Close Path layer is active. Press and hold Command/Ctrl and add a new layer. The layer appears under the Close Path layer. Name this **Gradient Strokes**. Press and hold Command/Ctrl+Option/Alt and drag the vector mask from the Close Path layer onto the Gradient Strokes layer. Fill the Gradient Strokes layer with solid white. Add a Gradient Overlay effect. Set the Stoke to **27** pixels Outside, Normal mode, Shape Burst style. You are able to see the gradient as you design it. Click the Gradient editor. Double-click the Color Stop on the left and set it to **RGB: 255, 0, 0**. Set the Color Stop on the right to white. Press Option/Alt as you drag a copy of the red Color Stop to location **23%**. Press Option/Alt as you drag a copy of the white Color Stop to location **23%** (yes, directly on top of it — that makes a hard stripe). That is the procedure to follow. Here are the other Stop locations and the color they need to have:

* RGB: **255, 255, 255** at **40%**
* RGB: **166, 21, 64** at **40%**
* RGB: **166, 21, 64** at **51%**

* RGB: **255, 255, 255** at **51**%
* RGB: **255, 255, 255** at **70**%
* RGB: **105, 123, 78** at **70**%
* RGB: **105, 123, 78** at **88**%
* RGB: **255, 255, 255** at **88**%
* RGB: **255, 255, 255** at **100**%

When you have created the gradient, click OK. Then click OK to exit the Layer Styles.

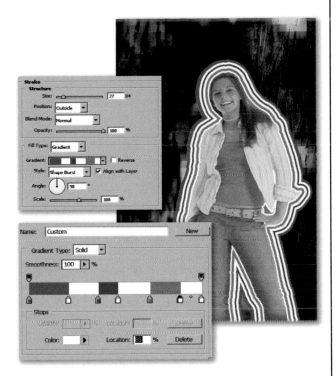

(**8**) Make the Close Path layer active. Add a Gradient Overlay style to the layer. Choose the Foreground to Background preset in the Gradient editor. Set the Foreground Color Stop to RGB: **255, 110, 2**. Set the Background Color Stop to RGB: **255, 255, 0**. Click OK Then change the Blend mode to Screen at **71**%. Use a Linear Gradient at the default settings. Click OK to exit.

(**9**) The gradient looks a trifle anemic to my eye. More density in the colors of the girl's garments would help. Press and hold Option/Alt and add a Hue/Saturation Adjustment layer. In the layer dialog box, select the Use Previous Layer to Create Clipping Mask option. Name the layer **Color Tone** and click OK. Set the Lightness slider to **-77** and click OK.

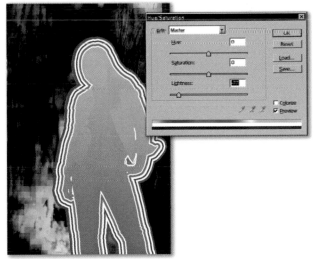

10 Now the girl's face is much too dark. Choose the Gradient tool and the Foreground to Background gradient. Make black the foreground color and white the background color. Place the gradient cursor on the green stripe above her head and press and hold Shift as you drag the cursor down to the bottom of her belt. Release the mouse button. Much better!

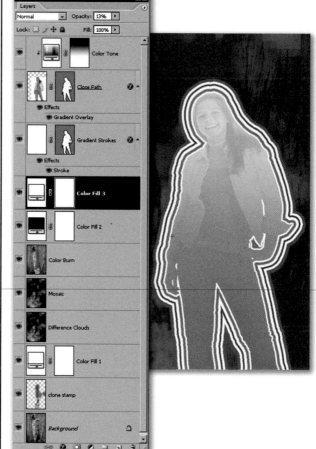

11 Time to finish the background. Make the Color Burn layer active. Press Command/Ctrl+A to select the whole image. Add a Solid Color Fill layer and choose RGB: 55, 55, 55. Click OK. Set the layer opacity to **75%**. Then add a white Solid Color Fill layer and set the opacity to **13%**.

12 Choose Image⇨Canvas Size and add **100** pixels to the width and **50** pixels to the height with the Relative option selected. Anchor in the center-bottom square. Set the Extension color to white. Click OK. Add a new layer above the white Color Fill and name it **Frame**. Set your foreground color to black. Command/Ctrl-click the Color Burn layer thumbnail in the Layers palette to load the layer opacity as a selection. Choose Edit⇨Stroke, **12** pixels, Inside, and click OK. Then choose Filter⇨Blur⇨Gaussian Blur, **4.0**, and click OK. Deselect.

TIP

The trick with a blurred stroke emulates a photographic vignette that darkens the edges of the photo. It's not always desirable in a camera, but it looks great when you create it on purpose.

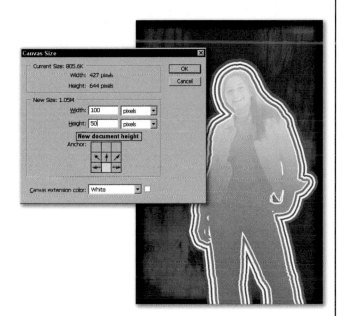

(13) Add an Outer Glow to the Frame layer. Just select it and then click OK in the dialog box. It is a simple, default glow, but it lights up the whole image.

(14) Select the Color Tone, Close Path, and Gradient Strokes layers and move the girl so that her sleeve cuff comes out of the frame on the right side. Also, sink her farther down in the bottom of the frame so that her knees are just visible.

(15) The borders need a bit of cropping to balance the image. Leave the full border on the right of the image but trim just a bit off the top and left sides. Click Commit. Make the Color Fill 3 layer active and Command/Ctrl-click the Color Fill 3 layer icon to load the selection. Choose Select⇨Inverse. Add a Solid Color fill layer and choose one of the muted tones in the background of the image as the new border color. Save your work.

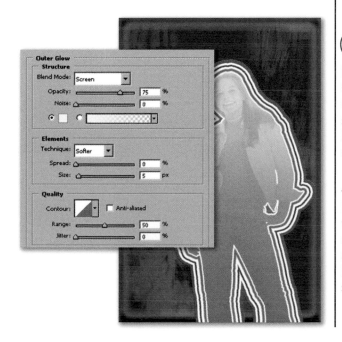

A short recap

Use this technique to make portraits stand out. The variations are endless. You can create an infinite variety of gradients. You've just seen how easy it is to create stripes against white. It is just as easy to create transparent stripes if you prefer that look. Try turning off the Mosaic layer to see more of the original trees. Almost any background or background-creation technique works here. All you need to do is to control the colors. The stripes are loud and bright. The background should be subtle and dark. However, you can also alter the gradient overlay color as well as the stripes. If you change the blend mode on the Gradient Overlay to Overlay mode, for example, you get a much more realistic-looking subject. I like the abstract or stylized look in images, but you know how they talk about different strokes...

Totem Pole

A totem pole is really a story-telling stick that recounts a story that those already familiar with it can read. It generally tells the tale of a person or a family. In this task, you develop the story of a very special, very brave little boy. His name is Sammy, he is 4 years old, and he has cancer. He was recently operated on to remove the tumor growing in his abdomen. Sammy's parents told him that he was having surgery because he'd won his fight during the chemo, to which he replied that his parents and his baby brother had helped, too. This is the story to tell — how Margot and Neil and baby brother Andy let Sammy sit on their shoulders to fight the bump in his tummy. Let's all root for a happy ending.

THE PLAN

- Create a stylized, low color version of Sammy's picture
- Create the embossed wood plaque of Sammy's face and colorize it
- Prepare the other plaques and the totem pole
- Arrange the images on the totem pole and finish up

1 Open the image Sammy.psd from the book Web site. It contains both a layer and a vector mask already. The other figure is a family portrait of Sammy, Andy, mom Margot, and dad Neil the summer before Sammy became ill.

Photo: Neil and Margot Hutchinson

2 Duplicate the Sammy layer and name it **Stamp**. Set your colors to the default of black and white. Choose Filter⇨Sketch,⇨Stamp and set the Light/Dark Balance to **25** and Smoothness to **1**. Click OK. Turn off the eye on the Sammy layer.

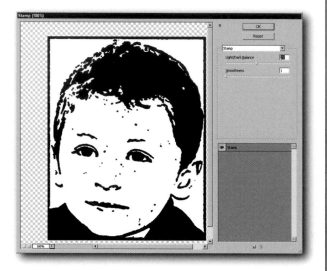

3 Add a blank layer at the top of the layer stack and name it **Cover Up**. Sammy has a lot of freckles, but you don't want him to look like he has a skin disease. With white, paint over the random black spots. Then press Shift+Command/Ctrl+Option/Alt+E to create a merged layer. Name it **Blur**. You need to smooth the shapes a bit. Choose Filter⇨Blur⇨Gaussian Blur, 2.0, and click OK. Add a Levels Adjustment Layer and set the Black Input point to **84** and the White Input point to **193**. Click OK.

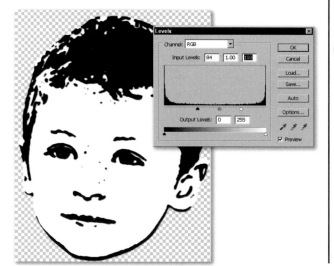

4 Open the image Wood.psd. This is a piece of Photoshop-generated wood. Drag the wood onto the Sammy image at the top of the layer stack. Name the layer **Wood Base**. Duplicate the Wood Base layer and name it **Face**. Turn off the eye on the Wood Base and Face layers and make the Levels 1 layer active. Command/Ctrl-click the RGB channel thumbnail in the Layers palette to load the values in the image as a selection. Make the Face layer active and turn the eye back on. Press and hold Option/Alt and add a Layer Mask to the Face layer. I know that you see nothing different yet — just a blank solid piece of wood.

5 On the Mac, double-click the SammyStyles.asl on the companion CD-ROM. On Windows, drag the SammyStyles.asl styles document from the enclosed CD-ROM into the open Photoshop application. The Styles attach to the Styles menu. In the Styles menu, click the Sammy Face style. Now you can see his face. However, you can also see the background. Take advantage of the masking on the Stamp layer. Starting with the Cover Up layer, make it and each layer above it active one at a time and on each layer, press Command/Ctrl+Option/Alt+G to create a Clipping Mask that uses all but the Sammy layer. Now you see just the face and the embossing.

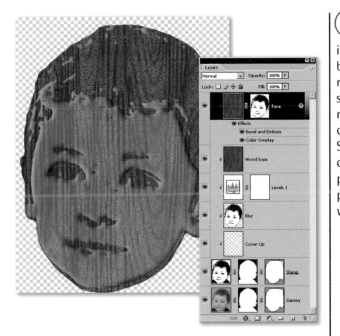

7 Now you have a bit of clean up to do. Option/Alt-click on the Layer Mask thumbnail for the Hair layer in the Layers palette to view only the Layer Mask. With black, remove any freckles in this mask. Click the RGB channel. Then Option/Alt-click the Face layer mask. You can add some more freckles here with a 5-pixel hard brush. Then make the Vector Mask for the Stamp layer active and choose the Direct Selection tool. Turn off the eye on the Sammy layer. The Stamp filter creates a roll under Sammy's chin that needs to be removed. Carefully move the Bezier points back to remove this rolled edge. You need to add a point with the Pen tool on the left side — it is obvious where it's needed.

6 Duplicate the Face layer and name it **Hair**. Make the layer mask active and press Command/Ctrl+I to invert it. Add it to the Clipping Mask if that does not automatically happen. Choose the 5-pixel hard brush and scribble in Sammy's hair area in the Layer mask using black. This leaves indentations in the embossing that resemble curls. Also, add some detail to Sammy's eyes. After you have added some curls, click the Thom_Chisel style in the Layers palette (it's one of the ones you just loaded and was developed by Thom La Perle). The curls stand out a lot more.

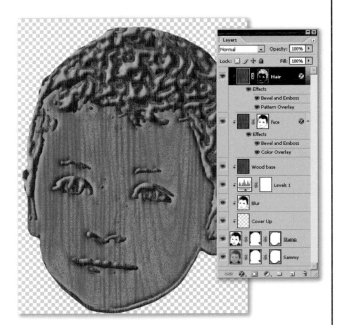

8 Make the Wood Base layer active and add a Solid Color Fill layer of RGB: **48, 36, 27** above it. Name the layer **Shadows**. Make the Face Layer Mask active. Then choose Filter⇨Other⇨Minimum, **1**. Click OK. This adds more space in the layer mask and lets more of the shadow layer underneath show through.

9 You next want to get some color into the face — as if it were either painted or using different tones of wood. Add a new layer to the top of the layer stack and name it **Desaturate**. Choose Image⇨Apply Image and set the Layer to the Sammy layer. Set the Blending mode to Normal and click OK. Duplicate that layer and name it **Equalize**. Choose Image⇨Adjustments⇨Equalize. Add a Hue/Saturation layer above it and set the Lightness to **+25** and the Saturation to **–100**. Click OK. Select the Desaturate, Equalize, and Hue/Saturation layers. Ctrl/right-click the layer entry for one of the selected layers and select the Group into New Smart Object option. Then press Command/Ctrl+Option/Alt+G to add the Smart Object to the Clipping Group. Change the Blend mode to Overlay. Name the Smart Object **Saturation**.

TIP

The Equalize adjustment is what makes Sammy's face start to look 3D.

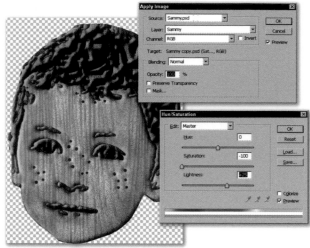

10 Add another layer to the top of the layer stack. Name it **Cutout**. Set your colors to the default of black and white. Choose Image⇨Apply Image and set the Layer to the Sammy layer. Set the Blending mode to Normal and click OK. Then choose Filter⇨Artistic⇨Cutout. Set the Number of Levels to **4**, the Edge Simplicity to **4**, and the Edge Fidelity to **1**, and click OK.

11 Change the Blend mode to Overlay. Sammy's hair gets nice and red (which it was before it fell out — and will be again). However, you lose the wonderful 3D shading that looks like a skillful woodcarving on polished wood. Add a Layer Mask and paint over Sammy's face in black. Take a very large soft brush and bring back a soft version of the dark shadow on the bottom right.

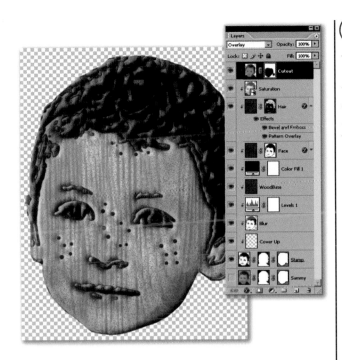

(13) Repeat the same steps for Andy.psd, Margot,psd, and Neil.psd — or open my finished versions. The thing that's interesting about redoing these images is to see how my instructions need to subtly change. Andy doesn't need the Eyebrows or Lips layers. Neil needs a more muted lip color. Margot needs a lighter brown eyebrow. At least look at what I did to each of the images. Save the versions that you want to use.

(12) The next step is to add some color to Sammy's eyes, lips, and hair. Add a Solid Color Fill Layer at the top of the stack and set the color to RGB: **96, 102, 63**. Click OK. Name the layer **Eyes**. Change the Blend Mode of the layer to Color. Fill the Layer Mask with black. Use a 5-pixel soft brush and zoom in. Paint over Sammy's eyes in white on the Layer Mask. Add a Solid Color Fill layer (in Color mode) named **Lips** and use RGB: **171, 90, 90**. Paint over his lips. Paint over his eyebrows in a Solid Color Fill layer (RGB: **184, 93, 56**) in Color mode. Name the layer **Eyebrows**. Save the image.

(14) Open the image TotemPole.psd from the book Web site. As you can see, a lot of work has already been done on it. You can figure out what it was very easily, so I see no need to take time to have you re-create it.

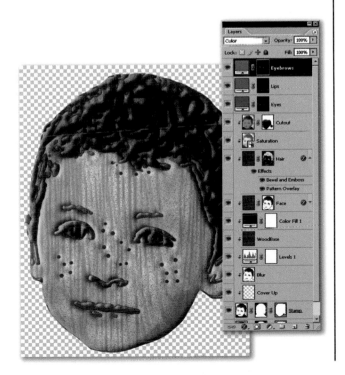

Photo: Sherry London

(15) Duplicate the TotemPole Smart Object and rasterize it. Name the layer **Texture**. Trash the layer style and the Layer Mask and create a Clipping Mask. Change the Blend Mode to Hard Light. Choose Filter⇨Stylize⇨Emboss. Set the Angle to **–50** degrees, the Height to **2**, and the Amount to **100**%. Click OK.

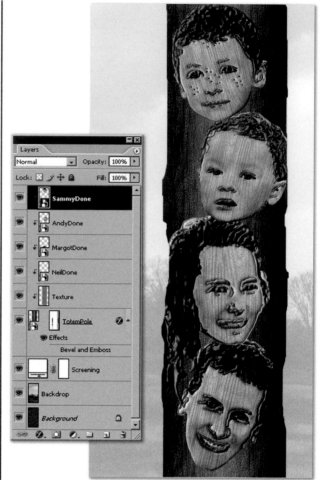

(16) Now you need to place the four people on the pole. Start with Neil and choose File⇨Place⇨Neil.psd and resize Neil to about 77 percent and 13 degrees of rotation. Click OK. Place Neil near the bottom of the pole. Place Margot at **81** percent. Place Andy at **61** percent and **14** degrees rotation. Place Sammy at **61** percent and **–15** degrees rotation. Add each layer to the Clipping Mask.

(17) The figures look as if they were pasted on — not carved on yet. You can change that. Drag the Woodgrain.pat file from the book Web site into the open Photoshop application. Make the SammyDone layer active. Press and hold Option/Alt and add a Pattern Fill layer. In the dialog box, select the Use Previous Layer to Create Clipping Mask option. Name the layer **Sammy Emboss** and click OK. Choose the Woodgrain pattern that you just loaded. Click OK. Fill the Layer Mask with black to hide it. Add the Sammy_Andy Emboss style from the Styles palette. Choose a 35-pixel brush with a Hardness of **55** percent. Paint with white around the outside edges of Sammy's face. You are actually painting on the embossing and you can control how it carves. Paint with black after you spread some on to create cracks. Repeat the same process with Andy.

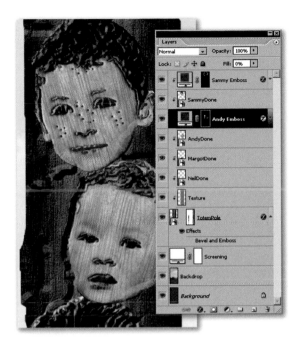

19 Make the Texture layer active. Add a Pattern Fill layer and choose the Woodgrain pattern. Name the layer **Pole Cracks**. Fill the Layer Mask with black. Attach the TotemPole Bevel style. Use a small version of the 55 percent Hard brush. You can drop down to a 3-pixel brush with this or go up to about a 20-pixel brush. Paint in the mask with white to reveal and black to hide. You will leave cracks on the pole. Repeat this same process by creating a Pattern Fill layer above the Sammy Emboss layer as well. This time, leave the mask white. Paint cracks in it in black over the people's faces — but follow the grain lines in the wood and use a 5-pixel brush.

18 You use the opposite procedure to add embossing to the adults. Make the MargotDone layer active and click the Neil_Margot Emboss style to attach it. Press and hold Option/Alt and add a Layer Mask. You remove Margot at the same time. Paint over her in the mask with white to reveal her again and then spread some of the embossing on the outer edges of her head. Repeat with Neil.

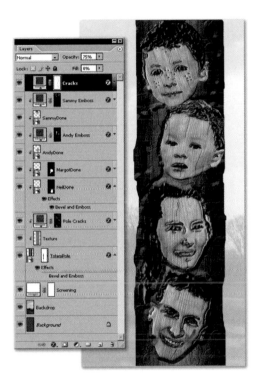

20 Double-click the TotemPole Smart Object to open it for editing. Put the file where you can see both it and the larger file. Click the large file to make it active and make the Cracks layer active. Click the Smart Object file and then press and hold Shift and drag the Reflected Gradient layer into the large file. Press Command/Ctrl+Option/Alt+G to add it to the Clipping Mask. Close the Smart Object file without saving it.

21 The remaining layers seem odd, but they are to even out the pole and make it look more rounded. Turn on the Bevel and Emboss effect on the Totem Pole layer. We now need to almost hide the layer effect. Add a Solid White Color Fill layer at the top of the layer stack. Don't add it to the Clipping Mask. Fill the Layer mask with black to hide the layer and apply a Pattern Overlay effect. Choose the Woodgrain pattern. With white and a 27-pixel soft brush, paint in the layer mask just along the left edge of the bevel. Keep the painting inside the bevel edge and try to leave just

a smidge of it on the left edge. Select the Background and the Screening layers and then drag them to the New Layer icon at the bottom of the Layers palette. Drag them both to the top of the Layer stack. Make the Screening Copy layer active, and make it into a Clipping Mask. Make the Background copy layer active, and press and hold Option/Alt and add a hide all layer mask. Use the same white brush on the outer edge of the bevel on the right side to make a soft edge for the totem pole.

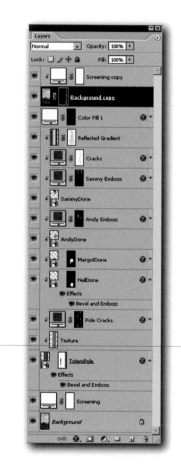

22 Save your work.

A short recap

The Photoshop theme of this task is to create wooden versions of friends and family. There are a number of different ways to add color to material sprinkled through this book. You might want to try Tasks 25 and 28 to see more of them. Here, you added contour to the wood by overlaying the original image back on top of it to get a 3-D effect. You can do much the same thing with other materials as well. If you prefer a flatter look to the figures, you can reduce the various overlay layers. Although it makes a very large file, you can also still edit any of the people on the pole. On my first design pass, I left the hard lines around Margot and Neil's mouths (the one that on adults runs between the mouth and nose to define the cheeks). When I got the entire image built, I felt that it was much too harsh. I was able to go back into the Smart Objects and edit the Face and Hair layer masks to hide those lines. If you want to follow Sammy's story, you can read it in progress at www.teamsam.com.

chapter
4

places

Oh, the places you'll go! You'll travel from China to the Southwest, to the coast of Greece with stops in New Jersey, Pennsylvania, and Downtown, USA. Along the way, you'll change a photo into a woodcut, carve a logo into rock, and see how easy it is to add a low depth-of-field effect to a photo shot at a small aperture (f/22). You'll make a carousel horse look as if it's running a race, create believable window reflections, and find Atlantis at the bottom of the sea. You'll also add a moody glow to etching as you hand-paint it. Have a good trip!

Woodcut

Woodcuts have been a popular, if time-consuming, look since at least the fifteenth century, but this digital version is really fast. It's almost a magical technique that looks great on stunning originals, but can also make a powerful statement from a less-than-stellar original (of which most of us have many). You'll learn a nearly nondestructive way to create the woodcut — a way that makes it very easy to modify and tweak your final result.

THE PLAN

- Prepare starting image
- Add Threshold layer and High Pass layers
- Blur then alter blend modes

(1) Open the image Chinatown.psd. It is from the Comstock library, so I'm not sure exactly where it was taken. However, whether in China or the U.S., it is a wonderful, colorful image.

Photo: www.comstock.com

(2) Add a new blank layer to the image and use the Clone Stamp tool to remove the partial figure on the left of the image. Leave his shadow as it makes the final image more interesting. I find the original stark white shirt a bit distracting. Make sure that you select the Sample All Layers check box. Name the layer **Clone Stamp**.

3 Select both the Background and the Clone Stamp layers and choose Group into New Smart Object from the Layers palette menu. Name the Smart Object **Corrected Original**. Then duplicate it by dragging it to the New Layer icon at the bottom of the Layers palette. Name the duplicate **Multiply**. Change the blend mode to Multiply.

4 Press and hold Option/Alt and choose Threshold from the New Fill or Adjustment layer icon at the bottom of the Layers palette. Click Use Previous Layer to Create Clipping Mask and click OK. Accept the default threshold value and click OK.

TIP

The Smart Object layer gives you a fast way to create the duplicate images you need without altering your base image or merging the two corrections layers together. If you discover that you don't like part of the correction you've made, it's easy to fix.

TIP

The Layer Options are automatically set to Blend Clipped Layers as a Group, so the blend mode of the base layer in the clipping mask determines the result. If you don't see black on top of the original image, open the Layer Properties dialog box and check the Blend Clipped Layers as a Group check box.

(5) Make the Multiply layer active and rename it **High Pass**. Choose Filter⇨Other⇨High Pass. Click OK to rasterize the layer. Choose a High Pass amount of **2.0** or the setting that you prefer. Click OK. Update the layer name with the High Pass Radius.

TIP

The High Pass filter is the magic behind the woodcut. Once you alter the Blend mode to multiply, you can judge the result as you apply the High Pass filter. The filter itself is destructive. Once you filter, you're mostly stuck with the result. However, try out a variety of settings before you decide on the final one. Lower values make the woodcut more detailed. You need to judge what you prefer for each image.

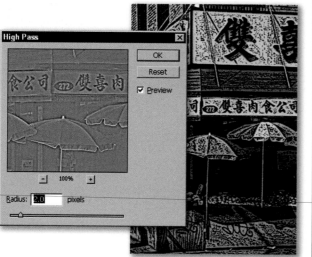

(6) Duplicate the Corrected Original layer by dragging it to the New Layer icon at the bottom of the Layers palette. Choose Filter⇨Blur⇨Surface Blur. Click OK to rasterize the layer. You may choose your own settings. I used a Radius of 63 and a Threshold of 71. Click OK. Rename the layer **Surface Blur 63, 71**.

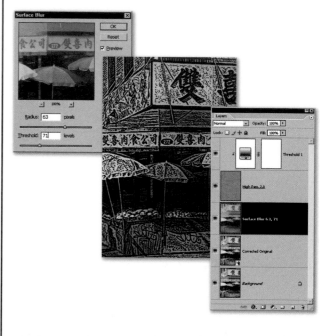

TIP

The higher the Threshold on this filter, the more the image is blurred by the Radius setting.

7 Duplicate the Corrected Original layer by dragging it the New Layer icon at the bottom of the Layers palette. Drag this layer above the Surface Blur layer. Change the blend mode to Lighten. Choose Filter⇨Blur⇨Gaussian Blur and click OK to rasterize the layer. Watch the preview and increase the Radius until you like the results. I like the overall effect at 60 pixels. Rename the layer **Gaussian Blur, 60** (or the value you used).

9 I miss the original flag color as well, but that's harder to add back as the flag's colors are darker than the Gaussian Blur layer. This trick works, though. Add a new blank layer, named **Give Back**, at the top of the layer stack. Double-click to open the Bending Options dialog box. Change the Fill Opacity to 0. Change the Knockout to Deep. Drag the Black slider on the Blend-If: Underlying Layer control to about **8**. Click OK. Wow! It looks like nothing happened.

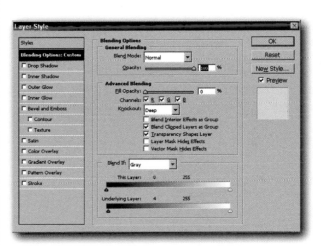

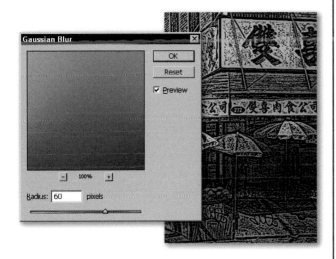

8 We need to bring back some of the original color in the fruit, so add a layer mask to the Surface Blur layer. With black, paint over the fruit on the fruit stand. Most of the fruit is lighter than the blurred layer so the color pops back up.

10 Okay, now the trick really happens! Using a small brush and any color that's sitting around, paint on the empty layer over anything whose original color you want to get back. I brought back the color of the flags, the green on the grocery shelves, the top Chinese letters, the red on the overhang, and a few spots on the umbrella. If you bring back too much, you can either erase it or mask it out.

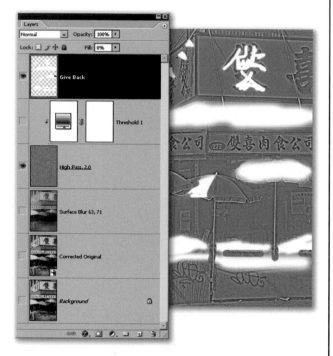

11 You can alter the Threshold layer to adjust the woodcut at any point in the process. The default Threshold amount is 128. Make the Threshold layer active and double-click to open it. With the Threshold Level field highlighted, press the up and down arrows and watch how the image changes. The figure shows a Threshold Level of 124. I prefer 127 as the value for this.

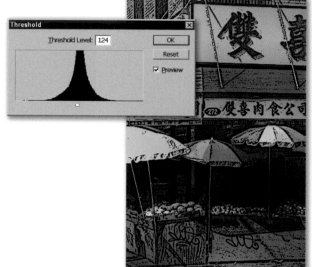

12 Now you see the finished image with a Threshold Level of 127.

A short recap

I could probably spin this task into a book, but I know the publisher would strongly object! It's a technique that can take you as far as creativity and imagination permit. At its most basic level, you apply a High Pass filter to a copy of the image, change it's blend mode to Multiply and then Threshold it. You blur the layer below. The way we did it, however, gives you ultimate flexibility to adjust the Threshold and to alter the blur layers and combine them. Try substituting a totally different, highly blurred image under the woodcut. Instead of Lighten mode on the Surface Blur layer, try Luminosity or any other blend mode. Try out different types of blurs, including Radial and Dust and Scratches. Experiment, experiment, experiment.

Intense Focus

Sometimes you take a photo and later say, "Gee, I wish I had only focused on the foreground." Never fear — this is a job for Photoshop. I really think that Photoshop should not be an excuse for poor photography. "I'll fix it in Photoshop," are not words I like to hear. However, Photoshop can create shallow depth-of-field effects that aren't physically possible in a camera, and for that I will stretch a good many deeply held beliefs. So, let's grab an image that does not look good in sharp focus and see how we can fix the design and composition by using multiple types of blurs. Oh yes, the place in this image is Longwood Gardens in Kennett Square, Pennsylvania (www.longwoodgardens.com).

THE PLAN

- Decide which part of the image remains in focus
- Filter and mask
- Build up filters and masks

(1) Open the Tulip.psd image from the book Web site. The image is in sharp focus but it looks unbalanced. There are too many flowers along the top of the image and only one tulip at the bottom. If the image features only two tulips in sharp focus and a third at a slight blur, the rest of the image could fade into a deep blur. Then the special tulips stand out from the crowd. The color of the tulips, however, is spectacular and should be preserved.

(2) Duplicate the background layer and name it **Lens Blur**. Choose Filter⇨Blur⇨Lens Blur and enter these settings: Depth Map Source: **None**; Iris Shape: **Square**; Radius: **100** Blade Curvature: **53**; Rotation: **194**. For Specular Highlights, use Brightness: **57** and Threshold: **205**. Leave the Noise at **0**. Click OK. How did I choose these settings? I fiddled with them and watched the preview until I found something I liked. There's no magic to this — just move the sliders and look at the image! I only knew that I wanted a lot of specular highlights.

Photo: Sherry London

TIP

The Lens Blur filter lets you simulate depth of field. The expected way to use it is to create a depth map. Much like some varieties of displacement maps, a depth map shows black where you want the image to be in focus and then moves into white the farther you get from your point of focus. I prefer to not use a depth map for the first pass of this technique. That way, you treat the whole image as background. I love the ability that the Lens Blur filter has to create specular highlights and shapes that are, at best, uncommon in cameras — such as the square that we use here.

③ Duplicate the Background layer again and bring the duplicate to the top of the layer stack. Name the layer **Sharp Focus**. Press and hold Option/Alt and add a Layer mask to the image. It will hide the layer. Use a large soft brush and make white your Foreground color. In the layer mask, paint over the bottom flower and the tulip on the top left. Make the stem of the tulip sharp as well. Paint in 50 percent gray over the tulip that is just behind and to the right of the one in sharp focus. Don't be afraid to change the opacity of the brush or to swap your foreground and background colors until you get exactly what you want. Paint loosely; you don't need to make a precise selection.

④ I want to get a bit more definition and glow. Duplicate the Background layer again and drag it to the top of the layer stack. Name it **Surface Blur**. Set a Radius of **62** and a Threshold of **129**. Click OK.

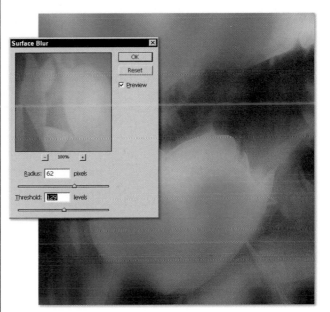

5 Command/Ctrl-click the layer mask of the Sharp Focus layer to load it as a selection. Then press Shift+Command/Ctrl+I to inverse the selection. Make the Surface Blur layer active and add a layer mask. The sharp image from the previous layer is still sharp, but the rest of the image only shows the Surface Blur. Painting in the mask with a large, soft 50% opacity brush, mask out most of the areas near the top of the tulips to bring back the specular highlights. Restore the specular highlights behind the lowest tulip and near the right edge of the image.

6 Duplicate the Background layer and bring the copy to the top of the layer stack. I want to spread some of the orange tones through the image and a heavy blur is one of the best ways to do that. You can use a Gaussian Blur of **250** pixels if you wish. However, try this one instead. Choose Filter⇨Blur⇨Box Blur. Set a Radius of **312** pixels. Click OK. This blur keeps the colors a bit better and creates some streaks that I like. Set the layer opacity to about 52%. Name the layer **Box Blur 312**. Bring the Sharp Focus layer to the top of the layer stack.

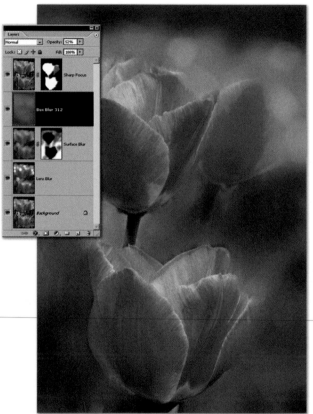

7 Add a layer mask to the Box Blur layer. With a 200-pixel soft black brush at 50 percent opacity, partially mask out the lower sides of the image to restore more of the Surface Blur layer. With 100 percent opacity, black, and a smaller brush, completely mask out the area between the sharp upper tulip and the slightly blurred tulip on to the right.

cursor from the center top of the image to just beyond the bottom left of the sharp tulip. (If you want to be very precise, the Gradient cursor is at an angle of **102** degrees as read on the Info palette. Decide which version you prefer and save your work.)

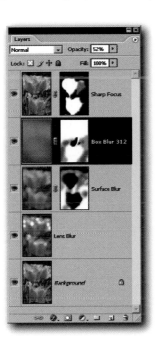

8 You could be finished at this point. The color is glorious. However, the color is a bit of a distraction from focusing on the major tulips. Try this. If you don't like it better, just toss away the layer. Make the Box Blur layer active. Add a Solid Color fill adjustment layer and choose RGB: **180**, **180**, **180** as the color. Click OK. Set the layer opacity to **62%**. Choose the Gradient tool and set your colors to a white Foreground and black Background. In the layer mask for the Color Fill 1 layer, drag the gradient

9 Decide which version you prefer and save your work.

TIP

You might want to try other colors in the Solid Color Fill layer. Try RGB: **106**, **112**, **84**, for example. You might also want to try black or a deep green.

A short recap

Photoshop gives you many ways to create and layer blur effects to produce an out-of-focus background for an image. If you really do want an accurate shallow depth-of-field effect, capture the image that you actually want with the camera (unless your camera won't let you set the aperture and shutter speed). However, you can get wildly creative in Photoshop to manufacture images that aren't possible to photograph. Now, you can let your imagination have free reign and focus on areas that can never have been in focus at the same time. You can also add motion blurs to the depth of field and play with masks until you achieve your artistic vision.

Panning

The place is Atlantic City, New Jersey, at the world-famous Steel Pier. The carousel is motionless on a cold April day. I really want a panning shot. (*Panning* is a traditional film technique where you move the camera at the same speed and direction as an object in motion. The result is that the object seems still but the background around it moves.) With the magic of Photoshop, however, you can make that shot happen. I exaggerate the effect (the merry-go-round does not have a top speed of 50 mph), but I like the look. I hope you do, too.

THE PLAN

- Create paths for the horse
- Apply several different Motion Blurs at different settings
- Put back a still copy at a lower opacity

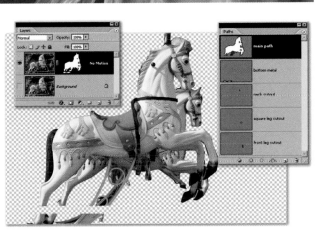

① Open the image Carousel.psd from the book Web site. Duplicate the Background layer as No Motion.

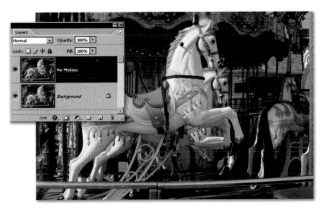

Photo: Sherry London

② Use the Pen tool to create as many paths and subpaths as needed to select the two center horses and the metal grating under them that makes them rise and fall. I create paths to select the horses and different paths to cut out the areas to get subtracted from the selection (such as between the horses' heads and legs). Load the main (positive) paths as selections and add a layer mask. Then load the negative path areas as selections and fill them on the layer mask with black.

TIP

If you have trouble using the Pen tool, you can use any selection method you prefer. However, you need a fairly precise selection. Try the Freehand Pen tool and see if that works better for you. When you create the Paths, make sure that you have Add to Path area active on the Paths Options bar.

③ Duplicate the Background layer and name the layer **Motion Blur 115**. Leave the layer behind the No Motion layer. Choose Filter⇨Blur⇨Motion Blur. Set the Angle to **0** and the Distance to **115**. Click OK.

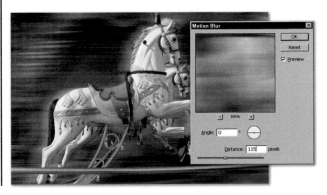

Choose the Brush tool with the 45-pixel soft brush and white. Start at the top-right corner of the image and press and hold Shift as you paint to the bottom of the image, thus revealing just a little of the offset edge. It looks like a slight double-exposure, but that's a lot better than the strange streaks.

4 Duplicate the Background layer and move it on top of the Motion Blur 115 layer. Name it **MB50**. Can you guess what's next? Right. Choose Filter⇨Blur⇨Motion Blur and set the Angle to **0** and the Distance to **50**. Click OK. This is more reasonable perhaps, but it covers the layers below.

6 Make the MB50 layer active. Click the Add Layer Mask icon at the bottom of the Layers palette. Choose the Gradient tool and set your colors to a white Foreground and a black Background. Make sure that the layer mask is active. Place the gradient tool at the center-right edge of the image and press and hold Shift as you drag to the edge of blurred horses' back ends. This keeps a lesser amount of blur over the front of the carousel.

5 The motion in front of the horse is actually not quite as pronounced as the motion behind the horse, so we really only want to save the right-most portion of the MB50 layer. However, there is also the problem of much too much streaking at the right edge of the image. Let's fix that one first. Duplicate the MB50 layer and name the copy **Offset**. Choose Filter⇨Other⇨Offset and set the Horizontal Pixels Right to **+20**. Set the Vertical Pixels Down to **0** and choose Wrap Around. Click OK. Press and hold Option/Alt and add a layer mask. The layer mask hides the layer.

7 Duplicate the Background layer and drag the duplicate to the top of the layer stack. Name the layer **MB15**. Choose Filter⇨Blur⇨Motion Blur. Leave the Angle set to **0** and change the distance to **15**. Click OK. This layer puts a low amount of motion blur on the horses because it is not really possible to get the edge of the subject totally crisp on a panning shot — but yet have the background moving at a fast blur. So, press and hold Option/Alt and add a layer mask (hide all) to the layer. Now, take a soft brush (I make a 70-pixel brush) and white and brush over the back end of the horse. Brush over his mane and the plume on his head. Change the brush opacity to **50%** and brush over the horse's face — but just near the edge. Brush over the moving metal parts to blur them a bit. Then brush over the back horse (the center one behind the main horse). Finally, change the brush opacity to **20%** and brush over the other carousel horses in the image to give them the lower blur amount. The carousel is moving at the same speed and it is reasonable that the horses traveling with the carousel would be more in focus than the background (even though not in as sharp focus as the main element).

8 Finally, duplicate the Background layer again and drag the image to the top of the layer stack. Name the layer **Final Focus**. Change the layer opacity to 10 percent to put back a tiny bit of the original image.

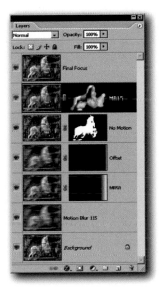

9 If you move a camera and don't move it continuously, the resulting image seems to sputter a bit and jump. That is what we are emulating on this last step. Save your work.

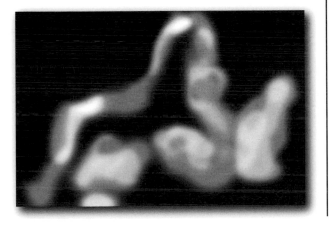

A short recap

Creating panning shots in Photoshop can be even more fun than photographing them. When you try to pan with a camera, it can be diabolically hard to get the right rhythm and travel at the same speed as your subject. You never have the problem in Photoshop and can get a good result every time. The technique is not complex — all you are doing is applying varying levels of motion blur and then masking to create the effect you want.

Window Shopping

Open any magazine and you see people inside on cell phones, on TVs, coming out of cameras. They weren't on the TV when the photo was taken, and their image wasn't on the cell phone either. However, we go a step beyond that effect to show what happens when you make a window with reflections of the shoppers — who aren't really there, either. I'll let you in on another secret — the images in the windows also aren't really there. They are a collection of shop photos from New Orleans to L.A. to Cape May, New Jersey, and points in between.

THE PLAN

- Create a layer sandwich for the windows
- Add the reflection scene and the people and mask them

alpha channel in the Channels palette to load it as a selection. In the Window Frame layer, click the Add Layer Mask icon at the bottom of the Layers palette to create a layer mask. The image shows no change at this point. All of the reflection images are added between the Background layer and the Light Version layer.

(1) Open the image Window.psd on the companion CD-ROM.

Photo: Sherry London

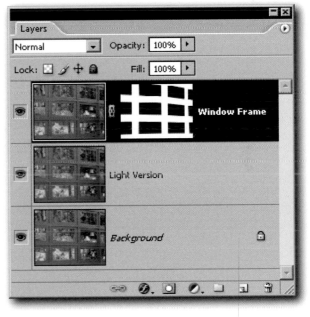

Photo: www.comstock.com

(2) Duplicate the Background layer by dragging its thumbnail to the New Layer icon at the bottom of the Layers palette. Name the duplicate layer **Light Version**. Change the Blend mode to Lighten and the Opacity to 25%. To complete the layer sandwich, you need to frame the windows at full opacity. The frame doesn't show a reflection at all. Duplicate the Background layer and drag it to the top of the layer stack. Name the layer **Window Frame**. Command/Ctrl-click the WindowFrame

TIP

Have you ever noticed that a reflection in a window doesn't seem to reflect everything equally? The lightest areas in both the window and the objects reflecting in the window tend to be most prominent. By setting a layer to Lighten and a lower opacity, you can simulate this effect.

3 Make the background layer of the Window image active. Open the image Shopper1.psd from the book Web site. Drag the image into the Window image and choose Edit➪Transform➪Flip Horizontal. Then press Command/Ctrl+T and change the Width to **200%**. Click the Maintain Aspect Ratio link between the Width and Height on the Options bar to set the Height to **200%** as well. Click Commit. Name the layer **Shopper1**.

4 Control/right-click the enlarged Shopper1 image and choose Group into New Smart Object. Double-click the Shopper1 Smart Object to open it for edit. Choose the Magic Wand tool and set it to a Tolerance of **25**, Anti-alias OnContiguous Off and Sample All Layers On. Click the white background to select it. Choose Select➪Inverse and then choose Select➪Modify➪Contract, **1** pixel and Select➪Feather, **1** pixel. Add a Layer mask. Leave the Smart Object file open.

TIP

You might wonder why I use the Smart Object here. If you are working nondestructively, you want to retain the original image. I find using Smart Objects — and hiding layers there — to be a much more manageable solution than leaving a lot of hidden layers in the main Layers palette. By tucking all of the parts of the shopper into the PSB .psb file in the Smart Object, any change that I make is recalculated in the image. I don't need to worry about moving multiple layers or masking them.

5 Drag the Shopper1 layer to the New Layer icon at the bottom of the Layers palette to duplicate it. Name the duplicate layer **Shear**. Turn off the eye on the original layer (Shopper1). Choose Filter➪Distort➪Shear. In the dialog box, add a control point at each grid intersection and nudge the points so that one goes just to the left of the center line, the next one goes just to the right, the next to the left, and so on. You want to gently bend the reflection — not make it unrecognizable. Click OK. Don't close the Smart Object file.

6 Duplicate the Shear Layer as **Ripple**. Turn off the eye on the Shear layer. Choose Filter➪Distort➪Ripple. Set the Amount to **35**% and the Size to Medium. Again, the idea is to introduce a bit of variation and shake — but not an earthquake. You see the ripples most across her shirt. Click the Close box on the Smart Object file and then click Yes to the prompt to save the file.

8 Open the Shopper2.psd image from the book Web site. Drag it into the Window Shopping image. Name the new layer **Shopper2**. This time, make the Smart Object first. Then on the Smart Object layer in the main file, press Command/Ctrl+T and enlarge the image to 200 percent in both width and height as you did in Step 3. Commit. No need to flip her as you did Shopper1. Then double-click the Smart Object to open it for edit. Create the Laser Mask as you did in Step 4 and then apply the same filters as in Steps 5 and 6. Click the Close box on the Smart Object file and then click Yes to the prompt to save the file.

7 Change the opacity of the Shopper1 Smart Object to **70**%. Position the shopper so that the top of her head is about halfway up the second window in the second row from the left. Her brown shopping bag should just barely be visible.

Photo: www.comstock.com

Photo: www.comstock.com

9 Change the Opacity of the Shopper2 layer to 60 percent. Shopper2's face needs to end up somewhere in the window on the same row as Shopper1 but the next window to the right (your right). As you try to position her, you can really see the effect of the Light Version layer. She shows up best in light areas, as a real reflection would. I put her face partially on the white lampshade in that window. You can choose the location that you prefer.

11 Double-click the Kids Smart Object to open it for editing. Don't add a mask here. Instead, choose Filter⇨Blur⇨Motion Blur. Set the Angle to **4** and the Distance to **5**. Click OK. This makes the kids' reflections — which come from a bit farther away — jitter a bit more. Click the Close box and click Yes to the Save prompt.

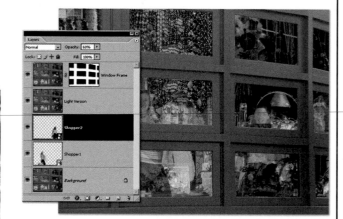

10 Open the Kids.psd image from the book Web site. Drag it into the Window Shopping image. Name the new layer **Kids**. Make the layer into a Smart Object. Then press Command/Ctrl+T and enlarge the image to 200 percent in both width and height as you did in Step 3. Commit.

(12) In the main image, move the Kids layer so that the child in the blue hat is in the center of the bottom-left window. The middle child's head should be fully visible in the next window. Add a Layer mask to the layer. With black at 50 percent opacity, paint out the areas that you don't want to see or leave some of the background areas partially visible. (I tried to preserve some of the details of the woman in the blue dress just to the right of the center child.)

(13) Open the Palm Tree image from the book's CD-ROM. It is the same size as the Window image.

Photo: Sherry London

(14) Make the Background layer active in the Windows image. Then make the palm tree image active. Press and hold Shift as you drag the palm tree image into the Window image. This registers the two images. Under the people is the logical place for this layer because the palm tree is physically the farthest reflection in the window. Name the layer **Palm Tree**. Add a Layer mask to the layer. Fill the Layer mask with 50 percent gray to make the layer partially transparent. This just gives it a head start. The real work is to decide which portions need to be more — or less — opaque. There is really no one right solution to this. Much as I like the puppets in the window on the top row, the reflections look best with the palm tree at full opacity in the right-most two windows on the top row. You can see my opacity decisions in the layer mask diagram shown here (the red is the window frame; black areas show the original window and white areas show the palm trees). I use a large, soft brush at between 30% and 50% opacity and add to or lower the visibility of areas as I paint.

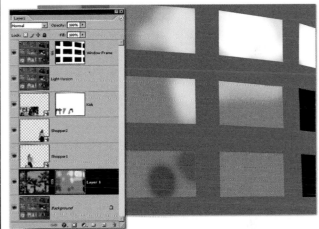

TIP

Your other location option is to place the palm tree in front of the people and then load each of them as a selection. You can then create a Hide Selection Layer mask. The advantage of this way of working is that you can have the palm tree reflect on top of a person a bit if you feel it is necessary without the need to adjust multiple masks. The main disadvantage is that you cannot move any of the people without fixing or altering the Layer Mask in the Palm Tree layer. I would rather have the ability to easily move the main players. It isn't all that logical anyway to have the palm trees cover some of the people when the people are in front of the trees.

(15) The final step is to tweak the positions of Shopper1 and Shopper2 if needed. I wanted to move Shopper 2 a little to the left and up. When you are satisfied with everything, save your work.

A short recap

The key to a realistic composite of window reflections is to pay attention to the way in which real reflections interact. The lighter image is the one that shows in the window. By adding a layer in Lighten mode at the top of a sandwich, you can model this behavior in your image. The other trick is simply to decide which reflections should rule in which areas of the window — and mask accordingly. The original window is built very simply by taking selections from a variety of images and placing them behind the window frame. No effects are added to the images that make up the original window. I show the use of several different filter possibilities on the various people in the image; these filters aren't the only possibilities. You can play with many other filters to get glass of different textures or to simulate motion in the reflections. Photographing reflections can be fascinating — but building them yourself can be even more fun.

Atlantis Found

Off the coast of Greece, not very far under the ocean, lies the lost city of Atlantis. If you're careful, you can hear the echoes of a drowned city or find the tops of forgotten towers poking out from the shallow sea. The unusual perspective of this image can be applied to many other images. Cross sections like this are a staple of technical illustration. I need to thank my friend David Xenakis, publisher of XRX books and *Knitters Magazine* (www.knittinguniverse.com), for the use of his wonderful photos of Greece.

THE PLAN

- Add the various images
- Size images and arrange them
- Add the water
- Add the light

Photo: David Xenakis

(1) Choose File⇨New and create an image that is 628 x 797 pixels at 72ppi with a white background. Name the image **Atlantis** and click OK. Open the image Columns.psd from the book's CD-ROM. Drag it into the empty image and place it at the bottom of the image. Name the layer **Columns**. Choose Filter⇨Other⇨Offset and move the image 15 pixels to the right and 15 pixels down. Select the Set to Transparent option button and click OK. Control/Right-click the layer entry in the Layers palette and choose Group into New Smart Object.

TIP

Did I use the Offset filter when I created this image? Of course not! I simply moved the image (a number of times) in the course of developing the example until it ended up in this position. However, the position does matter in the final image, so it's a lot easier to give you a precise way to get the image where I want it to go instead of trying to describe the image features that you need to use for guidance.

(2) Double-click the Smart Object icon to open the original image for editing. Choose the Pen tool and set it to Paths. Then make a path around the image that selects only the stonework and removes the greenery (which doesn't quite look the same under the sea). Once you make the path, save it as **Column** path in the Paths palette. Then leave it highlighted and Command/Ctrl-click the Add Layer Mask icon in the Layers palette. This adds a Vector mask to the layer. Don't close the Smart Object yet.

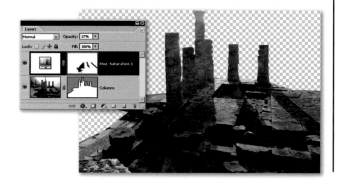

TIP

If you cannot use the Pen tool use the Polygon Lasso tool to make a hard-edged selection. However, this is a very simple Pen tool outline — you can just click at every corner point; the image has no curves.

TIP

You need to create the path while the Smart Object is open. That way, the path is part of the Smart Object file. If you create the path in the main image, it won't appear in the Smart Object when you try to use it as a Vector mask.

3 Add a Hue/Saturation layer to the Smart Object. Set the Hue to **-180** but don't change the other sliders. Click OK. Change the Opacity to **37%**. This merely tones the object and neutralizes it a bit Then use black with a soft brush in the Layer mask and paint over the three strong shadows from the columns to restore the blue shadows — that looks very good under the sea even though the original column color was too orange-yellow.

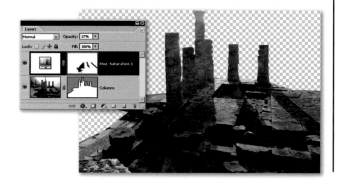

TIP

You can change any color to gray by moving the Hue slider to **-180** and setting the opacity at **50** percent. In pigment, you would tone a color by adding a bit of its complement. In Photoshop, setting the Hue to **-180** at values less than **50** percent accomplishes the same thing. You can also get close to the same look by setting the Saturation to **-100** and the opacity of that Hue/Saturation layer to **75** percent. If you are used to the behavior paints, altering the Hue is more intuitive.

4 Let's get a sense of the image that we're building by adding the ocean image now. Open the image Ocean.psd and drag it into the Atlantis image. Name the layer **Ocean**. Place the ocean at the top of the file (the width on both files is the same) and make it the top layer as well. Select the Rectangular Marquee tool and drag the marquee around the layer from the top-left corner to the right side of the image just under the small boat on the right. Add a Layer mask. Choose the Gradient tool with the Black to White gradient. Place your cursor approximately 40 pixels under the bottom of the small boat and then click. Press and hold Shift and drag to the bottom of the boat. Release the mouse. You should see a soft blend between the ocean and the white space below.

Photo: David Xenakis

5 Make the Background layer active. Open the image Temple.psd from the book's CD-ROM and drag it into the Atlantis image. Set it at the bottom of the image. Name the layer **Temple**. Choose Filter⇨Other⇨Offset and drag the Pixels Right slider to **-11** and the Pixels Down slider to **+99**. Leave the Undefined Areas at Set to Transparent. Click OK. Control/right-click the layer entry in the Layers palette and choose Group into New Smart Object.

Photo: David Xenakis

6 Double-click the Temple Smart Object to open it for editing. Make a Pen path around the outside of the temple, cutting off the sky. Then click the Subtract from Area icon on the Options bar and draw the paths to cut out the sky from the window areas. Save the path as **Temple** and Command/Ctrl-Click on the Add Layer mask icon in the Layers palette to add a vector mask. Don't close the Smart Object yet.

7 Add a Hue/Saturation layer to the Temple Smart Object. Set the Hue to **–180** and the Lightness to **+12**. Click OK. Leave the opacity at **100%** but fill the Layer Mask with black to hide the entire effect. Then use a soft white brush to bring the altered color back to the rocks area of the image and with a smaller, hard brush, add the color to the bush on the left of the temple. Click the Close box on the Smart Object and click Yes to the prompt to Save the changes.

8 Make the Background layer of the Atlantis image active again. Open the Monument.psd image and drag it into the Atlantis image. Name the layer **Monument**. Make sure that the entire circle image is visible in the Atlantis image and then Control/Right-click the layer entry and choose Group into New Smart Object. Double-click the Monument Smart Object to open it for editing. In the Monument Smart Object file, create a Pen path that cuts out the sky and trees as shown inside the yellow outline on the figure. Save the path as **Monument** and Command/Ctrl-click the Add Layer Mask icon on the Layers palette to add a Vector mask. Leave the Smart Object open.

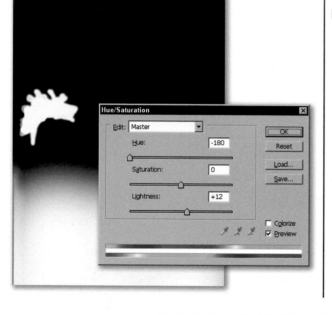

Photo: David Xenakis

9 Add a new layer above the Monument layer in the Smart Object. With the Clone Stamp tool, copy some of the background sand into the area of trees between the pillars. Then extend the small stone columns over the area of grass at the bottom left of the monument to complete the circle. Click the Close box on the Smart Object and click Yes to the prompt to Save the changes.

10 Press Command/Ctrl+T to transform the Monument Smart Object. Change the Width to **59**% and the Height to **64**% on the Options bar. Then choose Edit⇨ Transform⇨Flip Horizontal. Set the X field to **518** and the Y field to **382**. Commit the transform.

11 Open the Temple image again. Select the Rectangular Marquee tool and set Style to Fixed Size. Type **427** pixels wide and **232** pixels high as the dimensions. Click to set the marquee at the bottom of the Temple image. Choose Edit⇨Copy. Make the Background layer of the Atlantis image active and choose Edit⇨Paste. Name the layer **Rocks1**. Control/Right-click the layer entry and choose Group into New Smart Object. Double-click the Rocks1 Smart Object to open it for editing. Add a Hue/Saturation layer and change the Hue to **-180**. Click the Close box on the Smart Object and click Yes to the prompt to Save the changes. Drag the Rocks1 Smart Object until it touches the left side of the image and is lined up at the same height as the straight top of the front face of the Temple layer.

12 Duplicate the Rocks1 Smart Object layer by dragging it to the New Layer icon at the bottom of the Layers palette. Name this copy **Rocks2**. Drag the layer until it covers the white spot between the Monument and the Columns layers. Look at the various layers in your composite and adjust the Paths on the Smart Objects if you see white space in the image.

13 Turn off the Background layer and the Ocean layer. Make the Columns layer active. Press Shift+Command/Ctrl+Option/Alt+E to create a new merged layer. Name the layer **Merged** and choose Layer⇨Arrange⇨Send to Back. Turn on the Background layer and the Ocean layer. Press Command/Ctrl+R to turn on the Rulers. Drag a guide so that it is just below the extremely tiny sailboat near the horizon on the left of the image. Turn off the Ocean layer and make the Merged layer active. Control/right-click the layer entry and choose Group into New Smart Object. Don't open the Smart Object. In the main image, press Command/Ctrl+T to get the Free Transform command. Choose Edit⇨Transform⇨Flip Horizontal. Then move the image up until the top of the monument touches the guide. Grab the bounding box from the bottom-center point and drag it up until the bottom is about level with the top of the lower roofline on the Monument layer. Click Commit.

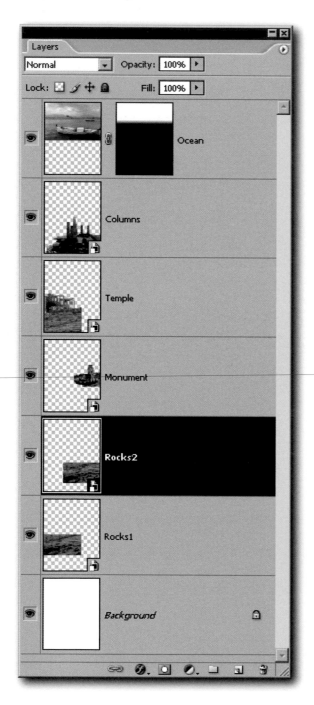

(14) Finally, it's time to sink our city under the ocean. Make the Columns layer active. Add a Gradient Fill layer. Click the Gradient Editor and choose a Foreground to Transparent gradient style. Double-click the left-most Color Stop and choose RGB: 21, 53, 63 in the Color Picker. Click OK. Double-click the right-most Color Stop and choose RGB: 57, 97, 106. Click OK. Press and hold Option/Alt and drag a duplicate of the black Opacity stop on top of the gradient bar to the 40 percent location on the Opacity gradient. This keeps the gradient totally opaque for 40 percent of the gradient distance. Click OK to close the Gradient Editor. In the Gradient Fill dialog box, set the Style to Linear and the Angle to –88 degrees. The Scale is 100%. Click OK.

(15) I want the top of monument in the Merged layer to peek out of the ocean. That's why you placed it where you did in Step 13. The most obvious way to revel the monument is to cut through the mask on both the Ocean and the Gradient Fill layers. However, that is very clunky and if you need to move the Merged layer, you need to repaint the layer masks. So, if obvious doesn't work, let's try tricky. Make the Ocean layer active. Press and hold Shift and the Rocks1 layer. All of the layers between are selected as well. Press Command/Ctrl+G to make a Layer Set Group. Name the group **Main Composite**. Make the Ocean layer active and add a new, empty layer above it by clicking the New Layer icon at the bottom of the Layers palette. Name this layer **Knockout**. Double-click the layer entry to bring up the Layer Style dialog box. In the Advanced Blending section of the dialog box, set the Fill opacity to 0%. Then change the Knockout to Shallow. Click OK.

TIP

Shallow Knockout works by revealing the area under the opaque portion of a layer. The layer that is used as the shallow knockout is either the base layer of a clipping mask or else the layer directly underneath a Layer Set Group in the Layers palette. The other condition that is needed is that the layer set to shallow knockout also has a 0 percent Fill opacity. Very tricky — but very useful. Step 17 would be a disaster if you did this using the other method. Of course, if you really want to wimp out, you can simply cut, paste, and mask the top of the monument from the Merged layer.

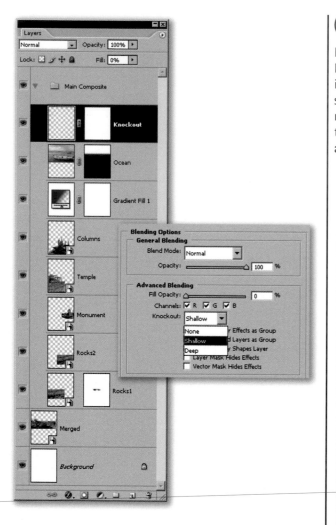

16 Command/Ctrl-click the Merged Layer to load the transparency of that layer as a selection. In the Knockout layer, paint in the selection marquee with your Foreground color until you reveal the top of the monument in the water. Then use a larger soft brush to brush over the same area again. This time, you're softly revealing just a bit more of the monument under the water. Add a Layer Mask to the Knockout layer. Using the Pencil tool and black, hide any white or light pixels that show out of the water.

17 The positioning of the monument out of the water is not quite right. It needs to move to the right so that it is not directly under the tiny sailboat. Click the Knockout layer and press Command/Ctrl and click the Merged layer to select both layers. Using the Move tool, slide the layers to the right. Unfortunately, you can start to see a blank spot in the image. Press Command/Ctrl+T and Command/Ctrl+drag the lower-left corner of the bounding box to the left. Then Command/Ctrl+drag the upper-right corner of the bounding box a bit to the right. Both layers are transformed at the same time. Click Commit. You can touch up the mask on the Knockout layer if needed, but you probably won't need to.

18 Next, you need to add the rays of light to connect the clouds to the bottom of the drowned city. Choose the Polygon Lasso tool. Click the right edge of the first shaft of light on the left side of the Columns under the sea and then click so that the line looks as if it is coming from the break in the clouds. Click 3 is high in the open area of the cloud and click 4 is at the left edge of the first shaft of light. Double-click to connect the selection. Choose Select⇨Feather, 10 pixels. Add a new layer above the Knockout layer. Name the layer **Ray1**. Fill the selection with white. Reduce the layer Opacity to **47%** and change the Blend Mode to Overlay. Deselect.

19 Duplicate the Ray1 layer as **Ray2**. Press Command/Ctrl+T. Press and hold Command/Ctrl and drag the bottom-center Control point to the right until the bottom of Ray2 is focused on the patch of light to the right. Then move the bounding box slightly to the right to get as much separation between the rays as you can, while still keeping the top of the ray coming from the cloud. Finally, press and hold Command/Ctrl and drag the lower-left Control point until the ray focuses back on that second patch of light. You can also drag the lower-right Control point while pressing Command/Ctrl to spread the ray a bit. Click Commit.

20 Open the Oceanlife.psd image and drag it into the Atlantis image. Choose Layer⇨Arrange⇨Bring to Front. Name the layer **Oceanlife**. This is likely to keep the layer inside the Layer Set Group, but that's okay. Control/Right-click the layer entry and choose Group into New Smart Object. Double-click the Oceanlife Smart Object to open it for editing. Choose the Magic Wand tool, set the Tolerance to **25**, Anti-alias checked and clear the Contiguous checkbox. Click in the blue-green background of the image. Then press and hold Shift and click to pick up the rest of the background. Hold the Option/Alt key and add a (hide selection) Layer mask. Option/Alt-click the Layer mask icon in the Layers palette to view the mask. Touch up the mask with white or black as needed to remove the rest of the background and get rid of breaks in the foreground object. Then choose Filter⇨Blur⇨Gaussian Blur, **1.0**. Click OK. Option/Alt-click to view the layer again. Now that you can see the layer again, in the layer mask, paint with black and remove the lettuce leaf at the top of the image. Add a Solid Color Fill layer to the Oceanlife Smart Object file. Choose RGB: **21, 53, 53** as the fill color. Press Command/Ctrl+Option/Alt+G to create a Clipping Mask. Drag the layer opacity to **38%**. Click the Close box on the Smart Object and click Yes to the prompt to Save the changes.

Photo: Sherry London

21 Press Command/Ctrl+T and set the Width to **243** px and then click the Maintain Aspect Ratio icon. Commit. Drag the Oceanlife Smart Object to the lower-left corner of the image.

22 Press Command/Control+G to create a Layer Set Group inside the Main Composite group. Name this group **Oceanlife**. Drag the Oceanlife Smart Object to the New Layer icon at the bottom of the Layers palette to duplicate it. Then drag the Oceanlife Copy layer to the right of the original Smart Object and down. Press Command/Ctrl+T and rotate and drag the object until the upper-right edge of the plant hits the bottom edge of the image and the upper-left edge is under the fan-shaped leaf from the original object. Commit. Drag the Oceanlife Smart Object to the New Layer icon at the bottom of the Layers palette to duplicate it again. Drag this copy below the original Oceanlife layer. Press Command/Ctrl+T and hold the Shift key to constrain the proportions as you make the object smaller. Put the object against the left side of the image so you can see the small cabbage head above the larger one from the original image. When you like the positioning, commit the transformation. Save your work.

A short recap

Atlantis Found is a fairly simple image composite with several twists. It shows you how you can turn four basic images into a very complex composition. It also shows you how to reveal something normally kept hidden. As I worked on this, I kept wondering if I could really find this perspective in the real world. Of course, as soon as I finished the image, I happened to look at photos I'd taken several years ago at the New Orleans Aquarium. In the photo, an alligator was lounging on a dock that was at the same angle as the boat image in Atlantis. The glass window that kept me safe formed a plane that cut straight down and showed the deep pool of water in which the alligator liked to swim. In the photo, one could see both the surface of the water (at an angle) and down below it at the same time. The moral: just pretend that you need to put a vertical glass window between you and your subject and then let the top image plane fall where it needs, to best show the top layer of your world.

chapter

5

faces

Human faces hold a strong fascination for other humans. The first thing that a baby learns to focus on is the human face. A newborn would rather look at a face than anything else. This chapter concentrates on faces of all varieties. You learn how to cover a woman's face with zebra skin and tortoise shell. You discover several ways to halftone or texture faces with type and with miniature copies of the original image. You play with duotone effects and change a man into a clown. Along the way, you pick up a whole new bag of tricks for displacing objects, warping and manipulating things, using Photoshop's elusive Knockout controls, and working with Smart Objects.

Be a Clown

All the world loves a clown. Clowns bring out the kid in everyone. Add a little face paint, and anyone can become a clown — even this clueless bystander. You paint his face and color his clothes, place some polka dots on his shirt, add a bowtie, color his nails, and presto... instant circus! You learn how adding many different Hue/Saturation, Gradient, and Solid Color Fills give you huge flexibility in coloring an image. You'll also learn a neat way to use the Calculations command to make a fuzzy selection of hair detail.

THE PLAN

- Color the skin
- Add paint to the face
- Make a costume
- Add a wig

(1) Open the image LrgClown.psd from the book Web site.

Photo: www.comstock.com

(2) The cherry on the sundae is a lovely touch, but that stem sticking up looks really strange when the clown act commences. So, choose the Magic Wand tool, set Anti-alias to On, Contiguous to Off, and Tolerance to 75. Click in the center of the top-left section of sky. If that doesn't quite pick up all of the blue, choose Select➪Grow. It's okay if the channel covers a bit of the man's hair. Then save the selection as a channel. Deselect. Make the alpha 1 channel active and paint over the cherry stem with white.

TIP

To change the color of the alpha channel overlay if you need to see colors in the image and the default red coating doesn't show it well, double-click on the channel entry in a blank area to open the Channel Properties dialog box. Click on the Color patch and select a different color in the Color Picker.

3) Make the RGB channel active. Using the Eyedropper, click the blue sky at the top center of the image to set your foreground color. Option/Alt-click the blue in the image just above the man's shoulder (near his neck). Try to find the lightest sky blue you can. Load the alpha 1 channel as a selection and add a Gradient Fill layer. Click the gradient bar to open the Gradient Editor. Choose the Foreground to Background preset and click the foreground color stop to see the Color Midpoint. Drag the Color Midpoint to Location 25. Click OK. Set the Angle to -90 degrees and click OK. Gee, the image looks remarkably the same for all that work — but the cherry stem is gone.

TIP

I can hear the "Why didn't she just use the Clone Stamp tool?" question that is hovering on all lips. The gradient in the original image is of such fine tolerance that matching the colors is close to impossible and no matter how I cloned, I could still see it slightly. This way, your background gradient is perfect.

4) Next, you need to widen his mouth. After trying this six or seven different ways, I prefer the Smudge tool. First, duplicate the Background layer as **Stretch Mouth**. Then use the Smudge tool with the 27-pixel brush to gently widen the mouth area. Don't add height to it though. Then use the History brush to put back some of his beard stubble.

5) Time to paint his face. Add a Solid Color Fill layer and choose RGB: **215, 22, 22**. Name the layer **Large Mouth**. Change the mode of the layer to Soft Light and fill the layer mask with black. Choose the 35-pixel brush and set a Hardness of **100** on the brush. Paint in the layer mask with white. Dab the paint on both his cheeks and then over the mouth and chin area in a loose heart shape.

6 Add a Hue/Saturation Adjustment layer and set the Hue to **0**, the Saturation to **25**, and the Lightness to **+85**. Click OK. Name the layer **Whiteface Mouth**. Fill the layer mask of the adjustment layer with black to hide the layer. Reduce the opacity to 93 percent. With the same 35-pixel hard brush that you used before, and with white, paint under his nose, and under and over his mouth. Duplicate the layer but fill the mask with black again. Name the copy **Whiteface Eyes**. Then use the Pen tool, with the icon set to create Paths, to make the selections over his eyes and around his cheeks. Load the paths as selections and fill the selections on the Whiteface layer mask with white. Then make additional subpaths on the same path entry to isolate his eyes. Load these selections (select both with the Path Selection tool) and fill the selections with black to show his eyeballs again.

7 Add a blank new layer named **Eye Outlines**. Choose the Brush tool with the 3-pixel hard brush. Set your foreground color to black. If you used paths for the eyes, load the paths again. Click the Stroke Path button on the Paths palette. If you don't have Paths, load the layer mask of the Whiteface Eyes layer as a selection. Then choose Edit⇨Stroke Path, 3 pixels, Center, and click OK. Deselect. Add another new layer and name it **Mouth Lines**. Use a 9-pixel brush and black and draw a straight line over the center of the clown's mouth and a shorter line under it. Then take the 13-pixel brush and click at each end of the longer line. Add a third new layer and name it **Eye Lines**. Use the 5-pixel hard brush to place a straight line over the center of each eye that goes above the center of the eyebrows as shown. Select the Eye Lines, Eye Outlines, and Mouth Lines layers. Press Command/Ctrl+G and name the new group **Face Lines**.

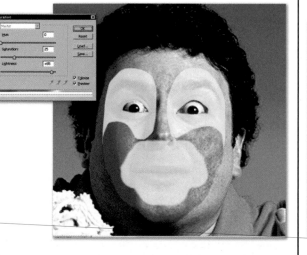

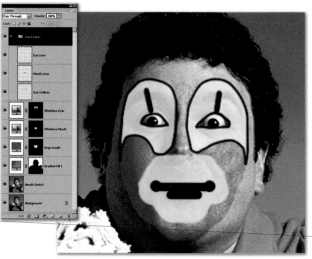

8 Seeing flesh tones rather breaks the clown illusion. So, let's turn our clown blue. Add a Hue/Saturation Adjustment layer and drag the Hue to **-168**. Click OK. Name the layer **Blue Notes**. Hmmm... Blue is certainly different for skin, but it's really a somewhat disgusting color for an apple (or the whites of the eyes). Not sure it's an especially flattering color for vanilla ice cream, either. Paint over those items with black in the layer mask to put back their correct colors. If you find the eyeballs now look a bit yellow, paint over them with white on the layer mask at about 20 percent opacity to bring back a hint of blue. Then drag the Gradient Fill 1 layer to the top of the layer stack to restore the sky (orange is not a great sky color, either, unless we're doing a sunset). Yes, I know the image looks too blue!

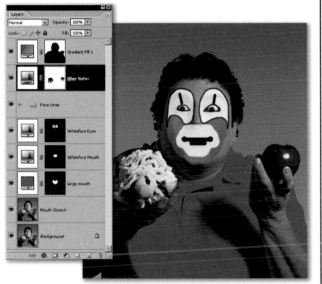

9 A clown needs a funny nose, too. Set your Foreground color to RGB: **255, 0, 0** and the Background color to RGB: **129, 0, 0**. Add a Gradient Fill Adjustment layer on top of the Blue Notes layer. Use the Foreground to Background preset and create a Radial Gradient. Click OK. Fill the layer mask with black to hide the layer. Use a 55-pixel brush at 100% hardness and click with the layer mask active where you want to place the nose. If you don't like the way the highlight looks, or you can't see it at all, double-click the Gradient Fill layer icon and drag the highlight where you want it. Add a Drop Shadow effect. Set the Angle to **30** degrees, the Distance to **6** px, the Spread to **3** px, and Size to **8** px. Click OK. Try setting the scale to 10%. Then, before you close the dialogue box, move the "dot" for the nose to where you want the nose to be. Then fill the layer mask with black and click with the white 55-pixel brush. If you need to move the highlight again, you need to first double-click to open the Gradient dialog box. You can only move a Gradient when the dialog box is open.

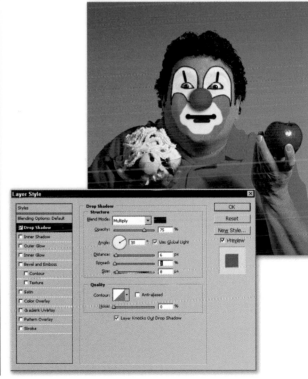

10 Choose the Polygon Shape tool with three sides. Set the Radius in the Polygon Options to **20** pixels. Change your foreground color to RGB: **232, 174, 45**. Click the Create Shape Layer icon on the Options bar. After you click just outside of the clown's right cheek, press and hold Shift to get the shape to sit with the point of the triangle down. Still holding Shift, press and hold the space bar and move the shape until it is just in the blue area of the clown's cheek and slightly overlaps the Whiteface Mouth area. When you have it properly seated, release the mouse button. Choose the Direct Selection tool. Click to select the shape. Press and hold Command+Option/Ctrl+Alt and place your cursor over an edge of the triangle. As you start to move the triangle to the right, press and hold Shift and constrain the copy to move horizontally to the left. Place the triangle on the other cheek. Name the layer **Yellow Triangles**. Command/Ctrl-click on the layer mask of the Whiteface Mouth layer to load it as a selection. Making sure that the Yellow Triangles layer is active, press and hold Option/Alt and click on the Add Layer mask icon at the bottom of the Layers palette. This removes the portions of the triangles that overlap the mouth. Change the Blend mode of the layer to Hard Light.

11 Let's turn the man's polo shirt into the basis for his clown suit. First, make the shirt white. Add a Hue/Saturation Adjustment layer. Change the Lightness to **95** percent. Don't worry; you put the tones back later. Click OK. Name the layer **Shirt**. Fill the layer mask with black to hide the layer. Either create paths or simply paint in the layer mask to bring back the white color over the clown's shirt.

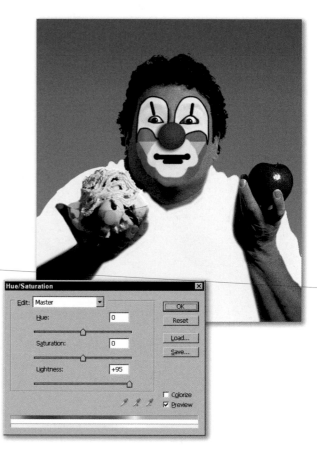

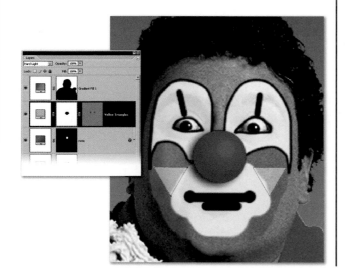

(12) Add a new empty layer above the Shirt layer and Option/Right-click on the layer. Choose Create Clipping Mask. Name the layer **Dots**. Using a 30-pixel hard brush and the same yellow-gold as the Yellow Triangles, sprinkle three or four dots over the shirt. Add more dots in red with a 45-pixel hard brush. Finish by adding some large dots (60-pixel hard brush) in green.

(13) Control/Right-click the Background layer and choose Duplicate Layer. Place the duplicate into a new file. Make that new file active and choose Image⇨Mode⇨Grayscale. Click OK. Choose Filter⇨Blur⇨ Gaussian Blur, Radius: **7** pixels. Save the file as **ClownDmap.psd**. Make the clown image with the Dots layer active. Then choose Filter⇨Distort⇨Displace. Displace

15 pixels horizontally and vertically, and click the Stretch to Fit and Repeat Edge Pixels check boxes. Click OK. Choose the ClownDmap.psd as the displacement map and click OK. Duplicate the Mouth Stretch layer and drag it above the Dots layer. Control/Right-click and choose Create Clipping Mask. Then press Shift+Command/Ctrl+U to desaturate the layer. Change the Blend mode to Hard Light and opacity to 54 percent. Name the layer **Tones**.

14 The clown suit needs a neck treatment and a wig. You can draw them in, but I like the realism that comes from borrowing (if a suitable image is available). Open the image Bowtie.psd. Choose Image⇨Duplicate⇨OK and close the original. Then press Command/Control+ Option/Alt+I to open the Image Size dialog box. Resize the image to 150 percent with Bicubic Smoother interpolation. Click OK.

15 Make a Pen path around the bowtie and change it into a selection. Drag the bowtie selection into the working clown image and rotate it so that it fits under the clown's chin. Add a layer mask and mask out the left side of the bowtie so that the bowtie seems to sit *behind* the banana split.

Photo: www.comstock.com

16 Back in the Bowtie.psd image, make a loose lasso selection around the clown's wig. Drag the selection into the clown image. Name the layer **Wig**. The wig is much too large and the angle and proportions are not correct. First, Control/right-click on the wig layer and choose Group into a New Smart Object. Name the Object **Wig**. Double-click on the Smart Object to open it. In the Channels palette, make the Red channel active. Choose Image⇨Calculations. Set Source 1 to Wig.psb; Layer: Merged; Channel: Red; Set Source 2 to Wig.psb, Layer: Merged, Channel: Green. Set the Blending mode to Color Burn at 100 percent opacity. Send the Result: to a new Channel. Click OK. Make the new channel active. Use black and paint in the areas inside the wig that are not fully black. Paint white around the outer edges but don't get close enough to lose any of the fuzz.

17 Choose Select⇨Color Range and click the gray area in the channel above the wig. Then press and hold Shift or choose the Eyedropper+ tool and add some of the other gray areas to the selection. Don't get into the black areas at all. Set the fuzziness to about 35. Click OK. Choose Select⇨Modify⇨Expand, 4 and Select⇨Feather, 4. Then fill the selection with white. Deselect and clean up any areas outside the wig. Press and hold Option/Alt and add a layer mask. Load the layer mask as a selection by Command/Ctrl-clicking on the thumbnail in the Layers palette. Make the layer mask active and choose Select⇨Inverse. Fill the selection with black (this just removes a bit more of the color spill on the edges of the wig). Deselect and click the Close box on the top of the Smart Object. Click Yes to save the changes.

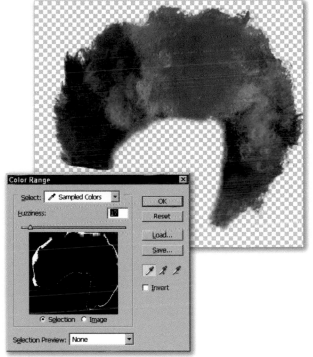

18 Press Command/Ctrl+T and rotate the wig so that the red section is straight up and near the top-center of the clown's face. Then press and hold Shift+Option/Alt and drag a corner handle to scale the wig from the center in proportion. Once you get it to a reasonable size, click the Warp icon. That way, you can individually adjust each side of the wig to tweak the fit. Click Commit when you're done.

19 The image can be considered done at this point, but the details matter and I think some changes are in order. To start, the clown's nails need painting. Make the Blue Notes layer active and add a Hue/Saturation layer above it. Change the Hue to **180** and click OK. Name the layer **Nail Polish**. Then fill the layer mask on the Nail Polish layer with black to hide it. Use a 9-pixel hard brush and paint over the clown's fingernails. Instant mustard polish!

20 I think the gold is a better background color than the sky blue. Double-click the Gradient Fill 1 layer and double-click the Color Stop on the left to open the Color Picker. Choose RGB: 233, 176, 48, and click OK. Then double-click the Color Stop on the right and choose RGB: 252, 245, 157 (or whatever two colors strike your fancy). Drag the Blue Notes layer until it is just above the Mouth Stretch layer. The clown's mouth gets pink tone. Change the Blend mode on the Large Mouth layer to Overlay. If you like the strong pink, leave it. If not, double-click to open the Solid Color Fill layer and choose RGB: 22, 27, 215. Try out some other colors and see what you prefer. Change the mode on the Yellow Triangles layer back to Normal.

Task 21 • Be a Clown

TIP

Try choosing a green for the mouth. You won't like the result. Because we use Overlay mode over a blue-toned skin, the colors aren't true in all of the color ranges. Some of them, such as the greens, change dramatically. Try out different color modes as well. Though you could use Normal, I like the face paint on the mouth area to react to the face rather than just cover it up.

21 Finally, make the Shirt layer active. You can alter the color of the clown's costume. If you alter the Hue in the Hue/Saturation Shirt layer, you won't see any change. You also need to alter the lightness. However, if you alter the lightness, you'll get back the very dark original shadows in the image. A better choice is to add a Solid Color Fill layer and clip it to the Shirt layer. Or even better... Press and hold Option/Alt and choose a Gradient Fill layer. In the dialog box, check the Use Previous Layer to create Clipping Mask. Then select a Linear Gradient at **0** degrees. You can pick any preset to start, but perhaps the Spectrum Gradient is the easiest to modify. Try creating stripes as I did. I used red, orange, yellow, and green. The stripes are created by duplicating the Color Stop (drag it with Option/Alt pressed) and moving the copy close to the next Color Stop. That gives a very small change zone and creates the illusion of stripes.

22 Open the Face Lines group and add a new layer called **Red Mouth** at the top of the folder. With a 3-pixel hard brush, paint a straight line between the two lines on his mouth. Have fun with the clown and try out as many changes you can think of. Save your work.

A short recap

I don't know how often you need to create a clown from images of friends or co-workers, though it is a great gift for children or co-workers (though I might not give it my manager). However, the various techniques you use here should be very useful. You have learned to manipulate color toning layers in various and sundry ways. You can move them, change them, use them, turn them off in almost any configuration you want. You can paint faces for sports events or create African masks with the same technique. You use the Calculations command to make an easy selection out of something that can take hours to mask unless you are willing to lose all of the fuzz detail. You've also done a nondestructive transformation using Image⇨Free Transform on a Smart Layer. Finally, you've seen how the Displace filter can make added clothing details cling to the values of the underlying layer as you made the dots appear to follow the garment folds. I'd love to see some of the images you create with these techniques!

Diffuse Glow Duotone

This tale tells a twofer. When the first image I try works perfectly, right away, I think that this technique is going to look fabulous on just about any image. It's so nice when things go well. Well, get real! Images don't always cooperate, so you need to figure out exactly why something works, and why it doesn't. Applying this technique is a simple six-step process if the starting image is in a good mood. Getting the image happy is the only tricky part.

THE PLAN

- Adjust your starting image
- Apply the Diffuse Glow filter
- Duplicate the layer and add color overlays
- Fine Tune

1 Open the image glow.psd from the book Web site. Duplicate it and close the original.

2 You're going to add a hat onto the model. However, I've built most of the new image for you. Choose Image⇨Canvas Size and make sure that the Relative option is not selected. Anchor in the lower-left corner. Set the new width to 488 pixels and the height to 716 pixels. Click OK. Then open The_Hat.psd from the companion CD-ROM.

Photo: Sherry London

Photo: www.comstock.com

3 Make the Glow Copy image active. Choose Image⇨Apply Image. Set the Source to The_Hat.psd and the Layer to Hat. The Channel should already be set to RGB. Click OK. The Background layer is now your original image and should not be altered.

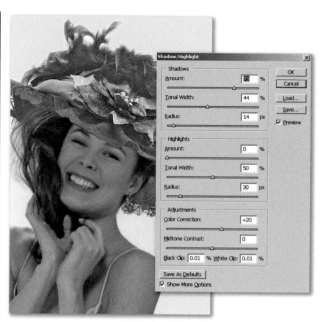

> ## TIP
>
> The Apply Image command makes it very easy to align and register the two images. It doesn't use clipboard RAM at all. The only requirement is that the two images have an identical pixel count.

5 While pressing and holding Option/Alt , click the Add Layer Mask icon at the bottom of the Layers palette to fill the mask with black. Then with white, paint over her hair in the mask. It's okay if the results look a bit unnatural. You did restore tone into her hair. The ending image will be fine.

4 The Diffuse Glow Duotone works best on lighter areas. You need to lighten the woman and her hair, but not the hat. A Shadow/Highlight adjustment fixes the hair. Duplicate the Background layer and name it **Highlight/Shadow**. Choose Image⇨Adjustments⇨Shadow/Highlight. Set the Shadow Amount to **73** percent, the Tonal Width to **44**, and the Radius to **14**. Click OK. Yes, I know those settings are too light, even on the hair. Just do it anyway!

6 Next, we lighten her skin. Add a Levels Adjustment layer and drag the Gamma slider to 1.87. Click OK. Again, this is much lighter than you would ever set the Levels under normal circumstances. Fill the mask with black and then paint over her skin with white. Don't include any of the hair in the white area of the mask. Her hair is light enough.

TIP

Use a large, soft brush so that the edges of her face stay a bit shadowed.

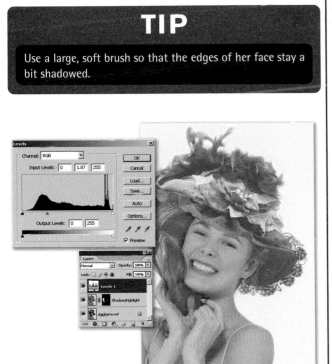

7 After I built the original effect, I realized that the woman needs softer shoulders. I could have simply gone back and fixed the image I gave you. But noooo.... I think you should fix the image I gave you. Make the Background layer active and make a loose Lasso selection around the model's left and right shoulders and the outside of her right arm. Choose Layer⇨New⇨Layer via Copy (Command/Ctrl+J). Name the layer **Shoulders**. Choose Filter⇨Blur⇨Gaussian Blur and a Radius of **4** pixels. Add a

Layer mask and gently remove some of the blur from her neck with a soft, black brush on the mask. Then add a new layer named **Bottom**. Choose the Brush tool with the 14-pixel spatter brush. In the Brush Tips section of the Brushes palette, change the spacing to 50 percent. Use the Eyedropper to pick up light blue background color on the Background layer. On the Bottom layer, drag the brush quickly across the bottom of the image. Filter using the same Gaussian Blur as before. The softness will pay off in the final result.

⑧ To create a composite that you can filter, select all the layers and choose Group into a New Smart Object. Name the Smart Object **Original Composite**. Duplicate the Original Composite layer.

⑨ Choose Filter⇨Distort⇨Diffuse Glow. Click OK to rasterize the Smart Object. Set the Graininess to 0, the Glow Amount to 5, and the Clear Amount to 10. Click OK. Rename the layer **Diffuse Glow 0, 5, 10-1**.

10 Add a Color Overlay effect. Choose RGB: **100, 52, 52** as the overlay color. Change the Blend mode for the color overlay to Color. Click OK. Color mode changes the Hue and the Saturation, but not the Value of the underlying image. Neither black nor white is affected by any color change in Color Mode, so that the midtones show the most change.

11 Duplicate the Diffuse Glow 0, 5, 10-1 layer as **Diffuse Glow 0, 5, 10-2**. Double-click on the Color Overlay effect to reopen the dialog box. Change the color to RGB: **0, 197, 111**. Change the Blend mode to Color Burn and reduce the opacity to 86 percent. Click OK. The Color Burn mode darkens the darker areas of the image, so it has less effect on the highlight areas. By controlling the opacity, you take charge of the radius of values affected.

12 Drag the Opacity slider on the top layer to about 50-55 percent. This amount is a totally free choice. I prefer 55 percent. The next figure shows the final image.

A short recap

You can vary this technique in many different ways. Change the blend modes on the Color Overlay. Change the blend mode on the top layer. Alter opacity in either location. The colors I used in the Color Overlay weren't true complements, but they were close to being so. The real trick was to prepare the image so that it took the diffuse glow well. To do that, you have to restore detail in some of the shadow areas and lighten the skin texture so that it glows without having to make everything in the image too light. To work for this, an image needs to have a good contrast with areas that you want to hold strong color and areas that you want to have gentle glows.

Recursion

Recursion is a computer-programming technique in which a program calls itself. If you put two mirrors across from each other and the reflection bounces back and forth into infinity; that too is recursion. You can also draw recursion. An image, when printed, needs to be broken into spots of ink on paper. These spots are called *halftones* and the pattern of black and white in the halftone gives the impression of grayscale color. But there is only black and white. For this technique, you create a halftone that is made from the image being halftoned so that it recursively reproduces itself.

THE PLAN

- Create a small version of an image and blur it
- Change the original image to grayscale mode
- Create a bitmap using the custom pattern

TIP

This is the rare technique in which a smaller original image is better than a larger one.

(1) Open the image bluelips.psd from the companion CD-ROM. It's almost impossible to work nondestructively when you're changing color modes and image sizes, so you'll leave a trail of duplicate images behind you on this technique. Chose Image⇨Duplicate⇨Bluelips Lrgpat⇨OK to create the basis for the grayscale halftone.

(2) Add a Channel Mixer Adjustment layer and click Monochrome. Move the Red Source Channel slider to about **+44**. Set the Green channel to **+120**. Leave the Blue channel at **0**. Move the Constant Slider to **–18**. Click OK. These settings force solid black behind the woman's head instead of leaving a really odd, disembodied ear.

TIP

Under normal circumstances, you want the sum of the Red and Green channels to roughly add up to 100. In this image, black is okay, but white looks even odder than the image subject! Watch the histogram as you adjust the Channel Mixer sliders to ideally leave no white in the image. For the halftone pattern portion of this technique, however, white is fine.

Photo: www.comstock.com

3 Add a Threshold Adjustment layer. Adjust to taste here. The figure below shows two possibilities. A level of 164 darkens the image to emphasize the third eye and a level of 136 shows more of the woman's face, but the eye is reduced in importance. Pick the look you prefer.

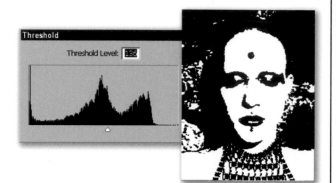

5 Choose Image⇨Duplicate⇨as **BlueLips Small**⇨ Merged Layers Only⇨OK. Then choose Image⇨Image Size. Set the Height to **30** pixels (yes, 30 pixels) and let Photoshop calculate the width (it is 23 pixels). Then set the Interpolation method to Bicubic Sharper. Choose the Resample Image and Constrain Aspect Ratio check boxes. Click OK. The figures below show the results on both versions of the small image. Very little difference remains. Then choose Edit⇨Define Pattern and name your pattern **BlueLips**. You may save and close the pattern image now.

4 Add a merged layer above the Threshold layer (Shift+Command/Ctrl+Option/Alt+E). Then choose Filter⇨Blur⇨Gaussian Blur, **2.3** and click OK. The halftone needs some gray values in it.

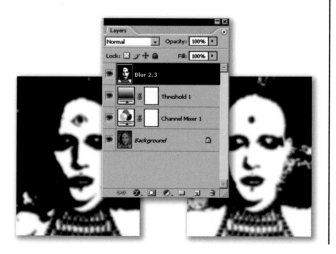

6 Make the BlueLips Lrgpat image active. Choose Image⇨Duplicate⇨**HaltonePrep**⇨OK. Turn off the top two layers (actually, you can — gulp — trash them). Double-click the Channel Mixer Adjustment layer to reopen it. The image as prepped for the pattern is too sharp to use for the actual bitmap. White areas stand out and shout on paper. Black areas do, too, but the image you're using is so strange that black adds a graphic element inappropriate on most other images. Set the Red channel to **70** and the Green channel to **32**. Move the Constant to **0**. Click OK.

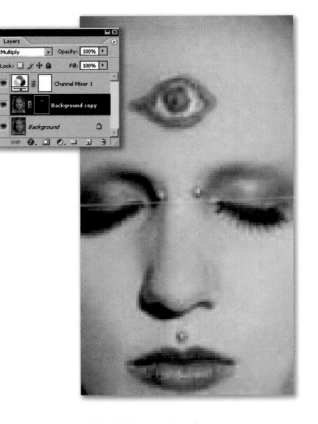

7 You need to emphasize the woman's third eye now so it doesn't get lost. Make the Background layer active. Duplicate the background layer of the image and leave it in position under the Channel Mixer layer. Change the Blend Mode to Multiply. Press and hold Option/Alt and click the Add Layer Mask icon. This adds a Hide All layer mask. Take a small brush with white and paint over the outlines of the third eye. Then take black and a larger brush and paint near the eye to localize the Multiply mode to just the outline of the eye. Add a Levels Adjustment layer and drag the White Point Output slider to **230** (that's the slider at the very bottom of the Levels dialog box) to keep the image from showing pure white.

TIP

When you prepare an image for print, you need to check the histogram very carefully to avoid true white or true black. You can compensate by changing the values of the White and Black Eyedroppers in the Levels or Curves command to keep the darkest image value to about 25 and the lightest value to no more than 240. Usually I also tell you to get rid of the black in the image for printing. When you try this with your own images, carefully set the maximum black and white in the image so that you don't get either solid black or paper white. It's not an attractive look at all.

8 Choose Image⇨Duplicate⇨**BlueLips Bitmap**⇨Merged Layers Only⇨OK. Then choose Image⇨Mode⇨Grayscale. Click OK to remove color information. Finally! Time to make the big switch. Choose Image⇨Mode⇨Bitmap. Set the Resolution to 1200 ppi. Choose Custom Pattern as the method and select the BlueLips pattern. Click OK. The image is bitmapped and huge. If you want to print it, choose Image⇨ Image Size and then clear the Resample Image check box. Type **8 inches** in the Width field and let Photoshop calculate the height and resolution.

9 To make the result a bit more funky (and screen friendly) go back to the Bitmap Prep image and repeat Step 8. This time, use a resolution of 300 ppi. Then choose Image⇨Mode⇨Grayscale, with a size of 1 (which retains the size of the image), and then choose Image⇨Mode⇨RGB. Now, go back to the original image and drag the color version on top of the 300 ppi bitmap. Press Command/Ctrl+T and move the color version to the top left of the image. Press and hold Shift and drag the bottom-right anchor point of the bounding box to the bottom-right corner of the image window. Commit. Change the blend mode to Screen. It doesn't matter that the original has become soft and yucky. It just lends color to the bitmap.

A short recap

Creating recursive halftones is a great way to deal with an original image that's way too small if you have the option of a fun approach. The process is very fast and easy — make a pattern, make a grayscale of the original, and convert to bitmap using the pattern. The only real decision points are correcting both the pattern and the original for tone and then picking the image resolution.

Zebra Woman

Zebra's are one of God's greatest graphics. Perhaps you don't want to wear one on your own face, but you can certainly dress up a model. She's already been paid and has no say in the matter! Technically, there are many ways to create the look. This technique uses Blend modes and transformations.

THE PLAN

- Alter the values of the model's face to whiten it
- Place the texture
- Change the blend modes
- Fine-tune the details by embossing and adding back some of the original

1 Open the image Zebrawoman.psd from the book's CD-ROM and duplicate the Background layer. Control/right-click on the duplicated layer and choose Group into New Smart Object from the pop-up menu. Name the Smart Object layer **Face Color**.

2 On the Face Color layer, press **Q** to enter Quick Mask mode. Paint with black, using a 50 percent hard brush, and change sizes as needed. Paint over the woman's mouth, eyes, eyebrows, and the black background as shown. Press **Q** to exit Quick Mask mode. Save the selection as a channel and don't deselect. Add a layer mask.

Photo: www.comstock.com

3 Double-click to open the Smart Object. Add a Hue/Saturation Adjustment layer. Drag the Saturation slider to **-100**. Click OK, then create a Levels Adjustment layer. Set the Gamma slider to **182** and the Input White point to **2.08**. Click OK. Click the Close box on the Smart Object image and then click Yes to save the changes. Your main image immediately updates.

4 Open the Zebra.psd image and use the Rectangular Marquee tool to select the zebra's body (minus head, tail, and legs). Using the Move tool, drag the selection into the Zebrawoman image. Change the layer into a Smart Object named **Zebra Skin**. Create a Clipping Mask with the previous layer. Fine-tune the mask on the Face Color layer if necessary. Drag the Zebra Skin layer around the woman's face to find the best location. You can see how I positioned the zebra.

Photo: zebra photo by Norman London

5 Choose Select⇨Color Range⇨Shadows and click OK. Add a layer mask from the selection. With black, paint in the layer mask to remove the zebra's skin from the left half of the woman's face. Make the mask follow the line of her nose. Then touch up the stripe areas missed by the Color Range command. Completely mask out the white of the zebra skin. Finally, use a 100-pixel soft brush at 20 percent opacity with black to partially remove the zebra's skin from the woman's right eye. Change the Blend mode to Multiply.

6 Duplicate the Zebra Skin Smart Object layer as **Left Skin**, and remove the layer mask on the new layer. With the Move tool, drag the layer to the left until the interesting skin near the tops of the zebra's front legs covers the left side of the woman's face. You don't have to be exact yet. Command/Ctrl-click on the Zebra Skin layer mask thumbnail. Using the Lasso tool and the Shift key, add to the selection so that it includes the entire right half of the face. Choose Select⇨Inverse and add the layer mask to the Left Skin layer. Change the Blend mode to Overlay. Unlink the layer and mask and move the layer (not the mask) into the desired position.

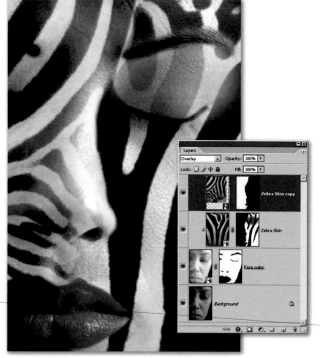

7 Make the original zebra image active and use the Lasso tool to select the zebra's mane. Drag the mane back into the Zebrawoman image and make it into a Smart Object named **Eye Lash**. Choose Edit⇨Free Transform and scale the mane proportionally until it is a bit larger than the right eyelid. Then move it under the eyelid and rotate it until the bounding box line from the top right to bottom-left corner is parallel with the top of the image. Click the Warp icon and apply an Arc warp of **70** percent. Then choose a Custom warp and manipulate the warp to make the mane into eyelashes. Commit the transform and move it if needed.

8 Create a layer mask on the Eye Lash layer. With black, get rid of the green on the eyelash. I used the 14-pixel spatter brush to leave lashes and remove green without making me totally crazy. If you enjoy getting the green out manually, feel free to have at it! I also touched up the top of the eyelash area in the mask so that the eyelid line was totally visible.

9 Duplicate the Background layer and drag it to the top of the layer stack. Name it **Texture**. Change the mode to Hard Light. (That actually looks interesting and you might want to stop at this point. But wait... there's more.) Choose Filter⇨Stylize⇨Emboss. Use the settings shown. Click OK. Choose Image⇨Adjustments⇨Desaturate to remove the color. Reduce the layer opacity to 52 percent.

TIP

If there's a chance that you ever want to keep the color in the emboss layer, you can create a Smart Object from the layer and add a Hue/Saturation Adjustment layer in the Smart Object file. I didn't do that because I see no reason, on an emboss layer, to ever want the color anomalies to remain.

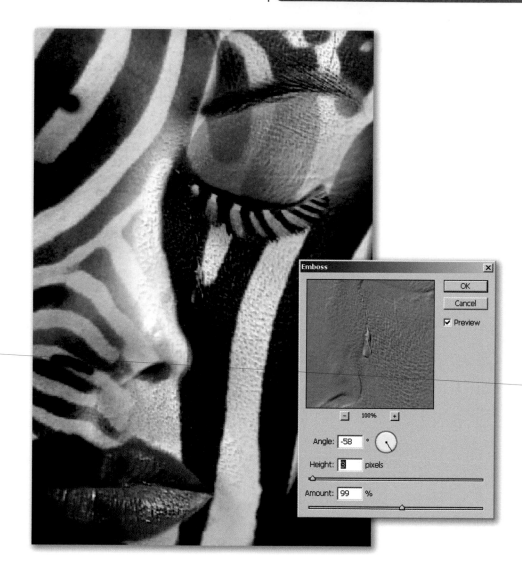

10 Duplicate the Background layer again. Drag it to the top of the layer stack and name it **More Color**. Change the layer opacity to about 27 percent or where you think it looks good. It cuts a bit of the black and white sharpness, so you can omit this step if you don't like it.

11 Finally, choose Layer⇨New Layer and set the mode to Overlay. In the dialog box, select the Fill with Overlay-neutral color (50% gray). Click OK. Name the layer **Tear Drop**. Draw a Lasso selection around the teardrop. Choose the Dodge tool using Midtones and a 10 percent Exposure. Increase the highlight on the teardrop. Then dodge over the dark left eyebrow a bit.

12 Save the image and admire.

A short recap

You have many ways to texture wrap an object. Zebra Woman uses perhaps the most basic of all texture wraps, just a simple blend mode change. However, the positioning of the wrapping material — in this case the zebra skin — is the critical issue. If you don't deform the material you're wrapping, then you need to match the textures to the basic shape of the object. You can let the white fur of the zebra remain, but I prefer to have a whitened version of the woman's original skin show through. In this instance, I feel it adds realism. That is also why I added back some of the original image coloring. It's a step that can easily be left out if you prefer.

Black and White — and Purple all Over

Recoloring images is a very popular technique. The idea is to start with a color image and then change it to grayscale. At that point, you can put back some of the color using the same — or totally different — colors. You can also blend patterns and shapes into the image. In this technique, imagine that you want to create a birthday gift for a friend who loves butterflies — and the color purple. I'm supplying the pattern files used in the image rather than asking you to build them — as they took me just as long to create as the final image!

THE PLAN

- Create the base image and background
- Remove the color
- Add new colors and patterns back into the image

① Open the image Bluetone.psd file from the book's CD-ROM. If you get a color mismatch warning, choose Edit in Embedded Profile Space. I've already cut out the hair areas for you. Press Command/Control+Option/Alt+C and change the canvas size to 562 x 703 pixels (with Relative Off). Anchor in the bottom-center square. Click OK.

WARNING

You need to edit this image in the Adobe RGB (1998) color space. If you are in a different RGB color space, you won't get the same colors, even if you use my color numbers.

Photo: www.comstock.com

187

② Add a new layer to the image. Name it **Hair Extensions**. Choose the Clone Stamp tool and check the Sample all Layers check box. Clone the dark tones of the hair to put back the areas that the camera cropped out. You need to clone from the original hair up so that you keep the highlights and shine. If you need dimensions, the finished hairdo should fit inside an ellipse that is 454 x 517 pixels. Select both women layers and Control/Right-click on the layer entry. Choose Group into New Smart Object from the drop-down menu. Change the name of the Smart Object to **Woman**.

③ Choose View⇨New Guide and add a Vertical guide at pixel 546. Drag the Smart Object toward that guide until the right side of the woman's hair touches it. Clear the Guides. Press and hold Option/Alt and add a Channel Mixer Adjustment layer from the Layers palette. In the New Layer dialog box, select the Use Previous Layer to Create Clipping Mask check box option. Click OK. Select the Monotone option. Set the Red channel to **+44**, the Green Channel to **+24**, and the Blue channel to **+42**. Click OK.

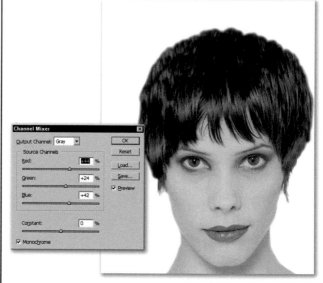

4 Press and hold Option/Alt and add a new layer to the image. In the New Layer dialog box, set the Mode to Hard Light and check the Fill with Hard-Light-neutral color (50% gray) and the Use Previous Layer to Create Clipping Mask check boxes. Name the layer **Eyes Burned** and click OK. Set the layer opacity to 79%. Duplicate the layer and name it **Cheeks Burned**. Make the Eyes Burned layer active and select the Burn tool set to Midtones and 15 percent Exposure. Choose a 65-pixel soft brush and paint over the woman's eyes to darken the lids and under her eyes. Make the brush smaller as needed. Then add a layer mask by clicking the Add Layer Mask icon. Take a small paintbrush and black and paint out her eyes in the layer mask. Use a 100-pixel soft brush at about 50 percent opacity to soften the edges of the under-the-eyes burning. You don't want her to look as if she fell down the stairs. In the Cheeks Burned layer, burn her cheek areas with a large brush and the Burn tool. Also, add some darkening to the sides of her neck and the bridge of her nose. Again, tone it down, if necessary, in a layer mask. Alter the layer opacity if needed.

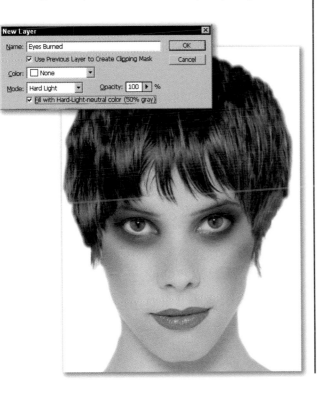

5 Press and hold Option/Alt and click the Create new fill or adjustment layer icon on the Layers palette. Choose the Solid Color Fill. Check the Use Previous Layer to Create Clipping Mask check box. Name the layer **Purple Tones**. Change the Mode to Color. Click OK. Choose RGB: **111, 95, 127** as the fill color. Now you've toned the face.

6 Make the Background layer active and add a Solid Color Fill layer in RGB: **200, 173, 204**. Click OK. This is the start of the background for the image. Choose View⇨New Guide and set a guide at Vertical pixel 200. Then add a new guide at Horizontal pixel 200. Turn Snap on (choose View⇨Snap, but make sure it's checked on the menu). Select the area on the top right from the vertical guide down to the horizontal guide and over to the right edge of the image. Then press and hold Shift and select the bottom-left area from the left edge of the image to the vertical guide and down to the bottom of the image. With this selection active, add another Solid Color Fill layer and choose RGB: **152, 177, 167**. Click OK. Now you have a slightly checkerboard background. Clear the guides.

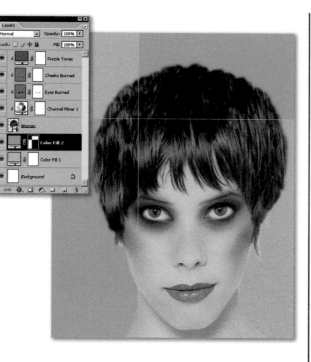

(7) Drag the pattern set ButterflyLady.pat into Photoshop. It is added to the Pattern presets. The Color Fill2 layer is active. Add a Pattern Fill layer and choose the WatercolorFlowers pattern. Name the layer **Watercolor Flowers**. After it starts to preview (but while the dialog box is still open), change the Scale to **331** percent. Click OK. Change the Blend Mode to Lighten and the Opacity to 63 percent. Press and hold Option/Alt and add another Pattern Fill layer. In the New Layer dialog box, check the Use Previous Layer to Create Clipping Mask check box. Name the layer **Grid**. Change the Blend Mode to Soft Light. Click OK. Choose the Grid pattern at 100 percent scale. Click OK.

TIP

You need to clip the grid pattern to the watercolor flowers pattern if you want the grid to show up only where the other pattern is visible. If you change the blend mode or opacity on the watercolor flowers, the visibility of the grid changes as well.

8 Make the Woman layer active and add a drop shadow effect. Set the opacity of the Shadow to 89%. Choose a Distance and Spread of **8** and a Size of **35**. Everything else is standard. Click OK. Above the Grid Layer add a Hue/Saturation layer named **Lilac**. Select the Colorize option and then set the Hue to **254**. The Saturation should automatically default to **25**. Click OK. Choose the 200 pixel soft brush and, using black, paint in the Lilac layer mask from the top of the Woman's head to the bottom of the image along the left side. Follow the contours of her head and paint so that the brush is half on and half off her face. This leaves a ring of color near the left side of her face, but the low saturation lilac shows up around the left edge of the image. Paint across the top of the head, restoring some color over her head. Finally, stamp a few brush strokes near the bottom-right edge of the canvas but don't get near the woman. Duplicate the Lilac layer and drag it to the top of the layer stack. Delete the layer mask. Rename the layer **Lilac Face**. Press Command/Ctrl+Option/Alt+G to add the layer to the Clipping Mask check box.

9 Press and hold Option/Alt and choose a Levels Adjustment layer. In the New Layer dialog box, check the Use Previous Layer to Create Clipping Mask check box. Name the layer **Low Contrast**. Click OK. Set the Input White numeric field to **219**. Set the Gamma to **0.88**. In the Output

fields, set the Black Output point to **74** and the White output point to **118**. Click OK. Reduce the layer opacity to 46 percent. This creates a very low contrast look on the woman's face, which is what I want here.

10 This next step is tricky. You bring back some of the original blue tones from her hair. Press and hold Option/Alt and add a new empty layer. In the New Layer dialog box, check the Use Previous Layer as Clipping Mask check box. Name the layer **KnockOut**. Click OK. Fill the layer with the foreground color regardless of what it is — it won't show. Double-click the layer entry to open the Layer Style dialog box. In the Advanced Blending section, set the Fill opacity to **0** and choose Shallow Knockout. The entire Woman Smart Object is revealed. Press and hold Option/Alt and click the Add Layer Mask icon to hide the effect of the layer. With the 100-pixel soft brush and white, paint in the mask over the woman's hair to bring back the highlight areas. These are the blue tones. Reduce the Layer opacity to 37 percent. Then use a much smaller brush at 20 percent opacity to bring back just a tiny bit of the blue as eyeliner on her eyelids (that's just above the eyes — for you guys who've never applied the stuff!). Then press and hold Option/Alt and add another new layer. In the dialog box, set the Mode to Hard Light, check the Use Previous Layer to Create Clipping Mask check box, and the Fill with Hard-Light-neutral color (50% gray) check boxes, and name the layer **Highlights**. Click OK. Change the Blend Mode for the layer to Color Dodge. Press and hold Option/Alt and click the Add Layer Mask icon to hide the effects. Set the layer opacity to 79 percent. Using a 65-pixel brush at about 30 percent opacity, brush over the unshadowed parts of the woman's face. With a smaller brush, lighten her lips and eyes. Go over the eyeballs a few times. Brush over the highlight areas on her hair. The highlights should be very subtle. All the areas I mentioned are actually in the layer mask, but you can see from the figure of the layer mask that only the eyes actually show a major change in value in the mask.

a new Shape layer. Choose RGB: **200, 199, 226** as the color for the shapes. Constrain the Properties of the Moon shapes and rotate them as desired. Set the Blend mode to Linear Burn. You should not have a stroke effect on this layer.

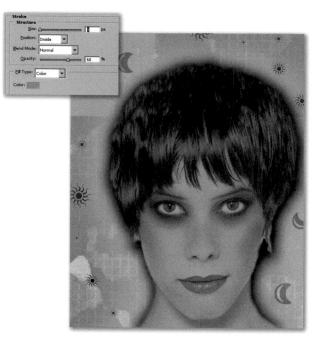

(11) Select the Custom shape tool and load the Nature set of shapes that ships with Photoshop. Click Append to add them to the currently loaded shapes. Choose the Sun1 shape. Set the icon on the Options bar to create a Shape layer. Then, in the Options bar, click the Custom Shape options and select Defined Proportions. Choose RGB: **228, 229, 148** as the foreground color. Make the Lilac layer active. Add sun shape to the lower–left quadrant of the image. After you add the one shape, make the layer mask active and click the Add to Shape Area icon on the Options bar. Add four more sun shapes of different sizes randomly to the lower–left area of the Image. Add 5 small sun shapes to the top–right quadrant of the image. They should all be added in the same Shape layer. After you've added the shapes, add a Stroke effect. Choose a 1 point Inside Stroke at **68** percent opacity in Normal mode. Using color as the Fill Type, choose RGB **230, 143, 33** as the Stroke color. Click OK. Change the Blend mode to Difference. Then add two Moon shapes to both remaining quadrants of the image in

(12) The next four steps add curves layers to colorize the woman's hair and face. Make the Highlights layer active. Add a new Curves layer. In the Red channel of the Curves dialog box, click near the center of the curve to open the Input and Output fields. Type **65** as the input and **38** as the output. Click OK. Rename the layer **Cheeks**. Click the layer mask thumbnail on the Curves layer. Press Command/Ctrl+I to make the mask solid black. With a 65-pixel soft brush and white, in the Cheeks layer mask at 10 percent opacity, add a hint of pink over the woman's cheeks and a bit less on either side of her neck. You can see my layer mask as well as the Curves dialog box.

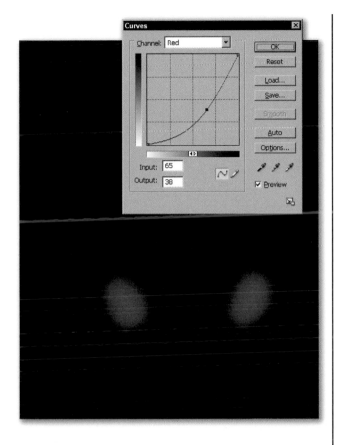

TIP

Inverting the Layer Mask is the fastest way to get it all black. You can press Command/Control+Delete/Backspace to fill the mask with black. Unfortunately, you can't add a Curves layer and automatically set the mask to Hide All.

(13) Add another Curves layer and name it **Blues**. Make the Blue channel active in the Curves dialog box. Click the bottom-left point in the curve and set the Input to **0** and the Output to **24**. Then click near the center and set the Input to **56** and the output to **38**. Finally, click the top-right point and set Input to **100** and Output to **82**. Click OK. Invert the channel to hide the color. Keep the opacity set to 10 percent or so and paint multiple strokes as needed to get the color. With white, paint over her eyes and eyebrows, her hair highlights, and her mouth. In the color figure, you can see a red coating where you should paint. The grayscale figure shows you the relative darkness of the mask. Neither figure shows you the resulting color.

(14) Add a third Curves adjustment layer. This time, use the Red channel. Set the **0** Input to **27** Output, set the **50** Input to **14** Output, and set the **100** Input to **46** Output. Click OK. Name the layer **Red Hair**. Invert the channel to hide the color. Keep the opacity set to 10 percent or so and paint multiple strokes as needed to get the color. With white, paint over the highlight areas in her bangs and the sides of her hair. This time, I do show you the results.

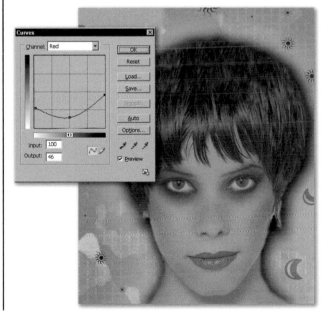

15. The final Curves layer is named **Greens**. In the Green channel in the Curves dialog box, drag the 0 Input/0 Output point over to the 25 line so that the graph reads Input **25**, Output **0**, but there is only one point on the graph there. Then drag that Output 0 point up until the fields read Input **25**, Output **67**. Click near the center and set Input **56** to Output **40**. Don't change the 100,100 point. Click OK. Invert the channel to hide the color. Keep the opacity set to 10 percent or so and paint multiple strokes as needed to get the color. With white, paint over some highlight areas in her hair. Paint very lightly over the area around her nose and mouth making a loose oval that avoids her lips.

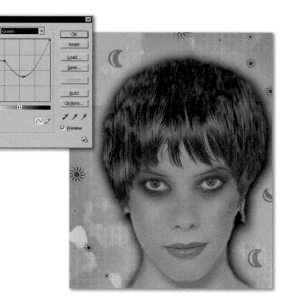

17. Add a Pattern Fill layer above the Butterfly layer. Choose the Grayedbutterflies pattern that you previously loaded. Name the layer **Butterfly Pattern**. Using the Move tool, move the pattern until a large butterfly sits over the woman's eye on your right. Change the blend mode to Linear Light at 40 percent opacity. With a soft, black brush, mask out the woman's face, leaving the butterfly on her eye and part of the butterfly on her cheek visible. You can use a 100-pixel brush to softly blend out some of the butterfly wings on her face and in her hair. The main object of masking the face and some of the hair is to remove the colors in the pattern so they don't change the curve layers you just laboriously created. The small figure shows the area that is painted out of the mask.

16. Select the Custom Shape tool and the Butterfly. In the Custom Shapes dialog box, set the Fixed Size to 257 x 166. Click to set a butterfly on the image. Name the layer **Butterfly**. Press Command/Ctrl+T and rotate the butterfly to -44 degrees. Click Commit. In the Styles palette, load the Abstract Styles preset that ships with Photoshop. Choose the Purple and Magenta style and apply it to the Butterfly layer. Change the Opacity to 60 percent. Position the butterfly so it sits slightly off the image at the top left of the woman's hair.

19 The final part of this technique is optional but just adds that finishing touch. Make the Butterfly Pattern layer active. Add a Channel Mixer channel above it. Check the Monochromatic check box. Set the Red channel to +44, the Green channel to +24, and the Blue channel to +42. Click OK. Name the layer **Lighting**. Turn off the eye on the layer to hide it. Command/Ctrl-click on the RGB channel thumbnail in the Channels palette to load the values of the image as a selection. Turn the eye for the Lighting layer back on and make the layer active again. Fill the selection marquee with black. Command/Ctrl-click on the Woman Smart Object layer to load the woman as a selection. Fill this selection (on the Lighting layer mask) with black as well. Press Shift+Command/Ctrl+I to inverse the selection. Press Command/Ctrl+H to hide the selection. Choose the Gradient tool. Set your colors to black and white and use the Foreground to Background gradient. Choose the Linear gradient at 100 percent opacity and Difference mode. Randomly drag the gradient cursor in different directions for different lengths. Each new gradient adds to the complexity of the color/grayscale mix on the image. When you like the pattern of light, stop.

18 Add a new Pattern Fill layer on top of the Butterfly Pattern layer. Choose the Purpletones pattern from the presets that you loaded earlier. Name the layer **Purpletone Pattern**. Cover the woman's face in the layer mask with black to hide the pattern. Remove the pattern in the layer from the top-left corner of the image as well. Then change the opacity of the brush to about 30 percent and use a 100-pixel soft brush to remove just a little of the pattern from the top-right and bottom-left areas of the image. Set the layer Blend Mode to Normal and the Opacity to 57% or to taste.

20 Save your work.

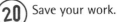

A short recap

Layers upon layers upon layers... You can build up very complex and unique imagery using this technique. The main trick is to keep going in and out of grayscale and to use masks to control the areas of color. I tried to show you how to build the image in a logical manner. That was not how I created it. I had the woman Smart Object near the bottom of the Layers palette, and I kept reusing the Woman mask in almost every layer. That makes no sense once you know what you want to do with the image. Put the layers that are logically under the woman, *under* the woman. Wherever you can, use the woman as the base layer of a clipping group so you don't need to keep making the same mask. If you want to refine the mask on the woman (as I do several times), you don't need to refresh or re-create seven other layers of the same mask. You learned how to add color to areas of an image by using Curves Adjustment layers that only change color in one channel. You have also learned a number of ways to combine blend modes, opacity, and pattern fills, and to control where a pattern fill lands in an image. If you want to colorize an entire image, making a Curves Adjustment layer for each color area is one of a number of different ways that will work.

Letterformed

Rob Day created one of my favorite pieces of typography ever. It looked like a continuous-tone grayscale dog, but it was made entirely out of type of different font widths and blackness. Although Rob's image was a piece of fine art, my technique works surprisingly well for something that can be done quickly and uses only a single font. I also need to thank David Xenakis, my writing partner on several books, who developed a method using Adobe Illustrator on which this technique is based. My original method for creating text art from a photo used 26 pattern layers and masks, but a 5 a.m. inspiration reduced it to only one pattern layer. Aren't you glad?

THE PLAN

- Prepare your starting image
- Create the pattern for the text replacement
- Build the basic text image
- Create a Displacement map and displace the type
- Add color back into the image

TIP

I like to close-crop images when using this technique. I also think they look best when there is some white around the face and color variation in the background. If the subject has dark hair, use the Image⇨Adjustments⇨Shadow/Highlight to lighten the hair. If that makes the original look funky, not to worry! You don't see it in the end result and the type values look better.

① Open the image Cara.psd from the book's CD-ROM. The image is already layered and contains changes that I made to the original Comstock image, which is the one shown here.

Photo: www.comstock.com

② Choose Image⇨Duplicate⇨Merged Layers only⇨OK. You may close the original now. Choose Image⇨ Image Size and set the image height to 2400 pixels and 300 ppi. Make sure that Resample Image and Constrain Aspect Ratio are checked. Set the Interpolation method to Bicubic Smoother. Click OK.

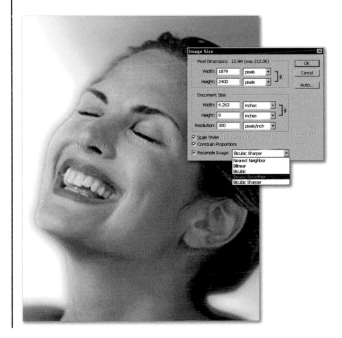

3 Add a Channel Mixer adjustment layer above the Background layer. Choose the Monochrome check box and set the Red channel to 54 percent and the Green channel to 30 percent. Choose Image⇨Duplicate⇨Merged Layers⇨OK. In the new image, choose Filter⇨Blur⇨Gaussian Blur, 8 and click OK. Then save the new file as **CaraDmap.psd**. Close the dmap file after you save it. Make the Cara image active again and minimize it for the moment.

so you need to adjust my example. My cropped type image is 384 x 90 pixels. You need to offset a second line of type. Press Command/Ctrl+Option/Alt+C and check the Relative box. Anchor in the center. For any size text image, add 8 pixels to the Width and 20 pixels to the Height. Click OK. This is one-half the height you need. Duplicate the type layer and type **RACA** and commit. Press Command/Ctrl+Option/Alt+C and with Relative checked, add 100 percent only to the image Height. Anchor at the center-top box and click OK. Press Command/Ctrl+T and click the Relative icon on the Options bar between the X and Y fields. Type one-half of the current image height in the Y: field (I typed **110** pixels) and click Commit. This pushes the second type layer to the bottom of the image. Turn off the eye on the Background layer of the image so you can only see the transparency under the type. Choose Edit⇨Define Pattern and name the pattern (I called it Cara).

TIP

You want to set fairly sharp contrast on the Channel Mixer. The Channel Mixer grayscale becomes a displacement map and values that differ from medium gray cause more movement in the filtered image. Blurring the displacement map image gives a smoother transition for the displace filter and creates better movement.

TIP

You can play around with the pattern as much as you want. I used a brick pattern method to offset the type, but could use a straight pattern repeat or set three lines of random letters or whatever and define it as a pattern. I also spaced this very closely, but you might prefer to leave a bit more room around the letters or even increase the letter spacing in the type. You could also just set the two lines of type by typing **CARA**, pressing Return, and typing **RACA**. Then just leave an equal amount of room around the type as you crop. If the space between the two lines of type is 14 pixels, for example, you would crop close and then add 7 pixels to both the top and the bottom of the image (14 pixels anchor in the center).

4 Time to create the text pattern. Create a new image about 400 pixels square at 300 ppi. You can use any text, any size, and type any phrase. I used the name CARA in Arial Black, Regular, 30 pts, Sharp (Helvetica on the Mac). After you set the type, crop the image around the type as tightly as you can. The numbers I give you are for my type,

5 Add a white Solid Color Fill layer on top of the Background layer. Leave the opacity at 100 percent. Then create a Pattern Fill layer and choose the text pattern that you just created. Set the Scale at 25 percent. Duplicate this layer and rasterize it. Turn the eye off on the Pattern Fill layer. Duplicate the Background layer and drag it to the top of the layer stack. Name it **Color**. Control/Right-click on the Background copy layer and choose Create Clipping Mask. The color image clings only to the type. This by itself could be a suitable ending image, but there's much more you can do.

6 Name the rasterized pattern layer **Displace**. Choose Filter⇨Distort⇨Displace. Set the Horizontal Scale to **10** and the Vertical Scale to **10**. In the Displacement map section, choose the Stretch To Fit option, and in the Undefined Areas section, choose the Repeat Edge Pixels option. Choose the Caradmap.psd as the displacement map. Click OK. Now some of the text follows and bends around the tones from the original image. Again, this is another suitable endpoint.

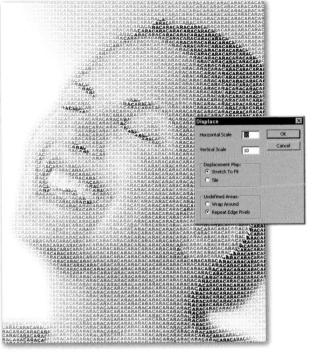

7 Let's take a detour for a moment. I'm moving Cara's image toward a color finish. However, it doesn't have to go that way. Move the Channel Mixer layer to the top of the Layer stack. This, too, is an excellent endpoint for the image. Control/Right-click the Color Mixer layer and choose Create Clipping Mask. Leaving the Color Mixer in place allows you to recolor the image in a few steps.

TIP

Part of my purpose in writing this technique is to show how the color of type (and here color really means value or degree of blackness) can create contour in an image. Leaving the Channel Mixer adjustment layer in place alters the final tonal range of the image. The best part is that sitting on the layer stack as it does, you can turn it on or off at any time. The choice to use it or not is yours.

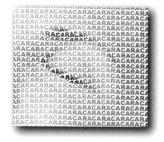

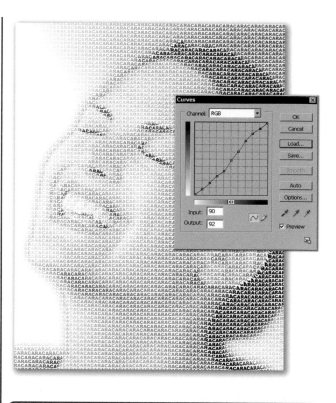

8 The next step lets you control the darkness of the text overlay and even out the tonal step in the Color Mixer adjustment layer. This is a holdover from my 26-pattern layer version where I individually set the opacity of each layer. Believe me, a Tone curve is much easier to create, and once it's done, you can reuse it every time you do this. Click the Color layer to make it active. Press and hold Option/Alt and add a Curves Adjustment layer. When the Layer Properties dialog box appears, Choose the Use Previous Layer to Create Clipping Mask check box. Set up the Curves so that it is divided into 10 vertical sections with the white of the graph to the left (Option/Alt-click on the grid to change four sections into 10. Click on the gradient bar under the grid to change from 0-255 to percentages).

Input 30	Output 26
Input 40	Output 33
Input 50	Output 48
Input 60	Output 60
Input 70	Output 75
Input 80	Output 85
Input 90	Output 92

Save the curve so you can load it again if you wish. Click OK to apply the curve.

TIP

The purpose of the curve is to make the light tones a bit lighter and the dark ones a bit darker. You can always adjust to taste or turn it off completely.

9 Duplicate the Background layer again and drag the duplicate up the top of the layer stack. Control/Right-click on it and choose Create Clipping Group. Change the Blend mode to Color. Instead of simply clipping the original values to the displaced text, this layer colorizes the existing values, a subtle but real distinction. Name the layer **Colorize**.

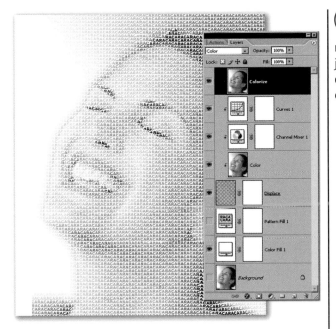

11 Duplicate the Background layer again and drag the copy to the top of the layer stack. Change the blend mode to Multiply and set the Opacity to 20 percent. This just adds back some detail in the image. Again, you can use or lose this step as you prefer. Here is a close-up of this change.

10 Press and hold Option/Alt and add a Posterize Adjustment layer. When the Layer Properties dialog box appears, check the Use Previous Layer to Create Clipping Mask check box. Again, the result is subtle. Try setting the posterize amount to **4** steps, then **6**, and then **8** or **10**. Try out the numbers and see what effect you prefer. I used 10 steps because I wanted to keep some amount of type everywhere on her face. It's your call, and you can change the result for as long as you keep the layers.

TIP

I didn't add this layer to the clipping mask because I wanted it to affect the entire image.

12 Let's add a layer style to the text to get just a bit of dimension in the image. Add a Bevel and Emboss. Most of the settings are standard. You want an Inner Bevel with a Smooth Technique. Set the Depth to **100** percent, Size of **3**, and Soften of **0**. Leave the other settings at their defaults. Then add a Drop Shadow style with the Distance of **2** and a Size of **3**. Click OK. Here's an extreme close-up.

13 Perhaps, after you've built the image, you discover that you need the type to be larger — maybe this image is now supposed to become a poster. What now? Not to fear. It's very easy to change. Turn off the eye on the Displace layer to hide the entire clipping group. Make the Pattern Fill layer active and double-click on the thumbnail to reopen the Pattern Fill dialog box. In the Scale field, choose 40 percent and click OK. Duplicate the layer and rasterize the duplicate. Apply the Caradmap in the Displace filter again.

(14) You can unlink and relink the entire clipping mask, but I think this is easier. Turn off the eye on the Color Fill Copy 1 layer. Make the Displace layer active and press Command/Ctrl+A. Then press Delete to clear the layer. Choose Image⇨Apply Image. Set the Source to your current image, the Source: Layer to Pattern Fill Copy 1, the Channel to RGB, and the Blending to Normal. Click OK. All of your effects are still there and no relinking is needed. You can change to any scale on the pattern that you wish just by repeating Steps 13 and 14.

(15) Finally, if you want to get a glowing look on the model's face, you can add a gradient to the Displace layer's layer mask. Press D to set your colors to the default. Choose the Gradient tool and select a Foreground to Background gradient. Make the layer mask of the Displace layer active. Drag the gradient cursor from the top-left corner to the cheek area between the model's nose and her ear. You can adjust this gradient as you wish until you get the right mix.

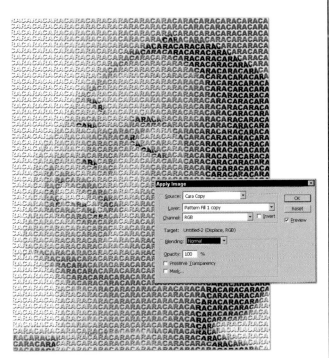

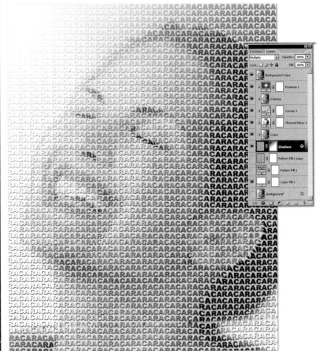

(16) Two more tweaks and you're done. Double-click the Color Fill 1 layer and choose RGB **236, 248, 255** as the color. Click OK. Then make the top layer active (Background Copy) and then choose Filter⇨Blur⇨Gaussian Blur, **50**. Click OK. Turn off the effects on the Displace layer. Save your work.

A short recap

You can make a great image using the letterformed technique from an original of almost any size. You can turn a substandard image (not that we used one here) into a stunning knockout. Experiment with different type treatments. After you build the type pattern, you need to add a pattern layer and clip a copy of the original layer to it. You then displace the rasterized type layer with a displacement map created from a grayscale version of your starting image. After the image is displaced, you can add some of the color back into it and finesse the tonal values of the image.

The Stages of Life

Usually, people want to look younger. However, by seeing how people age, you become more aware of the passage of time and the lines that time writes on the canvas of your face. I had a real-life encounter with this recently as I attended the 40th reunion of our class from the Philadelphia High School for Girls. It took a bit of time to find my classmates under this mask that time had painted on all of our faces. Actually, I think we look better today. We have character and maturity and our faces are much more interesting than they were 40 years ago. Of course, we are still a lot younger than you'll make the model in this exercise. However, you can add your own touches of character to her face. When you're done, your children and coworkers will love having you age their photos! Just think how much your boss would like to see how he or she will look in old age!

THE PLAN

- Use the Liquify command to alter the basic outlines of the model's face
- Create gray hair and age spots
- Tone and burn age lines
- Create neck veins

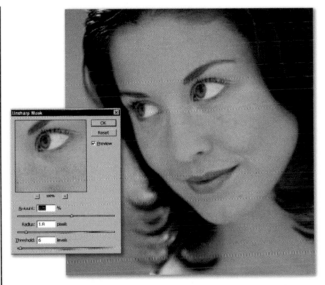

Photo: www.comstock.com

(1) Open the image Youth.psd from the book's CD-ROM. Press Command/Ctrl+Option/Alt+I to open the Image Size dialog box. Check the Resample Image and Constrain Aspect Ratio check boxes. Change the Interpolation Method to Bicubic Smoother. Set the Width to 200% (which should also change the Height to 200%). Click OK. Duplicate the Background layer by dragging its thumbnail to the New Layer icon at the bottom of the Layers palette. Name the new layer **Sharpen**. Choose Filter⇨Sharpen⇨Unsharp Mask. Set the Amount to about 105%, the Radius to 1.8 pixels, and the Threshold to 6. Click OK. Change the blend mode to Luminosity. Press and hold Option/Alt and add a layer mask. This hides the sharpening. Then paint over the eye area using white in the layer mask to reveal the sharpening. The eye is the most critical thing in a portrait to make sharp.

TIP

I prefer not to enlarge images. However, using Bicubic Smoother, you can usually get a reasonable enlargement to about 200 percent. The image becomes soft, but sharpening the eye seems to increase the apparent sharpness of the image (even if it doesn't get very sharp). Changing to Luminosity mode prevents the Unsharp Mask filter from creating color shifts.

2 Because you'll want to do a lot of work on the woman's neck, you need to remove her lovely flowing hair from it. Add a new, empty layer. Name it **Neck Clone**. Choose the Clone Stamp tool and Check the Sample All Layers check box. Using the skin on the lower area of her neck, clone over the hair and give her an enlarged area of exposed neck. You can use a fairly large brush (65-pixel brush works). Keep changing the Source point for the brush.

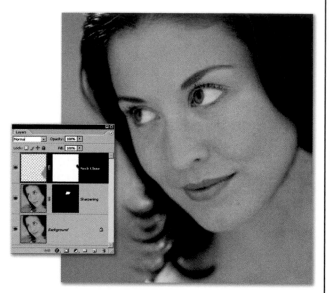

3 Make the Sharpening layer active. Choose Select⇨Color Range. Click on the woman's hair then press Shift until you see the Eyedropper get a plus sign (+) on it. Run the Eyedropper through the values in the woman's hair. Drag the Fuzziness slider until it picks up the hair area (to about **110**). Click OK. Press Q to enter QuickMask mode. Double-click the QuickMask layer entry in the Channels palette and set the mask opacity to **100%**. Remove the eyebrows and other areas that are selected but not part of her hair. Press Q to get out of QuickMask and then press Command/Ctrl+J to put the hair into its own layer. Name the layer **Hair** and change the Blend Mode to Normal.

4 As people age, things start to sag. The jowl line sags and creases; the eye no longer opens as wide, the eyebrow fades and drops, the cheeks develop crevices unknown in earlier years. We can replicate some of the changes of age using the Liquify command. First, turn off the Hair layer and make the Neck Clone image active. Then press Shift+Command/Ctrl+Option/Alt+E to create a new merged layer. Name the layer **Liquify**. Choose Filter⇨ Liquify. To start, choose a brush of about 250 pixels. Using the Forward Warp tool, grab the center of the woman's right cheek (that is your right) and pull the entire cheek down and to the left a bit. This deepens the slight line between her nose and cheek. Then pull the lower area of her right jaw to the left a bit as well. Push the slight dark line under the center of her neck just a bit to the left. Finally, make her right jowl sink down a bit. Don't close the dialog box yet.

5 Use the Freeze tool at a smaller size to paint over her right eye and lashes. Then use the Forward Warp tool and a 75-pixel brush to create the start of bags under her eyes. Just pull the pixels slowly down from the protected eye. Spread the color to the left and the pull it back toward her eye as shown in the figure. Lower the thin end of her right eyebrow a bit. Use the Pucker tool at 150 pixels on her lips to thin them slightly. Then use a very tiny brush (7 pixels) to push a bit of skin tone into the lips and a bit of lip color into the skin. The idea is to make the lip line less regular. You can use a slightly larger brush and very light pressure to partially restore the lip line so that color blending doesn't look quite so obvious. Use the Bloat tool at about 140 pixels on the tip of her nose and the right nostril to enlarge them a little. Turn down her nose a bit. You are going to make slight, gentle changes — not the wicked witch of the West! Save the mesh and click OK.

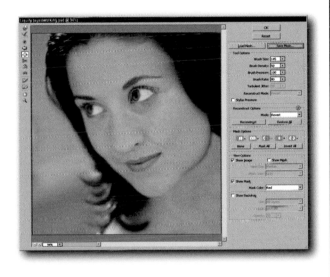

6 Next, we work on her hair. Turn on and duplicate the Hair layer and name it **Shadow/Highlight**. Press Command/Ctrl+Option/Alt+G to create a clipping mask. Choose Image⇨Adjustments⇨Shadow/Highlight. Accept the defaults and click OK. Press and hold Option/Alt and add a Hue/Saturation Adjustment layer. In the New Layer dialog box, name the layer **Gray Hair** and check the Use Previous Layer to Create Clipping Group check box. Click OK. Drag the Saturation slider to **-100** and the Lightness slider to **+21**. Click OK. Press and hold Option/Alt and add a Hue/Saturation Adjustment layer. In the New Layer dialog box, name the layer **Color Restore** and check Use Previous Layer to Create Clipping Group. Click OK Then check the Colorize checkbox. Set the Hue to **31**, the Saturation to **14**, and the Lightness to **-10**. Click OK. Fill the layer mask with black. Set the opacity to 44%. In the layer mask, with white and a small, soft brush, brush back some of the color in the top right of her hair. Finally, add a layer mask to the base layer and hide the unnatural-looking gray outlines of her hair — at least on the right side.

TIP

If you save your mesh before you exit the Liquify command, you can always start with the original Image and reload the mesh to get back to the point where you were when you exited Liquify. Then you can restore any areas that you don't like and reedit the image.

TIP

The left side of the woman's face stays young, so there is little reason to age it only to put it back again.

7 On the topic of hair... Add a new empty layer (name it **Eyebrow**) above the Color Restore layer. Using the Clone Stamp tool (with Sample All Layers checked), clone her forehead skin over the right eyebrow. Add a Layer mask and choose the 65-pixel Airbrush. Hold it gently under the eyebrow and hold the mouse a second or so to put back some color in the upper area of the eyebrow. Don't restore the full height — the eyebrows become less dense as one ages. Press and hold Option/Alt and add a Hue/Saturation Adjustment layer. In the New Layer dialog box, name the layer **Brow Desaturate** and check the Use Previous Layer to Create Clipping Group check box. Click OK. Drag the Saturation slider to **-100** and the Lightness slider to **+62**. Click OK. With black, paint in the layer mask to limit the area changed by the settings. Select the entire Clipping Mask and Control/Right-click to choose Group into New Smart Object. This makes a neat package out of the layers. Name the Smart Object **Hair**. If the colors get odd when you create the Smart Object, double-click to edit the Smart Object and then re-create the Clipping Masks. Click the Close box on the Smart Object and click Yes to save the changes.

8 Age spots usually occur when we reach our 70s and 80s, although they appear earlier on the hands and arms. Create a new layer at the top of the layer stack. Name the layer **Age Spots**. Choose the Brush tool with a 20-pixel brush at 50% hardness and 35% opacity. Use RGB: **173, 128, 99**. Randomly stamp the brush on the woman's face but not on her nose. Darken some of the spots by stamping over them a second time. Change the size of the brush to make it smaller and add more age spots.

9 The next step is to make a displacement map for the age spots. The easy way is to simply make a grayscale copy of the image and use it as the map. However, I want to randomize the shapes of the age spots as they are displaced, so we use a slightly more complex method. Turn off the eye on the Age Spots layer and choose Image⇨Duplicate⇨Merged Layers only. Name the image **Dmap** and click OK to create it. Choose Image⇨Mode⇨Grayscale. Then press Command/Ctrl+L to open the dialog box. Increase the contrast in the image by moving the Black and

White Input sliders toward each other until you force a little bit of the image to both true black and true white. Click OK. Choose Filter⇨Blur⇨Surface Blur, and set the Radius to **5** and the Threshold to **16**. Click OK. Choose Image⇨Mode⇨Multichannel.

Task 27 • The Stages of Life

TIP

A Displacement Map moves image pixels lighter than 128 in the dmap to the left and up and pixels darker than 128 to the right and down. So, the more the values vary in the dmap, the more your pixels move. In a Multichannel image, the first channel controls the horizontal and the second channel controls the vertical movement. Because you can set Horizontal and Vertical displacement scales to different values, using a Multichannel dmap lets you save two totally different images — one for the Horizontal and one for the Vertical displacement. A slightly blurred displacement map makes the pixels move more smoothly.

(10) The displacement map is halfway there. You need to create a small pattern and then make your second channel. Choose File⇨New and create a file that is **1** pixel wide and **12** pixels high. Double-click the Hand tool to enlarge the image. Using the Pencil tool and the 1-pixel brush, color the first four pixels black, color the next two and last two pixels medium gray (RGB: 128, 128,128) and the remaining four pixels are left white. Choose Filter⇨Blur⇨Gaussian Blur and set **0.8** for the Amount. Click OK. Choose Edit⇨Define Pattern and name it **Lines**. Close the pattern file. Back in the Dmap image, duplicate the Black channel in the image. Choose Edit⇨Fill, with

Pattern and select the saved Lines pattern. Click OK. Choose Edit⇨Fade Fill and drag the slider to **50%**. Click OK. You now see the image merged with the lines. Save the file as **Dmap.psd** and close it.

(11) In the aging image, make the Age Spots layer active and duplicate the layer. Name it **Displaced Age Spots**. Choose Filter⇨Distort⇨Displace. Type a Horizontal value of **20** and Vertical Displacement of **5**, Stretch to Fit, and Repeat Edge Pixels. Click OK. Choose the Dmap.psd image in the File Open dialog box and click OK to apply the displacement. Add a layer mask to the Displaced Age Spots layer and mask out any spots that land in a really odd place or that spread too much. Turn off the Age Spots layer; you don't need it any more, but I hate to delete it.

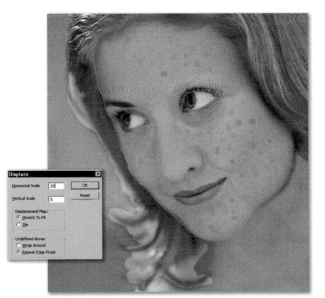

12. Next, give the shape of the face more definition. Press and hold Option/Alt and click the New Layer icon at the bottom of the Layers palette. The New Layer dialog box appears. Change the Mode in the dialog box to Overlay and select the Fill with Overlay-Neutral Color (50% gray) option. Name the layer **Major Burn Lines** and click OK. As you might guess, you now need to choose the Burn tool. Set the Exposure to 7 percent and choose a soft 17-pixel brush. Set the Range to Midtones. Darken the bag under her eye, the side of her nose, the major lines along her cheek, near the mouth, and under her face and chin. The grayscale image shows the lines I created as if they were in Normal mode.

TIP

The layer is only visible where it isn't neutral gray. This trick enables you to dodge and burn nondestructively. You can also try Soft Light mode to see if you prefer it.

13. Duplicate the Major Burn Lines layer and rename it **Major Burn Lines Blur**. Drag it under the original layer and turn off the original for now. Choose Filter⇨Blur⇨Gaussian Blur, **5.0**. Click OK. Make the Major Burn Lines layer active and change the mode to Darken. Then reduce the opacity to about **20** to **30** percent. Setting the mode to Darken also grays out the image a bit, which, in this instance, is good.

14. Press and hold Option/Alt and click the New Layer icon at the bottom of the Layers palette. The New Layer dialog box appears. Change the Mode in the dialog box to Overlay and check the Fill with Overlay-Neutral Color (50% gray) check box. Name the layer **Hollows** and click OK. Use a large soft brush (the 65-pixel brush is a good choice — turn off the Airbrush icon). Instead of the Burn tool however, use the Brush tool at 7% opacity and black as the foreground color. Brush over her neck, the side of her nose, under her eyes, and under her mouth. Reduce the brush opacity even more as needed to keep the effect from becoming grotesque. Don't go over the cheek area in this layer. Try Hard Light mode when you are done painting. I used Hard Light at **94**% opacity. Then make another Overlay filled layer and name it **Hollows2**. This time, paint in the hollows on her cheeks at about 3 percent opacity in black and leave the layer in Overlay mode.

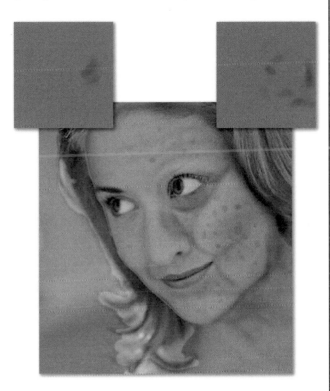

(15) Press and hold Option/Alt and click the New Layer icon at the bottom of the Layers palette. The New Layer dialog box appears. Change the Mode in the dialog box to Overlay and check the Fill with Overlay-Neutral Color (50% gray) check box. Name the layer **Fine Line Brush** and click OK. Get the SL-Agebrush.abr from the book's CD-ROM and drag it into Photoshop. It will place itself on the Brush menu. Choose the Brush tool and the Agebrush. Set the Master Diameter of the brush to 333. Use black at 7 percent opacity and stamp the brush over the image several times. You don't need to be careful about where the brush falls — just add a layer mask when you finish and then mask out the lines that are where you don't want them to be. Open the dmap.psd image and duplicate it. Trash the second alpha channel (the one with the lines in it) and save the new image as **dmap2.psd**. Close both dmap images. In the aging image, make the Fine Line brush layer (not the mask) active and choose Filter➪Distort➪Displace. Set both the Horizontal and Vertical amounts to 4. Click OK. Choose the dmap2.psd image and click OK. Now the lines bend to conform better to her face. Reduce the layer opacity to about **90**% (or to taste).

(16) Add a new empty layer in Normal mode. Name the layer **Veins**. Choose RGB: **138, 97, 97** as the foreground color. Using the 1-pixel brush and the Brush tool at 30 percent opacity, and scribble tiny veins on her nose and on the whites of her eyes. Add some fine lines under her eyes and then add some crow's-feet at the corner of her eye. Add a layer mask and use a soft brush with black at 30 percent opacity to control the darkness of the lines you just created. Then add another new empty layer (name it **Lip Lines**) and use a 1-pixel brush to draw some fine vertical lines over her lip. Add an Inner Bevel effect to the layer with a Depth of 720 percent, a Size of 7, and a Soften of 0. Set the Angle to 145 (deselect the Global Light option) and an Altitude of 5. Choose RGB: **163, 123, 124** as the Shadow color. Click OK to exit the Color Picker and OK to exit the Layer Style dialog box.

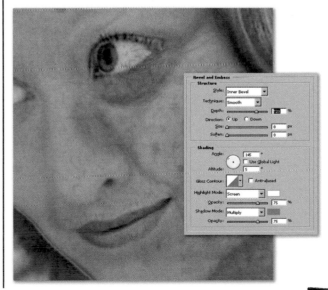

17 The model's skin still looks as if she's wearing too much face powder. Natural skin, especially older skin, reflects a bit more light. Press Shift+Command/ Ctrl+Option/Alt+E to create a merged layer. Name the layer **Plastic Wrap 9, 1, 13**. Then choose Filter⇨Artistic⇨Plastic Wrap. Set the Highlight Strength to **9**, the Detail to **1**, and the Smoothness to **13**. Click OK. Press and hold Option/Alt and add a Hide All layer mask. With white and a soft brush at **40**% opacity, paint the highlights you want to keep back into the image.

Strength to **20**, Detail to **15**, and Smoothness to **15**. Click the New Effect icon at the bottom of the Plastic Wrap dialog box three more times. Change the current effect settings to Highlight Strength, **13**; Detail, **1**; and Smoothness **11**. Click the New Effect icon again and change the settings to Highlight Strength **6**, Detail **15**, and Smoothness **11**. You have five effect layers stacked up. Click OK.

TIP

It can be hard to remember where the highlights are that you actually want to preserve. There are two ways to help you. You can choose Image⇨Duplicate⇨Merged Layers Only⇨OK before you add the layer mask. Then use this copy to show you the full image so you can see what to reveal. Or, you can add a Reveal All layer mask (solid white) and paint out the highlights you want to keep. After everything is painted, press Command/Ctrl+I to invert the mask to reveal the highlights and hide everything else. Either of these techniques works well if you have trouble with making the mask black at the start.

18 The final area that you need to touch up is her neck. Here is an odd way to make the veins on her neck stand out. You can experiment with the shapes and sizes, but this gets you started. Create a new file 221 x 314 pixels at 72 ppi named **Neck**. Click OK. This is approximately the size of her neck area. Fill the image with 50 percent gray. Choose Filter⇨Artistic, Plastic Wrap. Set Highlight

19 Drag the plastic wrap layer into the aging image. You may close the plastic wrap image; there's no need to save it. Control/Right-click on the new layer and choose Group into New Smart Object. Name the Smart Object **Neck Veins SO**. Press Command/Ctrl+T. Rotate the object until you have the bottom-left quarter of the object positioned over her neck, then stretch it to cover the area. Choose View⇨Fit on Screen to see the pasteboard area and the entire Transform bounding box. Once the plastic wrap covers approximately the needed area, click the Warp icon at the right of the Options bar. Warp the image to look like veins. Click Commit.

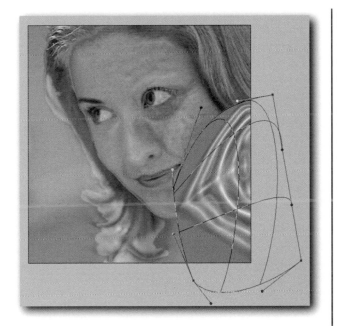

21 Finally, let's make the years pass swiftly over her face. Duplicate the Background layer and drag it to the top of the layer stack. Add a layer mask. Press D to set your colors to the default of black and white. Choose the Gradient tool and the Background to Foreground gradient. Press X to make white the foreground color. Drag the gradient cursor from the upper-lip area on the left side to the tip of her nose. You restore her youthful appearance on the left side of her face. You will need to experiment with the location and length of the gradient "drag" until you like the effect. Then, before you make yourself crazy trying to get it perfect, take a large soft brush and use black or white to fine-tune the effect. Save the image.

20 Add a layer mask and paint out the areas that are not needed. If you need to change the position of the veins and transform it again, disable the layer mask and then press Command/Ctrl+T and make your changes. Because you used a Smart Object, you can alter this as often as needed. When you are satisfied that the veins are in the right place, duplicate the Smart Object layer. Rename the layer **Neck Veins Pinched.** Rasterize the layer. Use the Lasso tool to select the neck area, then choose Filter⇨Distort⇨Pinch, 56 percent. Click OK.

22 Three more tweaks and then you're done. If the woman's right pupil (on your right) looks odd, it is because of the Liquify filter. In the Young Woman layer, paint over the pupil of her eye with white to restore the original pupil. Also, now that you can see the final composite, you can make her lips, when aged, a slightly more gray color. Add a layer under the Young Woman layer and use 50 percent gray at a low opacity to remove color from her lip. Name the layer **Lip Color Lost.** Save your work. Finally add a new layer at the top of the image. Command/Ctrl-click on the layer mask of the Young Woman image to load it as selection. Make black your foreground color. Choose Edit⇨Stroke, 1 pixel, Center and click OK. Add a layer mask and paint out the stroke around the eye and on the left and bottom sides of the image. Name the layer **Age Line.** Save your work.

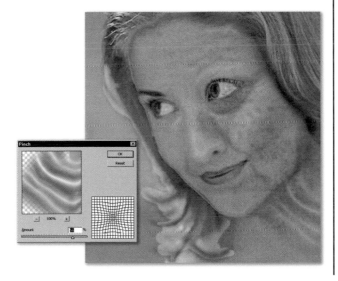

TIP

To add a layer *under* the current layer, press and hold the Command/Ctrl and click on the New Layer icon at the bottom of the Layers palette.

Liquify can be used to change the shape of a face; how you can create and use a displacement map to alter facial marks; how brush strokes can be made to blend in to create folds in the skin; and how the Plastic Wrap filter can provide both highlights and prominent veins. Another way, one you'll see on Photoshop contest sites like Worth1000, is to clone older skin onto a young person and match the skin and the color to the new recipient's face. That can give a more realistic appearance (and is also easier), but is much harder to do with a light and gentle hand. It's a better way to create a witch, but the techniques you've learned here give you much more control over which signs of age you actually want to create.

A short recap

Our old lady is a bit over the top, but you have learned a number of excellent ways to age someone. You don't need to make a person nearly as ancient as we did. You've seen how

chapter 5 · faces

groups

People enjoy associating with other people; hence people in groups. This chapter is all about groups. We have groups of people popping out of a picture frame, coming together to form a large composite playing basketball, and banding together (sorry about that!) to form a rock band. You will also meet kids (well, one kid) with super-human powers (and a wannabe). The Photoshop techniques are varied as well. You free the subjects of a photo from the confines of their picture frame in Task 28. Task 29 sparks your creativity by showing how to make a seamless composite of many images using photos embedded in layer masks. Task 30 shows a nondestructive way to stylize a photo by turning it into a combination of stamp and grayscale. Finally, in Task 31, you can play with gradient maps and the Posterize command to turn a photo into a comic strip.

Steppin' Out

One of the first lessons I learned in my first class on design was the power of the imperfect rectangle. An element that pops out of its frame and breaks that line is much more exciting than an image that stays neatly in its little frame. Many ways exist to break that frame. Here, you explore what happens when you decide to let people pop out of the frame (or, actually, make the critical area small enough that the people don't completely fit). This is a look that is popular in ads and fast becoming an exciting look for fans of scrapbooking. It's a fabulous way to showcase an image that has a fairly boring background.

THE PLAN

- Set up the image
- Create the main area
- Add a shadow

(1) Open the image Victory.psd. Choose Image⇨Image Size and increase the size by 160 percent. Set the Interpolation Method to Bicubic Smoother. Click OK.

Photo: www.comstock.com

(2) Add a white Solid Color Fill layer on top of the Background layer and set the opacity to about 40%.

(3) Choose the Rectangular Marquee tool. If you want to follow my measurements exactly, set the Style of the marquee to Fixed Size and the dimensions to **406 x 542** px. If you don't care to be quite so precise, make a selection similar to the one shown — or whatever you decide that you want as the main picture in the image.

(4) Add a new Solid Color Fill layer in black at the top of the layer stack. Name this layer **Knockout**. Set the Fill opacity for the layer to **0**. Double-click the layer entry to open the Layer Style dialog box. Set the Knockout to Deep. Click OK. Now you see the background layer through the hole made by the layer mask.

TIP

Knockout works by cutting through to the requested layer. Deep knockout always reveals the Background layer provided that the layer to which you assign the knockout has 0 percent Fill opacity. Shallow knockout reveals the base layer of a clipping group or the layer directly under a Group (layer set).

(5) The next step is to add the other areas that you want to appear at full opacity to the layer mask of the Knockout layer. The preferred way is to create Pen paths for each area; however, painting in the layer mask also works. In this particular image, I create a different path around each outer body part. I load each saved path as a selection, feather the selection by 1 pixel, and fill the selection with white in the Layer mask.

6 The next step is to widen the picture area by the width of a frame — the kind of frame you see (or used to see) on a photograph. Duplicate the Knockout layer and drag the duplicate layer under the Knockout layer. Name the duplicate **Frame and Shadow**. Double-click the layer icon and choose a shade of off-white as the new fill color. I use RGB **238, 238, 238**. Click OK. Set the Fill Opacity to 100 percent. You can change the Knockout back to None, but if you have the Fill Opacity set to 100% you won't knock out anything anyway. You can make a selection around the main frame area of the image as evenly as you can by eye. However, I prefer to append the Square Brush set of brushes to my available brushes and use that to help me get an even border. I use the 12-pixel square brush and stamp a brush stroke in white on each side of the image in the Frame and Shadow Layer Mask just outside of the original frame area. Then I position the Marquee tool to just enclose those brush strokes and fill the selection with white.

7 Fill the Marquee with white and deselect. Add a Drop Shadow layer style. Use a Distance of **8** and a Size of **27** with an Angle of **120** degrees — or whatever setting for the shadow that you prefer. Click OK. Touch up any areas that need it.

TIP

If you discover that the masking isn't as tight as it needs to be, fix it on the Frame and Shadow layer. Don't bother to also change it on the Knockout layer unless it makes a huge difference. Usually the shadow covers the problem areas.

8 The only thing left to do is to decide how light you want the background of the image. You could set the opacity of the Color Fill 1 to 100% if you wish. I prefer to see some of the original background however, and I use an opacity of 80 percent. The choice is yours.

9 Save your work. The figure shown here has the white Color Fill layer at 100% opacity.

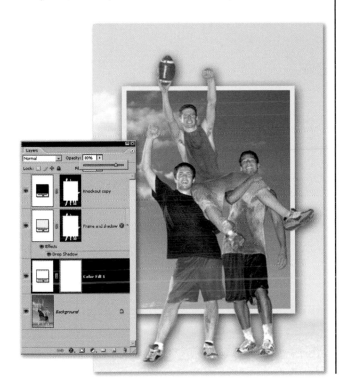

A short recap

If you want to make the frame look like an old scalloped photo frame, you can add that on the outside of the Frame and Shadow layer mask instead of just adding a plain outline as we do. If you have the AutoFx Photo/Graphic Edges filter (http://www.autofx.com), you can create a frame or edge treatment to use by loading it as a selection and then filling that selection on the Frame and Shadow layer mask. You can also create your edge treatment by hand with any number of Photoshop filters. Try this and soon you'll want to make everything jump out of its frame.

Photo Merge

Everyone loves a mystery. There's a universal fascination with things that are only partially revealed. Images that reveal themselves slowly are always more rewarding than those that present everything upfront and offer no more detail to the interested gaze. Photoshop gives you a tremendous ability to softly merge images together into a seamless composite. The shapes fade in and out of view and as you study the image, you begin to see more and more detail. While other techniques have given you steps to blindly follow, here you'll learn the method as you work to bring together your own interpretation of the starting photos. No two of these composites will be (or can be) identical pixel by pixel. Once you get the idea of what I'm doing, you are welcome to ignore my instructions and build a totally original composite from the same elements. All of the images in this technique are courtesy of Comstock (www.comstock.com).

THE PLAN

- Determine the composite size and images to use
- Add the first-level images and find masking images
- Build the remaining composite
- Add a frame, shadow, and glow.

TIP

You might find it easier to open all the images for this task from the CD before you start the exercise.

(1) Open the image Dribble.psd. Let's start this with two throwaway composites so you can understand the process before coping with a much more complex sequence. My compositing technique depends on the use of images in the layer mask. That allows you to create the subtle blending of two other images. In its most primitive form, you can develop an image in a layer mask between two solid colors. Choose File➪New and in the New Image dialog box, you need to click the Custom button and scroll to the bottom and select Dribble.psd. This gives you an image of the same size.

(2) In the new image, fill the Background layer with a dark color — black or any dark tone works. Add another new layer fill with a light tone — white, yellow, or anything light. Make the Dribble.psd image active and Command/Ctrl-click the RGB channel in the Channels palette to load it as a selection. You need to drag the selection marquee into the new image. To do that, choose the Rectangular Marquee tool. Place your cursor over the marching ants until it becomes a hollow arrowhead with a small marquee attached to it. Then press and hold the mouse button and drag the marching ants into the new layered image. If you press and hold Shift as you drag, the marquee drops into perfect alignment. Add a layer mask. Your totally solid image immediately gains a picture. You can save this or toss it — but now you know one way to merge layers.

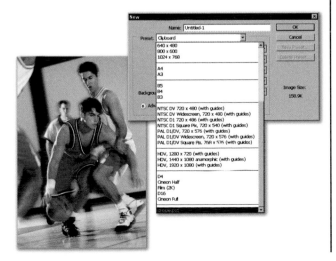

223

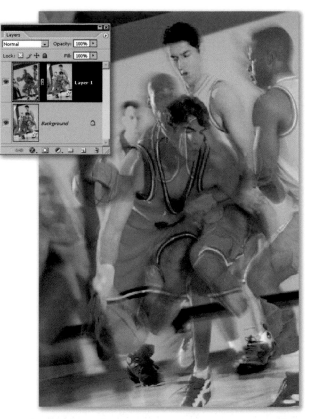

TIP

In order to develop a positive of the image, your bottom layer needs to be darker than the top layer. To give yourself maximum flexibility, you can use Solid Color Fill layers rather than regular layers. Then you can experiment with the color mix. However, you need to trash the automatic layer mask on the upper layer and then re-create it from the photographic marching ants. You can use Gradient fill layers or Pattern fill layers as well to try out other effects.

TIP

You can see this creates a much more complex composite. To vary it, you can invert the layer mask or you can use the Levels or Equalize commands in the mask to alter the values. Altering the values in the mask changes the image that is visible on each layer. Areas that are white or light in the mask reveal those areas on the layer; areas that are dark in the mask are hidden or only slightly visible in the resulting composite.

③ Leave open the Dribble image and then open the Pass.psd image. If you still have the marching ants visible in the Dribble image, let them remain. Drag the Pass.psd image into the Dribble image. Press and hold Shift as you drag to align the two images. Use the Move tool — not the Marquee tool — to drag the image. If the marching ants aren't visible, then briefly hide Layer 1 and Command/Ctrl-click the RGB channel to load the background layer as a selection. Turn on Layer 1 again and add a layer mask. You now have a blend based on the values in the Dribble image. Again, you can save this version or just drag Layer 1 into the Layers palette trash can.

④ Now you're ready to start to put together the various basketball images. Make the Dribble image active and click the snapshot in the History palette to restore the original image. Choose Image⇨Duplicate and name the copy **SportsComp**. Then click OK. Double-click the Background layer thumbnail in the Layers palette and name the layer **Dribble** in the New Layer dialog box. Press Command/Ctrl+Option/Alt+C to see the Canvas Size dialog box. With the Relative checkbox checked, type **100** in the Width field and change the Units to percent. Anchor in the center-right square and click OK. You may close the Dribble.psd image now. Command/Ctrl-click the Dribble layer thumbnail to load the layer as a selection. Click the Save Selection as Channel icon and name the new alpha channel as **Dribble**.

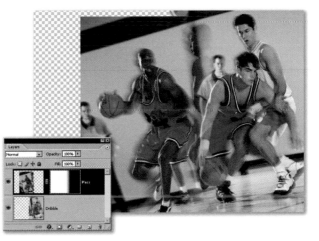

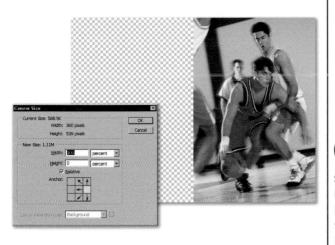

(5) Drag the Pass image into the SportsComp image and name the layer **Pass**. Drag it until the stripe on the ceiling seems to continue the same stripe on the Dribble layer and the right edge of the Pass layer is partially cutting off the player dribbling in the Dribble layer. Add a layer mask to the Pass layer. Choose the Gradient tool with the Foreground to Background gradient preset. Make the layer mask active and place your cursor at the upper-right corner of the Pass image (where it overlaps the image in the Dribble layer. Click, and with the Shift key pressed, drag the cursor just to the right of arm that remains visible at the top of the layer from the Dribble layer below. Release the mouse button. The two layers slide into one. You may close the Pass image now. Command/Ctrl-click the Pass layer thumbnail to load the layer as a selection. Click the Save Selection as Channel icon and name the new alpha channel **Pass**.

(6) Open the image Hoopshot.psd. Drag it into the SportsComp image and make it the top layer in the stack. Drag the image so that its left corner is exactly in the upper-left corner of the SportsComp window. Then add a layer mask. Choose the Gradient tool. Notice the player at the bottom of the image. Position your cursor over the inside of his elbow on your right side. Drag the Gradient cursor to the player's right eye (the one on your right). Then choose the 100-pixel soft brush. With white, click over the face of the player wearing the No. 33 shirt to fully reveal it. Then, with white at 30 percent opacity, click on the face of the player behind the one in the numbered shirt to bring back a bit of his opacity. You may close the Hoopshot image now. Command/Ctrl-click the HoopShot layer thumbnail to load the layer as a selection. Click the Save Selection as Channel icon and name the new alpha channel **HoopShot**.

7 Open the GreenBkg.psd image. Drag it into the SportsComp image so that the left edge of the image is even with the right ear (your right) of the bottom player on the Hoopshot layer. Then drag it to the bottom of the layer stack (where it's mostly hidden). Name the layer **GreenBkg**. You may close the GreenBkg image now. Command/Ctrl-click the GreenBkg layer thumbnail to load the layer as a selection. Click the Save Selection as Channel icon and name the new alpha channel **GreenBkg**.

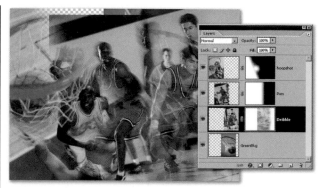

8 Turn on the eye on the GreenBkg channel but make the Dribble layer active. Open the Clouds.psd image from the book's CD-ROM. Command/Ctrl-click the RGB channel in the Channels palette to load the values in the image as a selection. Using the Rectangular Marquee tool as you did in Step 2, drag the marching ants into the SportsComp image until they are over the red coating from the GreenBkg alpha channel. Add a layer mask to the Dribble layer. Press Command/Ctrl+I to invert the Layer Mask. You have a hard edge on the right side of the layer. Using the 200-pixel soft brush with white at **100%** opacity, brush over the right edge of the layer so that the brush starts to eat away at the opacity. Brush mostly over the edge of the layer (which is outside of the masked area), but keep at it until you can no longer see the hard edge of the layer. Leave the Clouds image open because you might need it later.

9 Open the Web.psd image from the book's CD-ROM. Command/Ctrl-click the RGB channel in the Channels palette to load the values in the image as a selection. Using the Rectangular Marquee tool, drag the marching ants into the SportsComp image so that the left edge of the ants is to the left of the main player in the Pass layer (he's wearing orange). Make the Pass Layer Mask active and fill the selection on the layer mask with black. Leave the Web image open.

TIP

Filling the selection with black inverts the image in much the same way that Image⇨Adjustments⇨Invert does. However, here you invert only the selection and the rest of the layer mask stays as it was.

10 Make the GreenBkg layer active and add a layer mask. Turn on the eye on the GreenBkg alpha channel so you can see where its left edge is located. Use black and the 200-pixel soft brush at **100**% opacity. Hold the brush a bit to the right of the left edge of the green background (that is, most of the brush is on areas that arc transparent). Brush over that sharp edge to remove it. After you make one pass, turn off the alpha channel so you can see what you've accomplished. If you need more painting to get rid of the one sharp edge, continue to paint until it's gone.

11 Make the HoopShot layer active. Open the image Shoot.psd from the book's CD-ROM. Drag the Shoot image into the SportsComp image so that it hugs the left side of the file. It should be the top layer. Name the layer **Shoot**. Open the Basketball.psd image. Command/Ctrl-click the RGB channel in the Channels palette to load the values in the image as a selection. Using the Rectangular Marquee tool, drag the marching ants into the SportsComp image directly over the Shoot image. Add a layer mask. With black and the 100-pixel soft brush at **100**% opacity, paint over the right edge of the basketball texture in the layer mask to soften that edge. Again, you still see other hard edges for now. Then make the Pass layer active and click the New Layer icon at the bottom of the Layers palette. Name the new layer **Patch**. With black and the 100-pixel soft brush at **100**% opacity, paint the area along the top-left edge of the image where you can still see through to the transparency checkerboard. Also paint along the top edge of the Patch layer until you cover the small part of the arm still visible at the top of the Dribble layer. You may close the Shoot image, but leave the Basketball one available as you'll use it several more times.

CAUTION

You can't get rid of some of the other hard edges by painting in this layer mask. So just paint this one 200-pixel-wide line in the mask. Other steps will fix the remaining hard edges.

12 Finally, it's time to bring in the star player. Every image should have a focal point, and he becomes our focal point for this image. Make the Shoot layer of the image active. Open the image StarPlayer.psd from the book's CD-ROM. Press and hold Shift as you drag him into the SportsComp image (using the Move tool) so that he lands in the center of the image. Then press and hold Shift to keep him level as you drag him until the right edge of the image touches the shoulder of the player in the Dribble layer. Then drag the layer in the Layers palette until it's under the Pass layer. You can still see the hard edge on the right. You may close the Star Player image.

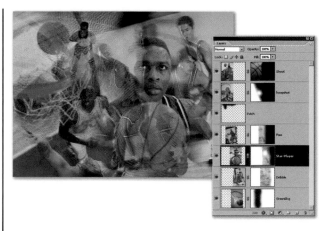

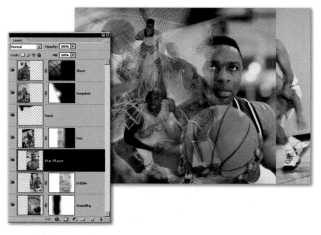

13 Make the Web image active again. If you deselected the image, then press and hold Command/Ctrl and click the RGB channel in the Channels palette to load the selection again. Drag the selection marquee into the SportsComp image all the way to the right edge of the canvas (need I say that you want the right edge of the selection — not its left edge — to touch the right edge of the canvas?). Then press and hold Option/Alt and click the Add Layer Mask icon. The hard edge where the Star Player image ends is still visible, so take the 200-pixel soft brush and black and hold the brush to the right of the Star Player in the layer mask. Gently paint with the brush up and down in the layer until you have softened that edge. Also, with black (this time at **50** percent opacity) in the Star Player layer mask, restore almost full visibility to the players at the right side of the image. Bring the opacity back to **100%** and change the foreground color to white. Click once or twice over the Star Player's face on the Star Player layer mask. You may close the Web image now.

14 Make the Layer Mask on the Pass layer active and with a black 200-pixel soft brush and **100%** opacity, click once or twice over the star player's face. This gives almost full opacity to the face. Again, paint with black, but use the 100-pixel soft brush at **100%** opacity, on a diagonal line from the head of the player on the bottom left of the image to the left edge of the basketball that the star player is holding. Now check the image for transparency. You should not be seeing any transparency checkerboard. If you do, turn the eyes on the layers off and on or turn the saved alpha channels on and off to identify which layer is causing the transparency. Paint with white in the offending layer mask to remove the transparency.

15 One major area needs more masking before we turn our attention elsewhere. The far right side of the image is strangely devoid of texture, especially considering the amount the texture on the left of the image. We need to balance that. However, the only layer that touches the right side of the image is the Dribble layer. If you add texture by masking it, you make it transparent. So, the solution is to add another layer under it. Make the GreenBkg layer active. Add a Solid Color Fill layer of RGB **128, 128, 128** and drag it to the bottom of the Layer stack. Make the Basketball image active. Command/Ctrl-click the RGB channel in the Layers palette to load it as a selection. Drag the marching ants into the SportsComp image until the marching ants that form the curved line at the top right of the basketball image are to the right of the right-most player's right shoulder (the shoulder on your right as you view the image). Click the Save Selection as Alpha icon on the Channels palette to create a new alpha channel. Name it **Basketball**. Make the Basketball alpha channel active, choose the 300-pixel soft brush with black, and just let the right tip of the brush come over the left edge of the image data in the Basketball alpha channel. You want to soften that edge so that you see no hard lines.

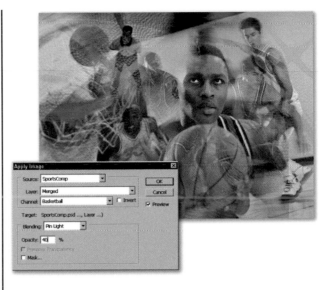

16 Make the Layer Mask on the Dribble layer active. Choose Image⇨Apply Image. Set the Source to SportsComp (not that you have much choice) and the Layer: to Merged. Set the Channel to Basketball. Change the Blending to Pin Light and the Opacity to **40**%. Click OK. This adds some of the basketball texture to the mask on the Dribble layer and helps to balance the image.

17 Make the Layer Mask on the GreenBkg layer active and with black, gently soften the sharp edge at the right side of the layer. Then, make the Pass layer active and, with black at 50% opacity, paint over the Star Player's hair and part of the side of his face. Look carefully to see if there are any other areas that need to have edges softened or texture added. If not, you're ready to add the finishing touches.

To check for unwanted hard edges, turn off all but the Color Fill1 layer. Then turn each layer back on from the bottom up and smooth the edges of the image in the mask layer if needed. I found it helpful to Option/Alt-click the Layer Mask thumbnail to view the mask directly. In that way, I painted out hard edges on the GreenBkg and the Dribble layers. On the Star Player layer, the spider web in the mask creates an unpleasant sharp edge. I marquee'd the area from the far left of the image to just to the right of the start of the web in the layer mask. I then feathered it by 5 pixels and made the value in the web my foreground color with white as the background color. I then used the Gradient tool to make a smooth transition. The hard edge where the Star Player ended on the left was covered over by higher layers and so didn't need any work.

By masking the group, you force the gray Color Fill layer not to expand when you enlarge the canvas. In addition, you keep the basic rectangle of the image together. The Pass layer actually extends below the original image and it reappears if the Group is not masked.

19 Choose the Crop tool and click the Front Image button on the Options bar to type the dimensions of the SportsComp image. Make the Basketball image active. Deselect if you still have marching ants. Choose Image➪Rotate Canvas➪90 degrees CW. Drag the Crop tool in the Basketball image from the upper-left corner to the bottom of the image as far to the right as it will go. Click Commit. With the Shift key pressed to register the images, drag the enlarged basketball image into the SportsComp image. Choose Layer➪New➪Background from Layer.

18 Select all of the layers and press Command/Ctrl+G to group them. Name the group **Main Image**. Press Command/Ctrl+A to select the entire image. Make the Group Folder the active layer and click the Add Layer Mask icon at the bottom of the Layers palette. Then press Command/Ctrl+Option/Alt+C to open the Canvas Size dialog box. With Relative checked, type **150** pixels in both the Width and Height fields. Click OK. Command/Ctrl-click the Main Image layer mask icon in the Layers palette to load the selection. With the Main Image Group folder layer selected and the group collapsed, add a Solid Color fill layer in black. Drag it below the Group but make sure that it doesn't fall into the Group folder. Name this new layer **Backing**. It will hold your effects.

(20) Make the Backing layer active. Add a Drop Shadow effect. Change the Angle to **127** degrees with a Distance of **41** px and a Size of **49** px. Then add an Outer Glow effect. Set the Size to **46** px. Click OK.

(21) Save your work.

A short recap

Layer masking generally hides or reveals areas of an image. You can make seamless composites using layer masks by simply hiding or showing the areas. However, you can add interest and mystery by using photos in the layer masks in place of simple gradients to solid black or white. By masking with photos, a whole new world opens up to you. You can do just about anything in a layer mask that you can do in an image. You can paint, filter, adjust Levels, posterize, equalize, make selections, and even set text. By using the Apply Image or Calculations commands, you can even combine images with control over opacity and blend mode. Why settle for simple black and white?

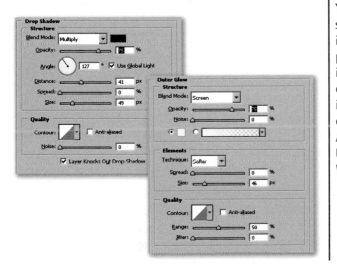

The '70s Rock Revival

Stamping is a hot craft right now and the look of stamps against a textured background is very popular. Abstracting and stylizing a photo so that it looks stamped is a surefire way to call attention to an image. Starting with a photo as the basis allows even the most drawing-challenged person the ability to produce graphic art. You can combine any photo and any background image using this technique to produce artwork that is unique. I like to use my own computer-painted backgrounds. The one I include here is a favorite, and you can download the layered texture — texturelayers.psd — from www.photoshopgonewild.com if you want to see how it was created. The best images to use are contrasty, so it's a great technique to use with a less-than-perfect original.

THE PLAN

- Create ragged edge on the image
- Prepare the background image
- Create the posterized, stamped effect
- Add the type

(1) Open the image theBand.psd from the book's CD-ROM. Choose Image⇨Duplicate⇨OK and close the original. In the duplicate image, double-click the Background layer in the Layers palette to create Layer 0. Name the layer **Original** and click OK. Then duplicate the Original layer by dragging its thumbnail to the New Layer icon at the bottom of the Layers palette. Name this copy **Edges**, and drag it below the Original layer.

(2) You want to fray the edges of the image without damaging the original image. That's why you create a copy of the original. However, you need to make room for the frayed edge. Press Command/Ctrl+Option/Alt+C to open the Canvas Size dialog box. With Relative checked, add 40 pixels to both Width and Height. Click OK.

(3) Photoshop provides many different ways to fray edges. The Wind filter works fairly well. However, we create a custom brush that does an ever better job of it. Choose File⇨New and set the new file Width to 2 pixels and the Height to 843 pixels. Name the file **SmudgeBrush** and click OK. Choose Filter⇨Noise⇨Add Noise, and set the Amount to **400**% with Gaussian Distribution and Monochromatic checked. Click OK. Then choose Image⇨ Image Size. Clear the Constrain Proportions checkbox and set the Interpolation Method to Nearest Neighbor. Leave Resample Image checked. Set the new Width to **4** pixels. Click OK.

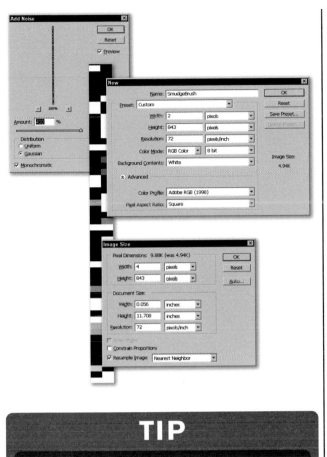

5 Open the image Texture.psd from the book's CD-ROM. You see only a Background layer in the Layers palette, but the figure shows the layered texture file as I created it. I just want you to get an idea of what is in this texture. I use brushes from the Graphicxtras brush collection (www.graphicxtras.com). I also use brushes to build the masks. I mix that with photographic masks and lots of blend modes. The layered file on the CD-ROM gives a better idea of the creation method.

TIP

In the file, the pixels that are darkest are more opaque when you paint with them. Brush opacity rules are the reverse of layer opacity rules.

4 Choose Edit⇨Define Brush Preset and click OK. The name is automatically set as **SmudgeBrush**. Make the Edges layer active. Choose the Smudge tool and set the Strength to **50%**. Place the brush so that it fits along the left side of the image. Place it just inside the left edge of the image area, press and hold the mouse button, and drag the brush to the left edge of the canvas. Repeat, starting the brush a pixel or two up or down from the original starting position. Repeat along the right edge of the Edges layer but stroke to the right this time. Then open the Brushes palette and make the Brush Tip Shape dialog active. Change the brush Angle to **90** degrees. Smudge the top and bottom edges of the Edge layer as you did the sides.

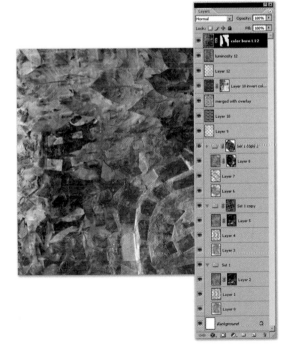

6 Double click the Hand tool on the texture image to fit the image into the window. Make theBand image active. Select both layers and Control/Right-click the layer entry on the Layers palette and choose Group into New Smart Layer. Name the smart object **theBand**. Press and hold Shift and Command/Ctrl keys and drag it into the Texture image. It should appear in the exact center of the image.

7 Duplicate theBand Smart Object by dragging it to the New Layer icon at the bottom of the Layers palette. Turn off the eye on theBand layer. Drag the duplicate below the theBand Smart Object layer and name it **High Pass**. Rasterize the layer. Change the Blend mode to Multiply. Press and hold Option/Alt and add a Threshold layer above it. In the New Layer dialog box, check the Use Previous Layer to Create Clipping Mask check box. Click OK. Set the Threshold to **124**. Click OK. Make the Background layer active, and add a white Solid Color Fill layer above it. Set the Opacity to **50** percent.

8 Turn off the eye on the High Pass layer. Turn off the eye on the Solid Color Fill 1 layer as well — you no longer really need the layer, but don't bother to trash it. Turn on the eye on theBand layer and make the layer active. Double-click theBand Smart Object layer entry to see the Layer Style dialog box. Move the Blend If–This Layer black point slider to **25**. The darkest values drop out. You can experiment with other settings, but use mine for right now — you can change it later if you want. Set the Blend Mode to Dissolve and the Layer Opacity to **87** percent. Click OK.

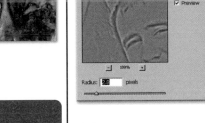

TIP

The look that you want for this image is a combination of stamp and grayscale. The Dissolve mode adds a grainy texture. The only setting that you can't change once you've set it is the High Pass filter. Once the layer is filtered, the only way to alter the setting is to re-create the layer. So, it pays to set up the entire image before you do the High Pass. Step 7 basically sets up the layer that is used for the High Pass filter. Now you need to get the top layer setup. You needed to keep the High Pass layer off because you would not see the result of setting the Blend-if slider when you drop out black but the layer underneath is also black!

⑩ Make theBand layer active. Press and hold Option/Alt and add a Solid Color Fill layer. In the dialog box, check the Use Previous Layer to Create Clipping Mask check box. Then change the Blend mode to Color. Name the layer **Color Tone**. Click OK. Choose RGB **249, 229, 250** in the Color Picker (it's a light pink) and click OK.

⑨ Turn the High Pass layer back on and make the layer active. Choose Filter➪Other➪High Pass. Watch the preview as you slide the Radius field. The smaller the radius, the finer the detail and the more detail you see. However, the fine detail is very light. As you increase the radius, you need stronger lines to emerge. I like the setting of 2.8, but 4.0 also looks good. You can set it where you like it best. Because of the way you set up the image, you can judge the final effect very accurately as you preview the filter. When you like the settings, click OK.

11. The background of the image is a bit busy. If you stretch part of the background to cover the entire image, you tone it down a bit. Choose the Rectangular Marquee tool and set the Style on the Options bar to Fixed Size. Set the Width of the Fixed Size marquee to **850** pixels and the Height to **858** pixels. Option/Alt-click the eye on the Background layer to make it the only visible layer. Make the Background layer active. With the Rectangular Marquee tool, click in the image and without releasing the mouse button, drag the marquee to the lower-right corner of the image. Release the mouse. Press Command/Ctrl+J to create a new layer via copy. Name the new layer **Stretched**. Press Command/Ctrl+T and drag the top-left corner of the bounding box into the top-left corner of the image. Don't worry about keeping the aspect ratio. Commit.

12. Turn on all of the layers with the exception of the white Solid Color Fill. The background is still a bit too busy. Duplicate the Stretched layer and name it Surface Blur. Choose Filter⇨Blur⇨Surface Blur and set the Radius to **31** and the Threshold to **44** (or your preferred settings). Click OK. If you feel that it's too blurred, reduce the opacity of the Surface Blur layer. (I backed off to about 80%.)

13. What's a band album without a name? This debut album is called Malaga Road. We need to add it to the album cover. Choose a grungy font (if you have one). I use Kab, a Typo5 font from Myfonts.com. Type the word Malaga in your font of choice. I use 100 points as the size, but a different font might need a different font size. Click the Warp icon and choose the Arc style. Give it a Bend of **0** and a Horizontal Distortion of **–60** percent. Commit. Set the word Road under it using the same font and size. Add an Arc warp but choose a Bend of **0** and a Horizontal Distortion of **+60** percent. Commit. Select both layers and press Command/Ctrl+T. Rotate the type about **–19** degrees. Commit.

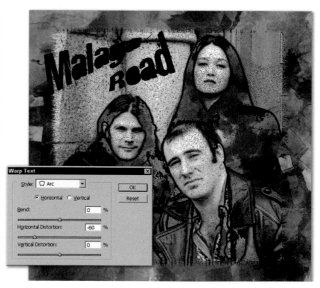

(14) Add an Outer Glow effect to the word Malaga. Set the Size to **21**. Click the Color swatch and choose RGB **234, 226, 32** or the color you prefer. Click OK. Then click OK to close the Layer Style dialog box. Make the Road layer active and add an Outer Glow effect. Set the Size to **21** and choose RGB: **29, 237, 60** as the glow color. Click OK and then click OK again.

A short recap

You don't have to be able draw to be an illustrator. All you need is a photo and a great idea. That turns a less-than-stellar photo of the band into a stunning album cover. Change the proportions a bit, and you can get a business card from the same image. If you prefer just the stamped look, you can open theBand Smart Object and add a Threshold layer inside of it. Click the Close box and click Yes to save it. Remove the Blend-If setting from the layer. Then, with this layer the only visible layer, Command/Ctrl-click the RGB channel in the Channels palette to load the selection. Press and hold Option/Alt to reverse the selection and add a layer mask to the Smart Object layer. Then you can open the clipping mask layer (Color Tone) and choose a dark color to use. You need to change the blend mode of the layer back to Normal. Now, the only thing you need is a quiet place to enjoy some loud rock.

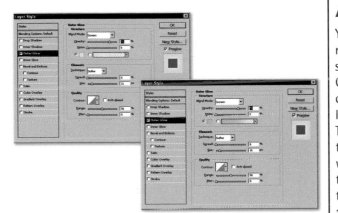

(15) Save your work.

Superhero Sam

The bold lines and rich coloring of comic book art appeal to most everyone of all ages. Whether or not you believe that comic books are truly an art form you can agree that the ability to imitate this popular style is a handy skill. Even if you are graphically challenged in terms of drawing ability you can create full-color comic book-style images with Photoshop. This technique is written and designed by Rhoda Grossman.

THE PLAN

- Combine two source images
- Develop line art using a combination of filters and Adjustment Layers
- Create bold color with more Adjustment Layers, filters and Gradient fills

MY KNUCKLES ARE REALLY GETTIN' SORE PUNCHIN' THE PANEL!

(1) Open the files KarateKid1 and KarateKid2. To qualify for inclusion in this chapter I put these two boys together. Use the Image Size command on each original to double the pixels in each image (Resample to 200 percent).

Photos: www.comstock.com

(2) Eliminate the gradient background behind KarateKid1. A few clicks with the Magic Wand followed by Delete/Backspace should do it. Add about an inch of blank space to the right of the figure by choosing

Image⇨Canvas Size. With a combination of the Magic Eraser and the Background Eraser, eliminate most of the leafy stuff at the edges of KarateKid2. Then it is easy to make a freehand Lasso selection of kid-without-background and drag him to the other image. Or, if you're proficient with the Pen tool, create a path; it's even easier.

(3) Flatten the image and duplicate the new background as a layer. Keep the colorful composite pristine, while working on the copy. The first step in developing the black-and-white line art is to eliminate color. Do this nondestructively with a Hue/Saturation Adjustment layer. Drag the Saturation slider to the extreme left.

(**5**) To emphasize those edges even more, add a Levels Adjustment Layer. Pull both the white and black triangles closer to the center of the histogram.

(**4**) Use the High Pass filter in the Filter⇨Other group to emphasize the edges in the image. I set the Radius to about 7. Notice that this filter replaces most of the pixels with gray. You fix that in the next step.

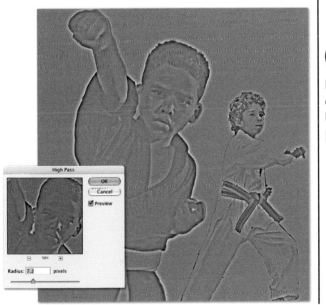

(**6**) The last step in this recipe for making high-contrast line art is achieved with a Threshold Adjustment Layer. Drag the slider back and forth until you find the optimal point for converting gray pixels to either white or black. Afterward, you might need to clean up a few stray pixels here and there.

⑧ The colors on the original KarateKid in the foreground are so dramatic, this looks pretty good already. But you create even better color effects. Once again, duplicate the background layer by dragging it to the Create a New Layer icon. Select the white background with the Magic Wand at a low threshold setting and save the selection to a new channel. Fill the selection with a radial gradient. I made a custom gradient called Yellow, Red, Violet, and I began to drag at the boy's fist, so it was the center of the fill.

⑦ When you are ready to commit to the settings for your various adjustment layers, merge them into one layer. Do this by turning off the visibility of the original colored image and use the Merge Visible command. Rename the merged layer **black line** and switch to Multiply mode so you can see the colors combined with the line art.

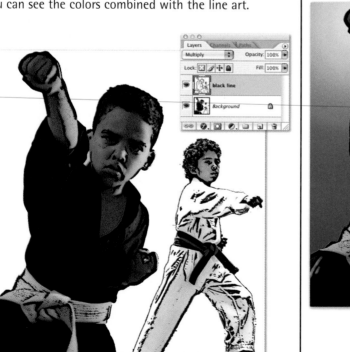

9 Inverse the selection and apply Filter⇨Artistic⇨ Cutout, using the settings shown. You now have just a handful of flat colors you can change with a simple click of the Paint Bucket. Visibility of the black line layer is off for now.

10 Of course, you can pick and choose each color fill individually. If you prefer an instant color treatment that can be changed in another instant, use a Gradient Map Adjustment Layer. All of the gradient preset libraries are available. I picked Violet, Green, Orange from the default presets for this example. Experimentation with other presets yields exciting variations. When you're happy with your color transformations, apply a Gaussian blur to smooth out the edges of the color fills.

11 Adding a "POW!" or "BAM!" isn't amiss at this point, but that's for another day. At least you can provide the "speed whiskers" traditionally used to indicate movement (or power or tension). These ghosted lines can be made with the Clone Stamp tool on the black line layer. Be sure the Aligned option is deselected or turned off.

(12) Simplify and clean up the black line layer by erasing unnecessary pixels. Pay special attention to the boys' faces, eliminating all but the minimum lines for facial features. This helps make them look more generic and less like recognizable photos. Yes, you can do this in Step 6 if you had thought of it then.

(13) You can change the contents of the Gradient Map Adjustment Layer at any time. This one shows a custom gradient made to include a white area for the highlights.

(14) Authentic comic book art often uses a few flat color fills under the black line work. You can imitate that effect with a Posterize Adjustment Layer. The number of levels shown here is three. Only the black line, Posterize, and original background layers are visible. Yes, I eliminated the "speed whiskers," at least temporarily.

15 All layers are turned on at this point, and I move the Posterize Adjustment Layer up in the stack. Now the background gradient is also posterized for a bull's-eye effect.

17 For a finishing touch, add a talk balloon for the secondary character. Create the text in a font that imitates the hand-lettered look of traditional comics. When you're satisfied with the size, alignment, and position of the text, make a new layer for the balloon. Use the Elliptical Marquee while pressing Shift to make a series of overlapping ovals that enclose the text. Choose Edit⇨Fill with white and Edit⇨Stroke with black.

16 Give your main character some X-ray vision. Use the Polygon Lasso to make two very elongated triangles beginning at a pinpoint within each eye. Create a Hue/Saturation Adjustment Layer using these settings. To make those intense rays fade out gradually, use the Foreground-to-Transparent gradient on the layer mask, dragging from the outer edge of each triangle toward the eye. Add a spiky shape around the other character's fist to suggest the impact of a karate punch. Fill that selection in the layer mask with white to enable the Hue/Saturation effect for those pixels.

A short recap

Combining two source images requires using advanced selections. The recipe for teasing bold line art from a photograph serves you well in other techniques, such as creating the look of a woodcut relief print. You simplified continuous color into a few flat shapes with the Cutout filter and a Posterize Adjustment Layer. After exploring the power of gradient mapping to produce exciting color variations, not to mention using the esoteric X-ray vision feature, you earn at least a purple belt in Photoshop.

animal farm

Animals are the theme for this chapter, but, like the characters in *Animal Farm,* I don't suggest making pets of most of them. They are much too human for that. Rhino Woman certainly isn't a pet. She is definitely a strong woman with an attitude. The wolf isn't a really good pet, either. He doesn't want your dog food — he'd rather have sheep. Reiko the cat (featured in a bottle and on the strut) is supposed to be a pet, but the woman who is allowed to provide food and shelter thinks she's actually the pet! Finally, the kangaroo is a bit bouncy and awkward to keep in the house. However, all of these examples show different ways to work with photographs and to manipulate them to tell a story.

Rhino Woman

Funny pictures should deliver a message of some variety. Graphic design is, after all, an exercise in communication. I must admit that I am not totally sure what the photographer of this original stock image was trying to say. I don't quite know what purpose is served by a half-dressed woman with a wizard's hat looking at the sea. However, by a little bit of change to the image, you can deliver a message about being different, and alone with your dreams. (Of course, if you're not into deeper meaning, you can just have fun messing around with a photo!)

THE PLAN

- Create channels and dmaps
- Texture map the rhino skin onto the woman
- Add the spiral type

(1) Open the image Hatlady.psd. Choose Image⇨Image Size and increase the size of the image to **160** percent. Make sure the Constrain Proportions and Resample Image options are selected as well and click OK.

Photo: www.comstock.com

(2) Choose the Polygon Lasso tool and make a selection around the outside of the woman's hat. Set the Magic Wand tool Tolerance to **50**, clear Anti-alias, and set ContiguousOn. Press and hold Option/Alt and click in the blue area between the marquee and the hat. The selection contracts to hug the hat. Repeat on the other side. Press Command/Ctrl+J to create a new layer via copy. Name the new layer **Hat**.

Click Here

3 You'll need to make a displacement map for the lady's skin, so it might as well be now. Choose Image⇨Duplicate⇨Merged Layers Only⇨HatLadyDmap⇨OK. Choose Filter⇨Blur⇨Gaussian Blur and choose an Amount of **3.0.** Click OK Save the file as **HatLadyDmap.psd**. You many close the document.

4 Use the Lasso tool to select the lady's hair. You don't need to make a precise selection. You won't be altering the background so having some of the background in her hair makes no difference. Therefore, why spend the time trying to isolate the wispies in her hair in a new layer? Name the layer **Hair**.

5 Open the image HatLadyMask.psd from the book's CD-ROM. I prebuilt the mask for you. Of course, if you'd rather do it yourself, be my guest! If you want to use my mask, just place your cursor on the Gray channel in the Channels palette with the HatLadyMask image active and drag the gray channel until it's on top of the HatLady image. Then release the mouse. The channel should now appear as Alpha 1. You may close the HatLadyMask image.

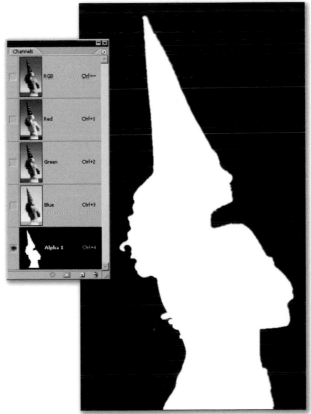

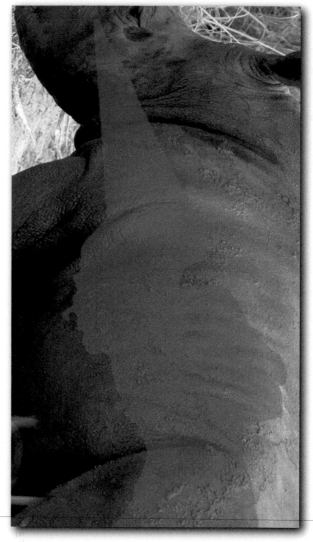

6 Make the Background layer in the HatLady image active and turn off the eyes on the Hat and Hair layers. Open the Rhino.psd image. This image has both the skin and head that you'll use for the lady. Some of the layers are just the real skin and some will be the displaced skin. However, every layer contributes to the final effect. First, choose Image⇨Rotate Canvas⇨90 degrees Clockwise. Then press and hold Shift and drag the rotated Rhino image into the HatLady image. Name the layer **Rhino**. Click the snapshot in the History palette to revert the image back to its original state. You may minimize for now.

Photo: Sherry London

7 Make the Alpha 1 channel active and press Command/Ctrl+I to invert it. Click the RGB channel to make it active and then click the eye next to the Alpha 1 channel to view the red coating inside of the lady. Make sure that the Rhino layer is active and then use the Move tool to position the layer so that the point of the lady's hat is just to the left of the rhino's eye and the dark crease where his hind leg starts is over the lady's waist. Once you have the Rhino image positioned where you want it, make the Alpha 1 channel active again and press Command/Ctrl+I to change the Alpha 1 channel back to the original. Make the RGB channel active.

8 Command/Ctrl-click on the Alpha 1 channel to load it as a selection. Make the Rhino layer active and add a layer mask. This layer becomes the bottom of a large clipping mask. Drag the Rhino layer to the New Layer icon at the bottom of the Layers palette to duplicate the layer. Name the duplicate **Screen**. Control/right-click on the Layer Mask thumbnail in the Layers palette and choose Delete Layer Mask. For right now, turn off the eye on the Screen layer.

9 Duplicate the Background layer and drag it above the Rhino layer. Name the layer **Darken**. Add a Hue/Saturation layer above it and change the Saturation to **-100**. Click OK. Select the Darken and the Hue/Sat layers and Control/right-click on the Layers palette entry for one of the selected layers. Choose Group into New Smart Object. Press Command/Ctrl+Option/Alt+G to create a Clipping Mask. Then change the Smart Object blend mode to Darken. Rename the Smart Object Layer as **Darken**.

TIP

You need to make the copy of the Rhino layer now because the next step creates a Clipping Mask. If you copy the base layer of the Clipping Mask, you break the Clipping Mask and need to redo it all.

You might wonder how I figured out the sequence of the blend mode layers to use. I could tell you it's because I'm brilliant (okay, I am, but that's not the point here). I didn't know in advance what I wanted to use. I knew I wanted to try the texture without displacing it right away; I really wanted to be able to see the skin surface of the rhino. The first layer was just the pure rhino skin and in Normal mode looked very good. However, it lacked the shadow detail. In Multiply mode, it lacked the rhino detail. My compromise was to use the Background layer in Darken mode (after desaturating it). I liked the slight deadening of the contrast. I needed to make a Smart Object of the copied Background layer and the Hue/Saturation layer though because the Hue/Sat layer had to affect only the copied image of the hat lady. As it's not possible to make a Clipping mask within a Clipping mask, the Smart Object was the perfect solution.

So, how did I invent these layers? Part of it was experimentation, but I knew where I wanted to go. The Screen layer adds some of the lighter tones lost by the Darken layer. Soft Light brings in more detail and the Multiply layer adds contrast.

(10) Make the Screen layer active and turn the eye back on. Change the Blend mode of the layer to Screen. Press Command/Ctrl+Option+Alt+G to add the layer to the Clipping Mask. Duplicate the Screen layer and change the Blend Mode to Soft Light at 100 percent opacity. Notice that the layer is automatically added to the Clipping Group. Name the layer **Soft Light**. Duplicate the Soft Light layer and change the Blend Mode to Multiply and the Opacity to **37** percent. Name the layer **Multiply 37**.

(11) Duplicate the Multiply 37 layer and change the Blend Mode to Normal at 100 percent opacity. (Yes, that defeats the purpose of the lower layers, but we fix it in a few minutes). Name the layer **Displace**. Choose Filter⇨Distort⇨Displace. Type **10** for the both the Horizontal and Vertical Displacement amounts and choose the Stretch to Fit and Repeat Edge Pixels option buttons. Click OK. Then choose HatLadydMap.psd as the displacement map. Click OK. Change the layer Blend mode to Multiply so you can see how it reacts with the layers below. I reduced the opacity to **74** percent, but you might prefer this to be darker or lighter — and you can keep changing your mind as you finish the image.

(12) The only part of the rhino skin that still has a problem is the lady's hand wrapped around her arm on the right side of the image. Duplicate the Background layer and drag it above the Displace layer. Name it **Hand Correction**. Change the Blend mode to Multiply at **37** percent opacity. Press and hold Option/Alt and add a Layer Mask. Make white your foreground color and use a large soft brush to bring back just the hand. With a much smaller brush and black, clean up the area so that only the hand is visible. The hand adds more color than really looks good — but a totally desaturated hand doesn't work well here, either. Choose the Sponge tool in Desaturate mode at **50** percent flow with a large, soft brush, and just dab the hand a few times until about half of the color bleaches out. The figure shows the before and after view of the hand.

(13) Make the Rhino image active. Choose Image➪ Duplicate➪OK. Command/Ctrl-click the Rhino Head Path in the Paths palette to load it as a selection. Choose Select➪Modify➪Expand, 25 pixels and click OK. Then choose Image➪Crop. Double-click the Background layer and name the new layer **Rhino Head**. Command/Ctrl-click the Rhino Head Path in the Paths palette to load it as a selection. Add a Layer Mask. Drag the entire layer into the HatLady image and Control/Right-click on the layer entry in the Layers palette to choose Group into New Smart Object. Close both the Rhino.psd and the smaller cropped copy. You don't need to save the cropped image.

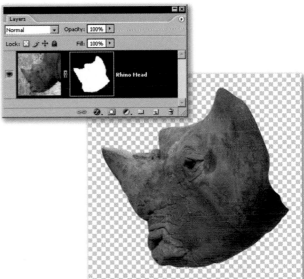

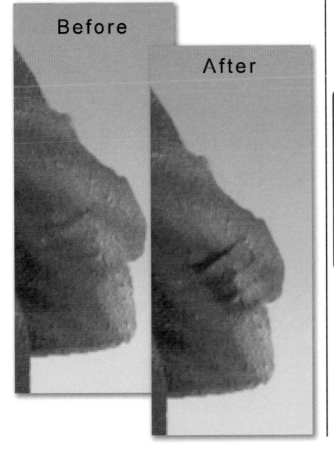

Before

After

(14) Press Command/Ctrl+T to select the Rhino Head Smart Object in the HatLady image. Choose Edit⇨Transform⇨Flip Horizontal. Then make the head smaller and rotate it. You can see the results of my transformation in the Options bar in the figure. You should probably like a size of somewhere between a **52** percent and **46** percent reduction for the head (I use 46 percent). The technique I use places the head just to the left of the lady's head and then tries to size it approximately to match. I also try to match the angle of her mouth with the rhino's mouth and then position the rhino's eye approximately over her eye.

(15) Next, you need to enlarge the canvas. Press Command/Ctrl+Option/Alt+C to open the Canvas Size dialog box. Clear the Relative check box and type **649** pixels as the width. Anchor in the center box on the right. Click OK. Make the Background layer active. Using the Rectangular Marquee tool, make a selection from the top to the bottom of the image of the Background layer from the start of the original image to the lady's hair; you only want the sea and sky in the selection. Once you have the marquee set, press Command/Ctrl+J to make a new layer via copy. Name the new layer **Sea Extension**. Then press Command/Ctrl+T. Drag the center-left handle until it reaches the left edge of the image. Commit. Select the ocean area on the layer with Rectangular Marquee tool. This area has gotten very soft. Choose Filter⇨Noise⇨Add Noise and add 1.5 percent noise, Gaussian Distribution. Click OK. Deselect.

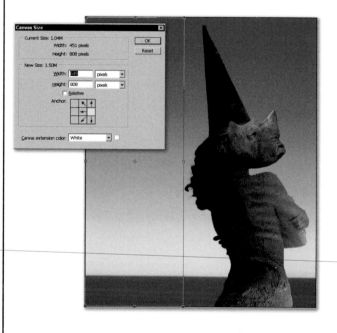

NOTE

The Noise filter adds back some of the grain that resizing the image segment removed. I rarely filter and image directly, but this change is subtle enough that it's really much more complex to add the noise nondestructively.

16 Set your foreground color to RGB **194, 108, 81**. Press and hold Option/Alt and choose a Solid Color Fill layer from the Add New Fill or Adjustment Layer icon. In the New Layer dialog box, check the Use Previous Layer to Create Clipping Mask check box. Change the Mode field to Color. The color is set to your Foreground color by default so just click OK.

17 Turn on the Hair and Hat layers again. You see that you seem to have an outline around it. That is coming from the Rhino layer because the mask is a bit larger than the original figure. However, you don't need the rhino skin on the hair or hat areas. Make the mask in the Rhino layer active and use black and a soft brush to remove that outline/halo around the hair. Then add a Layer Mask to the Hat layer and brush out some extra hair over what would have been her ear. Make the hair look as if it is growing on the rhino but blending in any rough spots. Add a Layer Mask to the Hat layer and with a small, hard brush and black, hide the area of the hat that covers the small rhino horn.

18 You can now add the sea mist to the image (an odd color sea mist, but I like the effect). Your foreground color needs to be set to RGB: **131, 73, 34**. This is a muted color but still related to the color used in Step 16 for the left side of the image. Add a Gradient Fill layer. Accept the default Foreground to Transparent Linear gradient and change the Angle to **-17.53** degrees. Leave the Scale at **100** percent and click OK. Name the layer **Sea Mist**.

19 A seashell and a spiral share a spine — the same basic shape runs through both. What, therefore, could be more appropriate a device for text on this scene than placing it around a spiral? Make the Shape tool active and choose the Custom Shape. Click the arrow to the right of the Shape field on the Options bar and drop down the menu in the Shape field. Choose the Ornaments shape set to load and click Append when prompted. Select the Spiral shape from the set by clicking its icon. Open the Custom Shape options and click the Fixed Sized option. Type **602** px for the Width and **499** px for the height. Click OK. Set the Shape tool to create Paths by clicking on the center icon on the Options bar. Then click the image with the Shape tool to create the shape.

20 Choose the Horizontal Type tool. Use a font that seems appropriate to the setting and not too fussy to be legible. I used Coquette Regular (available at www.myfonts.com) at **45** points. News Gothic Std also works well. Move your cursor onto the spiral. As you move over the shape, the cursor changes from the standard I-beam to a text-on-a-path cursor. You want to start the type on the lower edge of the spiral just where the lady's hair begins. See the figure for a close-up.

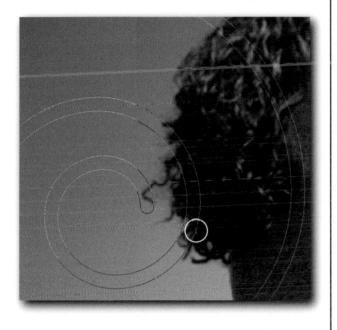

21 Once you find the spot to start your text, click and then type **Magic is believing in yourself; if you can do that, you can make anything happen.** Change the font size to about 24 points and type the attribution, **Johann Wolfgang von Goethe.** Click Commit. If you're lucky, the type will fit and not wrap around the shape. To adjust the location of the type if you need to move it around the spiral, choose the Path Selection tool. There are only two or three spots where you can typically insert the cursor easily. If you look at your type on the path very carefully, you should see a tiny circle and a tiny X near the start of the word "Magic." If you need to move the type to make it tighter on the spiral, move the circle (the cursor gets a left-pointing arrow) closer to the start of the spiral (more toward the center of the spiral). Then grab the text at the X (the cursor looks like an I-beam with a right-pointing arrow) and drag it toward the circle marker. Make sure that you don't cross the path or the type flips. You can also select the type and reduce or increase the font size as needed (but use the Type tool to select the type in order to alter the font size).

TIP

Setting this type is tricky. The spiral shape you use as the path allows type around both edges of the shape. You need to make sure that you only use one edge when you set the type or it becomes illegible. Most sans serif or casual handwriting fonts work well here. The image has lightness to it, so a heavy, wide font would be the wrong choice. After you select your font, experiment to find the size type that works.

22 Add an Outer Glow layer style to the text layer. In the dialog box, leave the standard opacities and blend modes. Just change the Size to 5 and click OK.

23 Add a new layer at the top of the layer stack. Name it **Glints**. Make white your foreground color and choose the Brush tool and the Star 70-pixel brush. Click on top of the dot on the first *i* in "Magic," "is," "believing," "in," and "anything." Then add a glint to the starting corner of the *m* in make.

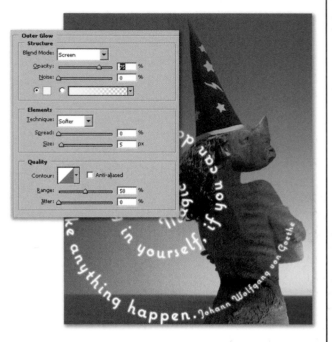

(24) Only a few tweaks remain. Zoom all the way into the image on the rhino lady's hair and head. Fix the layer mask on the hair layer if you discover you have some ear or some hard edges showing. Add a Drop Shadow to the Hair layer that puts a very soft shadow just to the right of her hair. If you see a line where the head starts or get too much of a shadow on the top right, mask it out in the layer mask. Add a layer mask to the Rhino Head layer and blend her face and neck seamlessly into the body. Double-click the Rhino Head Smart Object to open it for editing. In the open Smart Object, make the layer mask active and give it a Gaussian Blur of 1. Click the close box on the Smart Object and click Yes to the prompt to save the file. Make the layer mask on the Rhino layer active and add a Gaussian Blur of 1 to that layer as well. Add a Bevel and Emboss to the Rhino layer. Leave everything at the default except: change Depth to **101**%, Size to **1** and Soften to **8** px. Click OK. Finally, duplicate the Hand Correction layer and name it **Back Shadows** (it becomes the top layer in the clipping mask). Fill the Layer Mask with white to make the whole layer visible. Then use black to mask out all but the darker shadow on the rhino lady's back. Change the layer opacity to **40**%. Make the layer (rather than the mask) active. Press Shift+Command/Ctrl+U to desaturate the layer. Undo this and look at it both ways to decide if you prefer the slight reddish color on her back or the desaturated version. Duplicate the layer again as **Light** and make the Layer Mask active. Press Command/Ctrl+I to invert the mask. Change the Blend mode to Screen at **30**% or Vivid Light at about **10**%. If you didn't desaturate the previous layer, you still might want to desaturate this one.

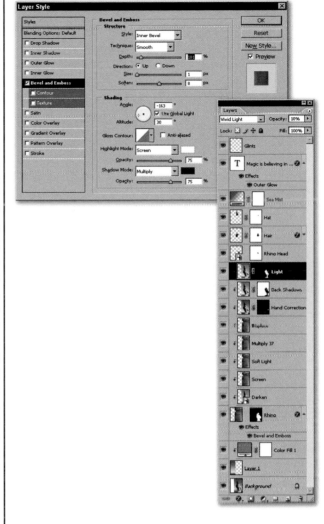

 (25) Save your work.

A short recap

Rhino lady is a combination of the absurd with the philosophical and says something, I hope, about the power of arranging an image to convey a message. It is what the movies would call a "concept shot." The content that is technically different in this technique is the many-layered approach to building the rhino skin on top of the woman's body. Here, we used a number of copies of the body without the displacement before multiplying a displaced copy into the mix. As you can see, you can also go back and tweak the final image to perfect it. The only other thing of note here is that we frequently had to contend with an unpleasant change in the way that Photoshop creates clipping masks (I won't be so unkind as to call it a bug). However, if you duplicate either the base layer or any internal layer in the clipping mask, you break the clipping mask and need to relink all of the layers. It isn't a major problem — but it is a major nuisance.

Magic is believing in yourself, if you can do that, you can make anything happen. Johann Wolfgang von Goethe

Meow Mix

Please pass the *cat*????

Maybe it's revenge for chasing Reiko, my friend's Siamese cat, around my studio. I collected 224 photos for the afternoon's effort. Most of them show only part of the cat or show unintended motion effects (translation: they're totally blurred). Oh well... Why put a cat in a bottle? At least the bottle stays still while being photographed! On a more practical note, however, you also learn how to insert something so that it looks enclosed in glass. You can use this to put goldfish in a bowl, create an ice cream parfait — or stuff your boss in a jar on a bad day.

THE PLAN

- Prepare the bottle and/or image background
- Distort and position the object(s) inside of the bottle
- Create the correct bottle highlights and shadows

1 Open the Bottle.psd image from the companion CD-ROM and duplicate it. Close the original. Add a new layer named **Bottle minus Back**. Using the Clone Stamp tool (Sample All layers checked) clone out parts of the inside of the bottle to get rid of the bottle back. Select the inside of the bottle and create an alpha channel named **Inside Bottle** from the selection.

TIP

Use the Pen tool because it gives you a smoother selection. Set it to create paths instead of a shape. Load the path as a selection to create the alpha channel. If you don't know how to use the Pen tool, then select the inside of the bottle with the Lasso tool or in QuickMask mode and save the selection as an alpha channel.

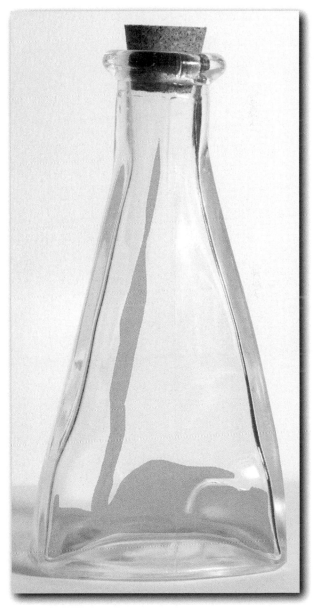

Photo: Sherry London

(2) Choose File⇨Place and pick Paws_and_Body.psd to add the cat image as a Smart Object. Set the W: field on the Options bar to **1547** pixels (the actual cat image size) and click the Maintain Aspect Ratio link icon to the right of it. Commit. Click the eye on the Inside Bottle alpha channel to see the red coating and then move the cat over the bottle. Choose Edit⇨Free Transform. Rotate the cat so that his body is straight and centered in the bottle alpha but don't commit yet.

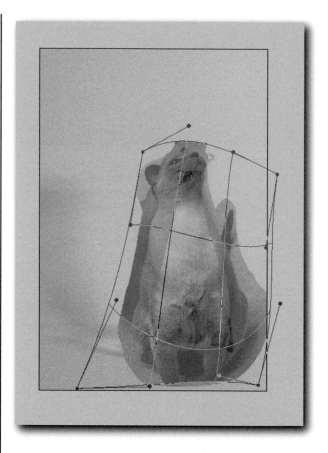

TIP

If you need to edit the live warping on the cat's body, you need to unlink the cat from the mask. This mask is the shape of the bottle, so don't warp that bottle-shaped mask.

TIP

The Place command defaults to making the new image the same size as the current file. To avoid resampling the placed image, always know the number of pixels in the width of the original image.

(3) Choose Edit⇨Transform⇨Warp. Get your image as close to the figure as possible and then commit the transform. Load the Inside Bottle channel as a selection and add a layer mask to the cat layer. Rename the layer **Kitty Body**. Turn off the eye on the Inside Bottle channel. Finally, click the Link icon between the mask and the layer thumbnail to turn it off.

(4) Double-click the Smart Object icon on the Kitty Body layer to reopen the original cat image. Make the Match Color Layer active in the cat image and press and hold Command/Ctrl+Option/Alt+Shift+E to create a new layer at the top of the layer stack. Name the layer **Liquify Layer** and then choose Filter⇨Liquify. Using very short strokes, a brush size of 600 pixels, and the Forward Warp tool. Nudge the belly fur down and out to both sides. Pull the hair beyond the outlines of the cat and obliterate the area where his legs begin. Try to keep the character of his fur. Click the Revert brush a few times in random areas. Change brush sizes as needed. Click OK to exit Liquify.

TIP

Saving the mesh before you exit the Liquify filter is a great timesaver. To change your effect, start with a fresh copy of the Liquify layer as it looked before being filtered. Go into Liquify and load the saved mesh. Your last effect is reapplied, and you can edit it by restoring the parts you hate and try something else.

TIP

Use the set of KB Brushes designed by Kathryn Bernstein to help you blend the hair on the cat. Load the KB_Brushes.abr file from the included CD-ROM by double-clicking the file on the Mac or by dragging the file into the open Photoshop application window on Windows. I used the KB_38 brush and altered the master Diameter to 60. This brush creates a more natural look to the cat's fur.

 Click the Close button on the Paws_and_Body.psd image and click OK to save the Smart Object file. Your warp effect immediately updates with the liquified cat. Paint out the neck of the bottle by using black in the layer mask of the Kitty Body layer. Then apply a Gaussian blur of 9 pixels to the layer mask to soften the edges. Add a new layer named **Bottom Fur**. Clone out any portions of the cat's original legs or any areas where the fur from the Liquify filter looks too wonky (such as the areas near the bottom corners of the bottle). Change the Blend mode to Lighten.

6 Now add the cat's paw. Double-click the Smart Object icon on the Kitty Body layer to open the original image. Choose Image⇨Duplicate⇨OK then close the original. In the copy, turn off the eye on the Liquify and Color Match layers and flatten the image. Make a loose Lasso selection of the leg area of the cat's left leg and drag the selection back into the bottle image. Name the new layer **Front paw 1** and drag it to the top of the layer stack. Control/right-click on the thumbnail and choose Group into New Smart Object from the pop-up menu. Close the **Paws_and_Body copy** image without saving it.

8 Choose the Brush tool and a very soft large brush (the 65-pixel brush works well). With black, paint on the mask to remove the extra area around the cat's paw. Leave some shading. Use a KB hairbrush to blend into the mask at the top of the leg. Don't worry if it isn't purrfect yet; you can fix that later.

7 Rotate the leg until it's pointing up and toward the left. Move the leg so the line that runs through the center of the bounding box lines up with the inside neck of the bottle. Then press and hold Shift and drag the bounding box down until one of the corners touches the bottom of the bottle. Widen the leg slightly. Commit. Load the Inside Bottle alpha channel as a selection and create a layer mask for the Front Paws layer.

9 Open the image Pawview2.psd. Make a loose lasso selection around the cat's right paw. Drag the selection into the bottle image and close the original. Control/right-click on the layer thumbnail and choose Group into New Smart Object. Name the layer **Front Paw2**. Next, choose Edit⇨Free Transform and move the leg into the bottle. Without committing, choose Edit⇨Transform⇨Flip Horizontal. Then rotate the leg to about -60 degrees. Widen the leg slightly and click the commit checkmark in the Options bar. Load the Inside Bottle alpha channel as a selection and create a layer mask for the Front Paw2 layer.

TIP

If it's easier to see where the edges of the bottle fall, turn on the eye on the Inside Bottle channel before you use the Edit⇨Transform command.

10 Choose the 65-pixel soft brush. Paint on the mask with black to remove the extra area around the cat's paw. Make a soft edge along the edge of the bottle by painting with white over the bottle edge in the layer mask to reveal more of the paw. Then switch to black and paint along the edge of the bottle to bring the paw back inside.

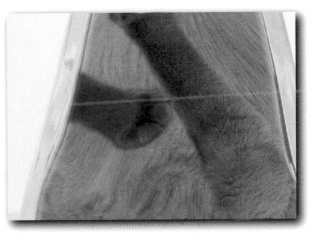

11 Choose File⇨Place and select the Tail.psd image. Change the Width on the Options bar to **1140** px and then click the Constrain Proportions link icon to the right. Click the Commit check mark. Name this Smart Object layer **Tail**.

12 Turn on the Inside Bottle Alpha channel. Choose Edit⇨Free Transform and move the tail to the bottom of the bottle. Rotate the tail to make it connect to the right side of the bottle. Widen it slightly. Then click the Warp icon on the Options bar. Curve the tail by pulling down on the center-bottom grid as shown. Click the Commit check mark to finish up.

13 Load the Inside Bottle alpha channel as a selection and create a layer mask for the tail. Turn off the eye on the alpha channel. Work on theTail layer mask to make the tail blend in. Again, leave a soft edge where the tail meets the bottle. Then add a Drop Shadow effect. I used a Distance of **22** and a Size of **70**.

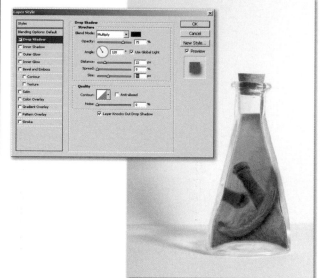

14 Choose File⇨Place and select the cat_head.psd image. Set the width to **1000** pixels and then click the link icon to set the height to the correct aspect ratio. Commit the place command. Name the Smart Object layer **Cat Head**.

15 Choose View⇨New Guide and add one horizontal guide at pixel **1395** and another one at pixel **1915** to create guides that help to size the cat's head. Turn on the Inside Bottle alpha channel. Drag the head to the bottle and press and hold Shift as you drag a corner point to size the head proportionally until it is the same height as the guides. Press and hold Option/Alt and drag the two sides of the head slightly closer. Then choose the Warp tool. Make the bottom of the cat's head a bit wider and bend the ears until they mostly fit inside the bottle as you see in the figure. Commit the transformation.

16 Turn off the Inside Bottle alpha channel. Load the alpha channel as a selection and create a layer mask for the head. Before you actually paint the layer mask, choose White as your foreground color. Add a new layer named **Whiskers**. Select the 5-pixel brush. In the Brushes palette, click the text on the left that says "Other Dynamics." In the Control field, click to drop down the menu. Choose Fade and set **75** as the fade amount.

TIP

I prefer to keep my units in pixels as pixels don't change regardless of image resolution. Even if you don't, and you prefer to work in inches, you can still add guides at a specific pixel by typing **px** after the number.

(17) On the Whiskers layer, start at the cat's face and drag out whiskers by tracing over the ones that are actually there. Exactitude isn't required. The white is much too bright, but not to worry. Click the Cat's Head layer to make it active. Click the layer mask thumbnail in the Layers palette. With a soft black brush, mask outside the cat's face to hide the background. Cover the whiskers that are in the real image. Add a drop shadow effect using the settings shown. Click OK.

(18) Double-click the Cat_head Smart Object icon to open it. Duplicate the Background layer. Change the cat's expression by choosing Filter⇨Liquify. With the Forward Warp tool and a brush about the same size as the cat's eye, pull the left side of the cat's face out just a bit. Move his eyes just a little bit closer together. Then use the Bloat tool near the top of his pupils to make his eye bulge a bit (wouldn't yours, if you were being stuffed in a bottle?). Save the mesh and click OK to exit. Don't close the original cat-head image yet.

(19) While still working in the cat-head image, Lasso the top of the cat's left ear and drag it into the main bottle image. Name the layer **Cat's Ear**. Close and save the original Cat_Head image. Make the new Cat's Ear layer active. Drag the ear tip in position at the top of the cat's left ear. Rotate the tip of the ear to make it bend into the bottle. Add a layer mask and mask the ear tip to blend into the main ear. The ear should look as if it bent when the cat was forced into the jar.

(20) Make the Whiskers layer active. Press and hold the Option/Alt and choose a Solid Color Fill layer from the New Fill or Adjustment Layer icon at the bottom of the Layers palette. Click the Use Previous Layer as Clipping Mask check box. Choose a medium gray for the fill color. Click OK. In the layer mask of the Fill layer, choose a 100-pixel soft brush and black. Just brush over the very tips of the whiskers with the very large soft brush to tone the whiskers from gray at the cat's face to near white at the tips.

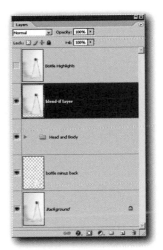

(22) The trick to making something look as if it's inside of a bottle is to add the bottle's reflections to the object inside. Double-click on the Blend-If layer to open the Layer Options dialog box. Set the White Blend-If: This layer slider to 203-239. Set the Black Blend-If: Underlying Layer to 52-80 as shown. These values should reveal a bit more of the darks in the cat body and out a film of white over the rest of the bottle. Click OK.

(21) Now for some housekeeping: To simplify the layers palette, select all the cat's body and head layers in the Layers palette and choose New Group from Layers in the Layers palette menu. Turn off the eye on the Head and Body group folder. Make the Bottle Minus Back layer active and press Shift+Command/Ctrl+Option/Alt+E to create a merged layer. Turn the eye for the Head and Body group folder back on and drag the folder below the new layer. Make Layer 1 active and rename it **Blend-If**. Duplicate that layer and name the duplicate **Bottle Highlights**. Then turn off the eye and make the Blend-If layer active.

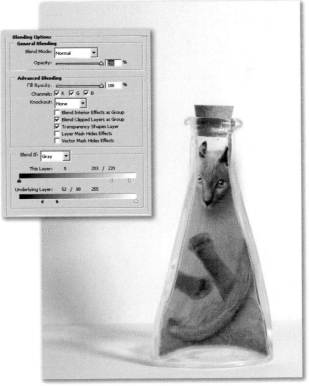

23 Make the Bottle Highlights layer active. To create a special mask for this layer that only lets the brightest spots through, Command/Ctrl-click on the RGB channel in the Channels palette. This loads the values in the Bottle Highlights layer as a selection. (It creates a grayscale selection with the lighter shades selected.) Add a layer mask to the Bottle Highlights layer and make the mask active. Then load the Inside Bottle alpha channel as a selection. Choose Select Inverse and fill the selection with black to hide it. Deselect. Leave the layer mask active and choose Image⇨Adjustments⇨Levels. Set the Black Input point to 222, the Gamma to .55, and the White point to 255, or use the values that best say "bottle on top" to you.

24 Drag the opacity on the Blend-If layer to 58 percent. Make the Head and Body folder layer active. Option/Alt-click on the eye for that folder layer to make it the only visible layer. Press Shift+Command/Ctrl+Option/Alt+E to create a merged layer. Name the layer **Color Restore** and drag it to the top of the layer stack. Option/Alt-click on the Add Layer Mask icon to create a "hide-all" mask (filled with black) on the Color Restore layer. Use a 200-pixel brush at **30 to 40** percent opacity and paint with white to restore some of the color and detail on the cat's body. Then switch to an opacity of **10 to 20** percent and cut down the intensity of the bright white highlights just a little bit.

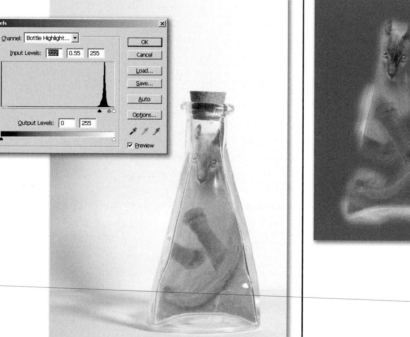

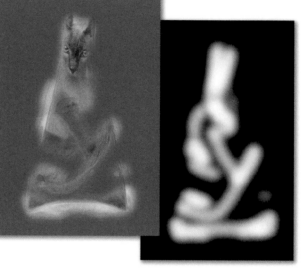

25 Add a Gaussian Blur of about **11** to soften the layer mask.

26 Only the gentle reflection for the bottom of the bottle remains undone. Choose the Pen tool and set the icon to Create Paths. Make a path around the inside of the glass bottom of the bottle and then load it as a selection.

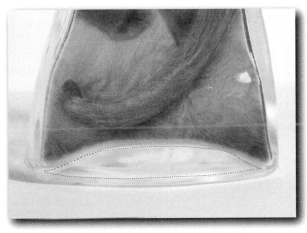

27 Drag the selection marquee up until it is on top of the cat's tail area and only contains cat. Choose Select⇨Transform Selection. Then choose Edit⇨Transform⇨Flip Vertical. Commit the transform. Choose Edit⇨Copy Merged and the Edit⇨Paste Into. You'll get a new layer and a layer mask. Name the layer **Reflection**. Make sure that the layer and the layer mask are linked and choose Edit⇨Transform⇨Flip Vertical. Drag the layer back to the bottom of the bottle. Add a Gaussian Blur of **11** to the layer mask. Change the Blend mode to Linear Light and the opacity of the layer to **50%**. Admire and save the result! You might want to add some additional glints or highlights as your artistic sense dictates, but it probably isn't necessary. A good brush should remove all the cat hairs on your clothes!

A short recap

What else can you stuff in a bottle? Probably just about anything else that won't land you in jail. The basic technique is to get your bottle image and make a selection of the inside of the bottle. Using that selection, deface, deform, liquify, or warp your object to conform to the shape of the bottle. Then put your bottle layer back on top and use a combination of Blend-If and highlight extraction to make the bottle look as if it's really on top of the object.

If you're using a round (cylinder) bottle such as a canning jar, you might also want to take a combined image of the bottle contents and add a Spherize filter to deform the object so that it looks rounded as well. To do this using the best nondestructive practices, make a Smart Object of the entire bottle contents and place your merged layer as the top layer of the Smart Object. Then filter that top layer. When you close the Smart Object, the deformed layer is the layer under the bottle.

A Wolf in Sheep's Clothing

The secret of success in a realistic (or surrealistic) image composite is paying attention to every tiny detail. The process can be tedious, but it isn't particularly hard; it requires basic Clone Stamp and layer masking skills — and a lot of patience. Here, you put the proverbial wolf into a sheep's skin. If this were a 3D program, you'd be able to manipulate both the wolf and the sheep and position them so that they face the same direction and have the same body lines. However, we don't have that luxury, and the images of the wolf were not taken with the composite in mind. Most of the wolf images come to you courtesy of Dan Bacon, who has been photographing wolves for many years at the Lakota Wolf Preserve in northern New Jersey (www.lakotawolf.com). I took all of the sheep images at the Sheep and Wool show in Howard County, Maryland.

THE PLAN

- Put the sheep in the field
- Add the main sheep
- Add the wolf's features and blend
- Touch up, perfect, and frame and crop

TIP

I already selected the scene for you to make this easier. I could have (and probably should have) masked the image rather than deleting, but you have enough to work with — and I have the original layers safely tucked away. My first file composite was 130MB, and didn't want to really over-burden your computers.

(1) Open the image Field.psd from the book's CD-ROM. Here's where the action takes place. Then open the image Flock_of_Sheep.psd. These are the poor innocent victims of the big, bad wolf (okay, that's not very politically correct today when we need to preserve the wolf as an endangered species; but wolves still love sheep — even if people aren't really on the menu very often).

Photos: Sherry London

(2) Drag the Flock_of_Sheep image into the Field image. It fits well, but then there's no room for the wolf. Control/Right-click the layer palette entry and choose Group into New Smart Object. Press Command/Ctrl+T and type **528** px in the W: field in the Options bar. Click the Maintain Aspect Ratio link between the Width and Height fields to have Photoshop calculate the correct height and click the Commit icon. Move the sheep up on the hill for now. Name the layer **Flock**. You can close the original (on this and the other "drag into" steps) once you add it to the field image.

3 Open the image Sheep2Wolf.psd on the included CD-ROM. Drag the sheep image into the Field image. Name the layer **Sheep**. Group into a new Smart Object. Press Command/Ctrl+T and type **-648 px** as the Width. Click the Constrain Aspect Ratio link. Remove the minus sign from the Height field to make the sheep stand up again (a wolf dressed as a sheep that's on its back isn't even remotely threatening). Click Commit. Move the sheep fairly close to the flock. Double-click the Sheep Smart Object to open it for editing. Add a Layer mask. Using black, remove most of the background from the sheep. Leave edges of background around the sheep and leave the straw where the shadow is. Click the Close box on the Smart Object window and then click Yes to the prompt to save the changes.

4 Open the WolfBack.psd image from the book Web site and drag it into the field image. Name the layer **Tail**. Make it into a Smart Object. Double-click the Smart Object to open it for editing. Make a loose selection around the wolf's tail with the Lasso tool. Then add a Layer mask. Use black to hide everything in the image but the tail. You need to actually mask the hairs on the tail that go into the background. This time, we need a tight mask. You can put in tail wisps later if needed. Click the Close box and then click Yes. If the mask isn't correct, reopen the Smart Object. Continue to alter the mask until you can only see the wolf's tail from this image. Position the tail on the sheep and press Command/Ctrl+T. Press and hold Shift as you adjust a corner point to resize in proportion. Commit.

Photo: Dan Bacon

5 Open the RockWolf.psd image from the book's CD-ROM and drag it into the field image. Name the layer **Head**. Make it into a Smart Object. Double-click the Smart Object to open it for editing. Make a loose selection around the wolf's head with the Lasso tool. Then add a Layer mask. Use a very soft brush to prepare the left side of the wolf's head. Use the same soft brush under his neck. Leave the fur around his chest. Use a harder brush around his ears. Use a slightly softer brush on the right and mask fairly close. Don't close the Smart Object yet.

High Pass Sharpening

High Pass sharpening is very useful. Objects with tiny detail need a low radius setting and images that have coarser detail can stand a higher setting. So long as you change the layer mode to Overlay before you filter, you can always see the results in the filter preview. Each image will have a sweet spot that makes it look sharp. You only need to move the slider until you find it.

(7) Open the ComstockWolf.psd image from the book Web site and drag it into the field image. Name the layer **Mouth**. Make it into a Smart Object. Double-click the Smart Object to open it for editing. Make a loose selection around the wolf's mouth and snout area with the Lasso tool. Then add a Layer mask. Make a fairly tight mask with a semihard brush. Click the Close box and click Yes to save. Move the mouth into position on the wolf's head and press Command/Ctrl+T. Place a minus sign in front of the number in the W: field to flip the mouth horizontally. You need to enlarge this a bit — to about 112 percent. Make sure that the new snout covers the old one. Commit.

(6) Duplicate the Head layer in the Smart Object and Control/right-click on the layer entry. Name the layer **High Pass 1.8**. Delete the Layer Mask. Press Command/Ctrl+Option/Alt+G to create a clipping group. Change the Blend mode to Overlay. The wolf's head really needs to be sharpened. Use the High Pass filter to sharpen it. Choose Filter⇨Other⇨High Pass and choose a Radius of **1.8**. Click OK. Click the Close box on the Smart Object and click Yes to save it. Move the head over the sheep and press Command/Ctrl+T. Resize about **57** percent in both height and width. Slide the wolf's head so that it mostly covers the sheep's head. Commit.

Photo: www.comstock.com

(8) Open the StealthWolf.psd image from the book Web site and drag it into the field image. Name the layer **HandPaws**. Make it into a Smart Object. Double-click the Smart Object to open it for editing. Make a loose selection around the wolf's two hind paws with the Lasso tool. Select enough of the top of the legs to enable the legs to grow believably out of the sheep. Then add a Layer mask. Make a

fairly tight mask with a semihard brush. Click the Close box and click Yes to save. Drag the legs into position on the sheep's hind quarters. I moved the Smart Object layer so that it's just above the Sheep layer in the Layers palette.

Photo: Dan Bacon

9. To get the first front paw, you need to copy the Hind Paws layer by Control/right-clicking the HindPaws layer and choosing New Smart Object via Copy (see the following Tip). Name the layer **Front Paw 1**. Then open the Smart Object, trash the Layer mask, Lasso the front-most front paw, create a new layer mask, and so on (you should know the drill by now). Close and save the Smart Object. Then make a new Smart Object via Copy from this layer and rename it **Front Paw 2**. Repeat the same steps on the back front paw. You'll need to resize this paw however. Press Command/Ctrl+T and resize to about **84** percent. Download the RockWolf image from the book's CD-ROM. Make a New Smart Object via Copy from the Head layer and name it **Paw Patch**. Open it for editing and repeat the same steps. After you save it, move the Paw Patch under the Front Paw 1 layer. Resize to about **50** percent high and then widen the paw so that it looks like it fits properly. The color is different, but we can fix that later.

10. Now it's time to trim the sheep down to size. Double-click the Sheep Smart Object to open it for editing. In the layer mask, use black and a **30** percent hard brush to mask out the head and legs and then remove most of the background that still remains in the sheep image. Keep the irregular outlines of the wool but try to get rid of the dark areas. If you have to sacrifice one for the other, go for the irregular outlines. You can Clone Stamp wool back over these dark areas later. When you have the sheep cleaned up (but not sheared), click the Close box and then click Yes to save the result. Move the sheep Smart Object layer above all the legs layers in the Layers palette. Then select the Sheep, Head, Tail, and Mouth layers and position the sheep2wolf over the legs to a height that looks convincing. This animal is taller than the original sheep. The image is starting to look a lot better. And yes, I know that the shadow is weird now.

TIP

I'm not really sure what to call our camouflaged wolf. However, the Sheep and Wool show features popular contests that have a group of people shear a sheep, then spin the fleece and dye the wool and finally knit a shawl. The event is called Sheep to Shawl, so it seems appropriate to name our combined animal sheep2wolf! By the way, the Web site for the Sheep and Wool show is www.sheepandwool.org.

(11) Select the Front Paw 1 and the Paw Patch layers. Group into a New Smart Object. Open the Smart Object for editing. Make the Paw Patch layer active and add a new empty layer above it. Name it **Paw Patch Color**. Press Command/Ctrl+Option/Alt+G to make a Clipping Mask. Choose the Clone Stamp tool with Sample All Layers checked in the Options bar. Clone the fur from the Front Paw 1 layer over the Paw Patch leg that is exposed. Then reduce the opacity of the Paw Patch Color layer so you can see the original foot. Add a Layer Mask. Remove the area between the toes (so you can see the individual toes) and over the left stem. Return the layer opacity to about **64** percent and click the Close box on the Smart Layer. Then click Yes to save the object.

(12) Select the Hind Paws, Front Paw 1, and Front Paw 2 layers. Group into a New Smart Object. You now need to color correct the legs. Press and hold Option/Alt and choose a new Solid Color Fill layer. In the New Layer dialog box, name the layer **Leg Color** and click the Use Previous Layer to Create Clipping Mask check box. Select Color as the Mode. I chose RGB: **111, 100, 90** as the fill color, but you can pick a color from either the sheep's wool or the wolf's face if you prefer a different one. Click OK to close the Color Picker. You now have a choice to make (though you can change your mind as you wish). Do you want the wolf to have wolf-colored legs or sheep-colored legs? Wolf legs are light; sheep legs are dark. In either case, Option/Alt-click and add a Levels layer to the clipping mask (named **Leg Values**). For light legs, move the Gamma slider to about **1.30**. For dark legs, drag the Gamma slider to about **.58** or lower. If you opt for the light legs, add another Levels layer (named **Rear Front Paw**) to the clipping mask. Set the Gamma slider to **0.52** and click OK. Fill the mask with black and paint in the rear front paw with white. Change the layer opacity to about **64** percent.

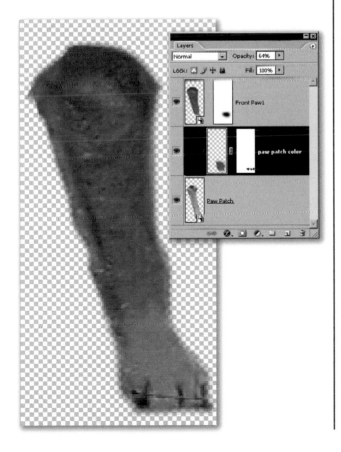

13 The rear hind paw needs fixing. Open the Paws Smart Object for editing and then open the HindPaws Smart Object. Lasso select the rear paw and press Command/Ctrl+J. Name the layer **Rear Hind Paw**. Turn off the eye on the layer. Make the Layer Mask on the HindPaws layer active and hide the leg you just copied. Then make the Rear Hind Paw layer active and add a Layer Mask. Remove the background. Drag the layer lower in the layer stack. Once the leg is in its own layer, move it up a bit and just to the left a tiny bit. Close and Smart Objects. You might need to do this a number of times until the leg is correctly positioned. In the Rear Front Paw Levels layer, paint over the newly positioned rear back paw with white as well. Rename the layer **Rear Paws**.

14 Make the Mouth layer active and add a new empty layer. Name the layer **More Wool**. Use the Clone Stamp tool to add more wool to the wolf's legs and under his belly (you need to have Use All Layers selected in the Options bar). You want to get the look of a fleece thrown over the wolf; and you want to accentuate the shaggy look of the wool. Clone more shaggies over the white sunlit area on the sheep's neck. Then work on his head area. Bring some of the fleece over his head between his ears. Blend his face fur into the wool by lengthening some of his fur and alternating with some locks of wool. Stamp some areas of the short curly wool on his back over his snout. For this, don't paint — just stamp and then move the Source location and stamp again.

15 The shadow on the sheep2wolf is the next thing to fix. With the Lasso tool, draw a selection around the current shadow. The shadow is much too far back. Use the Marquee tool to move just the selection ants to where they look right. With the selection active, click the Flock layer in the Layers palette and then add a Solid Color Fill layer filled with black. Set the layer opacity to about **46%**. Add to the shadow area as you think is needed and then choose Filter⇨Blur⇨ Gaussian Blur, and type a Radius of **7.5**. Click OK.

TIP

If you have a lot of trouble getting the legs in the right position, drag both layers from the Smart object back into the main image and position the rear hind leg in relation to front hind leg. Then Drag both layers at the same time back into the open Smart layer.psb file. Position the legs by moving both layers at the same time so that the front hind paw is directly on top of the original one. At this point then, you have the new legs in the correction location. Drag the two old leg layers to the trashcan and save the Smart Object.

16 Double-click the Flock layer to open it for editing. Duplicate the Flock layer and name it **Lens Blur**. Choose Filter⇨Blur⇨Lens Blur. Change the Radius field to 8 and click OK. Reduce the layer opacity to **75%**. Press Command/Ctrl+Option/Alt+G to make a Clipping Mask. Add a layer mask and fill it with black. Paint the effect back on in white in the Layer mask only over the sheep. When you paint the front-most sheep, use the brush at **50%** opacity. This keeps the front sheep a bit more sharp than the others. Make the Flock layer active and add a Layer Mask. With a very soft brush, remove as much of the grass as you can but leave the shadows. Don't reduce the opacity of the sheep by masking. Leave enough grass around the sheep that you can blend in with a layer mask in the image. Then click the Close button and click Yes to save the Smart Object. In the image add a Layer Mask to the Flock Smart Object and paint out any grass that looks odd.

17 On the stage, a spotlight indicates the main player and the place to look. It focuses your attention on the critical area. In this photo, a spotlight looks even less believable than our sheep2wolf. However, we can use the graphic device of fading back color in the less important areas so that we spotlight the wolf. Choose the Crop tool and drag the Crop marquee around the wolf and sheep. Keep some of the sky and some area on either side of the image beyond the main players. On the Options bar, select the Hide option so that you don't actually remove imagery. Commit.

New Smart Object via Copy

New Smart Object via Copy is significantly different than dragging the Smart Object to the New Layer icon to duplicate it. When you choose New Smart Layer via Copy, you break the link between the objects. You actually get an unrelated Smart Object that can be altered independently. All you are really copying is the original source object. We need to do this because each leg uses a different part of the same wolf. If masks on the Smart Object could be linked in the Layers palette, we wouldn't need to do it this way. But I want you to be able to rearrange the body parts without needing to remask (at least as much as possible), so this is the best way. If your file is getting to too large, you can crop the Smart Objects while they are open for editing to only leave the leg of interest.

18 Now to make the spotlight. Make the More Wool layer active. Add a new layer and fill it with your foreground color (the color doesn't matter). Name the layer **Knockout**. Press Command/Ctrl+T and type **55%** in the W: field. Then click the Constrain Aspect Ratio link to set the Height to 55 percent as well. Commit. Make the More Wool layer active again and add a white Solid Color Fill layer named **Screening**. Select the Screening and the Knockout layer and press Command/Ctrl+G to group them. Name the group **Spotlight**. Expand the group and make the Knockout layer active. Double-click the layer entry to open the Layer Style dialog box. Change the Fill Opacity to **0** percent and change the Knockout to Shallow. Add a Drop Shadow effect. Deselect the Use Global Light option. Set the Angle to **120** degrees and choose Distance of **20** px with a Size of **28** px. Click OK.

19 Make the Screening layer active and lower the layer Opacity to about **60%**. Then make the Knockout layer active. Use the Move tool and drag the layer to whatever portion of the image you most want to highlight. At the moment, it is perfectly centered.

20 Make any other adjustments that you feel the image needs and then save your work.

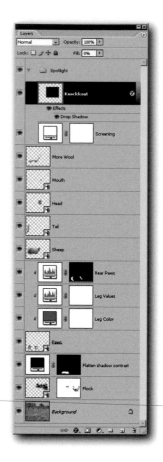

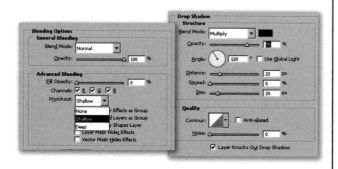

TIP

To use Shallow Knockout, you need to create the group. Shallow Knockout reveals the layer under a Group folder when the Fill opacity of the knockout layer is at 0 percent. The really useful thing about this is that you can move this layer anywhere to automatically change the image revealed.

A short recap

A Wolf in Sheep's Clothing is straight image processing—a lot of layer masking and fitting things together. Because many of the elements needed to be resized, the Smart Object technology provides the most nondestructive way to composite. The tricky thing with Smart Objects is trying to keep their layer masks together. The only way to make that happen is to mask the image inside of the Smart Object. You did learn a few other tricks though. Knockout has a lot of power. It seems odd, but it gives you a way to have a live window into the image. Even if something changes, you don't need to re-create the top two layers. You also saw how to work with the Smart Objects even if you need to redo something inside one of them. Finally, you tried out High Pass sharpening. Every image needs some type of sharpening and the High Pass method gives you incredible control over how the image is sharpened. Try it on your other images as well.

All Dressed Up

Magazines with pictures of dressed-up cats and dogs sit on the shelves of your local bookstores. But what do you do at midnight when you have the urge to dress up a pet to send in an e-mail to your friends? That's never happened to you? Oh well... You use the same skills if you need to change the clothing a model is wearing after the photo shoot. One key skill is cloning from clothing articles that are not quite the right size or in exactly the position needed. You have a straight boa for example and need it curved. After all, a cat's got to have feathers...

THE PLAN

- Add the dress
- Accessorize

(1) Open the image Icecreamgirl.psd from the book Web site. Choose Image⇨Image Size. Increase the image size by 140 percent. The Constrain Proportions and Resample Image check boxes must be checked. Use Bicubic Sharper as the Interpolation method. Click OK. Double-click the Background layer to change it into a 'real' layer. Name the layer BlueDress. Control/right-click the entry in the Layers palette and choose Group into New Smart Object.

(2) Double-click the BlueDress Smart Object to open it for editing. Set the Magic Wand to a Tolerance of 20 with the Contiguous and Anti-alias check boxes checked. Click the white background of the dress image. Press and hold Shift and click the unselected white background areas to add them to the selection. Press Shift+Command/Ctrl+I to inverse the selection. Add a layer mask. Choose the Pen tool and set the result icon at the left of the Options bar to Create Paths. Draw a path around the dress that selects the edges of the dress where you can see the inside of the back of the dress. However, the cat is wider than the child, so don't follow the outer edge the whole way around. Leave only curve points — the dress has no sharp edges. Once you have the path made, add a Vector mask.

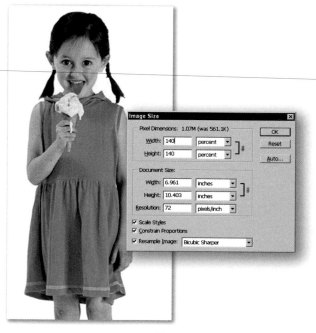

Photo: www.comstock.com

TIP

If you don't like to use the Pen tool you may certainly just adjust the layer mask. However, you need to use a hard-edged brush to get a sharp edge on the dress. Why not try the Freeform Pen tool with the Magnetic option selected and see that makes it easier for you to create the path.

③ Add a new layer (named Cloning) to the Smart Object image file. Press Command/Ctrl+Option/Alt+G to create a Clipping Mask. Choose the Clone Stamp tool with the Use All Layers option selected in the Options bar. Clone the dress over the ice cream and the arms. Carefully match the shadows on the dress. You need to use a lot of short stamping strokes and change location points frequently. Mostly, you need to preserve the folds in the dress as you clone. You also need to remove the shadows from the girl's arm on the dress. When you clone, follow a fold up and then down to make the folds work from the neck to the waist. Also make sure to remove the white arm-band from the right side (your right) of the dress. Click the Close box on the Smart Object file and then click Yes to the prompt to save the changes.

④ Open the Cat.psd image. Now that you can see both the dress and the cat, we have a problem. The cat is facing a different direction and isn't full front as is the child. Make the dress layer active and press Command/Ctrl+G to make it into a Group. Name the group **Blue Dress**. Drag the group into the Cat image from the icecreamgirl image. Expand the group so you can see the layer. Let's dig out the cat's front leg (on the right side of the image) first. Turn off the eye on the BlueDress layer. Draw a path around the cat's front leg where it overlaps the dress. When the path is complete, leave it selected. Add a Solid Color Fill layer above it (the color doesn't matter). The path becomes the vector mask to the layer. Double-click the layer entry away from the text on the entry to open the Layer Style dialog box. Change the Fill opacity for the layer to **0**. Then change the Knockout to Shallow. Voila! One leg revealed. Click OK to close the dialog box.

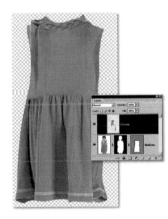

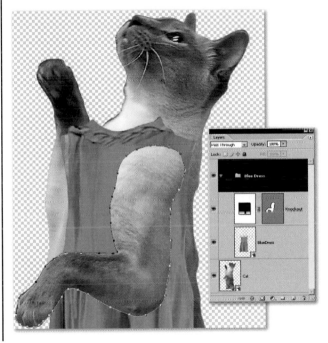

5 Duplicate the Blue Dress Smart Object layer as **BlueDress Rasterized** and rasterize it. Then make it into a new Smart Object. Press Command/Ctrl+T. Click the Warp icon on the Options bar. Pull on the warp grid to make the dress conform to the shape of the cat. To widen the neckline while compressing the shoulder, you need to drag toward the left from the top-center grid square on the Warp grid. You also need to lengthen the right side of the dress to end up with one that is even with the cat. Make sure that you pull the areas that contain the bottom inside of the dress hem so that they are outside the cat. Click Commit. The front leg has a problem, but let's see what remains after we add a sleeve.

TIP

The original BlueDress has a lot of hidden areas in it. You can't warp the dress effectively with all that unused space; you only get nine grid squares regardless of how large the object is. However, making the rasterized version into its own Smart Object preserves editablity on the warping and you still have the original as a safety backup.

6 Open the image Pinafore.psd from the book Web site. You need to prepare this image in its own file. We'll only use it in pieces, and it would be too confusing to prepare it in the same image. Duplicate the Background layer. Name the layer **Collar**. In this step, you're only going to borrow the collar area from the dress. Control/right-click the layer entry to choose Group into New Smart Object. You need to make a Smart Object because you need to adjust the collar on the dress. Double-click to open the Smart Object for editing. Very carefully remove everything from the layer but the collar and ribbon. I used a Path to select the collar and ribbon similar to what I did on BlueDress. When the path is complete, press Command/Ctrl as you click to add a Layer Mask so that you add a Vector mask instead. Then add an empty layer and press Command/Ctrl+Option/Alt+G to make a Clipping mask. Name the clipped layer **Cloning**. Clone out the shadows on the collar. Click the Close box on the Smart Object file and click Yes to save the file. Drag the Smart Object layer from the Pinafore file's layer palette into the Cat image.

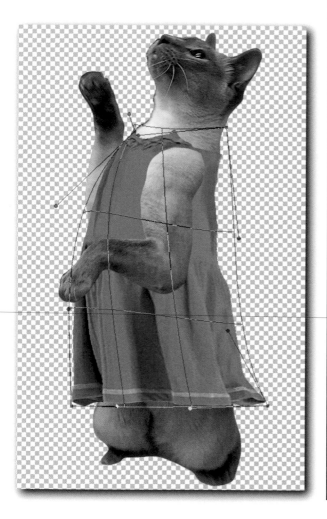

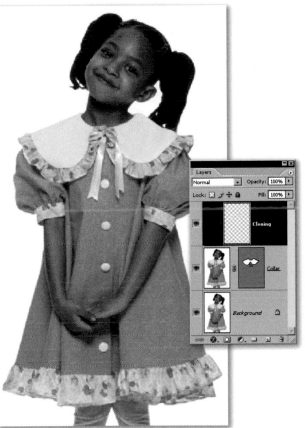

Photo: www.comstock.com

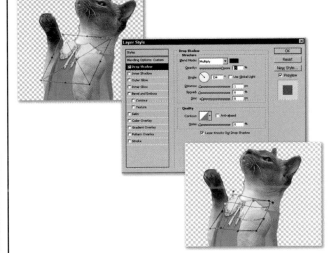

7 Duplicate the Collar Smart Object layer and rasterize it. Name the rasterized layer **Collar Rasterized**. Make that layer into a Smart Object and turn off the original Collar Smart Object layer. Press Command/Ctrl+T. You want to get the collar to fit the cat between the neck and the leg. Not much of the collar should end up to the right of the arm. I found that using normal scaling and a bit of Option/Alt moving of some corner handles gets me very close to where I want the collar to be. Then click the Warp icon to finish it up. Push the collar around until it fits on the dress. You want to try to keep the ribbon closer to the center of the real neckline. Commit. Add a Drop Shadow effect to the Collar Smart Object layer. Uncheck the Use Global Light check box and set the Angle to **134** degrees, Distance to **1**, and Size of **8**. Click OK.

8 Make the Pinafore image active. You can trash the Collar Smart Object layer. Choose Image⇨Image Size and enlarge to **140** percent as you did with the BlueDress image. Draw a Pen path around the flounce of the girl's dress. If you look closely at the flounce, you see that there is fabric that is attached to the front of her dress. You also see fabric that is actually attached to the back of the dress but that shows under the front flounce. You only want to select the fabric on the front of the dress. Save the path as Flounce. Command/Ctrl-click on the path to load it as a selection. Choose Select⇨Feather⇨Feather Radius:1 and click OK. Drag the selected flounce into the Cat image above or below the collar.

TIP

When you create the path, don't leave any corner points. Instead, leave a point on the straight area somewhat near the corner and drag a direction point then place a new point around the curve and pull out a direction point. Let the path form a curve as it goes around a corner.

9 In the Cat image, name the new layer **Flounce**. Make it into a Smart Object. Position the object on the hemline of the dress and try to match up the undulations on both dress and flounce. Your image is likely to differ from mine, but the figure shows how I made the first match. Duplicate the Flounce Smart Object as **Flounce2**. Repeat the same process to locate a part of the flounce that fits the other side of the dress. I scrunched up the flounce by dragging the side handle. Then I used the Warp control to try to get the gathers to fit the rest of the hemline. Commit. Add a Layer Mask to both Smart Object layers and mask out the parts of the flounce that are off the dress. Option/Alt-click the eye on the Flounce layer to make it the only visible layer. Than click the eye on the Flounce 2 object to turn it back on. Press Shift+Comnmand/Ctrl+Option/Alt+E to make a merged layer of the two layers. Name this layer **Second Flounce**. Add a Stroke effect of 1 pixel, centered, in Multiply mode at **36**% opacity. Choose a blue from the dress as a stroke color. Click OK. Move the stroked flounce up just a tiny bit as if it were another ruffle on the dress. Turn on all of the layers except the BlueDress and the Collar (you only need the rasterized versions of these layers).

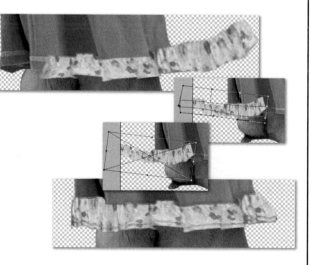

10 Make the Pinafore image active again. This time, we're going to create a sleeve. First, however, we need to recolor the dress to match the blue dress. Duplicate the Background layer as **Match Color**. Turn off the Background layer and make the Match Color layer active. Use the Magic Wand tool at Tolerance **20**, Anti-alias On, and Contiguous On, and click the white background. Press and hold Shift and click to add the other white areas to the selection. Then press and hold Option/Alt and add a layer mask that removes the selected areas. Make the layer active. Choose Image⇨Adjustments⇨Match Color. Set the Source to the Cat image and the Layer to BlueDress. Click OK. Make the mask active and brush out the lighter fabric attached to both sleeves.

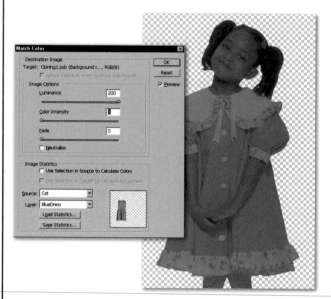

11 Press Shift+Command/Ctrl+Option/Alt+E to create a merged layer above the other two layers. Select each sleeve and copy each sleeve to a new layer (again, I used the Pen tool to create paths and I saved each path). Turn off the other layers. Rotate each sleeve so that the cuff is horizontal. Bring the Right sleeve over the left sleeve. Add a layer mask to the Right sleeve layer. Use the 100-pixel brush with black and hold it away from the left side of the sleeve. Press and let the soft edge of the brush just eat away at the opacity of the sleeve where it overlaps the left one. Create another merged layer. Use the Clone Stamp with the 19-pixel hard brush to just stamp in the area where the two parts of the sleeve don't meet at the top (you are trying to create one unified sleeve — and the shape is what you are interested in right now). Add a Cloning layer and clip it to the sleeve. Clone the blue fabric over the collar fabric on the sleeves. Leave the cuff alone. Make sure that you clone some of the shadows into the area. Finally, select all of the layers in the image and group into a new Smart Object. Name the object **Sleeve**. Open the Sleeve for editing and re-create the Cloning layer clipping mask that came undone when you created the Smart Object. Drag the Smart Object into the Cat image and place it above the Knockout layer.

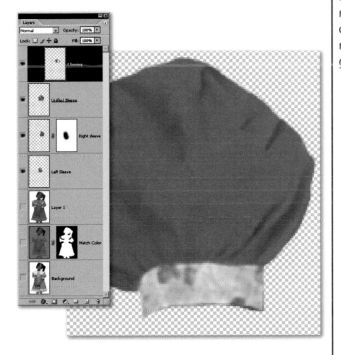

TIP

To make sure that you've not left any white edges on the sleeve, add a black Solid Color Fill layer under the unified layer in the Pinafore image, and if you see any white edges, just clone over them in the Cloning layer. Then delete the Color Fill layer before you make the pinafore into a Smart Object.

(12) Duplicate the Sleeve Smart Object as **Sleeve Rasterized**. Rasterize the Smart Object and Command/Ctrl-click the layer thumbnail to create a selection. Choose Select⇨Feather⇨3 pixels, and click OK. Add a Layer Mask. Then Group into a Smart Object. Press Command/Ctrl+T and enlarge the image about **180** percent. Then click the Warp icon. You need to try to position

the sleeve to cover up to the neckline and over the back of the dress. You also need to get the cuff on the sleeve to cover all of the width of the cat's arm. You need to move the sleeve down a little bit to cover the arm. Part of the trick is to force the cuff to be wide without making the entire sleeve huge. Keep pushing the top of the sleeve down and move the warp grid both by moving the image inside the grid and by moving the lines and points on the warp itself. When you like the result, commit. If you still need to move things around, press Command/Ctrl+T and choose the Warp icon again. You can repeat as often as you need with no image degradation. Collapse the BlueDress group. The dress is done.

TIP

The purpose of the layer mask is to soften the sharp edges of the sleeve. If you haven't used the Pen tool to select the sleeves, you can skip that step.

13 Now we need to accessorize. Open the Handbag.psd image. This image will do double duty. In this step, it's going to be a necklace. Duplicate the Handbag image (Image⇨Duplicate⇨OK). Choose Image⇨Rotate Canvas⇨ **180** degrees. Duplicate the Background layer and name it **Necklace**. With the Tolerance to **20** and Anti-alias and Contiguous On, click the white background on the Necklace layer. Click to pick up any other areas of white. Press and hold Option/Alt and add a layer mask. Then remove everything but the beaded handle of the handbag. Add a Bevel and Emboss layer style and accept the defaults but drag the Shadow opacity to **50%**. Click OK. Control/right-click the layer entry and choose Group into New Smart Object. Name the object **Necklace** and drag it into the Cat image just below the Knockout layer. Press Command/Ctrl+T and rotate it about 21 degrees. Push in the sides to about **86** percent and move the necklace down so that the bottom is under the ribbon on the cat's collar. Click OK.

Make a loose Lasso selection around the boa over the left shoulder (your left). Add a layer mask. Drag the layer into the Cat image. Now that you can see it in place; add to the layer mask to remove the image areas that should not be there and to make the boa fit nicely over the cat's left arm and around her neck. I like the sting of pearls thrown so casually over her arm, so I left it that way. Use a soft brush. Collapse the BlueDress group and then click the Cat layer to make it active.

Photo: www.comstock.com

Photo: www.comstock.com

14 Open the image RedHatBoa.psd. Choose Image⇨ Image Size and resample the image to **200** percent with Bicubic Smoother interpolation. Duplicate the Background layer as **Boa** and turn off the eye on the Background layer.

15 Open the BackBoa.psd file from the book Web site. This is also a piece of a Comstock image; however, I already created a Smart Object for you. Drag the BackBoa Smart Object into the Cat image. Drag the BackBoa Smart Object layer under the Cat layer. Position the boa to the right of the image and press Command/Ctrl+T. Rotate the boa so it looks as if it's a continuation of the front boa. Move it so that you don't need to mask anything and the edge of the boa is trailing nicely along, lower than the cat's hemline. Commit. Make the collapsed BlueDress layer active.

Photo: www.comstock.com

16 Open the Handbag.psd image again. Duplicate the Background layer as **Handbag**. Add a black Solid Color Fill layer on to the Background layer so you can judge the masking. Make the Handbag layer active and choose the Magic Wand tool with Tolerance of **20** and the Anti-alias and Contiguous check boxes checked. Click the white background. Choose Select➪Modify➪Expand, **1**. Click OK. Choose Select➪Feather, **1**, and click OK. Press and hold Option/Alt and add a Layer Mask. Then choose Filter➪Blur➪Gaussian Blur, **1**, and click OK. Press Command/Ctrl+L

to open the Levels command (the mask is still active). Move the White Point Input slider toward the left until you start to see white at the edge of the handbag. Then back off until the white just disappears. Click OK. Make the layer in a Smart Object and then drag it into the Cat image where it should appear above the BlueDress group. Move the handbag over the cat's wrist and press Command/Ctrl+T. Press and hold Shift to constrain the aspect ratio and reduce the handbag to about **67** percent. Commit. Add a Layer Mask. Brush out the left side of the beaded handle, and brush out the handbag areas under the cat's paw so that she is clutching the bag. Add a Bevel and Emboss layer. Set the Depth to **11**%, a Size of **8** px, and Soften of **3** px. Click OK.

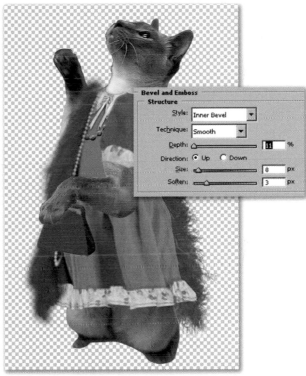

TIP

Using Levels in a blurred layer mask is an excellent way to tighten or loosen a mask. Move the black point or white point until you get the mask the size you want it to be. In the process, the outline of the mask gets very smooth. This is a very old trick courtesy of Kai Krause.

17 Open the Bonnet.psd image. Duplicate the Background layer as **Bonnet**. Choose the Magic Wand tool and select the white background of the Bonnet layer. Press and hold Option/Alt and add a layer mask. Load the layer mask as a selection and make the mask active. With black as the foreground color choose Edit⇨Stroke, **1** pixel, center, and click OK. This contracts the mask just enough to remove any white at the edges. Deselect. Press and hold Option/Alt and click to add a Hue/Saturation layer above the hat. In the dialog box, click the Use Previous Layer as Clipping Mask check box. Click OK. Set the Hue to **–126** and the Lightness to **+14**. Click OK. In the Layer Mask for the Hue/Sat layer, use black to paint back the original colors of the hatband and floral decorations. Select both the Hue/Sat and the Bonnet layer and group into a new Smart Object named **Bonnet**. Drag the Smart Object into the cat image.

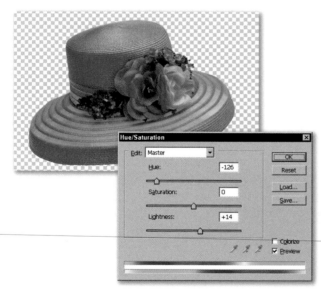

Photo: www.comstock.com

18 Press Command/Ctrl+T and flip the image horizontally. Then press and hold Shift and reduce to about 45%. Rotate it to an angle of **55** percent. Then drag the bottom handle up to look as if the hat is being rotated in 3D space (which we can't easily do in Photoshop unless you like to fuss with the 3D Transform filter). Move it into position on the cat's head and click the Warp icon. Just bend the hat to make it look as if it conforms to the shape of a head. Commit.

19 Open the Cat Smart Object for editing. Make the High Pass Sharpen layer active and press Command/Ctrl+Option/Alt+G to create a Clipping Mask. Make the Cat layer active and add a layer mask. With black, paint away the dark area between the hind legs and give her more shapely looking feet. Click the Close box on the Smart Object file and click Yes to save the changes.

Photo: www.comstock.com

20 It would be a fashion cat-astrophe (sorry about that!) for Mrs. Cat to be seen bare-pawed. Open the image RightShoe.psd and select the shoe on the left side of the image (your left). Select the shoe up to just above the ankle strap. You can make a loose selection and then drag the shoe into the Cat image above the Cat layer. Make the new layer Right Shoe. Use the Transform command to make the shoe fit on the cat's paw that is on your right side. Open the image LeftShoe.psd and select the shoe on the right-hand side of the image. I selected the shoe without the high heel in the first pass and dragged that into the Cat image, rotated, and sized in the LeftShoe layer. Then I went back and selected the heel of the shoe and positioned and sized that in its own layer (High Heel). Make the BackBoa layer active.

21 Finally, open the image Shop.psd and drag the image into the Cat image.

Photo: James Gerber

A short recap

If you can make the cat look good, you can retouch anything. I hope you enjoyed the exercise, but it was long and took a lot of fiddling to get it right. Because you built this nondestructively, you can go back and alter anything that still looks wrong to you at any time. You've learned a lot of tricks and really gave the Warp tool a workout. You need to experiment to see what happens to an image when you warp it by moving the image through the warp grid and when you move the points on the warp mesh or a specific mesh grid. You can exert tremendous control. The only real problem here is that Mrs. Cat is really Reiko, the cat in the bottle, and he would be humiliated to discover himself modeling the latest in cat haute couture!

(22) Name the new layer **Shop**. Drag it below the BackBoa layer. Create a white Solid Color Fill layer above it and set the Opacity to **50**% or to taste. Duplicate the Shop layer. Choose Filter⇨Blur⇨Gaussian Blur and set the Radius to about **3** pixels. Click OK. Save your work.

chapter

8

plant life

Plants give us the oxygen that we breathe. For many designers and photographers, they are also the breath of life. You get a chance to work with some of my favorite plant photos in this chapter. Try your hand at creating scrimshaw — an etching-on-ivory craft first practiced by American whalers in the 19th century. Plants and text go together, right? Well, they do. Hide a bunch of letters inside a lovely flower bouquet. Capture the spirit of nature in a tree.

Scrimshaw

Scrimshaw was the craft of the American whaler. Images were etched onto whale ivory. These images were characterized by soft color and glow. Ivory is no longer an acceptable material to use, but you can transform an image into a glowing softness on the computer without endangering any species at all. This image is of a floral showpiece designed to look like the stalagmites of a cave. Simply by placing one copy in Darken mode over a blurred version, you can create a wonderful glow. The technique works very well for any photo where you just want a soft effect and a bit of stylization.

THE PLAN

- Create the layers
- Apply the modes and filters
- Create a border pattern
- Add the border

(1) Open the image Caveplants.psd. Duplicate the Background layer and name it **Original**. Ctrl/right-click on the layer entry and select the Group into a New Smart Object option. Turn off the eye on the Smart Object. This is a safety copy of the starting image that won't be affected by the canvas size change later on in this technique. Just pretend this Smart Object doesn't exist — you won't use it for anything unless you need to get back to an unaltered starting image.

Photo: Sherry London

② Duplicate the Background layer again and name it **Darken**. Change the Blend mode to Darken. Because the images are identical, you see no change at all.

③ Duplicate the Background layer again and name this **Blur**. Choose Filter⟹Blur⟹Gaussian Blur and set the Radius to **10** pixels or to the amount that looks best to you. Click OK. This is all there is to the basic Scrimshaw technique: Duplicate and change to Darken mode and then duplicate and Gaussian Blur.

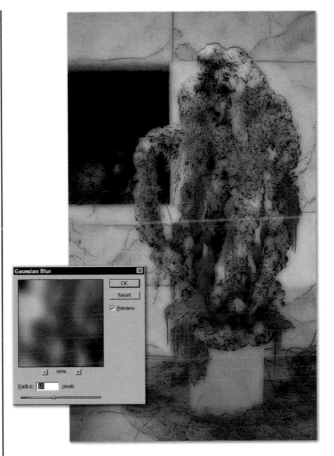

TIP

The blur amount changes with every image that you use. The size of the image matters as well. The larger the image, the more blur you need. By creating the Darken layer before you blur, you can accurately preview the effect in the Gaussian Blur filter dialog box.

④ Let's finish the image by creating a border and frame treatment that also works as a great framing technique for a whole portfolio of images. This first step is called Fun with Math. You want to create a border that repeats evenly. In order to do that, you need to adjust the image size. The border is a 100-pixel border on each side of the image. A border pattern tile that is 100 pixels square repeats perfectly, but your image dimensions also need to be evenly divisible by 100. The current dimensions are 894 x 1542. You need to resize the image to a height of 1500 pixels and then trim away the extra pixels on the width. Press Command/Ctrl+Option/Alt+I to open the Image Size dialog box. Type a Height of **1500** px. Change the Interpolation mode to Bicubic Sharper and click OK. Then press Command/Ctrl+Option/Alt+C and type **–70** px in the Width column (you can see the original number of pixels on the dialog box, which helps to figure out how many pixels to remove). Click the center-right anchor box and click OK. Click OK again to the message asking if you really want to make the image smaller.

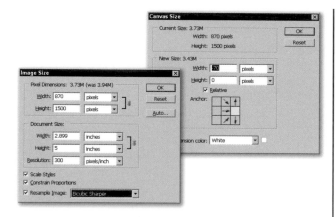

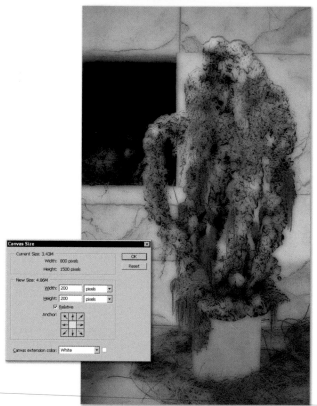

TIP

When you use the Canvas Size command to make an image smaller, Photoshop only hides the pixels; it doesn't remove them. If you don't crop the image, the pixels bounce right back into the image.

TIP

You can't use the Image Size command to change both height and width when you want to get dimensions to a specific multiple. If you change one value to the multiple, you then either get the wrong second value or you need to scale the image disproportionably (which looks odd, to say the least). So, you resize the image so that one dimension is correct and the other one still too large. Then you can use the Canvas Size command (or the Crop command from a fixed-size Rectangular Marquee) to get the second dimension down to size.

5 Choose Select⇨All and then Image⇨Crop. This physically removes the image data that you hid with the Canvas Size command in the previous step. Deselect. Press Command/Ctrl+Option/Alt+C to increase the Canvas Size to create the border. Check the Relative check box and add **200** pixels to each dimension. Set the Extension color to white. Leave the anchor in the center. Click OK. Select the Original, Darken, and Blur layers and press Command/Ctrl+G to create a Layer Set Group. Name the folder **Plant**. This step just helps to organize the Layers palette.

6 Make the Background layer active and add a new layer. Name the layer **Border Pattern**. Press Shift+Command/Ctrl+Option/Alt+E to create a merged layer that appears in the Border Pattern layer. Then choose Filter⇨Pattern Maker. Set the Tile Generation to **100** pixels Wide and **100** pixels High. Choose a Horizontal Offset with an Amount of **50%**. (This makes the border a bit less regular and adds interest.) Set the Smoothness to **3**. Drag the marquee in the center of the image to select a square area that is larger than 100-x-100-pixel tile size. Pick any area that seems to hold interesting detail. The filter is random, so you have no way to repeat my results. Click Generate. You may click Generate multiple times and store up to eight tiles temporarily. If you hate a tile, click the trashcan on the dialog box to remove it. You can scroll back and forth between stored tiles until you decide which one you prefer. Try a Sample Detail of **17** or try out some other sizes as well. When you find a tile you like, click OK.

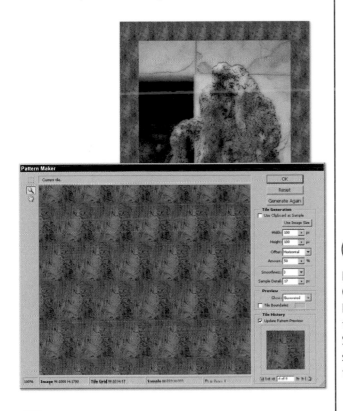

(7) Duplicate the Border Pattern layer and drag the duplicate below the original. Name the duplicate **Surface Blur**. Change the Blend mode of the Border Pattern layer to Darken. Make the Surface Blur layer active and choose Filter⇨Blur⇨Surface Blur. Set the Radius to **30** and the Threshold to **38**. Click OK. Now the border matches the character of the scrimshaw image.

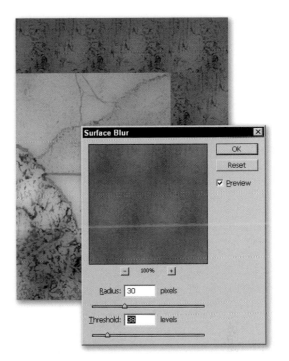

(8) Twirl down the arrow on the Plant group to view the layers. Command/Ctrl-click the thumbnail of the Blur layer to load the layer transparency as a selection. Collapse the Plant group again and click the Plant folder layer. Add a white Solid Color Fill layer. Command/Ctrl-click the Solid Fill layer mask icon to load the selection. Choose Select⇨Modify⇨Contract, **35** pixels and click OK. Fill the selection with black to reveal the scrimshaw again. Reduce the layer opacity to 60%.

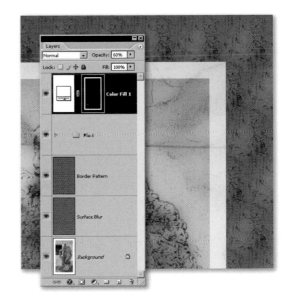

9 Add a Stroke effect to the Solid Color Fill layer. Choose black as the color and make the stroke **4** pixels, inside. Don't click OK yet.

10 Add an Outer Glow effect. Use the default yellow glow, but change the Blend mode to Linear Dodge at **26** percent opacity. The Technique is Softer with a Spread of **0** and a Size of **144** px. Choose the Half Round Contour with a Range of **50**% and a Jitter of **0**. Click OK.

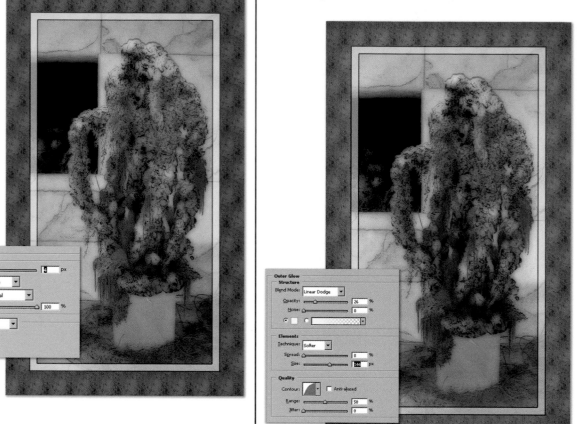

TIP

You can vary the Outer Glow in many different ways. I like the Blend mode of Screen on this as well. Try changing the opacity and the Contours. Try different glow colors. You can alter the border color based on the color of the glow and the Contour that you use. This Outer Glow effect pays a good dividend for experimenting. Because your pattern is different than mine, you will probably want to change to my settings. You can always go back and adjust these settings after you work the final step.

(11) Twirl down the arrow on the Plant group to view the layers. Make the Blur layer active. Add a Drop Shadow effect. Set the Blend mode to Multiply at **100%** opacity. Use Global Light to set the Angle. Choose a Distance of **37** pixels and a size of **43** pixels. The Spread is **0**. Use the Linear Contour. Click OK. Save your work.

A short recap

Scrimshaw can make attractive images from almost any original. If you have a photo that just doesn't quite have the needed quality or detail, it is still usable — and very attractive — as a piece of scrimshaw. Greeting cards are stunning in this technique. Borders also look well in it. The small frame treatment of a whiter edge to the image with just a small black stroke gives an elegant finish to any image. You can play with using blend modes other than Darken (try Lighten on a very dark image, for example). However, the Darken blend mode is particularly suited for this technique. Another attractive variation is to give your image a monochromatic color scheme before adding the blend modes or by adding a Hue/Saturation and a Levels Adjustment layer at the end. Delft blue and white is also a stunning combination. Of course, once you have a low-color version, you can then print it as a Duotone.

Hidden in Plain Sight

Text is always fun. Images that communicate clearly and hit their target audience over the head are always effective. However, subtlety can also be effective. If the viewer needs to think a bit about an image, the message sinks in even more. The trick is to interest the viewers long enough for them to keep looking at the image until it reveals itself. Here, the color should hold attention until the viewer deciphers the text. You'll also try some neat construction methods. You can move the letters all over the image when you're done and the displaced image always matches the main image. You can even change the font completely — and the image still stays together.

THE PLAN

- Set up the background image
- Prepare and use the Displacement map
- Build the letters and effects
- Arrange the letters and change the font

(1) Open the image Blooms.psd from the included CD-ROM. Duplicate the Background layer and name it **Original**.

(2) Choose View➪New Guide and set a Horizontal Guide at pixel **450**. Click OK. Choose View➪New Guide and set a Vertical Guide at pixel **85**. Click OK. Choose View➪New Guide and set the final Vertical Guide at pixel **550**. Click OK. Choose the Elliptical Marquee tool. Place the cursor at the intersection of the horizontal and vertical guides. Press the mouse button and hold it. Before you move the cursor, press and hold Shift and Option/Alt as well. Keep the keys and the mouse button pressed and drag the cursor until the marching ants reach the guide at pixel **85**. Release the mouse button first and then release the modifier keys. Don't deselect.

Photo: Norman London

(3) Duplicate the Original layer. Name it **Flower Base**. Click the Add Layer Mask icon at the bottom of the Layers palette. Make the Original layer active and add a Solid Color Fill layer in black. Name the layer **Backdrop**. Choose View⇨Show and uncheck Guides to hide them for a while.

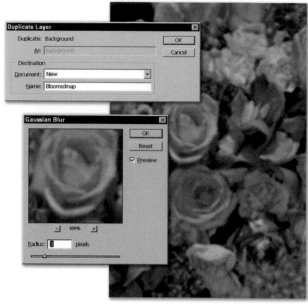

TIP

The Gaussian Blur filter setting that works best depends on the size of the image. As the file size increases, you need to use a larger blur. However, you only want to blur the image enough that it doesn't shred when you displace it. A small blur (small relative to the file size) works. Leave the file in RGB mode. The displacement won't be even as the filter uses the Red channel to displace horizontally and the Green channel to displace vertically. If you want a completely diagonal displacement, change the image to a Grayscale.

(4) Next, you need to make a displacement map. Make the Background layer active. Ctrl/right-click and choose Duplicate Layer from the pop-up menu. Set the Destination of the File to Document: New and name the file **Bloomsdmap**. Choose Filter⇨Blur⇨Gaussian Blur, **3.0** and click OK. Make sure that the file contains only the Background layer. Save the file as **Bloomsdmap.psd**. You may close it.

5 Make the Background layer in the Blooms image active. Option/Alt-click the eye on the Background layer to make it the only visible layer. (I know; this isn't needed, but it's much more comfortable to see what's happening.) Choose Filter➪Distort➪Displace. Type a Horizontal Scale of **25** and a Vertical Scale of **25**. Click the Stretch to Fit and Wrap Around option buttons. Click OK. Choose the Bloomsdmap file as your dmap. Click OK. Turn the rest of the layers back on.

6 Make the Flower Base layer active. Choose the Horizontal Type tool and select a Serif font that is on the wide side. I am using Hopeless Heart (a Pizzadudc.dk font: $22 from www.myfonts.com). I don't get a commission on sales of that font, and Minion Std, which should be on most systems, also works well. It's just a bit more rounded. Click the upper left of the flower area and type an uppercase **B**. I used a font size of **90** points. Set the Anti-aliasing method to Smooth. For the color, click the Color Patch on the Options bar to open the Color Picker. Choose a green from the green leafy patch in the center of the image. Click OK. Commit.

TIP

The Displacement amount also changes depending upon the image size. I first built the image on my original photo (1365 x 2048 pixels) before I decided to have pity on you and not give you a 7MB file to download. I used a 50-pixel displacement on the original file.

7 Duplicate the layer and name the duplicate **Styled**. Double-click the layer entry to open the Layer Style dialog box. Set the Fill opacity to 0% and change the Knockout to Deep. Click OK. Press and hold Command/Ctrl and press the left arrow key four times and the up arrow key two times. Hmmm... I know I said subtle but this is a bit too subtle! Not to worry. I never intended the text to be this close to invisible. You fix it in a minute.

8 Add a Bevel and Emboss style to the Styled layer. Choose an Inner Bevel. Smooth, with a Depth of **231** percent going Up. Set the Size to **18** px and the Soften to **7** px. The Angle should stay with Global light (**120** degrees angle and **30** degrees altitude). The rest of the dialog box is also just standard (linear Gloss Contour, Screen Highlight of **75**% and Multiply Shadow of **75**%). Click OK. Make the B layer active. Add a Drop Shadow effect. Leave the Blend Mode set to Multiply at **75**% opacity and the Angle set the Global Light of **120** degrees. Set the Distance to **26** px, the Spread to **0**, and the Size **25** px. Click OK. Select the B and the Styled layer and press Command/Ctrl+G to create a Layer Set Group. Name the group **B**.

9 Now that you have the one letter completely done and styled, the rest of the type becomes very easy — you just duplicate and then change the letter. Drag the B group to the New Layer icon at the bottom of the Layers palette. Name the duplicate group **L**. Make the L folder layer active and use the Move tool to drag the letters in the group to the right and up from the first letter B set. In the Layers palette, expand the group so you can see the individual layers. Choose the Horizontal Type tool. Click the bottom type layer to make it active and drag the Type cursor over the letter B. Type an uppercase L in its place. Click Commit. Make the Styled layer active and select the letter B and change it to an L as well. Commit.

10 Duplicate the L group and change it to an O and drag it below the L. Duplicate the O group and just drag it below the B. Finally, duplicate the top O group and make it into M. Position the M somewhere near the bottom of the image on the flowers. Reposition the letters as needed by making the group folder layer active and then moving the entire group.

TIP

If the Type tool misbehaves (as it can, unfortunately) and refuses to select the layer you want long enough for you to change the letter, just turn off the eye on the layer that Photoshop wants to select. Make the change, and then turn the eye back on. It isn't worth arguing with the program; Photoshop always wins.

How to Change Your Mind

The letters you type are always covered with flowers that match the Flower Base layer. As you drag the text, the knockout setting simply picks up whatever is on the Background layer at that location in the image. I've also tried adding the Displacement layer as a Smart Object clipped to each letter. That works as well and is probably a tossup so far as file size is concerned. The only time it gives you a major advantage is if you need to alter the displacement image in the Background layer — to filter it again or color tone it. You can't knock out multiple layers and if you want to alter the displacement image nondestructively, you need to stack the layers in a Smart Object and then make a clipping mask of that Smart Object on the Styled layer in each of the letter Groups. Because I just wanted the plain, unadorned, displaced image on the type, I chose the simpler approach in the Groups for this technique.

⑪ On the Mac, with Photoshop open, double-click the Graphicxtras_flowers.abr file on the enclosed CD. On Windows, drag the Graphicxtras_flowers.abr file from the enclosed CD and drop it into the open Photoshop program. The brushes install themselves in the Brushes palette and Brush Preset Picker palette. These are some flowery-shaped brushes from the huge Graphicxtras collection of brushes, given to you with the permission of Andrew Buckle, their creator (www.graphicxtras.com). Select the Brush tool. Choose Brush0465 (it is one with the default size of 176 pixels) or choose a different one of the new brushes if you prefer. Then open the Brushes palette and click the Brush Tip Shape section. Set the Master Diameter of the brush to **25** pixels and the Spacing to **200**%. You may then close or collapse the Brushes palette.

your foreground color. Check again to make certain that you have the layer mask on the Flower Base layer active and then click the Stroke Path icon at the bottom of the Paths palette. The flower image pops through where you stroked in the layer mask. Save your work.

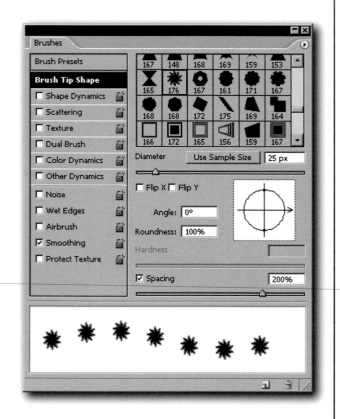

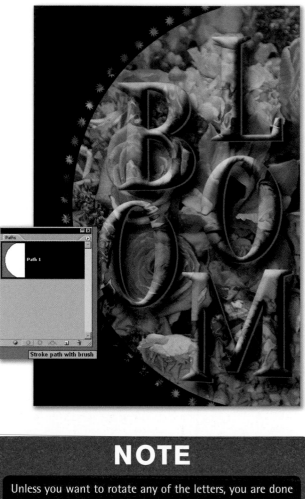

⑫ Now, you add a border around the flower panel by stroking a path in the layer mask of the Flower Base layer. Ctrl/Right-click the Flower Base layer mask in the Layers palette to load the mask as a selection. Choose Select⇨Modify⇨Expand, **15** pixels. Click OK. In the Paths palette, choose Make Work Path from the Paths palette menu. Click OK to the Tolerance of **2.0** that is the default value. Double-click the Work path to save it. Make white

NOTE

Unless you want to rotate any of the letters, you are done at this point. The remaining steps are for extra credit.

The next steps can use any font you want, the wilder or more decorative, the better. I use a font called Novak-Spring, again purchased from Myfonts.com. I fell in love with this font because it has flowers already embedded in it. Semiotics is the study of the relationship between words and their visual representation, and this font just carries on the theme of blooming. (Some less successful choices of matching words and their meanings would be to use a striped font to illustrate the word "Dots" or a thin, condensed font to illustrate the word "Heavy".)

13 Expand all of the groups so you can see all of the individual layers. Click the B layer to select it. Command/Ctrl-click every text layer in the Layers palette to select them all. Choose the Type tool but don't select any text. Choose a new font (I use Novak-Spring). Change the font size to 100 or make it large enough that the letters begin to overlap one another. Commit.

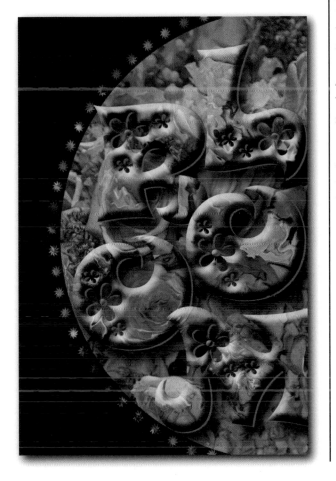

14 Collapse all of the groups. Arrange the letters as you want and rotate some of them (by pressing Command/Ctrl+T while the group layer is active). You can expand all of the groups when you rearranged everything and then select just the bottom layer in each group. Choose the Type tool and click the Color Patch on the Options bar. Choose a different color from the image for the accent color. I chose a strong orange. Click OK to close the Color Picker. Save this version with a different name. Because of the flowery font that I use, my image somewhat resembles a crowded flower bed.

A short recap

The displacement of the original image with itself gives a subtle rhythm to the flowers when you have an embossed letter covered in the displaced version. The original image looks as if it is flowing under and over and around the letters, giving them dimension and movement. If you displace the Background layer (and save your original layer in a different layer for safety), you can set all of the letters to knock out to the Background layer (Deep Knockout). That means that they will pick up the image on the Background layer wherever they are placed in the image. (To use Deep Knockout, you only need to set it in the Layer Style dialog box and set the Fill opacity of the layer to 0.) This technique gives you maximum flexibility to change fonts, sizes, and colors.

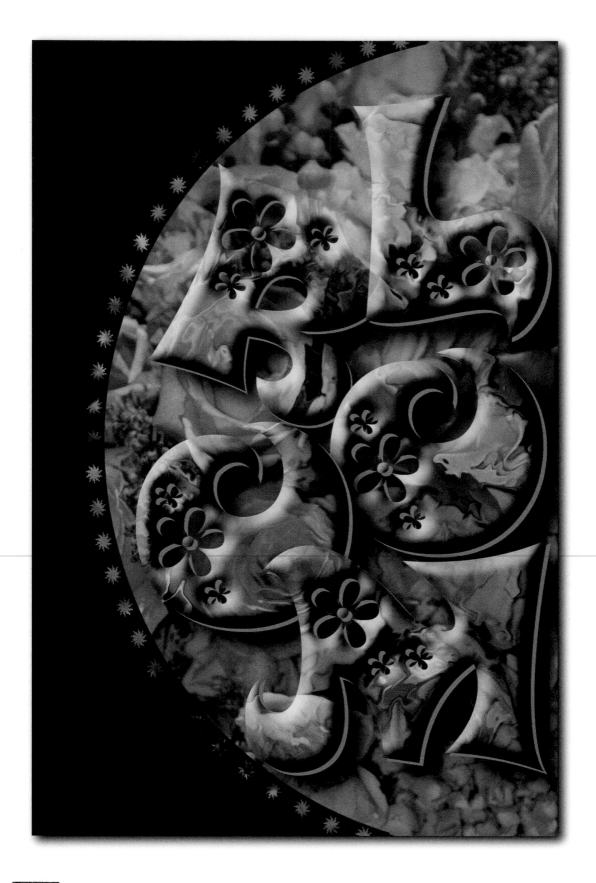

Living Tree

Guardian spirits who watch over the woods have been a staple in folktale and fiction, in genres as diverse as the apple trees in *The Wizard of Oz* and the Ents in *The Lord of the Rings*. I find the Displace filter to be one of the most useful filters in all of Photoshop. However, it gets very tricky when you need to displace something using a dark texture. Here, I use a wonderful African statue as the displacement object for the tree texture. It has the advantage of having sharp detail and good light play because it is a statue and not a photo of a person. However, the dark metal of the statue causes its own problems.

THE PLAN

- Build the displacement map
- Displace and build the layers
- Alter blend modes and blend the face into the tree

1 Open the image Statue.psd from the included CD-ROM. Choose Image⇨Duplicate and work on the duplicate image.

2 Add a Levels Adjustment layer from the New Fill or Adjustment Layer icon on the bottom of the Layers palette. You need to push the values to get more white into this image. Set the White point to **116** and click OK.

Photo: Sherry London

TIP

When you create a displacement map, you want to have the main areas of the map be close to neutral gray with some blacks or darker tones and some whites or light tones.

(3) Press Shift+Command/Ctrl+Option/Alt+E to create a merged layer above the two layers in the file. Name the layer **Blur 4**. Choose Filter➪Blur➪Gaussian Blur, **4.0**. Click OK. The blur helps keep the values in the displacement map smooth. Choose Image➪Duplicate➪Merged Layers only and click OK. Save the image as **Statuedmap.psd**. You may close it. Save the layered file as **Statuedmap_layers.psd**. You may close this image as well.

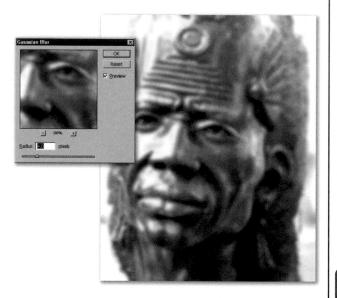

(4) Make another duplicate of the original Statue image. This copy becomes the image that you place as the base for the face in the tree. Choose Image➪ Adjustments➪Equalize. The command does a very good job of evening out the tonal values in the image. Save the image as **Equalized.psd** and leave this image open for now.

TIP

The results from the Equalize command are somewhat different than the results of the Levels adjustment. You burn out much less on the image. The burning works on the dmap but doesn't work as well when you try to multiply a layer. So, the best solution is to use the equalized version to create the face and the leveled version to create the dmap. Although you can use the equalized version for the dmap as well, it doesn't produce as crisp a displacement.

5 Open the image Tree.psd from the included CD-ROM.

Photo: Sherry London

6 Drag the equalized statue image into the tree image. Name the layer **Statue**. Control/Right–click the layer entry and select the Group into a New Smart Object option. Press Command/Ctrl+T. Press and hold Option/Alt and Shift as you drag a corner point on the bounding box to make the statue smaller. This keeps the proportions correct as you scale from the center of the statue. Scale the statue until it is the same size as the width of the tree trunk. Then move it until the bottom of the statue is just above the diagonal gashes on the left side of the tree. The left side of the statue's head then seems to fall in place against the tree trunk. Commit the transformation.

(7) Duplicate the Background layer and drag it to the top of the layer stack. Name it **Displacement 25**. Press Command/Ctrl+Option/Alt+G to create a clipping mask. Command/Ctrl-click the thumbnail of the Statue Smart Object on the Layers palette to load the size of the statue as a selection. Make sure that the Displace 25 layer remains the active layer.

(8) Change the Blend mode of the Displace layer to Multiply. Choose Filter⇨Distort⇨Displace. Set both the Horizontal and Vertical Scale fields to **25**. In the Displacement Map section select click the Stretch To Fit option; in the Undefined Areas section, click the Wrap Around option. Click OK. Choose the Statuedmap.psd image as the Displacement Map. Click OK. Deselect.

9 Duplicate the Displace 25 layer. It should automatically become the top layer and be clipped to the Displace layer. Name this layer **Overlay** and change it to Overlay mode. This layer puts back the light tones in the face.

10 Duplicate the Overlay layer and name it **Color**. Change the Blend mode to Color. Make the Displace 25 layer active and reduce the layer opacity until the value of the face matches the general value of the tree (to about 20 percent).

11 Make the Statue layer active and add a Layer mask. Paint with black in the layer mask around the edges of the statue to blend the statue into the tree. Use a soft brush and alter the opacity of the brush as needed.

12 To put back a bit of the original tree bark, duplicate the Background layer and then drag it to the top of the layer stack. Name the layer **Tree**. Press Command/Ctrl+Option/Alt+G to add it to the clipping mask. Reduce the layer opacity to the level that looks best to you. I chose 29 percent. Save your work.

A short recap

If you can use a statue in a displacement map, you get a huge advantage from the start. The statue generally has no extra colors on it and the shading there represents the way the light falls on the object. Under conditions of normal lighting, the highlights are raised and the shadows are indented — which translates perfectly into everything you want a displacement map to do. However, when the statue is very dark, as this one is, you get an unnatural displacement by using the statue's original values — just about

everything in the displaced image moves. The ideal is to get most of the image adjusted around neutral gray. That is the reason for both the Equalize and the Levels steps. You can build this image many different ways. When you multiply the tree before you displace it, you can see that you might not even want to displace it — the multiply step already shows the face in the tree. Displacement mapping is hugely powerful. How many other places can you think of to project a face?

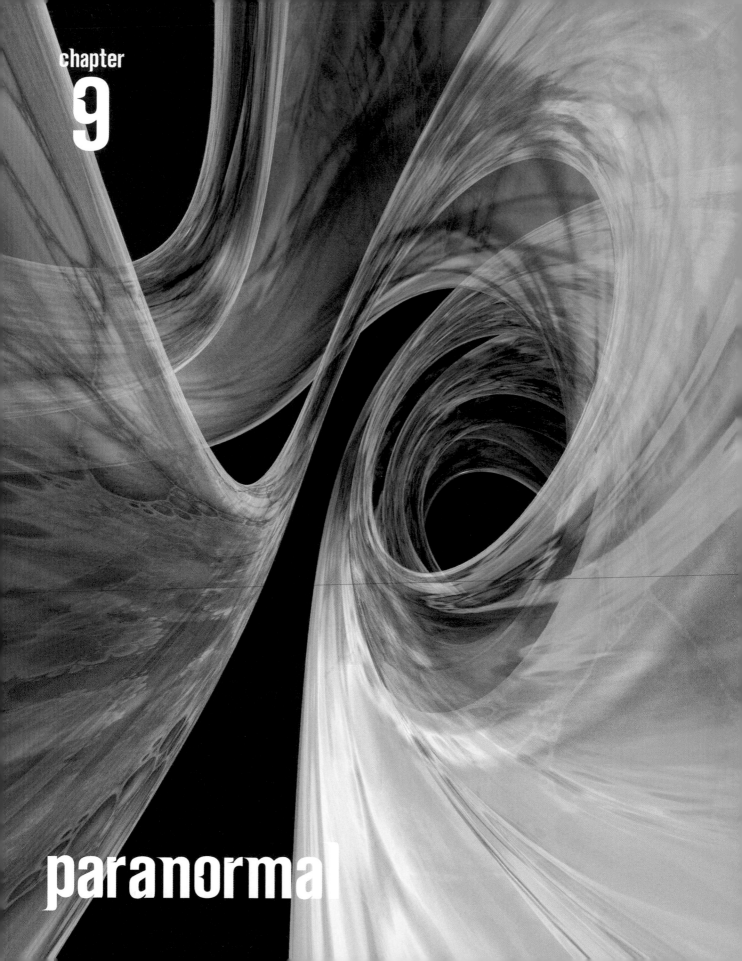

paranormal

Paranormal, fantasy, sci fi — whatever you want to call it, the images here are not everyday things. From Rhoda Grossman's strange sister merge that creates a green monster to Darren Winder's alien with glowing eyes, this is strange stuff, and Thom La Perle's winged lady is also not a common sight at the beach. The tasks are varied as well. Rhoda shows you how to disfigure lovely ladies and Darren's task shows you how to work with shapes, styles, and visible light. Thom's winged lady is mostly masking and compositing but it is done both seamlessly and nondestructively.

Jekyll & Hyde

Retouching to remove blemishes and imperfections on a headshot requires basic Photoshop skills you might already have mastered. But what if you want to create imperfections on a flawlessly beautiful face? You give these ladies a wide range of skin problems. Asymmetry and distortion effects are applied until you end up with faces only a mother (or a dermatologist) could love. This task is written and designed by Rhoda Grossman.

THE PLAN

- Distort facial features with filters and Liquify tools
- Create moles, blisters, and warts
- Add discolored blotches and unpleasant textures
- Combine two disfigured faces into a single monster

(1) Open Two-heads.psd from the CD-ROM. Choose Image⇨Duplicate and work on the copy. If you want the image to be larger, you can choose Image⇨Image Size and resample to **200**% with Bicubic Smoother.

Photo: www.comstock.com

(2) For the distortion portion of the project, you work on one face at a time. Crop out the lovely lady on the right, so you can work more efficiently. Make an elliptical selection around her right eye and choose Filter⇨Distort⇨Pinch at **100**%.

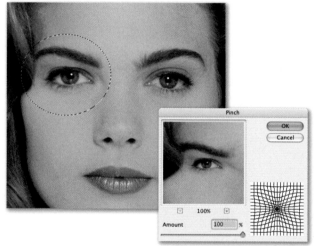

(3) Drag the elliptical marquee to the nose and choose Filter⇨Distort⇨Twirl using an Angle of **−102** degrees.

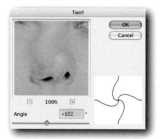

(4) Make a fresh elliptical selection around the mouth and choose Filter⇨Distort⇨Shear with the settings shown. Deselect and use the History brush to restore the skin around the edges of the effect.

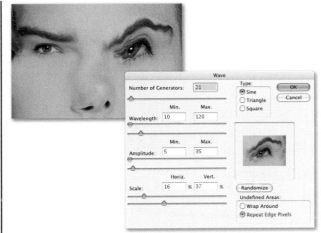

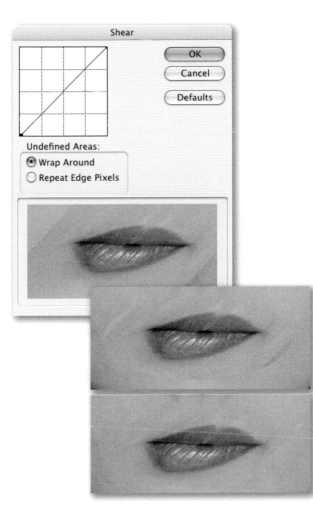

(5) Select her unfiltered eye and apply The Wave distortion filter using these settings for a wonderfully wicked eyebrow! Use the History brush in the corner of the eye to restore some pixels that got too weird.

(6) If you agree that the mouth isn't quite distorted enough, apply the Spherize filter with the settings shown.

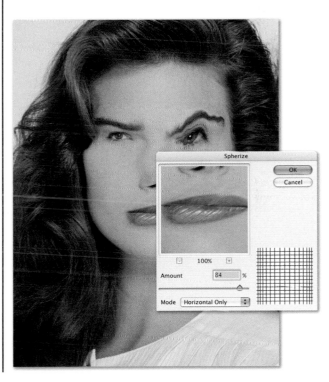

7 That smooth jaw needs to get lumpy and bumpy. Make a horseshoe-shaped selection around the jaw and apply the Wave distortion filter, using these settings. Deselect and repair the hair with the History Brush.

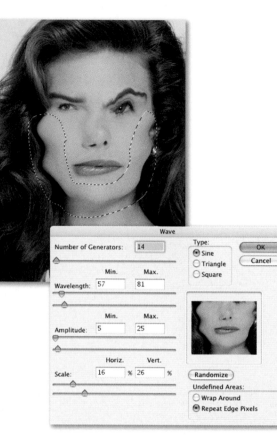

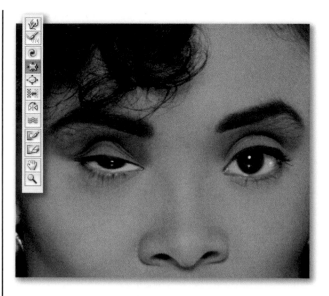

9 Use the Turbulence tool for a broken nose effect, similar to that achieved earlier with the Twirl filter. Some pushing and pulling with the Warp tool should result in puffy and irregular lips. I want to preserve these changes without dismissing the Liquify dialog, so I use the Freeze tool to paint over the parts that need protecting. Now I can safely experiment with changes to the jaw.

8 Let's turn our attention to the woman on the right. Open your copy of the original Two heads.psd and crop it so you have only the dark-skinned beauty ready for her makeover. This time we do all our damage with the Liquify filter. My brush size is about 100 pixels, and I reduce Brush Pressure to 50 for more control. Try a horizontal drag through the center of her eye with the Pucker tool.

TIP

The work you do in the Liquify environment is, of course, much more free flowing than using Distort filter effects with their precise settings. It's unlikely you'll get exactly the same results I do, even with the same Tool and Options choices. Liquify gives you the power to work very freely and organically. You can easily make all your distortions to this face with one visit to the Liquify filter, switching between tools. The Reconstruct tool is a great safety net, like the History Brush.

10 With a bit of practice, the Push Left tool enables you to carve out a new jaw. This tool is influenced by the direction of your stroke. Working on the remaining untouched eye, I continue with the Push Left tool, using a downward diagonal stroke on the inside corner of the eye and an upward diagonal on the outside corner, to get the squeezed look. In the next example, which I decided to keep, a single horizontal stroke from left to right results in the shrunken upper lid and sagging lower lid. The twisted eyebrow is the result of a bit of scribbling with the Twirl Clockwise tool. Finally, that glaucoma is what I got with a tiny circular stroke of the Bloat tool.

11 Splice the two women back together so they can share some skin problems. We make a simple pimple on a separate layer, which can be duplicated and altered several times. I begin, arbitrarily, with a small elliptical selection on the dark woman's cheek. Sample the highlight on her nose for the foreground color and a medium burgundy shade from her upper lip for the background color. Use the Foreground to Background Gradient with the Radial style to fill the selection. This basic blemish serves us well. Make several copies of the blemish layer (Command/Ctrl+J) and move them into suitable positions. Name each one in the Layers palette according to its new location.

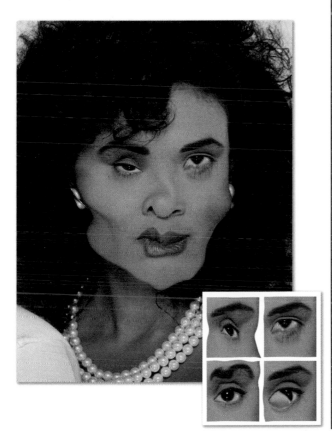

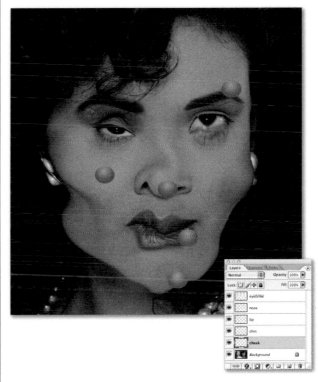

(12) Let's work with the original blemish on the cheek. I make it smaller and darken it with the Burn tool to simulate a mole. A drop shadow is a nice touch, too. Change to a warm brown for the shadow color. So she doesn't feel left out, Option/Alt drag a copy of the mole to the fair-skinned lady on the left.

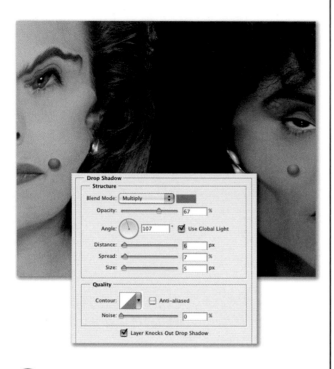

TIP

Be sure you have not locked transparency on these layers, or you will not be able to drag pixels outside the original elliptical fill.

(14) The blemish on her lip can easily be turned into a cold sore or fever blister. Use Free Transform to stretch it slightly and rotate to match the angle of the lip. To blend the upper edge of the blemish into her lip, make a layer mask and drag a Black-to-White gradient diagonally through the blister. Switch from the Radial style used earlier to the Linear style. Make the bottom edge of the blister irregular using the Smudge tool, this time dragging inward from the outer edge. A few dabs with a small Dodge tool enhance the effect. Now let's find a spot for the copy on our other victim. With a slight rotation and opacity reduced to about **75%** this makes a creepy, discolored area under the eye.

(13) The blob on the tip of her nose needs to be anchored in place with several strokes of the Smudge tool, dragged radially outward. Once again, we give the other woman a copy of this excrescence. It looks fine hanging from her chin.

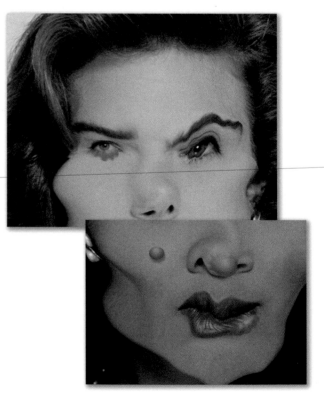

15 We turn one of the remaining pimples into a wart. This requires a roughened texture, achieved with the Add Noise filter, followed by a Gaussian Blur. Fine-tune the wart by making the edges irregular and adding a drop shadow. Reduce opacity to about **75%**. For a change of pace, don't copy this wart to the other face. Instead, make another of those radially smudged growths like the one we put on our fair lady's chin. Use the Hue/Saturation command to make it a sickly green.

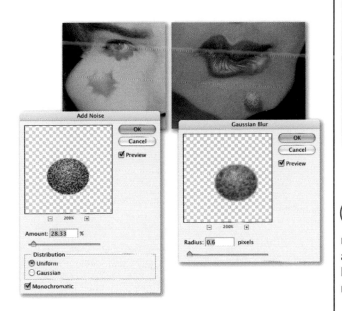

16 Let's damage the remaining smooth complexions by applying a different Pattern fill adjustment layer to each face. Make a rough selection of the skin on the dark woman's face, neck, and shoulders with the Lasso. You can refine the areas affected by the Pattern fill later, with the Brush tool, or gradient fills on the layer mask. I use Textured Tile from the Rock Patterns library with Color Burn as the

Blending Mode and opacity reduced to **70%**. The seriously blotchy effect on the other face is achieved with the Clouds pattern from the default collection. Color Burn mode works well once again, but at **45%** opacity.

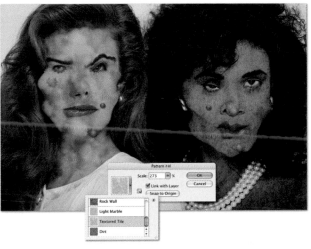

17 Before you begin this step flatten the image. We combine the two disfigured faces into one. Make a rectangular selection of the head on the right, then copy and paste (Command/Ctrl+J). Reduce transparency of the layer to about **50** percent and move it so that the features match up reasonably well.

18 Make a layer mask and, using default colors, drag a Linear Foreground-to-Background gradient horizontally from the left cheekbone to the right cheekbone. Some painting on the layer mask is necessary to make the composite more convincing.

19 Create a Hue/Saturation adjustment layer and move the Hue slider to about **+60** for greenish skin. Paint black on the layer mask where you want to eliminate the green shift. For excellent control in revealing the original color of blemishes, eyes, and portions of the lips use a Radial style Foreground-to-Transparent gradient (with Black as the foreground color).

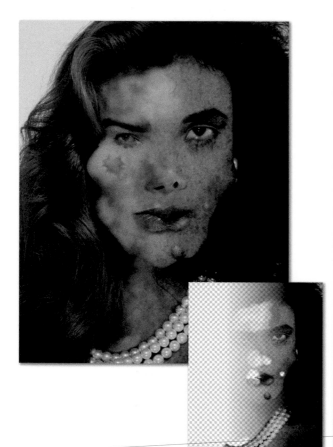

TIP

Recall that you can assign any blending mode to an adjustment layer. Here's the result of switching to Darken mode. We lose color purity (saturation) but we gain enhancement of the skin blotches through the unexpected interaction of greens and reds.

A short recap

There are so many choices to make when you want to create imperfection! You used precise controls as well as Liquify strokes to achieve distortion, and perhaps you learned that one or the other of these approaches suits you better. You created a wide range of variations on a simple pimple using Transform commands, Layer Styles, and the underappreciated Smudge Tool. It was efficient to make each blemish work on both faces, and that led to even more choices, because the same layer can look very different against a different background. So, using both a pale-skinned and dark-skinned model was not just for political correctness, but to stretch your Photoshop skills. Finally, you blended two disfigured faces together with the help of layer masks and adjustment layer effects.

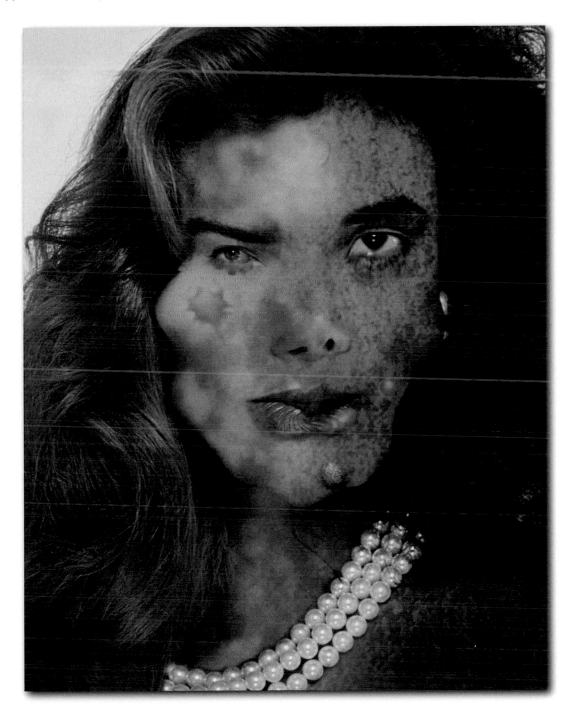

It Came From Outer Space

I had to have an alien in the book — a book on wild Photoshop, by law, has to have an alien. I also wanted to show how to make glowing taillights. I am indebted to Darren (Daz) Winder, California artist and TA extraordinaire, for bringing my concept to life (or more likely, figuring it out from scratch). Al, as he is affectionately known, sprang full grown from Daz's hand and mind. I've simplified Daz's work a lot — given much of it to you ready made. Daz's original artwork is amazingly complex. You can see his instructions about building the sky background and his original layered drawing by downloading them from the book Web site, www.photoshopgonewild.com.

THE PLAN

- Combine the background and the basic alien shapes
- Shade Al
- Build the eyes
- Make the eyes light up

TIP

Why did we create a shape? Why not just use the starting image? I want you to see how easy it is to create a shape from a drawing. If you decide to create your own cartoon character, you can either draw it and scan it or just sketch it on the computer. By changing that sketch into a shape, you allow it be resized to any size you want without loss of image quality. I just happened to give you the correct size image. I could have just given you a tiny image and let you create the shape and enlarge it to the needed size. You can take interesting brushes that you find and change them into shapes. The possibilities are endless.

(1) Open the image Al_the_Alien.psd from the CD-ROM. Choose the Magic Wand tool and set the Tolerance to 0, Anti-alias On, Contiguous Off. Click on the black to select the entire alien. Choose Select⇨Feather⇨1 and click OK. In the Paths palette menu, choose Make Work Path, and accept the default 2.0 Tolerance. Choose Edit⇨Define Custom Shape. Name the shape **AlienAl**. You may close the Al_the_Alien image now.

(2) Open the image Background.psd from the CD-ROM. Choose the Custom Shape tool. Then click the Custom Shape Options on the Options bar and choose Defined Size. Check to make sure that the first icon (Create Shapes) is selected. Choose black as your foreground color. Click in the image and set the shape. Before you release the mouse button, drag Al so that his bottom-right point is just below the spaceship portholes. There is really only a small range of places that he fits with only the very tip of his hands going out of the picture frame. Name the layer Base of Al.

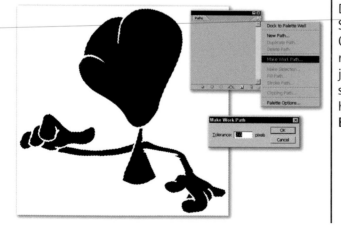

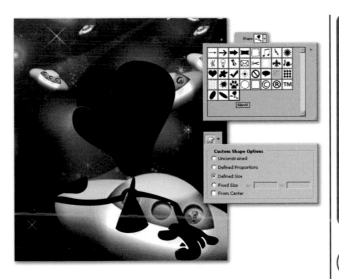

(3) Retrieve the AlienStyles.asl file from the book's CD and double-click it on the Mac or drop it into the open Photoshop application on Windows. The new styles immediately are available to you from the Styles palette. With the Base of Al layer active, click the DazAlien style in the Styles palette.

(4) Drag the thumbnail of the Base of Al layer to the New Layer icon at the bottom of the Layers palette. Name the new layer **GreenSkin**. Drag the Effects to the Trashcan at the bottom of the Layers palette. Double-click the thumbnail on the GreenSkin layer and choose RGB: **204, 255, 204** for the new color. Click OK. Change the Blend Mode to Linear Burn. Select the Base of Al and the GreenSkin layers and right-click the Layers palette entry on one of the selected layers and choose Group into New Smart Object. Name the Smart Object **AL**.

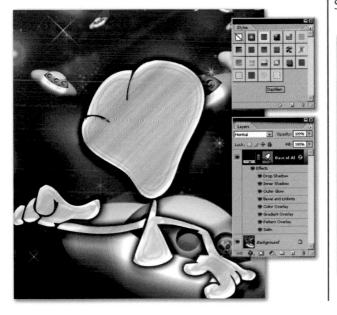

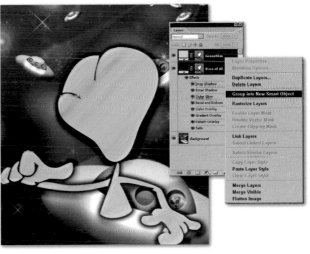

5 Double-click the AL Smart Object to open it for editing. Hold the Option/Alt key and click the New Layer icon at the bottom of the Layers palette. Name the layer **Shadows**. Click the Use Previous Layer to Create Clipping Mask check box. Change the Mode to Hard Light and click the Fill with Hard-Light-neutral color (50% gray) check box. Click OK. Choose the Burn tool and the **65-pixel** soft brush. Control/Right-click the Burn Tool icon at the far left of the Options bar and choose Reset Tool. Paint around the right edge of Al's face down to his chin. Stroke over the left brow ridge, both arms, the right side of his body, and the fingers on each hand. Reduce the layer opacity if you prefer softer shadows. (I have it set to **80**%.)

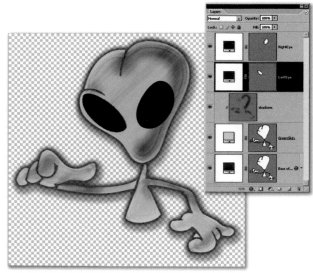

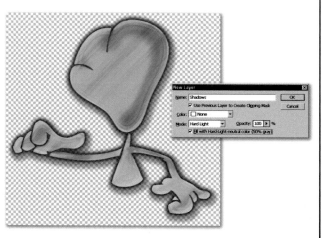

6 Drag the AlienShapes.csh from the CD-ROM and drop it into the open Photoshop application (on the Mac, double-click to open the file). The shapes attach themselves to the Shapes menu. Using the Custom Shape tool, black as your foreground color, and Deflided Size set in the Custom Shapes Options palette, choose the Left Eye shape and add it to Al so that it fits into the eye ridge. Name the layer **LeftEye**. Then add the RightEye shape as shown. Name the layer **RightEye**.

7 Add a new blank layer at the top of the layer stack and name it **Mouth**. Choose the **35-pixel** soft brush and open the Brushes palette. Click the Brush Tip Shape section. Change the diameter to **40 px** and the Hardness to **100**%. Change the Spacing to **10**%. Click the Shape Dynamics text on the left side to change the focus of the palette. Set the Size control to Fade in 10 steps. Set the Minimum Diameter to **33**%. Paint one stroke on the Mouth layer from the bottom to the top of the mouth area as shown. Create a new layer and name it **Nose**. Use the **5-pixel** hard brush but change the Master Diameter to **7** pixels. Paint a short, curved line midway between the mouth and eyes.

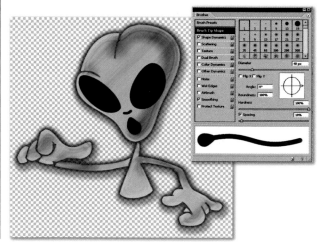

8 Add an Outer Glow style to the Mouth layer. Choose Black as the color, and Multiply as the Blend mode. Set the Opacity to 39%. Give it a Spread of **10** percent and a size of **18** pixels. Click OK. Ctrl/Right-click the Layers palette entry and choose Copy Layer Style. Make the Nose layer active and Ctrl/right-click and choose Paste Layer Style. Double-click the style entry and change the Size to **27** pixels. Click OK. Then click the Close box on the Smart Object and click Yes to the prompt asking if you want to save the changes. Now you can see what you've done in context. You can save and minimize this image; we come back to it.

9 It's time to start the taillight eyes. Create a new image **400** pixels square, RGB, **72** ppi, and fill with white. Name the image **EyeTexture** and click OK. Choose the Paintbrush tool and a **7-pixel** hard brush. Open the Brushes palette and click the text that says Scattering on the left side of the palette. This changes the focus of the dialog box. Click the Both Axes check box and move the slider to 1000%. Set the Count to 1 and the Count Jitter to 100%. Click the text on the left that says Color Dynamics. Set the Foreground/Background Jitter to **48%** and the Hue Jitter to 10%. Set the Saturation and Brightness Jitters to 100%. Set the Purity to **–22%** to get more muted colors. Now choose red (RGB: **255, 0, 0**) as the foreground color and black as the background color. In the new document, add a new layer (named **Painting**) and then scatter the paint all over the file. Leave small patches of white.

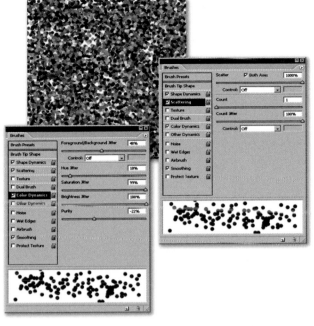

10 Duplicate the Painting layer as **Blur** and then choose Filter⇨Blur⇨Gaussian Blur, 2. Click OK. Change your foreground color to white and uncheck the Color Dynamics box at the far left of the Brushes palette. Then move the Master Diameter in the Brush Tip Shape section of the Brushes palette to **7 px** and move the Spacing to **100%**. Add a new layer to the file and name it **White Dots**. Brush some white dots all over the image, but don't let them build up.

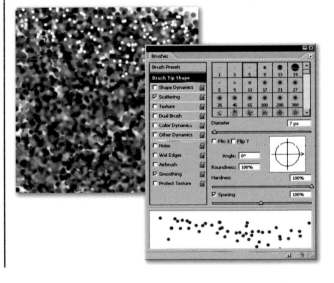

11 Make red your foreground color and white the background color. Add a Gradient Fill layer. Choose a Linear Gradient and then click the Gradient Editor field in the dialog box (the gradient preview image). Choose the Foreground to Background gradient. In the Gradient Editor, drag the red Color Stop to the **43**% location on the bar. Then click to add a new Color Stop on the left side of the gradient bar and choose RGB: **121, 24, 24** in the Color Picker. Click OK. Then click OK to close the Gradient Editor. Set the Angle for the Gradient to **180** degrees. Then click OK. Change the Blend mode to Multiply at **65**% opacity. Name the layer **Glass**.

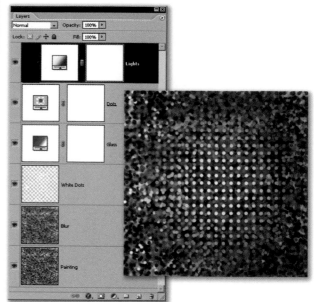

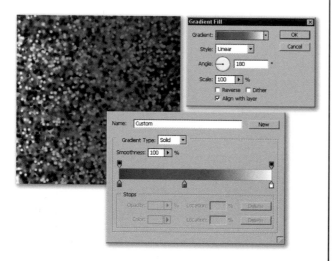

12 Drag the AlienPatterns.pat from the book's CD-ROM into the open Photoshop application. Add a new Pattern Fill layer at the top of the layer stack, and choose the Circle pattern that you just added. (It will be one of the last patterns in the Pattern palette.) Name the layer **Dots**. At this point, so that the clipping masks don't come undone, select all of the layers except the Background layer. Control/right-click one of the layer entries and choose Group into New Smart Object. Name the object **TailLight**. Then double-click the Smart Object to open it for editing. In the Smart Object file, hold the Option/Alt key and add a Gradient Fill layer. In the New Layer dialog box, check the Use Previous Layer to Create Clipping Mask check box. Name the layer **Lights**. Choose a Radial gradient at an Angle to **90** degrees. Click the Gradient Editor to open it. Choose the Black to White gradient preset. Click the black Color Stop and choose RGB: **254, 255, 205**. Click OK. Click the white Color Stop and replace it with RGB: **83, 47, 47**. Click OK. Click in the center of the Gradient slider to leave a new Color Stop. Drag the Color Stop to the **36**% location. Choose RGB: **219, 224, 62** for this color. Click OK. Then click OK to accept the gradient. Click OK once more to close the Gradient Fill dialog box. The clipping mask and the circle gradient help to create points of light.

13 Add another Pattern Fill layer above the Lights layer but don't add it to the clipping mask. Choose the Grid pattern for this layer. Click OK. Name the layer **Grid**. Add a Solid Color Fill layer in RGB: **255, 0, 0** (solid red) above the Grid layer. Name the layer **Red Glass**. Set the opacity to **34**%. Click the RGB channel in the Channels palette. Choose Edit⇨Define Pattern and name it **TailLight**. Then click the Close button on the Smart Object file. Click Yes to save the changes. Save the EyeTexture image as **EyeTexture.psd**.

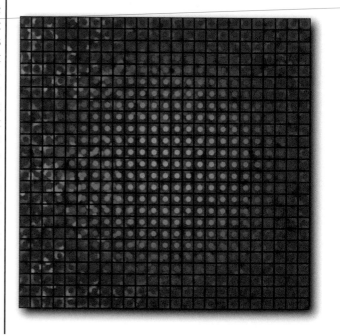

14 Make the Background image (that contains the AL Smart Object layer) active. Double-click to open the AL Smart Object. Make the RightEye layer active. Drag the TailLight Smart Object from the EyeTexture image into the AL Smart Object file. Select both the RightEye and the TailLight layers and Group into New Smart Object. Name the Smart Object **RightEye**.

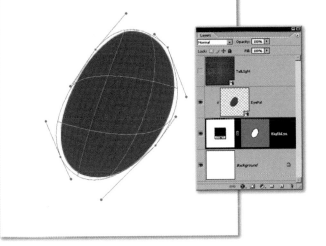

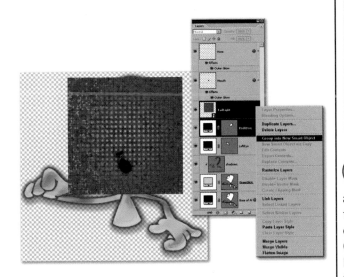

15 Double-click to open the RightEye Smart Object for editing. In the Smart Object file, turn off the TailLight layer. Make the RightEye shape layer active. Add a new Pattern Fill layer. Choose the new TailLight pattern that you just created. Set the Scale to **5** and click OK. Name the layer **Eyepat**. Make this layer into a New Smart Object — which is the only way that you can distort it. Name the Smart Object **EyePat**. Press Command/Ctrl+Option/Alt+G to create a Clipping Mask. Press Command/Ctrl+T to transform the object. First, scale it to about **47%**. Then click the Warp icon. First, move each corner warp point so that it's near the eye shape. Then move the corner Direction points so that they encircle the object. You can see from the figure how I arranged them. They need to almost hug the eye object. Make sure that you keep the EyePat larger than the object, however — no black should show through. Move the grid squares on each side of the center to make the eye bulge slightly in the center. Click OK.

16 Turn on the TailLight Smart Object layer and make it active. Press Command/Ctrl and scale the layer to about **37%**. Then click the Warp icon and warp it as you did the EyePat layer. The only difference is that you want to concentrate the yellow lights in the center of the eye. Click OK. Duplicate the layer as **EyeCenter**. Make the TailLight layer active and change the Blend Mode to Vivid Light. Set the Opacity to **62%**. Make the EyeCenter layer active and double-click the layer to open the Layer Styles dialog box. In the Advanced Blending Options section, hold the Option/Alt key and move the right half of the Blend If This Layer black slider to **195**. Click OK

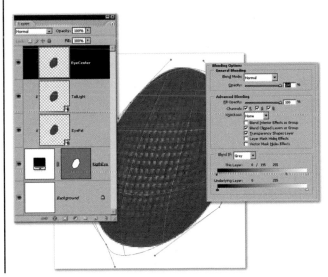

Sizing Smart Objects

It took me a while to figure out how to size the eye Smart Object to give me the additional room that I needed for the transformations. I wanted to build the Smart Object for the eye inside the AL Smart Object file. If you change the RightEye shape into a Smart Object before you add the TailLight or if you clip the TailLight before you make the Smart Object, your Smart Object file is only the size of the eye. You need more room in the file to put the taillight eye together. By using both the RightEye and the TailLight layers together to create the Smart Object, you can get that room. The resulting Smart Object becomes the size of the TailLight Smart Object. You might wonder why you can't just enlarge the canvas inside the Smart Object file when you edit it. You can; but the entire object, no matter how large it gets, still occupies the same amount of space in its original location. So, the larger you make the RightEye Smart Object file, the smaller the eye becomes when it gets back into the AL Smart Object. Smart Objects are fabulous; but they do require some mental gymnastics.

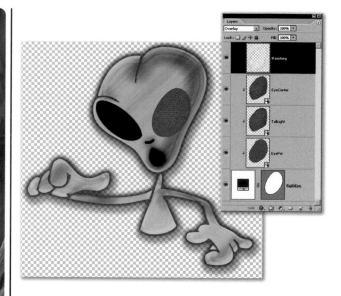

17 Add a new layer named **Painting** and press Command/Ctrl+Option/Alt+G to add the layer to the clipping mask. Choose the Brush tool and create a **2-pixel** hard brush with Scattering turned on. Make white your foreground color. Sprinkle white pixels around outside of the eye area, leaving the yellow-dotted area in the center, plain. Change the Blend mode to Overlay. Change the foreground color to black and paint in the same area, but even less than the white that you added. Select all of the layers except for the Background layer and Group into New Smart Object. Yes, the clipping mask all comes undone. You need to double-click to edit the Smart Object and then press Command/Ctrl+Option/Alt+G on each layer above the shape layer to reestablish the clipping mask. Then click the Close box and click Yes to save. Finally, AI has one taillight eye (even if it's not quite done yet). The Layers palette shown is the way it looked in the RightEye Smart Object file before you closed it.

18 Repeat Steps 14–17 to create the Left Eye. Begin by making the LeftEye layer in the AL Smart Object file active and placing the TailLight object from the EyeTexture image directly above it. Group into a New Smart Object. Then work through the other steps to wrap the textures around the eye. When the eye is complete, click the Close box on the file and click Yes to save your work.

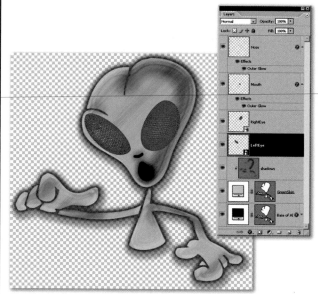

(19) Duplicate the Right Eye Smart Object and name the copy **RightEyeFrame**. Apply the EyeFrame style that you loaded in Step 3. Create a clipping mask with the RightEye layer. Repeat this for the left eye.

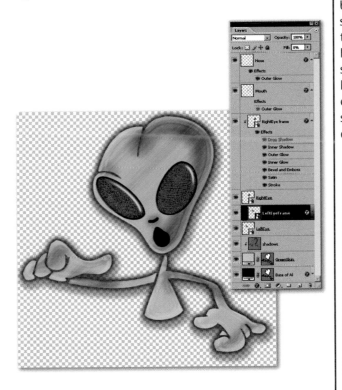

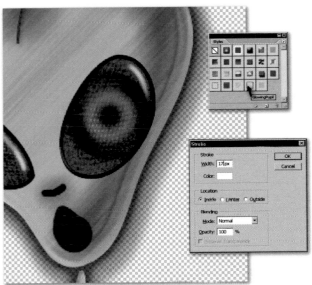

Size style option in the Options bar. Set the Width and Height to **62** pixels. Set the Marquee in the center of the right eye. Make white your foreground color and choose Edit⇨Stroke, **17** pixels, Inside. Click OK. This gives you a black ring in the center of the eye. Click the GlowingPupil style in the Styles palette to add it to the layer (you loaded this in Step 3 with the DazAlien style). Choose Filter⇨Blur⇨Gaussian Blur, 5. Click OK. This softens the selection in the layer mask. You can adjust this where you like it — or not use it if you prefer the harder eye ring. You can then decide on the Layer opacity to use (Fill opacity should stay at 0). The figure shows the pupil at 100% opacity.

TIP

If you prefer not to make a copy of the Smart Object, load the eye as a selection and fill the selection on a new layer. You need to have transparency around the eye for the style to work. It won't work on either a Solid Color Fill layer or a regular layer that is filled completely and then either masked or clipped.

(20) Next, it's time to make glowing pupils. Make the RightEye Smart Object layer active. Hold the Option/Alt key and add a Solid Color Fill layer. Name this layer **Right Pupil** and check the Use Previous Layer to Create Clipping Mask check box. Click OK. Choose black as the fill color. Click OK. Fill the layer mask with black to hide the fill. Choose the Elliptical Marquee tool and the Fixed

(21) Duplicate the RightPupil layer and place it on top of the LeftEye layer. Press Command/Ctrl+Option/Alt+G to create a clipping mask. Name the layer **LeftPupil**. Move the pupil into position over the left eye on the image.

I like an opacity of **41%** for both pupils, but it's your decision. Click the Close box on the AL Smart Object and click Yes to save your changes.

22 Al is supposed to cast a glowing light from his body as well as from his eyes. But first, we need to tuck him into the spaceship. Add a Layer mask to the AL Smart Object layer. Choose a **45-pixel** semihard brush (about 50 percent hardness) and paint in black over the lower portion of Al's torso until he is firmly planted in the spaceship. A shadow comes up around as you mask him. Then, let's create his glow. Make the Background layer active. Using the Polygon Lasso tool, make a vaguely trapezoidal selection from his neck to the tip of his left hand, across his arm, and back up to his neck. Hold the Shift key and select his head — but very loosely and a bit of a distance outside of it on the right and left sides of his face. Add a white Solid

Color Fill layer from the selection. Then choose Filter⇨Blur⇨Gaussian Blur, 2.0 and click OK. This just softens the selection a bit. Change the Blend mode to Overlay at **100** percent opacity. Next, make a very loose selection of both of Al's arms so that the selection looks a bit like a bowtie. Again, add a white Solid Color Fill layer and blur it as you did before. This time, leave the Blend Mode at Normal but reduce the opacity to **20%** or to taste. (The coated figure shows the two selections; yellow shows the area of the first selection and red shows the second one.)

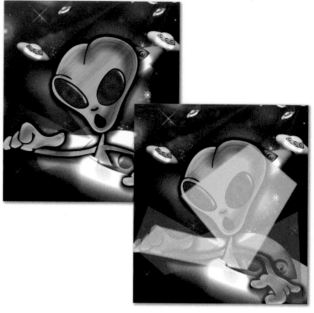

23 With the Polygon Lasso tool, make a selection from Al's right eye past the inside of his right arm down to the bottom of the image, across the bottom and about halfway up the right side of the image and back to the starting point. Choose Select⇨Feather, 25 and click OK. Make the AL Smart Object layer active. Make RGB: **133, 11, 11** your foreground color. Make RGB: **247, 159, 159** your background color. Add a Gradient Fill layer and choose the Foreground to Background preset. Choose a Linear Gradient at an Angle of **-60** degrees. Click OK. Change the Blend mode to Soft Light. It gives a subtle red glow. Name the layer **RightGlow**. Repeat this for the left side and just reverse the directions.

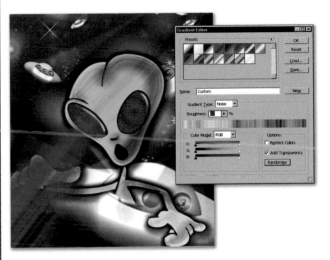

24 Load the LeftGlow layer mask as a selection by Command/Ctrl-clicking on the layer mask icon on the Layers palette. Choose Select⇨Modify⇨Contract, 20 pixels and click OK. Add a red Solid Color Layer. Name the layer **LeftBeam**. Command/Ctrl-click the Layer Mask on the LeftBeam layer to load it as a selection. Choose the Gradient tool. Click the Gradient Editor. Choose a Foreground to Background Preset. Then select Noise as the Gradient Type. Set the Roughness to **60%**. Click the Add Transparency check box. Click Randomize until you like the mix of transparency and then click OK. Drag the gradient

cursor across the width of the selection at its widest point. The gradient in the mask causes the beam to break up. You can reduce the opacity if you wish. You can also blur the layer mask slightly if you want a softer light.

25 You need to repeat this process for Al's right eye, but the selection is different. Choose the Polygon Lasso tool and make a selection from the center of his right eye, grazing his mouth and down to the bottom of the image. Come across the bottom to just past his right thumb, and then start the trip back up to his eye. Come across the eye to the starting point. Choose Select⇨Feather⇨10 pixels. Add the red Solid Color Fill layer and then load the mask as a selection. Use the same gradient as in Step 24 to break up the layer mask. Reduce the opacity of the layer as desired. I have the RightBeam at **70** percent and the LeftBeam at **62** percent. Save your work.

A short recap

Daz's artwork has an amazing amount of attention to detail. That is what makes it special. I hope this easier taste of his working methods shows you the reward for patience and perfection. There are still more modifications that you could make if you wanted. If you want to see more of a glow on the pupils, you can open the AL Smart Object again and load each Pupil layer as a selection. Add a yellow Solid Color Fill layer and either reduce the opacity to give the inner eye ring a yellow glow or change the Blend mode to Dissolve and make the opacity very low to leave yellow sparkles. You could even make each beam of light a different color. Because of the working methods, every part of Al the alien is easily changeable. Don't like green aliens? Turn him into the purple people eater! Remember that you can still make him bug-eyed, too!

Winged Lady

When I first saw this image designed by Thom La Perle, I was blown away. It fits the Paranormal topic of the chapter perfectly. I was delighted when he said that I could include it in the book. The image is of Toad the Mime (Toni Attell www.attell.com) and was photographed by Jeremy Mitchell under Thom's art direction. The sand snake is the work of photographer Karl Switak. This task is the bread and butter of Photoshop work. The skills shown here are critical to any day-to-day image processing. After a bit of cleanup, some color correction, and a lot of masking, the result is a stunning composite.

THE PLAN

- Prepare the Mime Image
- Gather the needed images
- Layer the images
- Mask the images

1 Open the image ToadMime.psd from the book's CD-ROM. Let's see if we can get a bit more dynamic range into the image without harming the true blacks. Choose Image⇨Adjustments⇨Shadow/Highlights. Click the More Options check box if you don't see the entire dialog box. Accept the default values but change the Color Correction slider at the bottom of the dialog box to **-100**. That helps to remove a tiny bit of the excess magenta.

2 Double-click the Background layer thumbnail in the Layers palette and accept the default name of Layer 0. Command/Ctrl-click the Alpha 1 channel thumbnail in the Channels palette to load the alpha channel as a selection. Make Layer 0 active and add a Layer Mask. Rename the top layer **Shadow/Highlights**. Press Command/Ctrl+Option/Alt+G to create a clipping mask. Now you can see if you want to back off the opacity of the Highlight/Shadow correction. I brought the layer opacity to **87%**. Add a Levels Adjustment layer. Click the Gamma Eyedropper (the center eyedropper) and search for a pixel (near Toad's collar bone on the left side of the image) that is close to value **128** in the green and blue channels. You can read the color numbers in the Info palette as you move the eyedropper icon over the image. Click on the chosen pixel and the image should neutralize. In the RGB channel of the Levels dialog box, move the Input White point slider to about **230** to create a bit more white. Change to the Red channel and move the Gamma slider just a small bit more back toward the red to restore a touch of the red cast that the midtone eyedropper removed. My final values are: RGB channel: White: **210**; Red channel: Gamma **0.95**; Green channel: Gamma **1.08**; Blue channel: Gamma **1.00**. Click OK.

Photo: Jeremy Mitchell

I always recommend doing your color correction before you start to clean up the image. That way, the cleanup doesn't come undone when you start moving values and color around.

③ You can now also see that the image needs a bit of touchup. It was scanned from film and has a lot of small areas of pixel dust that need to be removed. Hold the Command/Ctrl key and click on the New Layer icon on the bottom of the Layers palette to add an empty new layer under the Levels 1 layer. Name it **TouchUp**. Choose the Spot Healing brush and check the Sample All Layers check box. Have at it! Clean all the areas of visible damage (no need to fix the masked areas). When you have the image totally cleaned up, save the image as **ToadMime2.psd**. You may close it.

④ Choose File⇨New and create a file that is **1499 x 913** pixels, **300** ppi, white Background, RGB mode. Name the image **WingedLady** and click OK. Toad the Mime is the main element in the composite, so let's add her first. Choose File⇨Place and select ToadMime2.psd. When the bounding box appears, click OK. The file comes into your image as a Smart Object. Then press Command/Ctrl+T and type **61%** in the W: field on the Options bar. Click the Maintain Aspect Ratio button between the width and height fields. Then click the control between the X: and Y: fields so that it is set to use relative positioning. Type **–12** in the X: field and **+90** in the Y: field and click Commit.

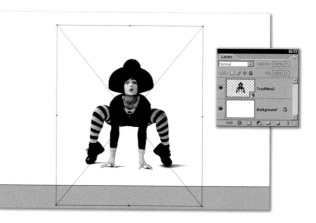

TIP

Why did I ask you to place the ToadMime file? I was being lazy! Well... only partially. You have a layer that is a clipping mask in the ToadMime file and if you make the layers of the ToadMime2 file into a Smart Object in that file, the clipping mask comes undone and you need to edit the Smart Object to repair it. However, by saving the file and then placing it, Photoshop accepts the clipping mask and embeds the file as is. It is not linked to the original image. The file is completely stored inside of the WingedLady image with no outside connections.

TIP

When you get near an area that spans multiple colors, the Healing brush smudges. To fix that, you need to make the brush smaller or else briefly switch to the Clone Stamp tool.

⑤ Open the image Sand.psd from the book's CD-ROM. Drag it into the WingedLady image. Name it **Sand**. Place it in the lower-left corner. Because you need to resize this, you might as well make it into a Smart Object first. Ctrl/right-click the Sand entry in the Layers palette and choose Group into New Smart Object. Then press Command/Ctrl+T. Hold the Shift key as you drag the upper-right corner of the bounding box until it reaches the height of Toad's nose. The release the Shift key and drag it by the center-right point until it reaches the right size of the canvas. Click Commit. Drag the layer below the ToadMime2 layer. Close the original Sand image.

Photo: www.comstock.com (sand photo)

⑥ Open the image BandedSnake.psd from the book's CD-ROM. This image was photographed by Karl H. Switak and is used with his permission. Make the Snake layer active. Click the Snake path in the file to make it active and then Command/Ctrl-click the Add Layer Mask icon in the Layers palette to add a vector mask to the Snake layer. Drag the Snake layer into the Wingedlady image. Name the layer **Snake**. Group it into a Smart Object. It's too big, but let's get more layers in place before we decide on the final size. Close the original BandedSnake image.

Photo: Karl H. Switak

⑦ Open the Sky.psd image from the CD-ROM. Drag it into the WingedLady image and place it in the upper-left corner of the image. Name the layer **Sky**. Group it into a New Smart Object. Press Command/Ctrl and drag the bottom-right corner of the bounding box until it reaches the right side of the image and the bottom-center control is approximately at the base of Toad's neck in the hollow of her throat. Commit. Close the original Sky image.

Photo: www.comstock.com

⑧ Open the image SharpMoon.psd from the book's CD-ROM. Hold the Shift key and drag it into the WingedLady image. Choose the Magic Wand tool with a Tolerance of 10, Anti-alias On, and Contiguous On. Click the black background of this image. Then hold the Option/Alt key and add a layer mask. This hides the selection and reveals the moon. Name the layer **Moon**. Close the SharpMoon.psd image.

Photo: NASA

9 Open the SeaGullWing.psd image from the book's CD-ROM. If you open the image, you see that it's a sandwich of three layers — the original image, the Shadow/Highlights layer, and a Remove Noise filter (to get rid of the color noise). If you don't like some of these decisions about the original, feel free to reduce the opacity of any of the layers. The image already is masked with layers added to a clipping mask. The easiest way to get it into the WingedLady image is to place it. Choose File⇨Place. Select the SeaGullWing.psd image and change the W: field on the Options bar to **50%**. Click the Constrain Aspect Ratio control and click OK. Move the right side of the wing to the center of Toad's back. We still have a lot more work to do.

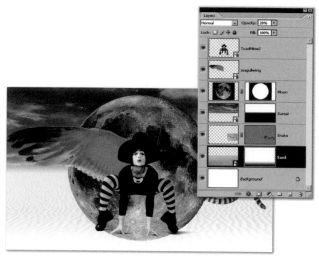

Photo: Norman London

10 Move the Snake layer until it is just above the Background layer. Command/Ctrl-click the thumbnail for the Sand layer to load the layer transparency as a selection. Save the selection to a channel named **Sand**. Deselect. Make the Sky layer active. Add a layer mask. In the Channels palette, click the eye to the left of the Sand channel; however, don't make the channel active — you just need to see the red coating. Choose the Gradient tool. Set your colors to the default and choose the Foreground to Background preset. Hold the Shift key and drag the Gradient cursor from just below the start of the Sky layer to just before the red coating starts. Release the mouse and the Shift key and click off the eye on the Sand channel. Make the Sand layer active and add a layer mask. Place the Gradient cursor at the bottom of the image under Toad's left shoe (the shoe on your left) and hold the Shift key as you drag the cursor to the top of her left shoe. Release the mouse and the Shift key. Change the layer opacity to **31%** (gee, you can see the snake again).

11 Make the Moon layer active. We added a fast layer mask before, but the outer edge of the moon is very rough and it should be smoothed a bit. Delete the current layer mask. Press Command/Ctrl+R to turn on the rulers. Drag a guide to just a tiny bit below the top of the moon and another one to just a tiny bit inside the left edge of the moon. Choose the Elliptical Marquee tool and position the cross-hair cursor at the intersection of the guides. Hold the Shift key and draw a circular marquee that is just a bit smaller than the moon. Release the mouse first and then the Shift key. Click to add a new layer mask.

12 Ctrl/right-click the Moon layer entry in the Layers palette and choose Group into New Smart Object. Then press Command/Ctrl+T. Type **128%** in the W: field and click the Maintain Aspect Ratio control. Move the moon so that it almost touches the top of the image and click Commit. Add a layer mask to the Moon Smart Object layer and choose the Gradient tool (Foreground to Background preset and default black to white colors). Place the Gradient Cursor near the 500-pixel mark on the side ruler and hold the Shift key as you drag the cursor to the top guide (the original height of the moon). Release the mouse and the Shift key. Choose the **300-pixel** soft brush and set the opacity to about **20%**. Remove some of the opacity in the center of the moon.

13 I want to get more texture into the moon. Double-click the Moon Smart Object to open it for editing. Add a new layer to the Smart Object and name it **Texture**. Then press Command/Ctrl+Option/Alt+G to create a clipping mask. Choose the Healing Brush tool (not the new Spot Healing brush) and choose a source point with a lot of texture. Make sure Sample All Layers is checked in the Options bar. Brush over an area of the moon near the top. Continue to brush texture over the top half of the moon.

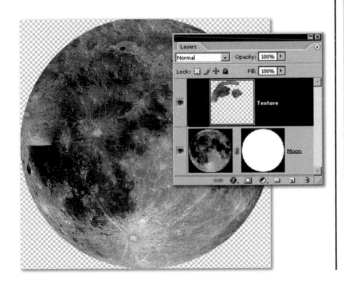

14 Add another new layer, name it **Craters**, make it into a clipping mask, and fill it with white. Change the Blend mode to Soft Light. Choose the Brush tool and open the Brushes palette. In the Brush Tip Shape section of the palette, choose the 19-pixel hard brush and change the Master Diameter to **45** pixels. Change the Brush Spacing to **110%**. Click the Shape Dynamics text to focus on the Shape Dynamics options. Change the Size Jitter to **100%**, the Minimum Diameter to **30%**. Change the Angle and Roundness Jitters to **100%** and the Minimum Roundness to **25%**. Click to view the Scattering Options. Scatter Both axes at **1000%** and set the Count to **1**. In the menu of the Brushes palette, choose New Brush Preset and save the brush settings as Moon Craters. Using black, paint over the top half of the moon — just one pass with the brush back and forth until you have sparingly sprayed craters. Choose Filter⇨Stylize⇨Emboss and choose an Angle of **–34** degrees, a Height of **1**, and an Amount of **100%**. Click OK. Click the Close box on the Smart Object file, and click Yes to save your work.

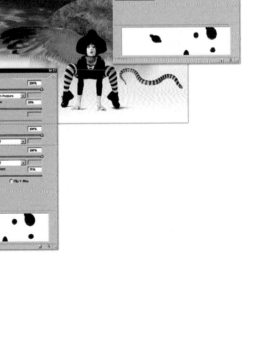

(15) Back in the WingedLady image, double-click the Moon Smart Object thumbnail to open the Layer Style dialog box. Add a Bevel and Emboss with the Inner Bevel style, Technique: Smooth. Set a Depth of 81% Up. Set a Size of **70** pixels and Soften of **9** pixels. Use Global light at the default of **120** degrees and **30** degrees Altitude. Change the Highlight opacity to **86**% and the Shadow opacity to **67**%. Click the Contour checkbox under Bevel and Emboss in the Styles list at the left side of the dialog box. Don't change the settings. You can preview and see if you prefer this control on or off. Then change the focus to the Color Overlay. Choose RGB **179, 179, 179** as the overlay color. Click OK to close the Color Picker. Set the Blend Mode to Screen at **70**%. Click OK to close the Layer Styles dialog box. Fine-tune the Layer Mask and make sure you can see some of the edges of the moon on either side of Toad and that the moon extends into the sand. You can use the **300-pixel** soft brush at **20**% opacity to make the changes.

(17) Make the Snake layer active. The snake is much too large for comfort! Make the Snake layer into a Smart Object. Then press Command/Ctrl+T and reduce the snake to **61** percent and rotate him **9** degrees (use the fields on the Options bar). Then click the Warp icon. You want to try to straighten him out a bit as shown. Click Commit. Position the snake just to the right of Toad's right knee. Add a Layer Mask. Make black your foreground color. Command/Ctrl-click the Snake thumbnail in the Layers palette to load it as a selection. Make sure that the mask is active and choose Edit⇨Stroke⇨5 pixels, Center. This is a very easy way to thin the snake to make him look as if he is belly-burrowing in the sand. However, too much of him got removed. Take the **9-pixel** soft brush and white to bring back the upper side of him and all of the mouth area. Then, to really bury his tail, use the **65-pixel** soft brush and black at **30**% opacity to cover the back half of him. Keep stroking from his tail to his midpoint but going less and less distance from the tail each time, so he just fades out. If you lose patience, increase the opacity on the brush.

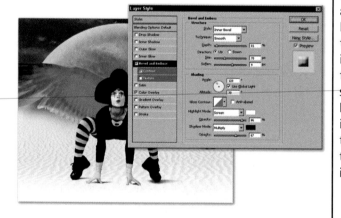

(16) Make the Seagullwing layer active. Press Command/Ctrl+T and then click the Warp icon on the Options bar. You need to concentrate on the center section of the warp mesh. Push that up to form the bend in the wing. Then push the other sections into position as shown in the figure. Click Commit. Drag the Seagullwing thumbnail to the New Layer icon at the bottom of the Layers palette to duplicate the Smart Object. Name the Smart Object **Wing2**. Choose Edit⇨Transform⇨Flip Horizontal. Hold the Shift key and move the wing into place.

(18) Let's tweak Toad's masking. Now that most of the elements are in place, you can see small areas of white around her hat. Double-click the ToadMime2 Smart Object to open it for editing. Command/Ctrl-click the layer mask thumbnail to load it as a selection. Make black your foreground color. Choose Edit⇨Stroke, 3 pixels, Center. This just tightens the mask enough to remove the stray areas of white. Click the Close box on the Smart Object file and click Yes to save your changes. While we are tweaking... The wings could use a contrast boost as well. Open one of the wing Smart Objects for editing. In the Smart Object file, add a Levels adjustment layer above the other layers. Set the Input Black Point to about **23**, the Input White Point to about **192**, and the Gamma slider to about **1.60** to lighten the wing. Click OK. Click the Close box on the Smart Object file, and click Yes to save your changes.

(19) The one major remaining area to fix up is the sunset. It doesn't have the dramatic light that I wanted (and that Thom had on his original sunset with an image that was also unavailable for use). Make the Sky Smart Object layer active and hold the Option/Alt key and add a Hue/Saturation adjustment layer. In the dialog box, click the Use Previous Layer to Create Clipping Mask check box. Click OK. Set the Hue to **-4** and the Lightness to **-15** and click OK. Hold the Option/Alt key and click the New Layer icon to add a new empty layer. In the dialog box, name the layer **Color Clouds**, change the Blend Mode to Color, and click Use Previous Layer to Create Clipping Mask. Click OK. Set your foreground color to RGB: **133, 73, 50**. Set the Background color to RGB: **238, 197, 125**. Hold the Option/Alt key and choose Filter⇨Render⇨Clouds. Duplicate the Color Clouds layer as **Lumi Clouds**. Change the Blend Mode to Luminosity and the Opacity to **31%**. Then set your colors to black and white. Hold the Option/Alt key and choose Filter⇨Render⇨Clouds again. Now that the sky is in place, you can fuss with the mask on the Moon layer again.

20 We are near the final stretch. Make the ToadMime2 layer active. We have just a bit more touching up and color work to do on Toad. Thom thought at this point that the image needs a bit more color. Double-click to open the ToadMime2 Smart Object file. Use a soft black brush at **30%** opacity and remove some of the masking from over Toad's neck area on the Levels 1 layer. You want to put back just a touch of the colorcast you removed from that area. Hold the Option/Alt key and add a Solid Color Fill layer to the image. In the dialog box, name the layer **WhiterFace** and check the Use Previous Layer to Create Clipping Group. Click OK. Choose white and click OK. Fill the layer mask with black to hide the effects of the Fill layer. Then use the soft black, low-opacity brush to add some more white to Toad's face. Set the Layer opacity to about **47%**. Try to stamp some additional color out of the left side of her lips. Make the left side of her face a bit more white than the right side. Add a Solid Color fill layer (named **PinkCast**) of RGB: **190, 146, 146** to the Clipping Mask and fill the Layer Mask with black. Set the Blend Mode to Color. Bring back the color very gently over her face, neck, and lips. Add more color to the right side of her face than the left. Add a white Solid Color fill (named **WhiteLips**) in Normal mode at **47%** opacity as you did the other layers. This time, only paint the mask in white over the left side of Toad's lips. The lower lip should be lighter than the upper lip. Finally add a Photo Filter Adjustment layer the same way and choose Color. Select RGB: **205, 54, 143** as the filter color. Click OK. Set the Density to **55%** with Preserve Luminosity on. This layer shows up only over the right side of Toad's lip and a tiny bit on the top left of the lip. It is deepest at the right side of her mouth. The effect of these changes is very subtle. Hopefully you can see it in the before and after figure. Leave the Smart Object file open.

21 Add a new layer to the top of the layer stack in the ToadMime2 Smart Object. Name it **Button**. There is no reason to add it to the clipping mask. Let's add the layer effects to the layer this time before you paint in the layer. That way, you can see what happens as you paint. Remember, the layer is still empty so the style shows nothing as yet. Add a Drop Shadow to the layer. It is the standard Drop Shadow, but set the Distance to **2**, the Spread to **9** percent, and Size to **4** pixels. Click the Bevel and Emboss. Again, this is a standard Inner Bevel with Smooth Technique but set a Depth of **81%**, Size of **1**, and Soften of **5** pixels. Zoom all of the way into the black button that is below Toad's neck. Take a 13-pixel hard brush and red, and paint over the small black button. Click OK to apply the styles. Click the Close box on the Smart Object and click Yes to save your changes.

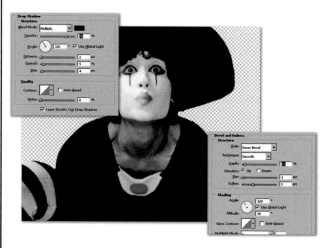

22 Save your work.

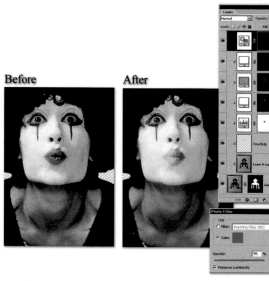

Before   After

A short recap

Attention to detail makes Thom's work special. The steps used in the task are not complex, but they bring together a number of dissimilar images in a unique and imaginative way. The thing that sets an ordinary composite apart from the fantastic is that awareness of the little things — such as four new adjustment layers just to fix the color on Toad's lips. The other factor that makes this artwork stand out is the selection of the original images. Jeremy Mitchell's photo of Toni Attell as Toad the Mine is one of the most striking photos I have ever seen. Thom's concept and composite make this special image into a showstopper. I am so grateful to all involved for sharing it with us.

playing with your food

No, we're not having a food fight! However, this chapter is major fun. Make over a shack into a cottage fit for a...well, you've got to read that one! You can also change the photo of a lobster into a neon menu decoration — I got a great dinner out of that project! The final task in the chapter lets you mix up some fruits for your otherworldly tastes.

Gingerbread Makeover

Once upon a time, there lived a young girl who had run away from her evil stepmother. When the young lady finally found her prince, the seven short people who had given her aid left their cozy cabin to live with her in the castle. For many years, the cabin stood empty. At one point, three furry residents occupied it, but they were evicted for terrorizing a little blonde girl. Finally, the landlord rented the house to a green-skinned lady who always wore long, black dresses. She seemed to be okay; at least she liked kids. She claimed that she wanted to remodel the old shack into a place that would attract lots of little children. Do you believe her tale? Do you believe my tale? No? Would you believe a great excuse to use the Vanishing Point filter?

THE PLAN

- Cover the house with graham crackers
- Add the porch and lawn
- Clean up
- Decorate

1 Open the image Cottage.psd from the book's CD-ROM. Also open the image Cracker.psd from the CD-ROM.

2 Our first concern is to get the new walls up and get a roof on; the garden can wait until later. Turn on the Color Fill I layer in the Cottage image. I draw this to get you started. It is the best that I can do to get the perspective of the front of the cottage. This image was taken at a flower show of a shack set up for display. I doubt it would pass the building code. Make a rectangular selection that is larger than the entire black color fill area and drag the selection marquee into the cracker image. Position the marquee on the largest section of crackers you can find. Choose Edit⇨Copy. Make the Cottage image active and deselect. Then add a new layer named **House Front**.

Photos: Sherry London

3 Make sure that the House Front layer is active. Choose Filter➪Vanishing Point. You are automatically in Create Plane mode. Set the first point by clicking at the top-left corner over the black Solid Color Fill layer. Then click at the top-right corner and the bottom-right corner. At this point, you see a rubber band line as you drag to set the fourth point. When all four corners are set, the grid turns blue if you have a possible plane. If the perspective is wrong, the plane turns yellow or red.

4 Now that you have the grid set up, press Command/Ctrl+V to paste the graham crackers that you copied earlier. They sit in the upper-left corner. Drag them down toward the grid until they get caught by the grid and snap into perspective. They are severely distorted Position them to about the right location and then choose the Transform tool (it's the fourth tool from the bottom along the left side of the interface). Use the bounding box on the tool to move the sides, top, and bottom to conform to the shape of the black Solid Color Fill selection. Leave a little bit over the shape — you can easily cut off extra material; you can't easily add more. When it looks right to you, click OK.

5 Press Command/Ctrl+Option/Alt+G to create a clipping mask. Turn off the eye on the Color Fill1 layer. Click the New Path icon on the Paths palette and use the Pen tool to outline the door and window. Command/Ctrl-click the Path thumbnail to make a selection. Turn the Color Fill 1 layer back on and Option/Alt-click the Add Layer Mask icon. Now the gingerbread looks like the front of a house. What a cheap witch — she can't even afford real gingerbread!

6 Add a new layer to the image and name it **Side**. Make the graham cracker image active and select as large a rectangle as possible without getting the background. Copy it to the Clipboard. Make the cottage active again and choose Filter⇨Vanishing Point. Look carefully at the right side of the existing plane and you see a center handle. Command/Ctrl-click that center handle and drag another plane from it as you pull to the right. It will be in perfect perspective to the original plane. That's the good news... The bad news is that it is only one of many possibilities for perfect perspective — and it happens to not be correct for this cottage. Without holding the Command/Ctrl key, bring the right-center handle back toward the front of the house so that it is within the area of the siding. (You need to have something against which to judge the perspective.) Drag the top edge of the side down and the bottom edge up until you at least have it positioned within a known area. Now you can make the perspective work. Hold the Command/Ctrl key as you move the top-right and bottom-right points to make the plane parallel to the planks on the side of the house. When you get a legal perspective, the plane turns blue again. You might need to readjust the front of the house now as well. Use the Zoom tool as you do in the main Photoshop application to get in close. Command/Ctrl+Z works for Undo.

7 When you finally get the perspective correct, just pull on the center handles on the top, right side, and bottom to extend the plane to the back of the cottage. Then paste the graham crackers and size them as you did in Step 4. In order to see to move the plane with the Transform tool, you need to zoom out a lot. Try to make the seams match on the crackers — even if you leave the top of the house uncovered. We can fix that later. Click OK.

8 You can't fix the roofline just by copying; cut and paste won't give you the correct perspective. (I know — I tried it!) Add a new layer named **Top Side**. Copy just two of the graham crackers to the clipboard. Go back into Vanishing Point and cover the rest of the side. Click OK to exit.

9 Turn off the Side and Top Side layers. Using the Pen tool, outline the side of the cottage. That sounds easy; the bottom line of the cottage is covered and not easy to judge. At that point, turn on the Side and Top Side layers so you can move the bottom point as needed. On the figure, you can see my selection stroked; don't stroke your path — that is just so you can see what I did. Save the path.

10 Make the House Front layer active. With the new path active, add a black Solid Color Fill layer. The active path automatically creates a vector mask. Name the new layer **House Side**. Then press Command/Ctrl+Option/Alt+G on the Side and Top Side layers to create a clipping mask. Once you have the layers clipped, you can judge your success at the side of the house. I found that I didn't have the correct roofline at the top point of the roof. It's easy to fix. Make the House Side layer active and use the Direct Selection tool to edit the points in the vector mask.

11 Make the Top Side layer active. Add a new layer and name it **Roof**. Copy the graham crackers to the clipboard (I selected all of the larger crackers). Make the Roof layer active and choose Filter⇨Vanishing Point. You need to create a new plane for the roof. Choose the Create Plane tool and outline the roof. Work small first and follow the known lines. Extend the roof plane to the right so that it covers the trim area that we left unoccupied over the side of the house. Paste the crackers into the filter and move them until they're caught by the plane. I allowed a bit of an overhang on the plane. Use the Transform tool to make the crackers fit the space. I had to zoom out a lot to be able to grab the points to resize the crackers. Click OK to exit. If you made the crackers fit the slightly oversized roof, you should not need to edit anything in the Roof layer.

(12) To give us a bit more sense of realism, add a Drop Shadow to the Roof layer. Choose an Angle of **124**, a Distance of **12**, and a Size of **24** pixels. Click OK. Make the Top Side layer active and hold the Option/Alt key as you add a Levels adjustment layer. In the dialog box, check the Use Previous Layer to Create Clipping Mask. Name the layer **Lighting**. Click OK. Drag the Gamma slider to **1.32** and click OK.

(13) Let's get a path laid on the side of the house. Open the image MM.psd. Copy a rectangular selection that only includes the candies. Make the Cottage image active and add a layer at the top of the layer stack. Name it **Path**. Choose Filter➪Vanishing Point. The path would be diabolical to use for perspective, but you can pull a plane off of the side of the cottage. Extend the cottage-side plane down (yank the bottom-center handle) so that it is low enough to meet the path (even though it won't touch the current path). Then hold the Command/Ctrl key and click the center-bottom point on the side plane and tear off a plane by dragging the point forward and to the right. Drag it out to cover. Then just drag the center points of the unconnected sides to fit over the entire path area. Paste the candies. Move the selection until it gets caught by the plane. Then choose the Transform tool and shape the selection to fit. The candies get flat like flagstones. Click OK.

(14) The next thing is to cover the porch with jellybeans. On the Mac, double-click the Gingerbread.pat file and on Windows, drag the Gingerbread.pat file from enclosed CD into the open Photoshop application. The patterns are immediately available to you. Make a Rectangular Marquee selection that is just larger than the porch (all three faces of it). The porch also extends behind the barrel on the right. Add a Pattern Fill layer into this selection and choose the Jellybean pattern. Set the Scale of the pattern to **25**% and click OK. Load the layer mask of the Pattern Fill layer as a selection. Choose Edit➪Copy Merged. Turn off the Jellybean Pattern layer and add a new layer named **PorchTop** to the image. Choose Filter➪Vanishing Point. Hold the Command/Ctrl key and click on the bottom-center point of the house front to tear off a grid for the porch. Size it to cover the porch, though you won't be able to get it to go back far enough. Paste the jellybean selection and transform it to perspective. Let it extend beyond the back of the plane. Click OK. Again, you get very flat, distorted candies. Turn off the PorchTop layer. Draw a Pen path for the porch top. Make the PorchTop layer active and visible. Hold the Command/Ctrl key and add the new path as a vector mask.

TIP

In order to copy a selection from a pattern fill layer, you need to use the Copy Merged command.

(15) Finish the porch construction by making two new layers: **Porch Face** and **Porch Side**. Tear off a grid from the center bottom of the PorchTop plane for the porch face and tear off a grid from the center side of the PorchFace for the porch side. You need to do this in two different trips into the Vanishing Point filter. Before each trip, turn off enough layers to be able to copy (merge) the selection from the jellybean pattern layer before you enter Vanishing Point. Make sure that a blank layer is active when you choose the filter. Leave the porch front visible when you create the porch side so that you can match the scale of the jellybeans. Create a path for each porch section and apply it as a vector mask to the correct layer.

(16) Before the Layers palette gets totally out of control, stop now and select the layers that form each part of the house and put each section into its own Group (select the layers and press Command/Ctrl+G) and then name it for what it contains. I create a Porch, Path, Roof, House Side, and House Front group. The occupant of the cottage labored hard and long. Seasons changed. She really hated the trees around the cottage and some of them were half-dead. She finally got the tree surgeons in to transplant some larger trees for her. Open the image NewTrees.psd from the book's CD-ROM. Drag the image into the top layer of the Cottage image (name it **New trees**) and then use the Pen tool or the Polygon Lasso tool to isolate the cottage and its grounds from the forest. Mask the trees.

Photo: Sherry London

17 Drag the New Trees layer to just above the Background layer. Add a layer mask to the Path layer and use a **65-pixel** soft brush at **50%** Hardness and change the candy flagstones into a curved path. Make another copy (Edit ⇨ Copy Merged) of the jellybean pattern selection. Add a new layer to the Porch group and name it **Foundation**. Choose Filter ⇨ Vanishing Point. Extend the plane for the porch side to the back of the house. Paste the jellybeans and transform to fit. Click OK. Drag the Vector Mask thumbnail from the PorchSide layer onto the Foundation layer (you can turn off the PorchSide as it is no longer needed). Edit the points on the vector mask with the Direct Selection tool to extend the mask over the whole foundation.

18 Open the image Fluff.psd. Select it and copy it to the clipboard. Make the Cottage image active. Collapse the Porch group and make it active. Add a new layer to the top of the stack. Name it **Lawn**. In the Vanishing Point filter, tear off a plane from the bottom of the Porch Face plane for the lawn. Stretch it to cover and paste the fluffy stuff. Transform the fluff to fit, and save and exit. Add a layer mask and mask the image to cover the lawn. Add a new layer to the image above the House Front and name it **Door-Window**. Make the door and window out of the Fluff selection. Use the House Front plane in the Vanishing Point filter. Load the Layer mask of the House Front as a selection and Option/Alt-click to add a layer mask to the Door-Window layer.

TIP

You need to turn off the other layers in the Porch Group in order to view the selection to copy.

Photo: Sherry London (Fluff.psd)

19 Now comes the fun stuff. Add a layer at the top of the stack and name it **Icing**. Drag the Icing.asl file from the book Web site into Photoshop. Attach the Icing style to the Icing layer. Use the **19-pixel** hard brush in white and outline the house in icing.

20 On the enclosed CD, you find a variety of candy images. Select, paste, and ice your own special creation. Don't forget to add shadows under the roof line and on the right side of the house for realism. Save your work.

A short recap

The Vanishing Point filter is one of the highlights of the Photoshop CS2 release. It is the "wow" feature. Some critics have called it the ultimate demoware — catchy and showy for demos and totally useless. Not so. You can put it to very useful work. If you need to retouch anything in perspective, this feature is priceless. The icing is made from a Shape Burst stroke around a bevel. Take a good look at how the style is created. Now, do you think someone needs to warn Hansel and Gretel to stay out of the forest?

Neon Bright

It's really not about the neon — or at least, not all about the neon. Neon is a very popular look, and it generally comes in two flavors: realistic or graphic. I prefer the graphic style and integrating neon into an overall design. So, we're not making a neon sign; we're making a menu cover that contains something that looks like a neon sign. Photoshop is the premier program for working with photos, but it also is a fabulous program for graphic design. It's easy to change a photo into a resizable shape; it's fun, and it's extremely useful as well. Mr. Neon Lobster started as a photo. He also made a great meal! I need to thank Kathryn Bernstein for the original design of this piece and for her neon style.

THE PLAN

- Create the lobster shape from a photo
- Create the neon effect on the lobster
- Create the type
- Add the Layer Style

1 Open the image Lobster.psd from the book Web site. Double-click the Background layer and name the layer **Lobster**. Click OK. Ctrl/right-click the Lobster layer entry in the Layers palette.

2 Choose the Magic Wand tool and set the Tolerance to **55**, Contiguous On, Anti-alias On. Click the white background behind the lobster. Hold the Shift key and click to add each of the shadow areas around the lobster to the selection. Then hold the Option/Alt key and click the Add Layer Mask icon at the bottom of the Layers palette to add a Hide Selection Layer Mask. With black and a small, hard brush, finish removing any of the shadow areas from the lobster. You need to be as clean and precise as possible. Remove the pixels in the mask that make the lobster's top-right leg attach to the top-right claw. Check the lobster carefully for areas of transparency inside of the shape. Remove any transparency you find by painting with white.

Photo: Norman London

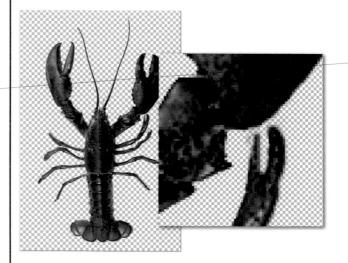

3 Draw a loose Lasso marquee around the lobster's two antennae. Press Command/Ctrl+J to create a new layer via copy. Name the layer **Antennae**. In the Layers palette, hold the Command/Ctrl+Option/Alt keys and drag the Layer Mask thumbnail from the Lobster layer onto the Antennae layer to add it to that layer. Command/Ctrl-click the Layer thumbnail of the Antennae layer to load it as a selection. Make the layer mask in the Lobster layer active and fill it with black. This removes the antennae from the Lobster layer. Turn off the eye on the Antennae layer.

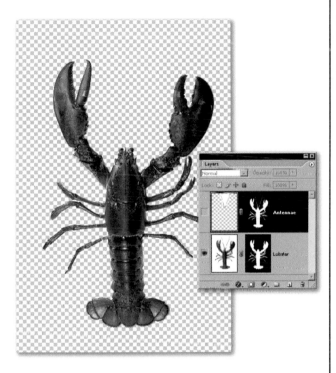

4 Make the Lobster layer active and Control/right-click the Layer entry in the Layers palette and choose Group into New Smart Object. Press Command/Ctrl+Option/Alt+C to access the Canvas Size command. Uncheck the Relative check box. Set the width to **515** pixels and the height to **783** pixels. Click OK. Press Command/Ctrl+T to transform the lobster. Scale the lobster **150**% in the W: field on the Options bar and then click the Maintain Aspect Ratio link icon to automatically set the Height to the same scale. Click the Warp icon. Choose View⇨Fit on Screen. You are trying to curve the lobster but not really distort the lobster. It takes a bit of playing and fiddling with the handles to get the lobster curved. I both moved the image in the mesh and kept moving the grid control handles to force the shape where I wanted it. Click Commit when you are satisfied.

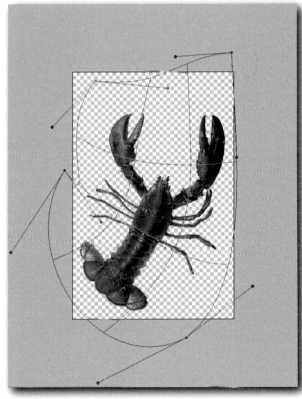

⑤ Add a white Solid Color Fill layer at the top of the layer stack. Change the layer Opacity to **50%**. Command/Control-click the Lobster thumbnail in the Layers palette to load the shape as a selection. Make the Color Fill layer active and add another Solid Color Fill layer — this time in red. The lobster shape appears in the Fill layer in red. Name this layer **Lobster Segments**. Change the Blend mode of the layer to Soft Light. You are now set up to see the lobster at the bottom of the image so you can create a segmented shape.

⑥ You now need to leave voids where you want breaks in the lobster shell. The lobster is a great choice for this technique because of his natural segments. You can respect those areas or totally ignore them — it's your lobster! I painted with a **5-pixel** hard black brush over the natural breaks in the lobster shell. Because of the changed blend mode, I could see the original lobster and see where I painted. Make sure that you detach all of the legs. You can leave wiggles in the lobster that aren't really there. If you don't like the edit, paint over it in white and redo it. Try to create segments with rounded corners. You might want to exaggerate the bumps on the lobster's legs. Stamp brush marks in black for the lobster's eyes and a smaller brush inside of that in white for the center of the eyes.

TIP

There are two ways you can create the template for the shape from this point: You can draw over the lobster or you can remove areas from the already masked lobster. I prefer the latter approach, and that is what I show in the instructions. If you prefer drawing, fill the entire layer mask with black and just draw with white in the mask where you want the lobster segments to be.

TIP

Editing the layer mask makes it much easier to correct what you paint. Instead of having to reach for the Eraser tool, you can just switch between black and white paint. Press X to exchange the foreground and background colors. I keep my left hand on the X key as I paint.

7 Draw a loose Lasso selection in the layer mask of the Lobster Segments layer around the left part of the right claw (the pincer that opens and closes). You want to open it. Press Command/Ctrl+T and drag the Reference point from the center of the selection to the center of the bottom edge of the pincer. This forms the new rotation point. Now rotate the bounding box to open the lobster's claw. Click Commit and deselect.

8 Duplicate the Lobster Segments layer and name it **Blur**. Change the Blend Mode to Normal. Turn off the eye on the Lobster Segments layer and change the Opacity of the Color Fill 1 layer to **100%**. Make the Blur layer active. Choose Filter⇨Blur⇨Gaussian Blur⇨1.0. Click OK. The object of this step is to smooth the layer mask. You are actually blurring the layer mask. Then press Command/Ctrl+L to open the Levels command. Again, you affect only the mask in the layer. Drag the Black point slider to about value **127**. Click OK. Now check the image carefully for shapes that are touching each other. Edit these areas (the legs are the usual suspects here) to remove the places where shapes touch. If any areas in the legs got too thin or humps that you want have gone missing, draw them back in.

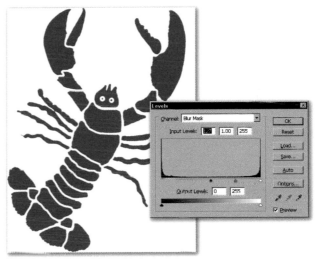

9. Next, we fuss with the antennae. Kathryn designed the right antenna to bend around and it really adds to the shape of the lobster. If you have a steady hand or can easily draw the path and stroke it with a brush stroke that fades, do it that way. However, my way works even if drawing skills are not part of your repertoire. Copy the lobster's right antenna into a new layer (without any white background) and make it into a new Smart Object. Transform the Smart Object to be **200** percent in width and **150%** in height. Click OK. Duplicate the Smart Object. Then press Command/Ctrl+T again. Choose Edit⇨Transform⇨Flip Vertical. Rotate the Smart Object approximately **−147** degrees and drag it so that the antenna crosses the lobster's right legs. Click the Warp icon. Bend the top-left corner of the mesh until it touches the spot on the lobster's head where you want to put the antenna. Then pull on the handles and move the image to get a good bend. Click Commit. Add masks to both antenna Smart Object layers, and work back and forth between them to smooth out the antenna.

10. Turn off all the layers except for the two antenna Smart Object layer. Set the Magic Wand to Sample All Layers. Click on the transparent background and then choose Select⇨Inverse. Add a Solid Color fill layer at the top of the stack and choose Red as the color. The selection of the antenna becomes the mask. Turn off the Smart Object layers and turn on the Blur and Color Fill 1 layers. Paint in the mask for this new layer (name it **Curved**

Antenna) to leave a void between each leg of the lobster. You don't want the shapes to touch or overlap. You can make any other smoothing needed in this mask. Then duplicate the layer as **Curved Antenna Blur** and blur it and level it as you did in Step 8.

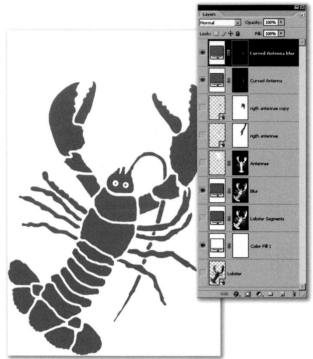

11. Now for the easier left antenna. Select the left antenna from the Antennae layer and copy it into a new layer. You can make the copy into a Smart Object, but it isn't really necessary because you aren't doing a huge amount of adjustment. Choose Edit⇨Free Transform and hold the Shift key as you drag the top-left control handle close to the top of the image. Click Commit. Turn off the Antennae layer. Load the transformed antenna as a selection and make the Curved Antenna Blur layer active. Add a new Solid Color Fill layer in red. Name the layer **Left Antenna**. Click OK. Blur and level this layer as you did for the other antenna. Fix the line if it is too narrow. Turn on only the Left Antenna, Curve Antenna Blur, and Blur layers.

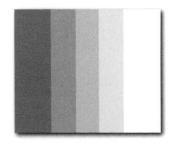

(12) Now is the time to give the image another good look and fix anything left that needs fixing. When you are satisfied, Command/Ctrl-click the Blur layer mask. Then hold the Shift key and Command/Ctrl-click the Curved Antenna Blur and Left Antenna layer masks to load all three layers as a selection. Choose Make Work Path from the Paths palette menu and set a Tolerance of 1 pixel. Click OK. Turn on only the Color Fill 1 layer so you can judge the path against solid white. If you don't like it, delete it and fix the problem and try again. When you think it's okay, choose Edit⇨Define Custom Shape and name it **Mr. Lobster**. Save this document as **Lobster Build** and close it.

(13) Create a new file **200 x 50** pixels, RGB mode, **72** ppi, with a white background. Press D to set your colors back to the default. Then press X to reverse them (so white is the foreground color).. Choose the Gradient tool and the Foreground to Background gradient. In the Options bar, uncheck both Transparency and Dither. In the alpha channel, drag the Gradient cursor from left to right with the Shift key held to constrain the gradient direction. Choose Image⇨Adjustments⇨Posterize and posterize to 5 levels. Click OK. Make the RGB channel active. Command/Alt-click the Alpha 1 channel thumbnail to load the values as a selection.. Command/Alt-click the Alpha 1 channel thumbnail to load the values as a selection. Set your Foreground color to RGB: **178, 97, 73**, (a strong coral). Fill the selection. The selection gives you an automatic five values of the orange, from hot orange to white. Deselect. Fill the background layer with white. These five values are your neon colors. Just keep the document open and accessible.

TIP

Unless you are also using the Adobe RGB color space, your neon colors won't look the same as mine when you use the same color numbers.

14 Choose File⇨New and create a new file, named **LobsterMenu**, that is 610 x 890 pixels in RGB mode at 72 ppi. Add a black Solid Color Fill layer. Choose the Custom Shape tool and select the Mr. Lobster shape that you just defined. In the Custom Shapes Options menu on the Options bar, choose Defined Size. Then click the first icon on the left of the Options bar to create a shape layer. Set the Style for the shape in the Options bar to None. Choose RGB: **255, 52, 0** as your foreground color (though it really doesn't matter — you won't see it anyway). Click in the image and drag the lobster close to the bottom of the image. Drag the Fill to **0** percent and add a Stroke effect. In the Stroke dialog box, choose a Stroke width of **10** pixels and Center position. Click the Color Patch and then click the foreground color patch in the Toolbox (or enter RGB: **255, 52, 0**). Click OK. Name the layer **Red**.

15 You are next going to add five more copies of the Red layer. In each copy, you need to edit the Stroke effect. This gives you a neon that is totally editable and that replaces the stroke path method I learned so many years ago in Illustrator (of course, in Illustrator, it always was editable; only in Photoshop was it a destructive set of commands).

* Duplicate Red as **Neon 1**. Stroke: **8** pixels using the color on the left of your color set.

* Duplicate Neon 1 as **Neon 2**. Stroke: **5** pixels using the second color from the left.

* Duplicate Neon 2 as **Neon 3**. Stroke: **3** pixels using the center from the color set.

* Duplicate Neon 3 as **Neon 4**. Stroke: **1** pixel using the second color from the right.

* Duplicate Neon 4 as **Neon 5**. Stroke: **1** pixel using white at **50** percent Opacity.

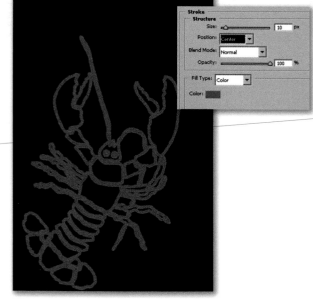

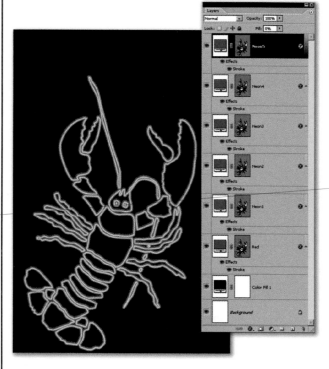

16 The neon is a bit too sharp. Stroking the path with the Blur tool will fix that. Drag the Neon5 vector mask to the New Path icon at the bottom of the Paths palette. This creates Path 1. Add a new layer to the top of the layer stack. Name it **Blur Stroke**. Choose the Blur tool with the **5-pixel** hard brush. Set the Options bar to Sample All Layers and set the Strength to around **100%**. With Path 1 active, click the Stroke Path icon on the Paths palette. Then duplicate the Blur Stoke layer and name it **Gaussian Blur**. Choose Filter⇨Blur⇨Gaussian Blur, **1** pixel. Click OK. This softens it nicely.

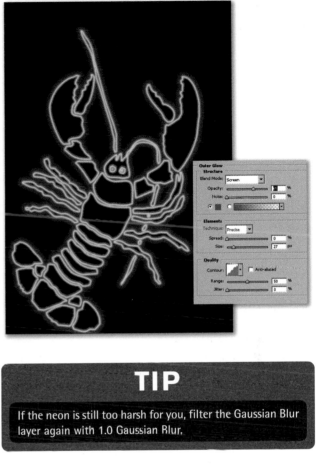

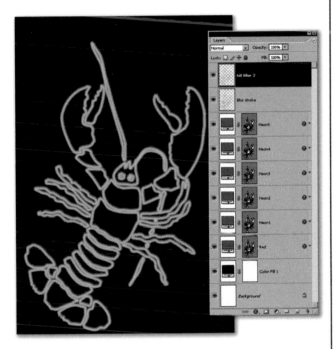

17 Add a Levels adjustment layer and drag the Black point to **100** and the White point to **215**. Click OK. Remove the Stroke effect from the layer. Then add an Outer Glow effect. Set the color to RGB: **255, 52, 0**. Set the Opacity to **65%**. Set the Technique to **Precise** and the Size to **27**. Select the Rounded Edge contour. Click OK. Add an Inner Glow effect of 50 percent Opacity in RGB: **255, 52, 0** Set the Technique to **Precise**. Click the Edge button. Set the Size to **32** pixels. Choose the Rounded Edge contour and click OK

TIP

If the neon is still too harsh for you, filter the Gaussian Blur layer again with 1.0 Gaussian Blur.

18 Duplicate the Neon 5 layer and drag it to the top of the Layer stack. Name it Glow. Remove the stroke effect from the layer. Then add an Outer Glow effect. Set the color to RGB: **255, 52, 0**. Set the Opacity to **65%**. Set the Technique to Precise and the size to **27**. Select the Rounded edge contour. Click OK. Add an inner glow effect of **50%** opacity in RGB: **255, 52, 0**. Set the Technique to Precise. Click the edge button. Set the Size to **32** pixels. Choose the Rounded Edge contour and click OK Duplicate the Neon 5 layer again and drag it to the top of the layer stack as Neon 6. Change the opacity to **75%**.

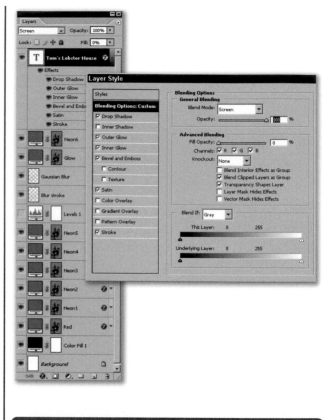

19 Choose the Type tool and type **Tom's Lobster**, then press Enter and type **House**. I used Liberty BT at 100 points Smooth. The type is right-justified. You can create neon in several ways. How much it looks like mine depends on the font. On Windows, drag the KB-Neon.asl file from the book's CD-ROM into the open Photoshop application. On the Mac, double-click the style file. The file then attaches itself (on both platforms) to the Styles palette. Add the style to the Type Layer.

TIP

Most slim fonts work well with the style as do the script fonts.

20 Save your work.

A short recap

Neon can be created by stroking a path multiple times with colors that range from the main neon tone to white at ever diminishing diameters. Because neon is a tube, many types of gradient-based neons are also possible. You can create a neon gradient stroke in a Shape Burst gradient. If you reverse the colors to make a thin back of white at the center and then take it back out to the main neon color, you get an effect very close to the one you just created. The Layers palette is much less complex, but the creation of the gradient itself is tricky. You can find a lot of different tutorials in books and on the Web about making neon. Everyone has a favorite way to do it. Making shapes from photos is fairly fast if you keep it less complex than the one we did. You can create shapes that are simple silhouettes of the image or that are just scribbles based on the outlines of the objects. One major advantage of the shape is that we can blow this menu up to billboard size with no loss of quality. Can you picture Mr. Lobster advertising Tom's Lobster House as you drive into your favorite seaport?

Melon Surprise

Have you ever bitten into an apple and tasted a lemon? Or cut open a cantaloupe and discovered that it looks, and tastes, suspiciously like a cucumber? No? Luckily, neither have I. But, through the wonders of Photoshop, you can do just that. Make yourself some mind-blowing images and be prepared to scoop up tabloid fame. The new Warp features make this ridiculously easy. It helps us to say, "Waiter, there's a watermelon in my pineapple."

THE PLAN

- Prepare the base images
- Swap the fruit
- Clean up any mess (and cover your tracks)

(1) Open the image FruitMix.psd from the CD-ROM. This is a composite of several still-life photos. It isn't put together, but the pieces (except for our traveling melon) are all there.

Photo: Norman London

(2) Let's start with a bit of tonal correction. Make the Pears layer active. Hold the Option/Alt key and add a Levels adjustment layer. In the dialog box, check the Use Previous Layer to Create Clipping Mask check box. Click OK. Drag the Input White Point to **211**. Click OK.

(3) Open the image Watermelon.psd. Use the Pen tool set to Create Paths and select the watermelon and its rind. Double-click the Background layer thumbnail in the Layers palette of the Watermelon image and create **Layer 0** (but name the layer **Watermelon**). Hold the Command./Ctrl key and click the Add Layer Mask icon to add a vector mask.

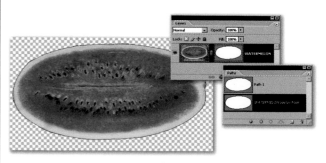

Photo: www.comstock.com

chapter 10 • playing with your food

4 Ctrl/right-click the Watermelon layer entry in the Layers palette and choose Group into New Smart Object. Drag the Smart Object into the FruitMix image. Position the watermelon over the cut pear.

5 Press Command/Ctrl+T. Hold the Shift and Option/Alt keys as you push on a corner handle to resize in proportion from the center of the shape. Make the watermelon smaller — but still just a bit larger than the cut pear. I resized to about **84** percent and rotated the watermelon **11** percent. Don't commit yet.

6 Click the Warp icon on the Options bar. Move the four corner points in toward the pear until you can see the outline of the pear. Then pull back on them if needed. You can work the control handles and push at the watermelon in the grid to shape the melon to fit the pear. Leave most of the watermelon rind hanging out of the pear. When you think you are close to having it right, click Commit. Because this is a Smart Object, you can retransform as often as needed.

7 Add a Layer Mask to the Watermelon layer. Choose the **17-pixel** soft brush and black. Paint over the edge of the watermelon until you actually reveal the edges of the pear. Then switch to white and paint back the watermelon on the inside of the pear until you reach the pear skin. You should still see the skin of the pear around the edges. You'll probably also see some watermelon rind inside the pear.

8 Make the Smart Object (not the mask) active and press Command/Ctrl+T again and click the Warp icon. You should see the warp mesh as you left it before (if you don't then you are trying to warp the mask). Now that you have the mask in place, pull on the warp handles and push the watermelon to get it to cover the entire pear. Try to keep the watermelon slice straight and not distorted. Click Commit.

9 Some of the pear is probably escaping from the mask. Clean it up. Then take the **65-pixel** soft brush with black and hold it outside the pear so that the soft edge just starts to eat away at the opacity of the watermelon. Go around the pear just barely feathering the edges of the watermelon.

10 Turn off all of the layers except the pineapple. Drag the watermelon Smart Object from the watermelon image into the FruitMix image again and place it directly above the Pineapple layer. Warp the watermelon to fit into the pineapple and mask it as you did before. When you rotate the watermelon to fit, you see that you also need to scale it disproportionally. This is definitely more of a challenge than the pear. You need to work back and forth between warping and masking until you get it the way you want it.

11 Make the Pineapple layer active and Command/Ctrl-click on the Pineapple alpha channel in the Channels palette. Add a layer mask.

12 Set the Pen tool to create Paths. Draw a pen path around the pears and the ceramic tiles. Include the shadow that goes on the wall as part of the path. Save the path as **PearPath** and then hold the Command/Ctrl key as you click the Add Layer Mask icon to add a vector mask.

13 Make the Watermelon Smart Object that is above the pineapple active. Rename the layer **Waterapple**. Select that layer and the Pineapple layer and group them into a Smart Object. Press Command/Ctrl+T and scale the waterapple to about **124** percent. Commit. Move it down so it appears between the pears.

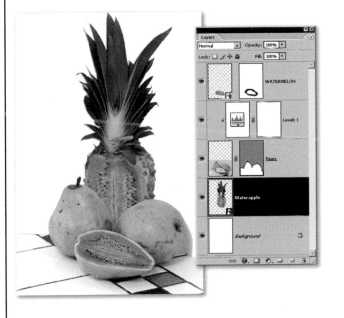

14 Make the Pears layer active. Command/Ctrl-click the vector mask thumbnail to load it as a selection. Add a layer mask. Choose Filter⇨Blur⇨Gaussian Blur, 4.0. Click OK. Take a **65-pixel** soft brush and keep it outside of the cast shadow area on the right of the image but let the soft tip eat at the opacity of the shadow to just blend it in a bit.

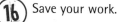

15 Make the Background layer active. Because the rest of the image is continuous tone, a solid background won't look natural or reproduce well. Choose Filter⇨Noise⇨Add Noise. Click the Gaussian option button and the Monochromatic check box. Add **1.00**% noise. Click OK. Then choose Filter⇨Brushstrokes⇨Crosshatch, and click OK to accept the default values. This just gives a bit of pattern and regularity to the noise. Finally, make the Watermelon layer at the top of the layer stack active. Add a Levels adjustment layer. Set the White Output Point to **232** and click OK.

TIP

When you prepare something for printing, it is generally a good idea to have no values lighter than 235 in the image. Paper white looks odd and ugly mixed with photos, and many presses can't hold less than a 5 or 10 percent dot. The coarser the line screen, the lower you need to make that white point value (and the lighter you need to set the maximum black). Several years ago, I had images with a 30 percent black area photocopied, and was astounded to discover that the 30 percent black dropped out of the image completely and changed to solid paper white.

16 Save your work.

A short recap

It's easy to create a mixed-up fruit salad. Using the Warp command, you can make just about any food fit into or onto another. Just think, you can mix an egg onto a filet mignon or fill hard-boiled eggs with lime slices. Just add some pork and you have a totally new interpretation of green eggs and ham!

index

continued

index

COMSTOCK®
IMAGES
We've just added 10,000 new images to our own collection, plus 40,000 more from these premium royalty-free providers:
· Thinkstock Images
· IT Stock Free
· Creatas Images
· Goodshoot
OUR COLLECTION HAS GROWN
www.comstock.com
© 2005 Comstock Images, a division of JupiterImages Corporation. Image # FL101100